The War Against Cliché

Essays and Reviews, 1971–2000

By the same author

MARTIN AMIS

The War Against Cliché

Essays and Reviews, 1971–2000

JONATHAN CAPE
LONDON

Published by Jonathan Cape 2001

2 4 6 8 10 9 7 5 3 1

First published in Great Britain in 2001 by Jonathan Cape
Random House, 20 Vauxhall Bridge Road, London SW1V 2SA

Random House Australia (Pty) Limited
20 Alfred Street, Milsons Point, Sydney,
New South Wales 2061, Australia

Random House New Zealand Limited
18 Poland Road, Glenfield,
Auckland 10, New Zealand

Random House (Pty) Limited
Endulini, 5A Jubilee Road, Parktown 2193, South Africa

The Random House Group Limited Reg. No. 954009
www.randomhouse.co.uk

A CIP catalogue record for this book
is available from the British Library

ISBN 0-224-05059-1

Papers used by The Random House Group Limited are natural,
recyclable products made from wood grown in sustainable forests;
the manufacturing processes conform to the environmental
regulations of the country of origin

Typeset by Palimpsest Book Production Limited,
Polmont, Stirlingshire
Printed and bound in Great Britain by
Clays Ltd, St Ives PLC

To Kingsley
and Sally

Contents

Acknowledgments

I would like to thank my editors, in whom I have been unusually fortunate: Arthur Crook, John Sturrock, Peter Labanyi and the late Nicolas Walter at the *Times Literary Supplement*; the late Terence Kilmartin at *The Observer*; the late George Gale at the *Spectator*; John Gross and Claire Tomalin at the *New Statesman*; Harvey Shapiro and Charles McGrath at the *New York Times Book Review*; Karl Miller and Mary-Kay Wilmers at the *London Review of Books*; Jack Beattie at *Atlantic Monthly*; Blake Morrison at the *Independent on Sunday*; Tina Brown, David Remnick, Bill Buford and (again) Charles McGrath at the *New Yorker*; Deborah Orr at the *Guardian*; and Jonathan Burnham at *Talk*. I would also like to thank Dan Franklin, Pascal Cariss and Jason Arthur at Jonathan Cape.

Pieces in this book were compiled by Professor James Diedrick. I gratefully salute his skill and acuity.

Foreword

While complacently planning this volume in my mind I always thought I would include a nice little section called – let us say – 'Literature and Society', where I would assemble my pieces on literature and society (pieces on F.R. Leavis and Lionel Trilling, and on lesser figures like Ian Robinson and Denis Donoghue). 'Literature and society' was, at one time, a phrase so much on everyone's lips that it earned itself an abbreviation: Lit & Soc. And Lit & Soc, I seemed to remember, had been for me a long-running enthusiasm. But when I leafed through the massed manuscripts I found only a handful of essays, all of them written, rather ominously, in the early Seventies (when I was in my early twenties). Having reread them, I toyed with the idea of calling my nice little section something like 'Literature and Society: The Vanished Debate'. Then I decided that *my* debate had better vanish too. The pieces themselves I considered earnest, overweening, and contentedly dull. More decisively, though, Lit & Soc, and indeed literary criticism, felt dead and gone.

That time now seems unrecognizably remote. I had a day job at the *Times Literary Supplement*. Even then I sensed discrepancy, as I joined an editorial conference (to help prepare, perhaps, a special number on Literature and Society), wearing shoulder-length hair, a flower shirt, and knee-high tricoloured boots (well-concealed, it is true, by the twin tepees of my flared trousers). My private life was middle-bohemian – hippyish and hedonistic, if not candidly debauched; but I was very moral when it came to literary criticism. I read it all the time, in the tub, on the tube; I always had about me my Edmund Wilson – or my William Empson. I took it seriously. We all did. We hung around the place talking about literary criticism. We sat in pubs and coffee bars talking about W.K. Wimsatt and G. Wilson Knight, about Richard Hoggart and Northrop Frye, about

Richard Poirier, Tony Tanner and George Steiner. It might have been in such a locale that my friend and colleague Clive James first formulated his view that, while literary criticism is not essential to literature, both are essential to civilization. Everyone concurred. Literature, we felt, was the core discipline; criticism explored and popularized the significance of that centrality, creating a space around literature and thereby further exalting it. The early Seventies, I should add, saw the great controversy about the Two Cultures: Art v. Science (or F.R. Leavis v. C.P. Snow). Perhaps the most fantastic thing about this cultural moment was that Art seemed to be *winning*.

Literary historians know it as the Age of Criticism. It began, let us suggest, in 1948, with the publication of Eliot's *Notes Towards the Definition of Culture* and Leavis's *The Great Tradition*. What ended it? The brutalist answer would consist of a single four-letter word: OPEC. In the Sixties you could live on ten shillings a week: you slept on people's floors and sponged off your friends and sang for your supper – about literary criticism. Then, abruptly, a *bus fare* cost ten shillings. The oil hike, and inflation, and then stagflation, revealed literary criticism as one of the many leisure-class fripperies we would have to get along without. Well, that's how it felt. But it now seems clear that literary criticism was inherently doomed. Explicitly or otherwise it had based itself on a structure of echelons and hierarchies; it was about the talent elite. And the structure atomized as soon as the forces of democratization gave their next concerted push.

Those forces – incomparably the most potent in our culture – have gone on pushing. And they are now running up against a natural barrier. Some citadels, true, have proved stormable. You can become rich without having any talent (via the scratchcard and the rollover jackpot). You can become famous without having any talent (by abasing yourself on some TV nerdothon: a clear improvement on the older method of simply killing a celebrity and inheriting the aura). But you cannot become talented without having any talent. Therefore, talent must go.

Literary criticism, now almost entirely confined to the universities, thus moves against talent by moving against the canon.

Academic preferment will not come from a respectful study of Wordsworth's poetics; it will come from a challenging study of his politics – his attitude to the poor, say, or his unconscious 'valorization' of Napoleon; and it will come still faster if you ignore Wordsworth and elevate some (justly) neglected contemporary, by which process the canon may be quietly and steadily sapped. A brief consultation of the Internet will show that meanwhile, at the other end of the business, *everyone* has become a literary critic – or at least a book-reviewer. Democratization has made one inalienable gain: equality of the sentiments. I think Gore Vidal said this first, and he said it, not quite with mockery, but with lively scepticism. He said that, nowadays, nobody's feelings are more authentic, and thus more important, than anybody else's. This is the new credo, the new privilege. It is a privilege much exercised in the contemporary book-review, whether on the Web or in the literary pages. The reviewer calmly tolerates the arrival of the new novel or slim volume, defensively settles into it, and then sees which way it rubs him up. The right way or the wrong way. The results of this contact will form the data of the review, without any reference to the thing behind. And the thing behind, I am afraid, is talent, and the canon, and the body of knowledge we call literature.

Probably some readers are getting the impression that I think these developments are to be deplored. Not so. It is the summit of idleness to deplore the present, to deplore actuality. Say whatever else you like about it, the present is unavoidable. And we, in the Seventies, were frequently ridiculous, too, with our Fallacies and our Seven Types (and Leavis's besieged intensity was ridiculous. His shaping embarrassment, however, was to nominate as his model for sanity the person of D.H. Lawrence). Emotional egalitarianism, for example, looks hard to attack. I honour it, in a way, but it has to me the pale glow of illusion. It is utopian, which is to say that reality cannot be expected to support it. Then, too, these 'feelings' are seldom unadulterated; they are admixtures of herd opinions and social anxieties, vanities, touchinesses, and everything else that makes up a self.

One of the historical vulnerabilities of literature, as a subject for study, is that it has never seemed difficult enough. This may come as news to the buckled figure of the book-reviewer, and to the literary critic, but it's true. Hence the various attempts to elevate it, complicate it, systematize it. Interacting with literature is easy. Anyone can join in, because words (unlike palettes and pianos) lead a double life: we all have a competence. It is not surprising, therefore, that individual sensitivities come so strongly into play; not surprising, either, that the discipline has rolled over for democratization far more readily than, for example, chemistry and Ancient Greek. In the long term, though, literature will resist levelling and revert to hierarchy. This isn't the decision of some snob of a belletrist. It is the decision of Judge Time, who constantly separates those who last from those who don't.

Let me run, for a while, with an extended simile. Literature is the great garden that is always there and is open to everyone twenty-four hours a day. Who tends it? The old tour guides and sylviculturists, the wardens, the fuming parkies in their sweat-soaked serge: these have died off. If you do see an official, a professional, nowadays, then he's likely to be a scowl in a labcoat, come to flatten a forest or decapitate a peak. The public wanders, with its oohs and ahs, its groans and jeers, its million opinions. The wanderers feed the animals, they walk on the grass, they step in the flowerbeds. But the garden never suffers. It is, of course, Eden; it is unfallen and needs no care.

Readers of the present book are asked to keep an eye on the datelines which end these pieces, for they span nearly thirty years. You hope to get more relaxed and confident over time; and you should certainly get (or seem to get) kinder, simply by avoiding the stuff you are unlikely to warm to. Enjoying being insulting is a youthful corruption of power. You lose your taste for it when you realize how hard people try, how much they mind, and how long they remember (Angus Wilson and William Burroughs nursed my animadversions – and no doubt the animadversions of others – to the grave). Admittedly there are some critics who enjoy being insulting well into middle age. I have often wondered why this spectacle seems so undignified. Now

I know: it's mutton dressed as lamb. I am also struck by how hard I sometimes was on writers who (I erroneously felt) were trying to influence me: Roth, Mailer, Ballard.

You proceed by quotation. Quotation is the reviewer's only hard evidence. Or semi-hard evidence. Without it, in any case, criticism is a shop-queue monologue. Gallingly for the lit-crit imperialists (especially I.A. Richards), there is no means for distinguishing the excellent from the less excellent. The most muscular literary critics on earth have no equipment for establishing that

Thoughts that do often lie too deep for tears

is a better line than

When all at once I saw a crowd

— and, if they did, they would have to begin by saying that the former contains a dead expletive ('do') brought in to sustain the metre. Yet quotation is all we have. To idealize: all writing is a campaign against cliché. Not just clichés of the pen but clichés of the mind and clichés of the heart. When I dispraise, I am usually quoting clichés. When I praise, I am usually quoting the opposed qualities of freshness, energy, and reverberation of voice.

London, October 2000

On Masculinity
and Related Questions

Zeus and the Garbage

Iron John: A Book about Men by Robert Bly;
The Way Men Think: Intellect, Intimacy and the Erotic Imagination
by Liam Hudson and Bernadine Jacot;
*Utne Reader: Men, It's Time to Pull Together: The Politics
of Masculinity*

In 1919, after prolonged study, the Harvard ethologist William
Morton Wheeler pronounced the male wasp 'an ethological nonentity'. An animal behaviourist had scrutinized the male wasp and
found – no behaviour. We can well imagine the male wasp's response
to such a verdict: his initial shock and hurt; his descent into a period
of depressed introspection; his eventual decision to behave more
intriguingly. For nowadays, according to a recent *Scientific American*,
'interest in the long-neglected male is flourishing, a tribute to the
animal's broad array of activities'. Male humans will surely feel
for their brothers in the wasp kingdom. After a phase of relative
obscurity, we too have rallied. In fact, we seem to have bounced back
pretty well immediately, with all kinds of fresh claims on everyone's
attention. Male wounds. Male rights. Male grandeur. Male whimpers
of neglect.

What is the deep background on the 'deep male'? From 100,000 BC
until, let's say, 1792 (Mary Wollstonecraft and her *Vindication of
the Rights of Woman*), there was, simply, the Man, whose chief
characteristic was that he got away with everything. From 1792
until about 1970, there was, in theory anyway, the Enlightened
Man, who, while continuing to get away with everything, agreed
to meet women for talks about talks which would lead to political
concessions. Post-1970, the Enlightened Man became the New Man,
who isn't interested in getting away with anything – who believes,

3

indeed, that the female is not merely equal to the male but is his plain superior. The masculine cultivation of his feminine 'side' can be seen as a kind of homage to a better and gentler principle. Well, the New Man is becoming an old man, perhaps prematurely, what with all the washing-up he's done; there he stands in the kitchen, a nappy in one hand, a pack of tarot cards in the other, with his sympathetic pregnancies, his hot flushes and contact pre-menstrual tensions, and with a duped frown on his ageing face. The time is ripe. And now the back door swings open and in he comes, preceded by a gust of testosterone and a few tumbleweeds of pubic hair: the Old Man, the Deep Male – Iron John.

Iron John, a short work of psychological, literary and anthropological speculation by the poet Robert Bly, 'dominated' the *New York Times* bestseller list for nearly a year, and has made, as we shall see, a heavy impact on many aspects of American life. It has not done so well over here. For this there are many reasons, but let us begin with the most trivial. *Iron John* runs into trouble – into outright catastrophe – with the first word of its title. I don't know why I find this quite so funny (what's *wrong* with me?); I don't know why I still scream with laughter every time I think about it. Is it the spectacle of Bly's immediate self-defeat? Or is it because the title itself so firmly establishes the cultural impossibility of taking *Iron John* straight? Anyway, here's the difficulty: in England *iron* (iron hoof) means 'poof' – just as *ginger* (ginger beer) means 'queer', and *oily* (oily rag) means 'fag'. *Iron* means 'poof'.

At my local sports club in Paddington, where I do most of my male bonding, there is much talk about *irons*. Not long ago I joined in a conversation whose notional aim was to select an *iron* football team. The mood was earnest rather than hostile, and we didn't get very far with this particular team sheet. 'Chairman: Elton John. Elton *is* an *iron*, isn't he?' 'Centre-forward: Justin Fashanu. *He's* an *iron*. He came clean about it in the *Sun*.' So I can easily conjure the fickle leers that would await me if, one morning, I walked into the club saying: 'Well, guys – there's a new book about men and masculinity that's going to straighten out all the problems we've been having with our male identity. It says we should spend much more time together and exult in our hairiness and sliminess and zaniness. It says we should leave the women at home and go camping and take all our clothes off and rough-house in the woods. It says we should hang out more with older men. It's called *Iron John*.'

Naturally, it's much too easy to laugh at Robert Bly's vision. But why is it *so* easy? Partly because he is one of those writers, like F.R. Leavis and Hermann Hesse, whose impregnable humourlessness will always prompt a (humorous) counter-commentary in the reader's mind. Then, too, we are British, over here; we are sceptical, ironical, etc., and are not given, as Americans are, to seeking expert advice on basic matters, especially such matters as our manhood. But the main reason has to do with embarrassment. Being more or less unembarrassable, Americans are fatally *attracted* to the embarrassing: they have an anti-talent for it (the Oscars, the primaries, the hearings, the trials, Shirley Temple, Clarence Thomas, Andrea Dworkin, Al Sharpton, Ronald Reagan, Jimmy Swaggart). Whereas, over here, maleness itself has become an embarrassment. Male consciousness, male pride, male rage – we don't want to hear about it.

This of course is the very diffidence and inhibition that Bly wants to goad us out of. His exemplar is the old tale of Iron John, which 'could be ten or twenty thousand years old', or could be 'pre-Christian by a thousand years or so', but which is, at any rate, old. Let us quickly do Iron John, or its first and more interesting half, and without any of the twinkly demotic ('okay', 'there's no problem', 'yuck!') that Bly uses to keep his modern audience reassured. The King's hunters start vanishing in the forest. One day a man appears, and offers to investigate. He goes out there accompanied by his dog, which gets tugged into a pond by a naked arm. The pond is bucketed out. At the bottom lies a Wild Man. The King has him locked up in a cage in the courtyard. One day the King's eight-year-old son drops his best toy – a golden ball – into the cage of the Wild Man. A trade is arranged: the golden ball for the Wild Man's freedom. The boy agrees to open the cage – but he can't find the key. The Wild Man tells him that the key is to be found beneath his mother's pillow. The boy does as he is told but is worried about punishment. So the Wild Man hoists him on to his shoulders, and off to the forest they go.

The story trundles on from here – the golden spring, the trial, the descent into the world, horses, battles, ending with the usual stuff involving glory/princess/kingdom/treasure – and Bly trundles on alongside it, increasingly drunk on panoptic explication. Late in the book, encountering some conventional guff about the boy's white horse, Bly has us know that white stands for 'semen, saliva, water, milk, lakes, rivers . . . the sea, and priesthood . . . health, strength and all good things . . . fellowship and good company . . . the purity of children and brides . . . persons with high moral purposes . . . purification . . . [and] a sort of abstract, ideal state'. That's what white stands for. Bly takes the tale, in any event, as an allegory of male maturation.

Iron John, the Wild Man, smothered in his ginger hair, is the 'deep male', the embodiment and awakener of, variously, 'Zeus energy', 'divine energy', 'hurricane energy', 'masculine grandeur' and 'sun-like integrity', brandishing 'the Varja sword' of sexuality, courage and resolve, and championing 'the moist, the swampish, the wild, the untamed'. Iron John is hard to find and awkward to contain and dangerous to release; but his mentorship brings huge rewards (all his treasure). The story's single beauty – the location of the key to the cage – is also its crux, for the boy must put aside womanly things in his journey from 'soft' male to 'hard'. The rest of his development (learning to shudder, tasting ashes, warriorhood) comes over as a cross between adolescent fantasy and middle-aged encounter-group sessions, with many a crackup and primal scream. The forest is an arcadia splattered with mud and blood.

What emerges? Feminist writers have done their job on *Iron John*, and intelligibly. It hardly needs to be pointed out that Bly is phallocentric to the ends of his hair, and rollickingly tendentious even in his imagery:

'The King' and 'the Queen' send energy down. They resemble the sun and the moon that pierce down through the earth's atmosphere. Even on cloudy days something of their radiant energy comes through.

Yes, but the moon has no energy, and doesn't radiate; the Queen merely reflects the heavenly power of the King. Not that Bly is at all forgetful of women's interests. He wants to establish, or re-establish, a world where men are so great that women *like* being lorded over:

> We know that for hundreds of thousands of years men have admired each other, and been admired by women, in particular for their activity. Men and women alike once called on men to pierce the dangerous places, carry handfuls of courage to the waterfalls, dust the tails of the wild boars.

After a few hours of that kind of talk, the women will get their reward – in the bedroom:

> Sometimes in a love affair, the lovers make love with the Wild Man – and Wild Woman – right in the room; and if we are those lovers, we may feel certain body cells turn gold that we thought were made entirely of lead.

So there will be that: Wild Sex. Bly knows about women's ascensionism, but he thinks 'it is appropriate for women to describe it'. 'We will confine ourselves here to men's ascensionism.' The dialogue had better start soon, before the yodelling gets any louder.

Bly is a poet. He is a big cat, so to speak, and not some chipmunk or beaver from the how-to industry. Then again, maybe Bly is more like a stag or a peacock, contentedly absorbed in the 'display' rituals he so admires. To pick up a book like *The Way Men Think: Intellect, Intimacy and the Erotic Imagination*, a sober, chatty, palliative study of gender differences, is to be transported into another – dramatically blander – world; but it is the civilized world, the modern world, the real world. Bly's utopia is as remote in time as the story of Iron John, and can be recreated, now, only as a Rockwellian fantasy – the gruff dads, with their tools and their guileless dungarees. At the end of *Lady Chatterley's Lover* Mellors tells Connie that everything would be all right if men sang and danced every evening, dressed in tight red trousers. Bly, who likes his Lawrence, can think of nothing to do about the modern landscape except turn away from it. *Iron John* finally settles on the mind as a tangled mop of vivid and cumbrous *nostalgies*.

Turning to a quite elderly copy of the *Utne Reader* (a monthly digest of America's 'alternative press' – always informative, always revealing), we are confronted by an astonishing and unchallengeable fact: *Iron John* has transformed male consciousness in the United States. There can be no argument. It has already happened. The Wild Man Weekends and Initiation Adventure Holidays and whatnot, which are now big business, may prove ephemeral. But what does one make of the unabashed references to 'men's liberation' and 'the men's movement', and the fact that there are now at least half a dozen magazines devoted to nothing else (*Changing Men, Journeymen, Man!*). Men, the male argument goes, are 'oppressed', coming out second best on longevity, suicide rates, drug use, homelessness and work hours. The political platform being nailed together includes the Federal encouragement of boys' clubs and scout troops, male-only early-grade classes taught by men, right down to such things as male-friendly tax breaks for home-based employment. Now that men are just another minority, the way forward, or the way back, lies with 'eco-masculinity', an emphasis on husbandry which will 'affirm the "seedbearing", creative capacity of the male'. Actually, part of me always did suspect that there was something in it – in Blyism; and now I suppose I'll eventually have to act on that dawning conviction. When my boys reach a certain age, and the time comes to establish a distance from their mother and introduce them to the rugged lineaments of the male world, then I'll probably take them to the Hilton for at least a night or two.

It is relevant, I think, to ask what Iron John is like as a husband and father. How tight a ship does Captain Bly run? There he is on the back cover, assuming the stance of a man warming the backs of his legs over a log fire, with wispy white hair, with specs, tapestry waistcoat, crimson cravat, and tight, dutiful, chinny smile. He doesn't look like a man of iron, but there's definitely something steely about him. He is unironical about himself, and naïvely vain (*Iron John* features a book-length running joke on authorial pretension, in which quoted gobbets from such poets as Rilke, Antonio Machado, the Norwegian Rolph Jacobsen, and many others, including Dante, are all '*translated by R.B.*'). Mr Bly wants respect; he has plenty of bristles and prickles; like Bronco toilet-paper, he takes no shit from anyone. He is, in fact, that familiar being, the 'strong personality'. This kind of strength is innate and not acquired, and is always looking for ways to expand. 'Zeus energy is male authority accepted for the sake of the community.' It sounds like a marvellously elemental excuse for getting away with everything. Zeus energy, 'hurricane energy': here is something that sweeps all before it. Would you want to tell Zeus to take out the garbage? Would you want to ask a hurricane to wipe its feet on the mat?

Feminists have often claimed a moral equivalence for sexual and racial prejudice. There are certain affinities; and one or two of these affinities are mildly, and paradoxically, encouraging. Sexism is like racism: we all feel such impulses. Our parents feel them more strongly than we feel them. Our children, we hope, will feel them less strongly than we feel them. People don't change or improve much, but they do evolve. It is very slow. Feminism (endlessly diverging, towards the stolidly Benthamite, towards the ungraspably rarefied), the New Man, emotional bisexuality, the Old Man, Iron Johnism, male crisis-centres – these are convulsions, some of them necessary, some of them not so necessary, along the way, intensified by the contemporary search for role and guise and form.*

London Review of Books December 1991

* This piece became part of a lecture I gave at two American universities in the mid-1990s. At St Louis, Missouri, I feared that Robert Bly's daughter (who is on the faculty) might be in the audience. She wasn't there. Robert Bly's daughter wasn't there at Harvard, either. But Robert Bly was. At the close of the talk I invited his rebuttal. Standing tall, Bly asked me why I was so frightened of male grandeur. I wanted to say, 'Because it's so frightening'; instead I shrugged and mumbled, feeling I had already answered his question.

I Am in Blood Stepp'd
in So Far

Hollywood vs. America by Michael Medved

In the cinema, if not elsewhere, violence started getting violent in 1966. The films that marked the escalation, in my memory, were Arthur Penn's *Bonnie and Clyde* (1967) and Sam Peckinpah's *The Wild Bunch* (1969). And I was delighted to see it, all this violence. I found it voluptuous, intense, and (even then) disquietingly humorous; it felt subversive and counter-cultural. Violence had arrived. There was also, I noticed, a sudden flowering of sex and swearing. The future looked bright.

Before then, violence wasn't violent. People often talk, usually disapprovingly, about the way violence has become 'stylized' on film. But the old violence was stylized, too: it simply wore the soft gloves of much gentler conventions. Writing in the Fifties, Nabokov noted the ineffectuality of the 'ox-stunning fisticuffs' of an average cinematic rumble, and remarked on the speed with which the hero invariably recovered from 'a plethora of pain that would have hospitalized a Hercules'. Few of us are in a position to say which style is the more life-like: the cartoonish invulnerability of the old violence or the cartoonish besplatterings of the new. We imagine that reality lies somewhere in between – that it is less dramatic, less balletic, and, above all, quicker. In life, the average fistfight, for instance, lasts about a second and consists of one blow. The loser gets a broken nose, the winner gets a broken hand, and they both trudge off to Emergency. Thus the great Stallone joins the queue at the trauma unit, while Chuck Norris fumbles with his first-aid kit. It just wouldn't play.

What happens, now, if you drag out the old movies and look again at even their most violent violence? I gained my first solid

apprehension of earthly mortality not from the death of a relative or
a pet but from the death of Jim Bowie in *The Alamo* (1960). Richard
Widmark's skirling death cry haunts me still. I also remember my
audible 'Jesus' when I saw Paul Newman smash his rifle butt into
the raised glass of the saloon Okie, in *Hombre* (1967). And who
can forget the various torments meted out to Marlon Brando in *On
the Waterfront* (1954), *One-Eyed Jacks* (1961), and *The Chase* (1966)?
(Brando, always well known for having his artistic 'say', definitely
has a thing about getting beaten up.) Look again at such scenes
and you marvel at your earlier susceptibility. They seem tame partly
because they *are* tame (not dramatically but technically tame), and
also because, in the interim, you have yawned and blinked your way
through a thirty-year Passchendaele of slaughter. You have become,
in other words, irreversibly desensitized. Macbeth – and let's make
that Polanski's Macbeth – speaks for you when he says:

> I am in blood
> Stepp'd in so far, that, should I wade no more,
> Returning were as tedious as go o'er.

In real life, interestingly, desensitization is precisely the quality that
empowers the violent: empowers them to bear it away. In the
moments leading up to violence, the nonviolent enter a world
drenched with unfamiliar revulsions. The violent know this. Essentially they are taking you to where they feel at home. You are leaving
your place and going over to their place.

Screen violence, we might notice, has close affinities with the
weapons business, and, to borrow an ageing phrase from the
nuclear-arms community, is often technology-led. *Bullitt* (1968) is
justly remembered for its car chase, which, astonishingly, remains
unsurpassed, despite bigger budgets, bigger engines, and the existence
of furiously literal-minded actors willing to spend years of their
lives bonding with racing drivers and crash dummies. But there
was another standard-setting scene in *Bullitt*: the shotgun slaying
of the underground witness, which entrains the incomprehensible
plot. Suddenly, the door of the murky hotel room is kicked open;

the police guard is caught in the thigh; the camera glances at this wound and then turns on the swarthy stoolie, who retreats with his hands raised, clambering up on to the foot of the low bed. As the gun is fired he is lifted off his feet and jerked through the air, smashing back-first into the wall in a nebula of blood. Soon after the film appeared, I happened to meet its director, Peter Yates, and when I asked him about this scene he took me through the mechanics of it – the blood pouch, the steel wires. In the old days, an actor who stopped a bullet would merely crush a ketchup sachet to the supposed entry-wound and look indignant. If he was a bad guy, he would roll to the floor and decorously close his eyes. If he was a good guy, he would get really mad, then later assure the gasping blonde at his side that the bullet hole was just a 'scratch' or, better, a 'flesh wound'. Well, after 1968 there were no more scratches, no more flesh wounds. With the electronically ignited plasma-brimmed sandwich Baggie, the lurch cables and jolt harnesses, and so on, death by shotgun ceased to look like something you could quickly recover from.

In this context the recent *Schindler's List* marks a progression, or maybe a retrogression. Here the point-blank pistol shot to the head results in a tubular spout of blood followed by a tragic curtsy to the ground almost as girlish and theatrical as Uma Thurman's swoon in *Dangerous Liaisons*. One feels sure that this rendition was the result of close research, part of the carapace of verisimilitude that Spielberg needed to allow him artistic passage to the Holocaust. (Nearing the Holocaust, a trespasser finds that his imagination is decently absenting itself, and reaches for documentation and technique. The last thing he wants to do, once there, is make anything up.) In general, the escalation of violence in war films is not much questioned. Even the squeamish accept that a mechanized heartlessness forms the natural background – a civilian obedience, perhaps, to the hawkish axiom 'What did you expect? This is *war*.' We know more and more about the horror and pity of war, but we still seem to need persuading about the horror and pity of, for example, bank robbing, drug trafficking, serial murders, and chainsaw massacres.

To the extent that screen violence is technology-led, a specialized value system will tend to assert itself. As in the weapons industry, you will get no moral guidance from the specialist, the salaried expert. What you will get is the explanation 'Everyone *else* does it', because, when up against can-do, don't-do will always finish second. Still, the prop-shop eggheads at places like Praxis and Visual Concept Engineering, the morphers and animators at Industrial Light & Magic or Dream Quest Images are mere hirelings: somebody has to *want* that particular splat or spatter, that cute decapitation, that ginchy evisceration. There is this half-formed view of Hollywood as an acropolis of conglomerates, of marketers and targeters, unsmilingly supplying the public with what it has come to want and need: more violence. But it doesn't work like that. 'Projects' swim around the movie community until someone with power gets connected to them. Then they get 'developed' by writers, producers and directors, and then get sent upstairs to the 'suits' – these supposedly pitiless bottom-liners. But what happens up there remains a mystery to everyone, the suits included. Some projects go ahead, and some don't. 'The only films they make', a director once told me, 'are the films they can't get out of making.' The final decision, then, is the result of fatalism, embarrassment, or inertia – office politics, maybe, but not policy. So violence is director-led, or *auteur*-led. Films are violent because the talent wants it that way.

Who else does, apart from me? One of the few points that survives the battering of Michael Medved's beleaguered monograph *Hollywood vs. America* is that the moviegoing public *doesn't* like violence. In his introduction to the paperback edition Medved writes in heroic cadences about 'the passionate intensity of the public response to my work'; yes, he has taken his share of 'intemperate anger' and 'personal abuse', but on the whole, says Medved, 'I am grateful for whatever contribution my arguments have made to facilitating this discussion.' Certainly, *Hollywood vs. America* got Hollywood thinking, at least for a weekend or two (late nights in the dens of the Moorish mansions). And it got America thinking, too, and the controversy that gathered around it managed to trickle up as high as Janet Reno and Bill Clinton. It was a book, and a mood, whose time had come: the feeling that Hollywood had gone too far in its divergence from the American mainstream; the feeling that Hollywood loved everything that America hated (violence, sex, swearing, drugging, drinking and smoking), and hated everything that America loved (religion, parents, marriage and monogamy, plus the military, policemen, businessmen and America). Now, I'm sure that Mr Medved seldom, if ever, gets into fights, which is just as well. After three hundred pages of his pedantry and sarcasm, I imagine him tooled up like the loathed Schwarzenegger, and spray-firing from either hip. His argumentative style is so strident that even his own intelligence, you suspect, is cowed and deafened by it. Why oh why, he typically asks, is Hollywood so obsessed by Vietnam and so unmoved by the struggle in Kuwait, which, 'amazingly enough', has yet to be celebrated on film? If Dan Quayle were a lot brighter, this is what he would sound like.

Despite its contemporary attire, Medved's theme, or plaint, is as old as time. It is *Ubi sunt?* all over again. Where are they now, the great simplicities of yesterday?

> In years past, in the heyday of Gary Cooper and Greta Garbo, Jimmy Stewart and Katharine Hepburn, the movie business drew considerable criticism for manufacturing personalities who were larger than life, impossibly noble and appealing individuals who could never exist in the real world. Today, the industry consistently comes up with characters who are *smaller* than life – less decent, less intelligent, and less likeable than our own friends and neighbors.

Medved's 'beat is the entertainment industry'. He knows about the entertainment industry, but does he know about art – about literature, for example, which has been following exactly the same graph line for two thousand years? If art has an arrow, then that is the way it points: straight downwards, from demigod to demirep.

Cinema is a young form, and has been obliged to make this same journey in less than a century. I said earlier that violence got violent in 1966, because that was the year the Hay Production Code was revised, and film edged closer to being a director's medium, freer to go where the talent pushed it. As we now know, the talent pushed it away from the mainstream of America and towards the mainstream of contemporary art, while playing to its own strengths

– action, immediacy, affect. So the great current debate is caught in a confusion of categories. If cinema is just mass entertainment, then Medved is an eloquent awakener. If cinema is art, then Medved is just a noisy philistine.

We now enter a world of closed circles. After 1966, movie audiences halved, and they have stayed halved. Auteurism did more damage to the industry than the arrival of television. Medved, with his polls and his content-analysis, gathers plenty of evidence to confirm what he wants to believe: that Americans don't like violence – and violent themes and violent language – and won't pay money to see it. (A final analogy with weaponry: Americans have always been avowedly pro-gun-control but somehow never pro enough to make any difference.) Americans don't want violence. They probably don't want art, either. What Americans want is escape – escape from American violence. American violence 'travels', it's said, and enthralls audiences all over the planet, but Americans have to live in America, where all the violence is. Does screen violence provide a window or a mirror? Is it an effect or is it a cause, an encouragement, a facilitation? Fairly representatively, I think, I happen to like screen violence while steadily execrating its real-life counterpart. Moreover, I can tell the difference between the two. One is happening, one is not. One is earnest, one is play. But we inhabit the postmodern age, an age of mass suggestibility, in which image and reality strangely interact. This is now perhaps the most vulnerable area in the common mind. There is a hole in the credulity layer, and it is getting wider.

In Britain, in recent months, two of the most sensational murder trials of the century have involved discussion of the same rental video; namely, *Child's Play 3*. The first case was that of James Bulger, a toddler who was beaten to death by two ten-year-olds; the second case was that of Suzanne Capper, a teenager who was kidnapped, strenuously tortured, and finally set alight by a clique of young acquaintances. *Child's Play 3* has therefore been much in the news, and therefore much in demand. It, too, has been set alight, semi-ritualistically, by public-spirited managers of video-rental stores. When my two children (aged seven and nine) noticed *Child's Play 3* in its package, up on a high self, they regarded it with reverent dread.

In their schoolyard voodoo, *Child's Play 3* was considered potent, venomous, toxic. It was like angel dust – a ticket to frenzy.

So one afternoon I duly settled down to watch a routine little horror film about a children's doll called Chucky that comes to life and starts killing people. The modicum of horror it inspires can be traced back to Freud's definition of the uncanny: ambiguity about the extent to which something is, or is not, alive. Equally conventionally, such frights and shrieks as the film elicits have to do not with very scary things happening but with mildly scary things happening very suddenly. As the credits rolled on *Child's Play 3*, I felt no urge or prompting to go out and kill somebody. And I also knew why. It's nothing to boast about, but there is too much going on in my head for Chucky to gain sway in there. Probably the worst that Chucky could do to me is to create an appetite to see more Chucky, or more things like Chucky.

What we have to imagine is a mind that, on exposure to Chucky, is already brimful of Chucky and things like Chucky. Then, even if you mix in psychopathology, stupidity, moral deformation, dreams of omnipotence and sadism, and whatever else, Chucky is unlikely to affect anything but the *style* of your subsequent atrocities. Murderers have to have something to haunt them: they need their internal pandemonium. A century ago, it might have been the Devil. Now it's Chucky. When the killers tortured Suzanne Capper, they chanted the catchphrase 'I'm Chucky. Wanna play?' When the two ten-year-old boys began to throw bricks, James Bulger fell down and stood up again. 'Just stand there,' said one of the killers, 'and we'll get you a plaster.' And then he threw another brick. This is Chucky's way: the worthless joke, the worthless swagger. Here was a mind that had seen a lot of things like Chucky, and had nothing much in prospect but more things like Chucky. Perhaps, also, the child who spoke those words didn't understand the meaning of earnest. As a result, he was all too ready to play.

New Yorker May 1994

A PM, a President, and a First Lady

The Iron Lady by Hugo Young

Mitterrand thought she had the eyes of Caligula and the mouth of Marilyn Monroe. 'In her presence,' said Zbigniew Brzezinski, 'you pretty quickly forget that she's a woman. She doesn't strike me as a very female type.' In 1979, Tass called her the Iron Lady; but by 1984 Yasser Arafat was calling her the 'Iron Man'. When an interviewer told Gloria Steinem that the English never believed that they'd ever have a woman prime minister, Steinem replied: 'They were right.' So, as the grocer's daughter stalks around the Kremlin and the White House, as she traumatizes Helmut Schmidt in Luxembourg or wows Lech Wałęsa in the shipyards of Gdansk, onlookers seem to share the same anxiety: that one day Mrs T. will start heading for the wrong toilet. Hedging his bets, as ever, Ronald Reagan called her 'one of my favorite people'. And she herself later sought a kind of impersonality in the royal *we*.

Mrs Thatcher is the only interesting thing about British power politics; and the only interesting thing about Mrs Thatcher is that she isn't a man. Tricked out with the same achievements, the same style and 'vision', a Marvyn or a Marmaduke Thatcher would be as dull as rain, as dull as London traffic, as dull as the phosphorescent prosperity, the boutique squalor of Thatcher's England (or its southeastern quadrant). A newspaper once cobbled together an item on the 'sexy' new voice Mrs T. had aired on a recent radio show. (In fact, of course, she had had a cold at the time.) 'Margaret,' said one of her ministers, 'I read in my paper that you have developed a sexy voice.' She answered: 'What makes you think I wasn't sexy before?' It is a good question, deserving a sincere and detailed response.* It is also one of perhaps three or four 'warm' moments in Hugo Young's very long, very solid, and unavoidably very gruelling book. British politics just isn't sexy the way Tehran and Pretoria are, the way Moscow can be, the way Washington always is. Oh, how one yearns, after 546 pages, for the banjos, the majorettes, the misappropriated campaign donations, the sweating vaudevillians of the American scene. Describing a gradient of sullen and insular decline, British politics has long ceased to be sexy. But for the time bring, at least, it does have plenty of gender.

The early years form a tale of almost macabre banality. A Young Conservative is one thing (and not a nice thing), yet Margaret Roberts was a reactionary from the cradle. Her adored dad was a Lincolnshire shopkeeper, an alderman, a justice of the peace, a pale and thrifty busybody. At school, little Maggie was 'a model pupil of demure habits and tediously impeccable behaviour'; she ran errands for the Tories in the 1935 election, at the age of ten. Having scraped into the subdued, war-torn Oxford of 1943, she studied chemistry, and gained entry into the tweed-lined sanctum of the Conservative Association.

* I once discussed Mrs Thatcher's feminine qualities with Christopher Hitchens, who had recently spent some time in her company. This was his verdict: 'Oh, she stinks of sex.' And this is my father, Kingsley Amis, in his *Memoirs*: her beauty, he writes, is 'so extreme that ... it can trap me for a split second into thinking I am looking at a science-fiction illustration of some time ago showing the beautiful girl who has become President of the Solar Federation in the year 2200. The fact that it is not a sensual or sexy beauty does not make it a less sexual beauty, and that sexuality is still, I think, an underrated factor in her appeal (or repellence).' Helplessly I reach for the commonplace about the glamour of power. I could further infuriate my father's shade by adducing another cliché: English nostalgia for chastisement. Philip Larkin shared his friend's enthusiasm for the Prime Minister ('I adore Mrs Thatcher'). Larkin was a great poet (see below), but in his personal life he was a clear example of UK toilet-training run amok. He once asked Mrs Thatcher, who had professed herself a fan, to quote a line of his. She blinked and said, 'All the unhurried day / Your mind lay open like a drawer of knives.' The quoted poem, 'Deceptions' (1950), is addressed to a Victorian waif who has been drugged and raped.

There followed two brief careers, one in spectacle-frame plastic, the other in cake fillings. Soon, dashing Denis is motoring through these early pages in his Daimler with its prestige number-plate, DT3. Quite a catch, Denis – his boyish good looks, his 'weed-killer and sheep-dip' fortune. Love bloomed at the annual dinner dance of his trade association. Their honeymoon was her first trip abroad. A year after the twins were born she was looking for a parliamentary seat: Orpington, perhaps? But no. 'Finchley Decides' is the riveting title of Hugo Young's third chapter. And thence to the impossible glamour of the Ministry of Pensions.

Around here the tenor of the story changes. Provincial grit and fresh-faced striving now give way to outright historical ascendancy. Or, to put it differently, phenomenal will was allied with phenomenal luck; and the alliance is still holding, after fifteen years. Thatcher's hot streak reveals itself most brazenly in the absence of any coherent opposition during her decade in power; and it finds its sharpest emblem in the three Argentinian shells which wedged themselves into task-force vessels and failed to explode. Throughout the 1970s there was only one dynamic in British politics, trade-union power, which had brought down – and, it seemed, eternally discredited – both factions of conventional governance. Mrs Thatcher broke the unions by dividing the class they represented. In 1980, unemployment made its largest single-year climb since 1930. And this wasn't what monetarism and the 'Chicago revolution' had in any way predicted. It was a brutal chaos that somehow resolved itself in Mrs Thatcher's favour. With hindsight, would she now claim feminine intuition? Her first act as Prime Minister, after all, was to create the ten-grand-a-year policeman, who could be trusted to keep the lid on the new underclass, once it started to boil. It started boiling in 1981. When she saw the first footage of the riots and looting, the urban Morlocks in their ecstasy of hatred and despair, Mrs Thatcher responded as follows: 'Oh, those poor shopkeepers!'

Women! But *is* she one? Well, yes and no. She has never been afraid to cry in public. Right from her early days at the Ministry of Pensions, if senior officials proved insufficiently right-wing then Mrs T. would avail herself of a refreshing little weep. I once saw her cry on television; I was in a London pub at the time, and was almost knocked off my stool by the ambient roar of foul-mouthed disgust. With her own people she is evidently forceful, fierce, vengeful, hortatory – and always right. 'You mean to say', whispered a newcomer to the Cabinet, 'that you've been putting up with this for four years?' On the other hand she could be recklessly loyal: a strategic hug from a colleague could win lifelong fealty from the melting Leaderene. Above all, her integrity expresses itself in responsibility-taking, in non-delegation. Although she adored Reagan, she was closer to Carter in her love of detail – and closer to Nixon in her resentment of a cultural 'establishment' supposedly ranged against her, in her settled philistinism, and in her passion for secrecy.

She has never expressed any admiration for the women's movement or shown any concern for women's rights. Far from it. 'I hate those strident tones we hear from some women's libbers.' Something of a bitch in the manger, she seemed to want women, or other women, to stay in their place, to become ever keener on 'the family' and its Victorian manifestations. When the Yorkshire Ripper was at his most active, in 1980, Mrs T. told the Home Secretary that she was going to Leeds to take charge of the investigation. This ridiculous proposal was until then her only gesture of female solidarity. When she said *we*, she was being *Queen* Victorian. What she meant was *I*: 'We are in the fortunate position, in Britain, of being, as it were, the senior person in power.' Nevertheless, her wardrobe came almost to engulf the Lady MPs' room in the Commons: 'There would be half a dozen garments hanging up there and underneath them a tidy row of at least eight pairs of shoes.' In 1986 she threw her home closet open to the viewing public on a show called *The Englishwoman's Wardrobe*. Here, in her innocent volubility, she was *all* woman. We will never know where Harold Wilson's Y-fronts come from; but it is a matter of public record that Mrs T. scores her underwear at Marks & Spencer.

It doesn't sound likely, or even a wise move, but Margaret Thatcher is the first British politician to have embraced the television age. In this area she was always entirely unfastidious. Media valets were hired early on and constantly deferred to. In her first campaign the gawky dowd was there for the photo-op, fondling a new-born calf or whatever else they had her do. After the Falklands War she invited David *Chariots of Fire* Puttnam and Andrew *Evita* Lloyd Webber to Chequers at Christmas, in an apparent attempt to coax them into some kind of celebration of her triumph. Her handlers found her femininity helpful; as Young says, a woman is 'well accustomed to manipulation for cosmetic effect'.

She took speech lessons from an instructor at the National Theatre, and did humming exercises to reduce the famous dentist's-drill effect of her voice. 'She achieved a reduction of pitch of 36 Hz.' The refashioning of Mrs T. (creepily apparent from the photographs included in the biography) is in my view crucial to her aura of near-pathological inauthenticity. The creature on the TV, with martyr's frown, pitying smile, saccharine tongue – what is she doing, exactly? Hamming, dissembling, dissimulating? Does *she* buy that tutored serenity?

'Most families have one like her,' wrote Ian McGregor, Mrs T.'s Scottish–American unionbuster. 'She was like my mother – who always had a clear idea of what she wanted to do.' Yet this mother was never loved by her extended family: never loved. Her first victory was secured despite a nineteen-point deficit in her personal-approval ratings (inconceivable in America). Two years later she was as unpopular as any PM since polling began. Even now public opinion spurns her, and shows a confused and wistful sympathy for all those 'wet' notions – consensus, compassion, collectivism – that she so stoutly opposed. Who is this 'dry' mother, whom people can't love, and what kind of children is she rearing? They all feel guilty – this mother can make *anyone* feel guilty. But they feel guilty in the wrong kind of way. They miss the old kind of guilt. They want an aggregation that points towards something better than 'acquisitive individualism'. Something better than mere *human nature*. They don't want someone who just monitors its workings, with a saintly smile.

Elle October 1989

Lincoln by David Herbert Donald

He is more to our taste than he ever was to theirs. Lincoln now commands a consensus of sober admiration and gratitude that was quite unavailable to him or to anybody else during America's bloody adolescence. Changes in aesthetic fashion have even rehabilitated his physiognomy, and drastically. Old Abe was not a *plug-ugly* (a thug, a ruffian), but that's how everyone thought he looked: plug ugly. 'The ugliest man I ever put my eyes on,' said one well-disposed observer, who could discern only a 'plebeian vulgarity' in his gaunt and haunted face. To us, nowadays, that face is a vision of forbidding authenticity.

Bark-hard, slanting and angular, Lincoln stands like Geronimo among his slackly epicene contemporaries; in comparison, supposed heart-throbs such as General McClellan and, indeed, John Wilkes Booth are no more than mustachioed doughboys. In 1854, Lincoln resembles a man of the frontier, but one sent there by Hollywood: lean, calmly illusionless – Robert Ryan rather than Ronald Reagan. A later photograph, taken in February 1865, two months before Lee surrendered his sword to Grant at Appomattox, shows the mouth and the eyes still human and humorous, while the rest of the face has been entirely parched by war.

This new *Lincoln* is a utilitarian biography of detail: a desk job about a desk job. David Herbert Donald, of set purpose, has denied himself the broad contexts, the big pictures of perspective and hindsight. America, convulsing and pullulating in the background, remains strictly undynamic; the South is altogether unexamined, and its president, Jefferson Davis, is merely a named adversary; the origins and aftermath of the civil war are not examined and neither is its strategic course. This is a history of memos and dispatches and late nights in the White House. The great social torments and exhilarations of these years do not buffet the narrative. What Professor Donald offers is the verisimilitude of marathon anxiety.

But before we get 300 pages of that, first we get 300 pages of this: Lincoln's obscurity. 'It is a great piece of folly', Lincoln once said, 'to attempt to make anything out of my early life.' And in truth only a few dabs of colour survive Donald's grinding chronicle. Kentucky, then Indiana, then Illinois. Hogwallows called Sinking Spring Farm, Pigeon Creek, Posey's Landing. The young Lincoln wrote with a buzzard's quill. He briefly attended a 'blab' school, where you chanted your lessons: 'No qualification was ever required of a teacher, beyond "readin, writin, and cipherin."' He worked the rivers, he slaughtered hogs, he split rails; he fought (or marched) in the Black Hawk War; village postmaster; surveyor; lawyer. Stuart & Lincoln, Logan & Lincoln, Lincoln & Lamon. Donald's method, here, often seems frivolously assiduous. Lard factories, waterwheel patents; Lincoln represents Robert Nuckles, who is suing Elijah Bacon for damaging his corn; Lincoln defends John P. Singleton, who is being sued for nonpayment of a debt to Pearly Brown. The reader sits there with Kent's Commentaries and Chatty's Pleadings coming out of his ears, or coming out of the ear they aren't going in at. Moreover, Donald seems to have got hold of The Complete Shopping Lists of Mary Lincoln: 'her purchases . . . included needles, buttons, thread, muslin, calico, cambric, whalebones, and corset lace'. Soon she will be wallpapering their little home in Springfield, Illinois: dark and boldly figured for the bedrooms, but with a lighter pattern for the parlours.

Lincoln's sudden political ascendancy was largely accidental and back-door. Donald's account of it, as we might expect, cleanses the tale of any vestigial glamour. The historical moment of the Whigs had passed, and the Democrats were in their traditional 'disarray', when, in 1850, the new territories of Kansas and Nebraska were opened up for pan-American settlement; hostility to the extension of slavery saw the formation of a new and exclusively northern party, the Republicans. Ten years later, after much massaging at the convention in Chicago (exhaustively documented in these pages), Lincoln, 'The Railsplitter', the green and gawky populist, abruptly became the Republican nominee. He took the presidency without winning a single electoral vote in ten southern states. Secession was entrained by the simple fact of his victory. America had entered a mood resembling clinical dissociation, as democratic hardboileddom came up against the illusions of oligarchy. The American civil war has been called the War Between the States and the War About Slavery. Certainly, it was the war made inevitable by slavery. But there was nothing inevitable about Lincoln.

Once we are in the White House, Donald's method (like Mary Lincoln's shopping) really comes into its own. In tragedy, the hero is first isolated, and then pummelled; and this looked to be the president's destiny. When the fighting began, Lincoln had insufficient troops to secure Washington. The Kansas frontier guards were quartered in the East Room of the White House. As defeat followed defeat, Lincoln borrowed military textbooks from the Library of Congress, attempting to master war in the same way he had mastered law – a measure of his desperation. His studies were interrupted when his two younger sons contracted typhoid. Tad survived, but Willie didn't (joining his elder brother, Eddie, an earlier casualty). Stepping into his office, Lincoln said to his secretary, '"Well, Nicolay, my boy is gone, he is actually gone!"' Then, and then only, Lincoln wept. The largest massacre of whites in American history (the Sioux uprising in Minnesota) was followed by the heaviest defeat in the history of its army, at Fredericksburg. Draft riots erupted in New York City. Republicans of all factions were agitating for Lincoln's court martial. Lincoln faced mutiny everywhere but not within himself. Tragic heroes are meant to fall. Lincoln did not fall.

The internal drama, like the national drama, was unquestionably and indivisibly bound up with Lincoln's evolving attitude towards the Negroes, or the African-Americans, as Donald calls them (anachronistically and perhaps provisionally, for they may soon be called something else). Lincoln was no congenital visionary. Like his father, he was always 'naturally anti-slavery', but he was by no means an abolitionist. America was formed 'on the white basis', and Lincoln was opposed to Negro suffrage, and to intermarriage. Well into his presidency he remained a colonizationist: Lincoln fancied Liberia, or some such spot, as a congenially sweltering homeland. Within sight of the (unfinished) Capitol, seven blocks away, stood the warehouse of Franklin & Armfield, the biggest slavetraders in the country. Lincoln seemed to accept this. He thought that slavery, if contained, would wither and die (soil exhaustion, overmanning). To him, apparently, slavery was above all legal: it was a given that the constitution could do nothing about.

War changed him. In the summer of 1862, on his way to the funeral of Edwin Stanton's infant son, Lincoln announced that he 'had about come to the conclusion that we must free the slaves or be ourselves subdued'. He then moved towards the Emancipation Proclamation and, crucially, towards black enlistment. At no point is the record wholly free of ambivalence and irresolution, but Lincoln's sensibility had clearly undergone a decisive shift. In the summer of 1864, a subliterate Pennsylvanian wrote to Lincoln with the reminder that 'white men is in class number one and black men is in class number two and must be governed by white men forever'. Lincoln replied, asking to be told 'whether you are either a white man or a black one, because in either case, you could not be regarded as an entirely impartial judge'. This is the voice we hear and trust. As the fighting became dirtier and wearier and crueller, Lincoln needed an ideal, a palpable good, to counterbalance 'the moral rot of war', in Churchill's phrase. He had to go back past the constitution to the Declaration of Independence.

Like the assassinated Kennedy, Lincoln was succeeded by Vice-President Johnson; but Andrew, unlike Lyndon, was a disaster. Donald's narrative stops dead on the night of 14 April 1865, after the visit to Ford's Theatre on Tenth Street between E and F. Reconstruction and all the other great questions are still up in the air, but Donald is true to his brief. This book has been praised for its happy congruence of author and subject. Although Donald may be as methodical as Lincoln, he is his junior not least in literary talent. The prose is continually defaced by that scurviest of false graces, Elegant Variation. Here is but one example of Donald's futile dexterity: 'If the president seemed to support the Radicals in New

York, in Washington he appeared to back the Conservatives.'*
Still, if merely by attrition, the book convinces us that only Lincoln
could have found a way through the vast cluster of catastrophes,
steering as the pilots on his western rivers steered, 'from point to
point as they call it, setting the course of the boat no farther than
they can see'.

Sunday Times January 1996

It Takes a Village by Hillary Clinton

Newt Gingrich called her a bitch. Rush Limbaugh called her a
feminazi. One New York weekly called her a scumbag. William
Safire, in the *New York Times*, called her a congenital liar. And the
President himself, it is rumoured, calls her the First Liability. Rumour
goes on to add that Hillary Rodham Clinton is a communist and a

---

* This point may need spelling out. 'The fatal influence', writes Fowler in
Modern English Usage, 'is the advice given to young writers never to use the
same word twice in a sentence ...' Such writers are 'first terrorised by a
misunderstood taboo, next fascinated by a newly discovered ingenuity, & finally
addicted to an incurable vice ...' You can almost hear Professor Donald's cluck
of satisfaction as he follows 'seemed to support' with 'appeared to back'. As
Fowler says, in such sentences 'the writer, far from carelessly repeating a
word in a different application, has carefully not repeated it in a similar
application; the effect is to set readers wondering what the significance of
the change is, only to conclude disappointedly that there is none.' Fowler then
goes on to fulfil 'the main object of this article': 'to nauseate by accumulation
of instances'.

carpetbagger, a wowser and a fraud, a floozie and a dyke. It has been repeatedly suggested that she had an affair with her financial conspirator Vincent Foster, who died, mysteriously, in 1993. At this stage, we don't want to know whether Hillary slept with Vincent Foster. We want to know how she killed him.

America is running out of patience with its First Ladies. In recent years, Barbara Bush alone has escaped whipping; perhaps because everyone assumed, subconsciously, that she wasn't George's wife but his mother. Similarly, the pious Rosalyn Carter came a poor second to Miss Lillian, who, in old age, symbolically reclaimed her virginity. If they're not prigs, they're tramps, like that Jackie, or that Nancy. It makes you wonder why we're so soft on *our* First Ladies. Nobody ever accused Audrey Callaghan, say, of putting out for Frank Sinatra. Mrs Lincoln was the first First Lady (the phrase being coined in her honour); and maybe she was the worst First Lady (profligate, hysterical). But it should have been clear back in 1860 that First Ladydom was a terrible notion, reeking of fake precedence and popularity contests. Our baser instincts will always want to turn the First Lady into the Last Lady. And the resentment would seem to have its sexual component. What these women have in common is that they go to bed with presidents. Hillary, we may be sure, is no exception. Chelsea proves the point.

Still, Mrs Clinton is the most unpopular First Lady ever; and, more substantively, she is the first First Lady to stand before a grand jury. She is clearly the brightest and ablest of her line. And, in all senses, she is the most exposed. As the author of the failed health-care plan, Hillary assumed quasi-ministerial power while remaining unelected and unaccountable. And unsackable, it was said, though the President now seems to have kicked her upstairs. She came to Washington, with her new broom, and the institutions duly defeated and deformed her. Everything she touches turns out to have the word *gate* tacked on to the end of it: Cookiegate, Cattlegate, Travelgate, Fostergate, Whitewatergate; and now Thankyougate.

Thankyougate, or better say Nothankyougate, has to do with the book under review. Evidently, *It Takes a Village* took a village to write, and Hillary neglected to acknowledge the village elder: Barbara Feinman of the *Washington Post*. It appears that Hillary also sought to underpay that villager; but the facts of the dispute hardly matter. What matters is the way things can be made to look. In American politics, you go through the gates and you get to the doors: the doors of 'perception'.

If this book had been written by someone with a different address, then of course I wouldn't be reviewing it. And neither would anybody else. A chatty manual about raising children along voluntarist and communitarian lines, it might have got a mention in the *Times Educational Supplement*, or in *Pregnancy* magazine. But, as the jacket copy patiently explains, Hillary Rodham Clinton is 'America's First Lady'; 'she lives in the White House with the President and their daughter, Chelsea'. Thus the book will be considered top-down rather than bottom-up. *It Takes a Village* looks like a book and feels like a book but in important respects it isn't a book. It is a re-election pamphlet or a stump speech; it is a 300-page press release. At no point did I find myself questioning the benignity of the author's original impulse; indeed, the book is as sincere, in its way, as anything I've ever managed to finish. And yet there is also something horrible about it. More subtext than text, ameliorative, harmonial, beamingly upbeat, it teaches an ugly lesson.

First, we have to imagine Hillary, in the Old Executive Office Building, with her staff of fifteen women (and one man: what is *he* doing there?), plus Barbara Feinman and other helpers 'so numerous that I will not even attempt to acknowledge them individually', marshalling her manuscript. Their object is to reduce it to a condition of pan-inoffensiveness. This is a big job, because being inoffensive, and being offended, are now the twin addictions of the culture. Chapter by chapter, *Village* goes over to Bill's people, to see if they have a problem with this or are uncomfortable with that, and Bill's people bounce it back to Hill's people with what they are unhappy about, and so it goes on, until in broad daylight and full consciousness you confront printed sentences which read:

A University of Chicago study showed that by the age of two, children whose mothers had talked to them frequently since infancy had bigger vocabularies than children from the same socio-economic backgrounds whose mothers had been less talkative.

The 1990 Census showed that young people without college degrees earn significantly less on average than those with degrees.

Brisk walking, hiking and bicycling are all good exercise and are great ways to spend time together.

In addition to being read to, children love to be told stories.

By the time everybody's done, we are out there on the cutting edge of the uncontroversial.

As for style, well, the First Lady should not be seen to be solemn. She can make jokes. But we don't want her sounding like a flake. Every joke, therefore, must wear a joke badge: it must be accompanied by a plump exclamation mark. As in 'Sometimes Mother knows best too!' Or: 'So much for her grasp of physics!'

Colloquialisms are appropriate only when they come with a tamper-proof set of inverted commas. To say 'All of us blow our tops' may give the impression that things sometimes get a little too ragged around here. But to say 'All of us "blow our tops"' suggests that the tendency is under control. The stories about Bill and Chelsea, and Hillary's 'kinfolk', establish the human context; we can then wind down into the sanitized anti-poetry of soft jargon, with its follow-up and outreach, its skills, tools, goals and roles, its giving and caring and ongoing caregiving.

Even the grammarian will remain unoffended by Hillary's syntax, though one might enter a few quibbles. A 'light-year' is a measurement of distance, not time. 'Nurturance' is a neologism we can muddle along without. 'Stomachachy', finally, is not a campaign stop on the way to Poughkeepsie but Hillary's epithet for a pain in the gut.

Properly decoded, then, *Village* is a portrait of a First Lady who deserves a second chance. And a second term. This is not the unsmiling feminist, the ballbreaking ambulance-chaser, who came to Washington four years ago. This is someone softer, gentler, homier, holier. As parents, Bill and Hillary could be said to have fallen at the first hurdle: they called their child Chelsea. But they've made up for it since. 'From the time she was a baby, Bill and I took turns reading to her and praying with her'; and home life in the White House, it seems, is now a full-time trance of piety. Toiling through all the cuteness and cant, I was struck by one sullen sentence: 'Life itself is the curriculum, as are history, literature, current events, and, especially, religious teachings.' With that measured 'especially', Hillary blows a kiss of farewell to the secular intellect and falls into step with the philistines.

One keeps turning disconcertedly to the photograph on the back flap. With her pearls, her cloth-buttoned suit top, her spryly waved hair and glazed maquillage, she looks like the wife of some sulphurous video vicar (who, any day now, will be found in a motel somewhere, under a heap of prostitutes). America has taken Hillary Rodham and bent her into a different shape. She stands there, smiling, dumbed well down, and purged of all quiddity.

Sunday Times March 1996

The World and I

The End of Nature by Bill McKibben

The Green Movement needs a holy book. So does Viking Penguin. So do I. So do we all. Our need survives *The End of Nature*, in which Bill McKibben fails to fulfil the rolling prophecies of his publicity kit. The book is honest, decent, salutary; also largely unresonant. Also callow, and painfully stretched. Perhaps one ought to be easier to please than usual, when the subject is the death of everything. But we are not yet reduced to scattered shouts of *Help* and *Whoah* and (above all) *Christ*.

Or not quite yet. This was meant to be the era of post-historical man. The species was just about to finish mastering the wilderness when it transpired, with sinister synchrony, that the wilderness had turned into a toilet. Although Mr McKibben knows about time-scales, he isn't much good at evoking their significance ('It always shocks me when I realize that 2010 is now as close as 1970 – closer than the break-up of the Beatles'). It is certainly hard for human beings to grasp that in a single century their planet has aged four-and-a-half billennia. This atrocious *coup de vieux* has effectively rearranged the four dimensions. The frontier we face is no longer spatial. It is temporal.

The holy book we mentioned would, of course, be a Bad News Bible. By now, most of us have a notion of the gloomier scenarios and models and loops and kick-ins. We have an image of this kind of future (shaped by the set-dressers of *Blade Runner* and *RoboCop*): wearing welder's goggles, and studded with skin cancer, the average Eskimo will spend all winter under the mosquito nets, playing host to successive bouts of malaria, ringworm, encephalitis and dengue fever. It was to allay such fears that Donald Hodel, Reagan's Secretary of the

Interior, urged Americans to counter ozone-depletion with the wider
purchase of sunglasses and baseball caps. Clearly it will take a new kind
of effort to imagine – let alone deal with – the grosser synergies that
are now in view. A further 2 billion tonnes of carbon await release
in the threatened forests; if ocean temperatures rise, then a further
ten trillion tonnes of methane await release in the polar tundras. Mr
McKibben discusses these matters with all due caution – indeed, with
sober distaste. He is trustworthy; he doesn't want nature to be over
quicker, just to give his book more punch.

Besides, his main point is that nature is *already* over, or that its
meaning, at least, has been irreversibly transformed. Nature isn't
'out there' any more, because out there is just like in here. Without
wanting to, without meaning to, we have altered the chemical
composition of the planet. The Arctic penguin, the Saharan wind,
the Patagonian mountain creek: all now bear man's taint. We rightly
regard this disaster as our own unpremeditated crime, and tend to
account for it in terms of profligacy, rapacity, and foul habits ('binge'
is the word Mr McKibben keeps using). Some things we do are
dirtier and more wasteful than other things we do; but it is difficult
to work up much indignation about paddy fields and farting cattle
(both of which produce methane). In fact we are incapable of any
real antipathy towards our own worst enemy: human numbers. We
look up from the campfire, alarmed by the growling and slavering,
the splitting branches. And the enemy is no longer 'nature'. The
enemy is us – ourselves.

If it's broken, how, then, do we get nature fixed? Do we Do
More, or do we Do Less? Aggressive solutions include various kinds
of atmospheric hose-downs and paint-jobs, with infra-red lasers and
fleets of jumbo jets. If you want to increase the earth's reflectivity,
for instance, why not coat the oceans with a layer of white styrofoam
chips? Do-More takes on a Promethean dimension when we look
at biotechnology or gene-splicing, which might give us 'elite' or
designer forests, not to mention designer lamb-chops and designer
chickens (minus wings, tails and heads). Mr McKibben, naturally,
wants to Do Less. He is additionally prepared to Buy Less and to
Drive Less. 'We screwed it up,' as he says, not untypically; but

perhaps it isn't too late 'to clean up our collective act'. He counsels humility, childlessness, a tremulous pantheism. He just wants us all to cool off.

The End of Nature has been compared to Jonathan Schell's *The Fate of the Earth*, which is certainly the set text on the nuclear question. But the two books have little in common apart from the necessary immodesty of their titles. To put it simply, Mr McKibben lacks weight of voice. Speaking on behalf of all human life, Schell attained a pristine impersonality, whereas Mr McKibben (or shall I call him Bill?) is throughout a puzzled and guileless presence: his thumbprints and inkspots, his false starts and rethinks, are visible in the margin of every page. Bill is always biking and hiking (though not always grammatically: 'A forty-minute hike brings the dog and I to the top of the hill'),* always swimming and paddling; he exults in 'the rippling muscular joy' of his body and is pleased too by his nice house in the Adirondacks with its many eco-conscious features, including a fax machine that 'makes for graceful, environmentally sound communication'. Bill's over-intimate admission that he and his wife 'try very hard not to think about how much we'd like a baby' prompts two contradictory thoughts. First, that it will take many generations, and many babies, before people evolve into not wanting them. And secondly that the future would clearly be the better for Bill's descendants. We wouldn't be in this fix, if we were all a bit more like Bill.

These pages read well enough, so long as Mr McKibben is sticking to his dignified summaries of the not very numerous books and reports he has read on the subject. The trouble begins when he gets personal, or thoughtful, or restless, and starts livening things up with his jokes and his hearty colloquialisms ('big deal', 'deep down and nitty gritty',

* It is chastening to see this rank genteelism in print (I recently saw it twice in the space of a week, from the pens of Eric Jacobs and Julie Burchill), because it means the editors and sub-editors don't know about it either. And it's really very simple: just take out the 'So-and-so and' bit, and your ear will do it for you. Bill wouldn't write 'A forty-minute hike brings I to the top of the hill', now would he?

'*Whew!*'). It may also be that the appropriate language is unavailable, or unavailable for now. There is something obsolescent and accusatory about the nature-ramble literature that Mr McKibben likes quoting from: fragrant, charming, russet, gilded, harmonious, clear, sweet, healthy. On the other hand, what can you do with *stressed* and *putrescible* and *biomass crashes*, with *feedback* and *dieback*, with *ips* and *thrips*. In *The Fate of the Earth* Schell had a murderous – or suicidal – mentality to oppose, with its institutions, its jargon, its pedantry and euphemism. He had the bang, whereas Mr McKibben is stuck with the whimper. He must deal with the slow accretions of human folly, human weakness, human accident.

One cannot determine how much Schell contributed to the revolution in consciousness that is certainly underway with regard to nuclear weapons. If you want to choose a single saviour, or prophet, then you would probably be on firmer ground with Mikhail Gorbachev. The Green Movement still lacks a bible, but Gorbachev may also serve here as an inadvertent figurehead. He declared that the global Emperor of Deterrence wore no clothes. The Emperor is nude now. And at last we have the leisure to contemplate the condition of his skin.

Independent on Sunday February 1990

Elvis and Andy: US Males

Elvis, We Love You Tender by Dee Presley, Billy, Rick
and David Stanley, as told to Martin Torgoff

'What happened, El?' said Vernon Presley to his son, one day in 1956.
Elvis was twenty-one at the time, and a multimillionaire. 'The last
thing I can remember is I was working in a can factory and you were
driving a truck.' Elvis laughed. 'I don't know what it is,' he later told
a reporter. 'I just fell into it, really.'

What happened was this. The Presleys were Depression-shoved
nomads from the deep rural South. Elvis's uncle, Vester Presley, was
a teenager before he owned his first pair of shoes. Looking for work,
the family straggled into Memphis. Elvis was a half-employed slum
spiv when he did his first audition. He recorded the rockabilly classic
'That's All Right, Mama' – and suddenly the tenement Okies found
themselves in Graceland, a Doric mansion at the far end of Elvis
Presley Boulevard.

It was during Elvis's much-publicized stint of military service in
Germany that the present writers came into the story. Dee Stanley
was the wife of a morose sergeant stationed in Bad Nauheim. On
a bored impulse Dee gave El a call, to offer him some Southern
hospitality. They arranged to meet for coffee. As it happened, Elvis
was on manoeuvres; but Dee was greeted and squired by the courtly,
personable and recently widowed Vernon . . . On her return to the
US, Dee got a divorce and ensconced herself at Graceland, with her
three small sons, Billy, Rick and David.

Elvis, We Love You Tender is their story, cobbled together twenty
years on with the excitable help of journalist Martin Torgoff. Elvis's
entourage was divided into TCBers and TLCers: those who Took
Care of Business and those who gave Tender Loving Care when

the exhausted menfolk returned from the road. One way or another, then, the Stanleys were seldom far from Elvis's side. In many respects their book is a sorry effort – coarse, sentimental and lurchingly written. But the vulgarity of its idiom provides some inadvertent literary interest, and the memoir is far too damaging to all concerned for one to doubt its authenticity.

'Elvis was an enigma,' writes Torgoff, 'a walking, breathing paradox.' Oh no he wasn't. Indeed, in the circumstances it is hard to imagine a character of more supercharged banality. Elvis was a talented hick destroyed by success: what else is new? All that distinguished him was the full-blooded alacrity of his submission to drugs, women, money and megalomania, and the ease with which these excesses co-existed with his natural taste for spiritual conceit and grandiose Confederate *machismo*.

First, the women. During his early days on the road, Elvis 'decided to see how many chicks he could bang just for the hell of it'. He liked women who were 'classically feminine', didn't drink or talk too much, and had 'that unbeatable combo of beautiful, rounded ass and long tapered leg'. These women were called 'foxes' – 'quality women' as opposed to 'dogs'. 'No dogs around the Boss' was a TCB rule. Some foxes were easier to catch than others; but then El would 'slap a Mercedes or a home on them and . . .' (His youthful wife Priscilla, incidentally, tired of Elvis's infidelities and ran off with one of his karate instructors.) There was, however, 'nothing kinky' about the King. 'Elvis', says Rick, 'was very proper.'

Similarly, Elvis was never a 'casual' user of drugs, and despised hippie concoctions like marijuana and LSD. He drank hardly at all. 'My head tells me I need a pill,' he would inform one of the captive quacks who tended him. Anything that came from a prescription seemed scientifically sanctified to Elvis. The uppers and downers he took souped up his bodyclock and probably contributed to the heart failure that caused his death. He tried drying out on numerous occasions; but minor TCBers would smuggle 'medication' into his room. 'They'd get stuff for it, you know, cars.'

On the road, Elvis carried a minimum of two guns on him at all times. He occasionally threatened fellow motorists with these if they honked or yelled at him too much. He enjoyed shooting up TV sets and hotel chandeliers. Never back down from a fight, he told his step-brothers, or else 'you're gonna feel like shit for the rest of your life'. 'A man has got to be a man,' he explained. Elvis elaborated tellingly on this theme in his song 'US Male': 'Mess with my woman, and you're messin' with the US Male. That's M-A-L-E, son, that's me.'

Meanwhile, Elvis would regularly repair to the quiet and elegance of Graceland. Here, all was matriarchal propriety: mild rough-housing with the boys, teetotal barbecues by the pool, communal prayers and a terrifying variety and intensity of familial emotion. Here, too, Elvis pursued his interest in religion and fringe parapsychology. He believed himself to be blessed with psychic powers; his entourage apparently spent many a tedious hour pretending that Elvis could read their minds. He was 'really into miracles'. Elvis pondered on the afterlife, entertaining tasteless reveries of his coming reunion with his dead twin and much-lamented mother. But he still lived the life, in a thickening mist of drugs and boredom. There was the usual eighteen-year-old in his bed on the last morning, as Elvis lay dying in the bathroom next door. 'My baby is gone. My *baby*, Dee,' said Vernon.

This is Rick's version of 'the paradox': 'He was a true believer who made his own rules so that his beliefs could blend with the way he lived his life.' Handy, that. 'Elvis *was* Elvis,' Torgoff concurs. 'He was *just* the King!' Does this remind you of any-thing? The world-view of a child-in-arms, for instance, a couple of weeks before the primal scream? Everyone who ever met Elvis, it seems, is currently writing a book about him, from his numer-ologist to his under-gardener. *Elvis, We Love You Tender* will not be the least lurid, but it will probably be by far the warmest – vivid testimony to the hysteria that the King still manages to inspire.

Observer August 1980

The Andy Warhol Diaries edited by Pat Hackett

Despite their virtuoso triviality, their naïve snobbery, and their incredible length, the diaries of Andy Warhol are not without a certain charm. Of course, they aren't even diaries; they are the 'Collected Cassettes' or the 'Collected Wiretaps'. On most mornings Andy Warhol called his former secretary, Pat Hackett, and rambled on for a while about what he did the day before. She made 'extensive notes', she explains, and typed them up 'while Andy's intonations were fresh in my mind'. So that's what we are looking at here: 800 pages – half a million words – of Andy's intonations.

But it works, somehow. 'Peter Boyle and his new I think wife were there.' 'Princess Marina of I guess Greece came to lunch.' 'Nell took her clothes sort of off.' 'Raymond [is] out there posing for David Hockney – Raymond takes planes just to go pose.' Ms Hackett's editing, one feels, is affectionate and scrupulous, yet correctly unprotective. And after a while you start to trust the voice – Andy's voice, this wavering mumble, this ruined slur. It would seem that *The Andy Warhol Diaries* thrives on the banal; for in the daily grind of citizenship and dwindling mortality, the nobody and the somebody are one.

Meanwhile, here comes everybody – or at least everybody who is somebody. 'We went over to Studio 54 and just everybody was there.' 'You go to places where people are sort of nobodies.' 'Everybody was somebody . . . just everybody came after the awards. Faye Dunaway and Raquel Welch and just everybody.' But who is everybody? Or who is everybody else? Everybody is Loulou de la Falaise and Monique Van Vooren and Issey Miyake, Peppo Vanini and Yoyo Bischofberger, Sao Schlumberger and Suzie Frankfurt and Rocky Converse, Alice Ghostley, Dawn Mello and Way Bandy and Esme, Viva, Ultra and Tinkerbelle and Teri Toye, Dianne Brill, Billy Name, Joe Papp, Bo Polk, Jim Dine, Marc Rich, Nick Love and John Sex.

Similarly Andy went everyplace, or everyplace that was any-place – or not even. He goes to the opening of an escalator at Bergdorf Goodman, to Regine's for Julio Iglesias's birthday, to an icecream-shop unveiling in Palm Beach, to Tavern on the Green for a 'thing' (this is a word that Andy has a lot of time for) to announce that Don King is taking over the management of the Jacksons, to the Waldorf-Astoria for the Barbie Doll bash, someplace else to judge a Madonna-lookalike playoff and someplace else to judge a naked-breast contest. It strains you to imagine the kind of invitation Andy might turn down. To the refurbishment of a fire exit at the Chase Manhattan Bank? To early heats of a wet-leotard competition in Long Island City? Some days, of course, nothing much happens. 'Had to go close on the building and we had to drink some champagne with the people', for instance, listlessly accounts for Oct. 19, 1981. Or take this eventful interlude in September 1980: 'I tried to watch TV but nothing good was on.' Ah, such striving. If you try, you can make Andy's life sound almost ghoulishly varied: 'I had tickets . . . to the rock kid who ate the heads off bats'; 'Lewis Allen came down with the dummy-makers who're making a robot of me for his play.' But really every day was the same old round. Occasionally he stayed in and dyed his eyebrows, or read the memoirs of some old movie queen, or met with success in front of the television (*The Thorn Birds* or *I Love Lucy*; this is the man who saw *Grease II* three times in one week). And every now and then a mention in the news media proves to be as good, or as bad, as the real thing: 'There was a party at the Statue of Liberty, but I'd already read publicity of me going to it so I felt it was done already.'

During the years covered by the diaries (from 1976 until Warhol's death in 1987), the planet was spinning, as it always spins, but Andy's self-absorption remained immovable. Events of world-historical sig-nificance are simply given a quick sentence here and there, before being engulfed by the usual gossip and grumbling. This isn't to say that Andy remains untouched by current affairs. The 1986 American raid on Libya seriously disrupts a live television show he's doing. The *Achille Lauro* hijacking in 1985 causes concern, because now 'everybody will be watching *The Love Boat* . . . with my episode on it'. The fall of the Shah of Iran spells a lost commission ('At dinner the Iranians told me that when I paint the Shah to go easy on the eye shadow and lipstick'). For Andy, as for Bellow's Citrine, history is a nightmare during which he is trying to get a good night's rest: 'Some creep asked us what I thought about the torture in Iran and Paulette said, "Listen, Valerian Rybar is torturing me here in New York." He's still decorating her apartment, she was complaining that it's been a year.'

Manners change too, though, and Andy is better placed, and better equipped, to reflect the general retreat, the increasing social distrust, of his final decade. In 1977 he can say of a woman dress designer: 'She acts like a businesswoman – she doesn't take much coke in the day.' But by 1987 it isn't just Andy who is drinking Perrier water and then curling up with a quarter of a Valium. AIDS makes its first appearance halfway through the book, in February 1982, where it is called 'gay cancer' (in contradistinction to 'regular cancer'). By June 1985 it is referred to as 'you-know-what'. The diaries show very clearly how the transcendentalism of the counterculture eventually turned in on the self, on the human body. Andy, already a fervent hypochondriac (he was shot in 1968 by a woman who had once appeared in one of his underground movies), shuffles on from beauty classes and pedicure into nutrition, collagen, shiatsu treatments, crystals, kinesiology and other desperate quackeries. By December 1986, AIDS itself is weirdly called 'the magic disease'.

It would be hard work, and a waste of energy, to do much disapproving of Andy Warhol. He doesn't take himself seriously enough for that – or for anything else. It is worth remarking that at no point does he say anything interesting (or even non-ridiculous) about art. He'll mention having 'a good art idea' or attending 'an art party'; he'll mention that 'art is big now'. 'We talked art,' he says, and the reader leans forward attentively, into this: 'Thomas told the story of the Picasso he bought from Paulette Goddard, it cost $60,000 and he brought it to one of the Picasso kids and they said it was a fake, and he said Paulette gave him a hard time, that she was "difficult," but she did give him his money back.'

It's all on that level. Andy's agent tells him 'not to take the wrinkles out too much on these old people'. There is a conference about Dolly Parton's beauty mark: is it in or out? 'I'd taken it out and they want it in, so I called Rupert [Smith, Andy's silk-screener] and told him it was in again.' Pia Zadora wants a painting and she'll 'take it with her if it fits into her husband's jet, so they were measuring it'. For the rest, it's desultory reports on how much his Marlons and Marilyns and Lizzes and Elvises are currently fetching. The Warholian apotheosis is duly reached when Andy does a commission for Campbell's soup. It troubles him – 'Me standing there twenty years later and still with a Campbell's soup thing' – but he doesn't quite appreciate the asymmetry. Once the artist urging us to re-examine the ordinary, Warhol is now the commercial portraitist celebrating the vendible. 'And for all the work and publicity, I should've charged them like $250,000.'

Plainly, Andy was funny about money. Throughout the diaries he dutifully records the cost of everything – everything claimable, anyway. These bracketed price-tags look odd at first – on page 1: 'phone call for directions (phone $.10)' – but we soon get used to them. Andy's crab soap cost $6, and his bulletproof vest cost $270. 'She said Matt didn't relate to her (dinner $600 including tip).' 'Drank and talked and looked out of the window ($180).' Money has a habit of making people seem lopsided. Andy pays for Grace Jones's dinner, despite the wad of hundreds she produces. And yet: 'Went to church and while I was kneeling and praying for money a shopping-bag lady came in and asked me for some. She asked for $5 and then upped it to $10. It was like Viva. I gave her a nickel.' Well, it could have been worse. It could have said: 'I gave her a nickel ($.05).'

Warhol was a fame snob, a looks snob, a weight snob, a height snob and an age snob. But he got older, and iller, and was obliged to wander the biological desert of middle-aged gaydom. Childish himself, he became a frustrated parent. His chaste crushes never seemed to work out: 'Looking back now, I guess I wasn't seeing what I didn't want to see. Again. Does it ever end? Do you ever get smart?' Towards the close, the invitations dry up, the photographers pass him by, the calls go unreturned. 'I like ugly people. I do. And anyway, ugly people are just as hard to get as pretty people – they don't want you, either.'

His most thoroughly sympathetic moments come in his dealings with animals. Even here he is habitually wounded and touchy: 'I took all my old bread to the park and tried to give it to the birds but they didn't come around and I just hated them for that.' Or with his dachshunds, Amos and Archie: when he returns home from work on a rainy day and finds that one of them has wet his bed, 'I beat him up. Amos.' Or, most appropriately, most comically, most hopelessly, when the Walt Disney film crew arrives and asks him who his favourite Disney character is, 'and I said, "Minnie Mouse, because she can get me close to Mickey."'

New York Times Book Review June 1989

Bad Dreams

*Blundering into Disaster: Surviving the First Century
of the Nuclear Age* by Robert McNamara

Our experience of World Wars is in a sense exhaustive, but our experience of how they get started is confined to just the two models – Sarajevo and Munich, critical accident and unappeasable psychosis. On a planet that now sports over 50,000 nuclear weapons, pure accident and pure psychosis are improbable contenders for the initiation of World War III; as the title of Robert McNamara's book suggests, it will more likely be some kind of mixture. The only thing that could precipitate general nuclear attack would be the fear of general nuclear attack. You would never go first unless the enemy looked like going first; and, in a crisis, he would look like going first, and so would you. Mrs Thatcher has dismissed the idea of a nuclear-free world as 'a dangerous dream'. In fact this would exactly and evocatively describe the status quo.

It should be said early on that this book contains almost nothing new. It feels weighty, yet such authority as it has derives, not from McNamara's writing, but from his former eminence as Secretary of Defense under Kennedy and Johnson. Two-thirds of the way through, the book fragments into Appendices plus Glossary, Notes, Acknowledgments and Index. The information in the *apparatus* you can get elsewhere. More surprisingly, the information in the body of the book you can get elsewhere too, pretty much. It is not what is said; it is who is saying it.

Certainly this isn't the book for lovers of the power anecdote and the geopolitical indiscretion. McNamara takes us behind the scenes, but in brisk and formal style, as if conducting a coach-party tour of the Pentagon. True, we glimpse, or overhear, a fuddled

Johnson summoned to the Hot Line: 'Goddam it, Bob, what is the problem?' (the problem was the Middle East, June 1967). True, we still stroll with McNamara to his car on 'that beautiful fall evening' (27 October, 1962: Cuba) when he feared he 'might never live to see another Saturday night'. The third nuclear crisis, Berlin in 1961 − the third occasion when nuclear war came close without anyone wanting it to − flits by in a colourless page and a half. No stand-offs in the Oval Office. No white-knuckle scenes in the (aptly named) Situation Room.

The remaining 'insider' stuff is carefully rigidified for the record, with McNamara emerging with dignity and steady credit. 'At that point I said to the President . . .' Two hundred words of impeccable McNamara grammar are then followed by: 'The President seized on this proposal as a way out of a very difficult position.' Or: 'I opposed the Air Force's recommendation. Kennedy accepted my judgment.' In 1962 the journalist Stewart Alsop asked McNamara to comment on CIA evidence that the Russians were hardening their missile sites. 'Stew,' drawls Bob (it is the book's one split-second of intimacy), 'I never comment on information relating to the CIA. But let me say this: if the Soviets are hardening their missile sites, thank God.' Several congressmen promptly demanded McNamara's resignation. They didn't realize, as he did, that *deterrence* requires a complementary element of *reassurance*. In office, Bob blundered a bit himself; but he was quick to intuit some unfamiliar nuclear realities.

What was prescient then, however, is now common ground: and the book isn't very much more than a respectable primer. Some of the emphases are new, or newish. One is grateful for his remarks on what has been called American 'angelization', or willed unblameability. According to Caspar Weinberger, the Russians 'know perfectly well that we will never launch a first strike on the Soviet Union'. How do they know this? Is it because, as Reagan once claimed, 'we have more regard for human life than those monsters do'? It is the current Administration's belief, writes McNamara, 'that the Soviets can trust us. At the same time, how-ever, a prime justification for SDI has been that we can't trust them.' Michael McGwire's point about 'cognitive dissonance' is relevant here. Reagan and Gorbachev may make some friendly overtures, but both happen to be packing several dozen tons of TNT for each 'enemy' citizen. You might as well expect a lasting concord between Godzilla and the Creature from the Black Lagoon.

In his valedictory pages McNamara offers Minimum Deterrence as a path through the next half-century. Five hundred each: any fewer, and successful cheating will tip the balance. Well, that is still the equivalent of 30,000 Hiroshimas, plus perhaps a million Chernobyls. A little later he is obliged to 'recognise that major changes in nuclear strategy are unlikely until they receive broad support from the American people and from the other members of Nato'. In other words, what is needed is a revolution in consciousness. While instinct tells us that the revolution will have to come from below, contributions from above retain a peculiar value. McNamara joins a distinguished list of senior politicians, strategists and soldiers who have woken from the dangerous dream. With them, the revolution seems to be one not of consciousness so much as conscience. The dream only ends when the career ends. Robert Jay Lifton has called this syndrome 'retirement wisdom'.

'That's the way you can have a winner,' said George Bush in 1980, gamely best-casing it on nuclear war. 'I find such comments incomprehensible,' says McNamara, 'as one who has confronted the possibility of nuclear exchanges.' These last words evoke a different book, one that McNamara hasn't produced here. Probably that kind of book could never be written by someone who has wielded that kind of power. The exclusion would seem to be mutual, with nuclear politics always stifling the human voice. This is why we listen to Gorbachev (who regards the nuclear situation as fundamentally puerile) with such bafflement. And perhaps we shouldn't be asking the question: is he sincere? Perhaps we should be asking the question: is he historically inevitable?

Observer June 1987

Blessed Assurance: At Home with the Bomb in Amarillo, Texas
by A.G. Mojtabai

A.G. Mojtabai's subject is 'the intersection of nuclear reality and religious vision'; and she isn't referring to papal encyclicals, pastoral letters, or the gentle activism of troubled divines. She is referring to American fundamentalism, to those Born Again Christians who have the nuclear holocaust firmly fixed in their calendars and anticipate it with the hottest zeal. 'Go understand people' is what Americans say when they can't understand people. Miss Mojtabai, at any rate, has given it a try.

She has gone to Amarillo, Texas, a panhandle railhead town, a place of flash floods, dust-devils and polar winds. Amarillo has known boom and bust, and now clings to a hard-won prosperity. About 25 per cent of the local economy depends on Pantex, the final assembly plant of all American nuclear weapons. The arms race would therefore seem to be 'good for business', 'good for Amarillo'. Pantex also qualifies Amarillo as 'a class 1, 2 and 3 target' for Soviet missiles, and makes it a likely spot for nuclear accident, terrorist attack, and so on (in addition, Amarillo is now being teed up for a nuclear-waste 'facility'). Pantex's motto: *Pantexan: We believe that peaceful coexistence is best maintained by being Too Tough to Tackle.*

'AMARILLO', says the sign on the way into town: 'WE LIKE WHO WE ARE'. One suspects that people who like who they are, and like saying that they like who they are, are soon going to be saying that they don't like who *you* are. But after a while the town opens up to Miss Mojtabai, with her gently persistent interrogations, her uncensorious female presence (and her novelist's eye and ear). It opens up, like any American town, with generosity, candour, vigorous community *esprit*. The place teems with bake sales and kiddie clubs; on Sunday mornings 'joy buses' ferry the children to church. Why, Pantex itself has blood drives, car pools, educational grants for employees, and a fine record on the hiring of non-whites.

'In Naples,' says a local, 'they don't worry about Vesuvius. They're used to it.' Instead of 'worrying', Amarilloans simply find themselves leading lives of fantastic contradiction. Pantex official Jack Thompson, who coaches Little League and helps out at Kids Inc., breaks off from an hour of 'honey-dos' (chores for the wife) to tell Miss Mojtabai about Soviet infiltration in America's nurseries (infants with fake passports). Judy Mamou, ex-hooker, now an evangelist, gives an interesting slant to the Red/dead axis: 'If you're Red, you *are* dead.' A dead Red is just dead, whereas a dead Judy Mamou would simply 'go home' and 'be in heaven with the Lord'. Royce Elms, a preacher at Jubilee Tabernacle, has the end of time pencilled in for 1988, but carries life insurance – 'in case the Lord tarries'. Royce's morning sermons, or matinees, are about 'success principles', as laid down by the Bible ('God don't sponsor no flops'); in the evenings it's Armageddon – the Tribulation, the Second Coming, the Rapture.

The *mise-en-scène* for the end of the world is not Hieronymus Bosch so much as Walt Disney. Just before the destruction of the planet by (nuclear) fire, the Rapture occurs. Believers become astronauts, whisked up to heaven at 186,000 miles per second. On Earth, life goes on as usual for a while, though you will notice that the more devout members of the community are, rather ominously, no longer around. The Antichrist soon comes to power, via a United World Church, or a cartel of corporations, or possibly the EEC.

Nuclear Tribulation follows. After seven years Christ returns and defeats Satan in the Battle of Armageddon near the hill of Megiddo in Israel. On top of sores, seas of blood, fire, darkness, drought and unclean spirits, we get the seventh vial of wrath, 'poured out into the air' – nuclear fallout, perhaps. Then a further sifting of unbelievers and the binding up of Satan, who, one thousand years later, stages his final doomed revolt. Then a new heaven and a new earth.

For most of its length *Blessed Assurance* reads like an analysis of the richest, the most elaborate brew of credulity that human beings have yet concocted. Along the way, though, the phenomenon starts to look more familiar. It looks like religion. An implausible quest for implausible solace, outlandish suffering set against outlandish reward, a way of thinking (or emoting) about the unthinkable. Here, religion has adapted to the nuclear reality. As a result it looks preposterous. But everything that adapts to the nuclear reality is going to look preposterous – or ugly, or insane, or just preternaturally trivial.

Miss Mojtabai suffers, in her vivid exploration, from an embarrassment of riches, or an embarrassment of embarrassment. She takes no pleasure in gloating over human stupidity; and the wistful gloom of her conclusion feels accurate. After all, in this maelstrom of terror and desire the only things with any objective reality are the weapons – the weapons, and the holy book of a Bronze Age nomad tribe. Consider these two quotes:

1   I have read the Book of Revelations and, yes, I believe the world is going to end – by an act of God, I hope – but every day I think that time is running out.

2   You know, I turn back to [the] ancient prophets in the Old Testament and the signs foretelling Armageddon, and I find myself wondering if – if we're the generation that's going to see that come about.

It would, I suppose, be neither here nor there if these remarks came from some summoner or pardoner, some Chaucerian huckster, some morons' pin-up or vaudevillian vicar of the Born Again circuit. But the first speaker is US Secretary of Defense Caspar Weinberger. And the second is Ronald Reagan.

Observer January 1987

With Enough Shovels by Robert Scheer; *Defence of the Realm*
by Alun Chalfont; *The New Maginot Line* by Jon Connell;
Star Wars in a Nuclear World by Lord Zuckerman;
Star Warriors by William Broad

The best time to deal with a nuclear missile is when it is on the ground and subject to negotiation – or, more generally, to diplomacy. The worst time to deal with a nuclear missile is when it is heading towards you at four miles a second. In the latter case, there is likely to be only one winner: the nuclear missile. But the error of SDI, or Star Wars, is far deeper than that. It presupposes a situation of unique desperation and catastrophic failure, one in which everyone has already 'lost'. It presupposes nuclear war. 'Well, things do go wrong,' the layman will say with a shrug. But this thing isn't like other things. For the first time in history, human beings have come up with something that may eliminate all second chances, something that therefore *must never go wrong*.

It is possible to read a very great deal of pro-SDI literature without encountering anything whatever to be said for SDI (or for the literature). Turning to the literature of the other side, one's sceptical murmur becomes a roar of disbelief. SDI-admirers allow that space defence would be the most complicated and expensive venture ever undertaken. But even if it could be achieved at a single snap of the President's fingers it wouldn't be worth having. It remains a bad idea because that is what it is: a bad idea. That SDI has gained such momentum is a mystery more exotic than the workings of the X-ray laser or the particle-beam weapon, a mystery to which we shall gingerly return. First, the context.

Ronald Reagan campaigned and came to power as a nuclear jingo. Denounced by the far right (after INF: the long-sought deal on intermediate nuclear forces) as 'a useful idiot' of the USSR, Reagan was unquestionably for many years a useful idiot of the far right.

His *apparat*, and his Vice-President, talked with ghoulish freedom about 'winning' or 'prevailing' in a protracted nuclear war: 'It would be a terrible mess, but it wouldn't be unmanageable'; 'Nuclear war is a destructive thing, but still in large part a physics problem.'

These proclamations, of which there are many, are usefully collected in Robert Scheer's terrifying book, *With Enough Shovels* (1982). Controversial at the time, the Administration's early recklessness is now largely forgotten, or put down to youthful exuberance on Reagan's part (talk of 'winnability', 'prevailing', and so on). The same hazing or tinting has happened over INF. Editorials in respectable newspapers now say that Gorbachev has at last 'come round' to Reagan's original proposal. But the original proposal was aimed at Gorbachev's predecessors, and was disingenuous, offered on the basis of a confidence that it would never be taken up. The new deployments in Europe were militarily insignificant, intended only as a demonstration of political will. Meanwhile Reagan has appointed career enemies of arms control to the key positions in arms control, denounced the USSR as an evil empire, and entrained the biggest military build-up, or spend-up, in world history.

Despite retrospective claims that SDI was a belated response to a clear Soviet lead ('the SDI gap'), the President's Star Wars speech of March 1983 caused consternation in all but a small section of the US strategic community. Reagan presented SDI as a way of *escaping* deterrence: protection of the people from nuclear weapons. Almost immediately Reagan's experts assured him that this was unachievable. So SDI was retouted as a way of *enhancing* deterrence: protection of nuclear weapons from nuclear weapons.

Somehow the notion survived this humiliating volte face. Indeed, the original goal subliminally lingers as the true justification of its compromised offspring. In June 1986 Reagan was still talking enticingly of 'a shield that could protect us from nuclear missiles just as a roof protects a family from rain'. 'Don't *you* want to be protected from nuclear missiles?' George Shultz asked a TV interviewer, not in 1983, not in 1986, but the other day. When Nixon came to power he vowed to find a cure for cancer. Billions were spent. Reagan has vowed to find a cure for nuclear weapons. He certainly isn't interested in preventive medicine. At best, he seems to be offering us an orgy of surgery; at worst, efficient corpse-disposal.

Among the many anomalies in the 1983 speech was Reagan's claim that SDI would 'pave the way' for significant arms-control. In fact SDI precludes significant arms-control. While in power Reagan has foreclosed the Comprehensive Test Ban Treaty and broken out of SALT II; SDI would dish the Nuclear Test Ban Treaty, the Outer Space Treaty and, most crucially, the ABM Treaty. And that would be that. When the USSR contravenes a treaty, it is called a violation; when the US does it, it is called an Initiative. Alun Chalfont, in his miserable new book, *Defence of the Realm*, contents himself with calling SDI 'an entirely new approach'.

SDI points in the other direction: it points towards a sign saying MORE. It points *up*, into space, a new and boundless arena. Lord Chalfont is unworried about the militarization of space because, he says, space is 'already' militarized. This is like ceasing to worry about ozone-depletion because the ozone is 'already' depleted. Changing the word defeats the cavil, which is why the Soviets refer to the *weaponization* of space. Many of these weapons would be lightspeed and, like all weapons, would have offensive capabilities. Warning periods would be so reduced that human beings might well be excluded altogether from the 'decision loop'. One fails to be reassured by this, even when the human being in question is Ronald Reagan.

There is a hole in deterrence theory, a hole so vast and unsightly that it seems tasteless to point it out. If the nuclear moment ever approached, *there would never be any point in going second*. Both sides would be massively primed to pre-empt, and SDI would simply add to that pressure. Useless against a first strike (and useless against bombers and cruise missiles), the space shield might yet absorb a ragged retaliation. The Soviets would fear this, and would act on their fear. SDI doesn't enhance deterrence. It just widens the hole. It enhances pre-emption.

The President's idea sounded good, and sounded simple, for

about ten minutes. Then it stopped sounding simple. Then it stopped sounding simple, and it stopped sounding good. How has it survived and what is its attraction? Jon Connell, in his cogent study, *The New Maginot Line*, argues that a kind of frontier technophilia accounts for its hold on the American people. In *Star Wars in a Nuclear World* Lord Zuckerman cites the subjection of 'the laws of physics . . . to political attitudes and a historical belief in the controllability of scientific breakthroughs'. And William Broad in *Star Warriors* shows us the weaponeers themselves: dreamy, lopsided idiot-savants, inspired by competitiveness, personal ambition, schoolyard anti-communism and bachelor *esprit de corps*. Here the SDI agenda takes its crassest form: pauperize the USSR; win the race, and win the war.

The weird blend of utopianism and sordid mugwumpery is best expressed in the person of the President. Reagan likes his idea, partly because it is the only idea he has ever had, but also because it chimes with his belief in the superiority of the American people and the American system. Nuclear capitalism must always prevail over nuclear communism. His is a Presidency during which almost anything might have happened. The thoroughness of the President's collapse — and the aspirations of the President's wife — have given us the INF deal. But the more important legacy is SDI.

It is a millennial notion, the 'dream' or 'vision' which has become the loyalty test of the Reagan administration. It is millennial in several senses, literally so in that it is timed for the year 2000, and more blearily in that it accords with Reagan's belief in the apocalypses of Revelation and Ezekiel. It also supposes that only the evil will perish, and only the good will prevail.

Here is a millennial valediction. What happens to the nuclear missiles once they are 'taken out' by SDI's lasers, smart rockets and death rays? Some will fall back to earth, some will go nuclear, some will explode 'conventionally', dispersing their plutonium into the atmosphere. The gunpowder for nuclear weapons, plutonium, is found, not in nature, but at the toilet end of nuclear reactors. It remains lethally toxic for 250 millennia, or 2,500 centuries, or a quarter of a million years. Technology, if there is anything left of it, will be obliged to mop up that problem too. Some kind of space shield, perhaps.★

Observer January 1988

★ Both the Democrats and the Republicans support SDI (or NMD – National Missile Defense – as it is currently known), the Democrats reluctantly, the Republicans enthusiastically. In fact America is stuck with the thing; and the explanation for this is eerily post-modernist, and eerily Reaganish. It has become politically impossible to tell the American people that they aren't going to get something which (the polls disconcertingly reveal) they believe they already have ... Victory in the Cold War was part of Reagan's legacy, but you couldn't really say that it was part of his achievement. The reckless aggression of his first term moderated into the diplomatic 'hardball' of his second. His policies perhaps hastened the Soviet disintegration by a year or two. And you could argue that his preparedness to think radically about nuclear weapons arose from a genuine revulsion – hence his eager response to Gorbachev's 'zero option'. But maybe the revulsion was supplied by Nancy Reagan, the failed actress who (we are now learning) ruled the world from 1980 to 1988.

What's Your Favourite?

The Best of Forum edited by Albert Z. Freedman

Since *The Best of Forum* is a collection of essays and correspondence rather than a specialist monograph the reviewer's task is largely one of enumeration, of alerting readers to their particular areas of interest. In the commissioned articles, frigidity, impotence, premature ejaculation, the tumescent properties of vitamin E, the perils of the high clitoris, vasectomy, sex in one's twilight years, masturbatory techniques – all get a decent airing from *Forum*'s sexologists. Vaginal orgasms are denounced for the shabby myths they are; the male is advised to delay entry (which women should always supervise) until the female climax is imminent; never be ashamed to confide in your partner about unusual desires, fantasies, needs. The contributors regularly lapse into a tone of oily Togetherness ('Why don't you try my "one night of love treatment"?') and are inclined to establish their anthropological credentials by off-hand references to such things as 'ancient fertility rites', but on the whole they seem tolerably empirical and unanxious.

Among the more recondite articles are: 'Penile Dimensions – What Women Really Think' (they think they like them big); 'Thank You For Having It', notes towards organizing a sex-party, which makes 'it' sound both clinical and unsalubrious (you scatter the floor with mattresses and 'essentials like Vaseline'); and 'Orgy, Porgy, Puddin' and Pie' by Jenny *Groupie* Fabian, which makes it sound pure hell (Miss Fabian, for one, 'needs a lot of love around'). Readers are asked also to complete a quiz called 'How Sexy Can You Get?'; your reviewer got fairly sexy, but was ticked off by Dr Martin Shepherd for being insufficiently bisexual. Indeed, utter, unquestioning catholicity appears to be the key to almost every problem. If it stirs, the suggestion is, you ought to want to go to bed with it.

Of course, the correspondence – The Forum Adviser and The Forum itself – is the heart of the magazine; here (we think) are all those nonagenarian transvestites, undersized hampton-flashers, manacle-and-dungeon artists. A young mother finds that her sex life has come to depend on breast-feeding sessions with her – practically teenage – son ('the fact that you feed him whilst naked and masturbate yourself', reasons the editorial answer, 'clearly has nothing to do with his dietary requirements'). An exhibitionist finds erection only when displaying himself to Arabs ('I would expose myself to almost any African delivery man who came to my flat'). One couple experience respiratory difficulties during soixante-neuf (triumphantly resolved by the purchase of a nose snorkel). Parents wonder how best to get their children masturbating early and with an adequately varied repertoire of techniques ('Johnny, if I catch you not masturbating in lots of different ways . . .'). Admittedly these letters form the lunatic fringe; most of the correspondents are pathetically ignorant and dislocatingly naïve: the pages are full of ponderous trouncings of non-prejudices, sarcastic recapitulations of imagined traumas, brave stands taken against such doctrinaire phenomena as repression and loneliness.

'How do you go about thanking a magazine for saving your marriage without sounding maudlin?' writes M.W., Newton, Massachusetts. An excellent question. Naturally, all readers of the *New Statesman* could afford to browse through these pages with a comfortable sense of irony. But if the letters are genuine – and despite their formula of tell-tale case-history plus guileless self-revelation some of them probably are – we would have to admit, along with Dr Albert Ellis, that *Forum*'s 'direct, no-holds-barred approach, together with its blatant lack of coy prurience, gives it a public power that is exceptionally potent'. Naturally enough, too, the liberated society tends towards its own brand of triteness, a tendency which this book ably enshrines.

New Statesman September 1973

Making Love: An Erotic Odyssey by Richard Rhodes

Sex, I gather, is a pretty popular topic; but 'hardly anyone', notes Richard Rhodes in the preface to *Making Love: An Erotic Odyssey*, 'has come forward to write about it intimately except behind the mask of fiction'. Certainly his bibliography is sufficiently thin to shore up this view. But there must be a good reason why no one is coming forward to write about it, because everyone is coming forward to talk about it. A widespread fear of writing a book like *Making Love* would perhaps be reason enough.

'Fiction is fine,' Mr Rhodes goes on, 'but using fiction as a disguise makes both the uniqueness of intimate experience and its common humanity easy to dispute.' This argument turns out to be spectacularly mistaken. When fiction works, the individual and the universal are frictionlessly combined. In real life, sex demotes individuality, leaving us only with the usual sorry quiddity of various personal fetishes and taboos. What Mr Rhodes gives us, in any event, is a cataract of embarrassment. *Making Love* is a hot book, right enough; but the heat is all in the armpits.

So we begin with virginity loss, and the hick scholarship boy from Yale tiptoeing forth to the local brothel. This is all very 'tenderly' told. But because it is 'fact' ('It happened'), Mr Rhodes permits himself the kind of clichés that even the most worthless novelist would impatiently discard: 'My heart started pounding. I was avid. I was also terrified . . . Gussie's body was a woman's body, generous and real . . . I lay on the bed filled with happiness, one with the universe . . . It was springtime. I jumped into the air and clicked my heels.' The prostitute, Gussie, we are astonished to learn, was golden hearted (or she was with him: maybe she was rather sharper with the elderly drunks who made up most of her clientele). But Gussie 'really' was a cliché. So what is Mr Rhodes to do – except go ahead and give us the cliché?

Next, masturbation, homosexual experiments at school, plus some deeply unshocked stuff about bestiality. But when it came to girls, 'I froze with panic,' Mr Rhodes writes, adding, for clarification, the striking simile, 'like a deer caught in the headlights of an oncoming truck'. Along the way he bungles several good chances, and now grieves for these near-misses: 'That's the loss I mean: of persons each a species, each unique, of gatherings of selves in my arms intoxicating me with essence.' As so often when Mr Rhodes gets grateful and reverent, you have to read the sentence twice, even though you didn't want to read it once.

On to the mysteries of the female orgasm. Mr Rhodes, who won both the Pulitzer Prize and the National Book Award for *The Making of the Atomic Bomb*, has so far presented himself as such a picture of sexual health that you start wishing the book had been written by someone more interestingly screwed-up – like a coprophagic pig farmer or a sadomasochistic funeral director. Despite the corny chauvinism inherent in his imagery, or his catchphrases ('fleshy as a ripe plum', 'fingers in the same pie', 'climbed aboard', 'bucked like a mustang'), Mr Rhodes keeps letting us know how strenuously P.C. he is. 'I valued my partners first and foremost as persons', for example. Or, 'I respect women and treat them accordingly.' Or, 'I've never found it easy to use people.' Needless to say, these clear-eyed avowals sound tremendously unrelaxed. The reader girds himself for confession, or confession of a kind, because (sexily) one's sexual truth is always furtive, always obscure, by definition. That's why it's sexy.

We duly arrive at the moment that, in bed, is sometimes broached with the question 'What's your favourite?' Here it is: the revelation of peculiarity. And at this point, strangely, *Making Love* takes on some inadvertent interest. If the first half of the book reminds you of nothing so much as a primitively autobiographical novel (*Portnoy's Complaint* shorn of all talent), then the second half resembles the much tricksier fiction of the 'give-away' dramatic monologue and the unreliable narrator. This is genuinely paradoxical. Unsuccessfully striving to be honest, to reveal, Mr Rhodes is at last being revealing – but without knowing it.

The author, it transpires, is a sex-on-the-brain merchant, an erotic obsessive of a more or less manageable order. He says he has written a book about sex because he wants to help and share, and so on, but a more convincing reason may be that he finds it very hard to think about anything else. We get a nineteen-page hint along these lines when Mr Rhodes describes, in incredible detail, his near-daily practice of masturbating to pornography. There he is, grimly assembling the Vaseline, the videos and the 'remote'. 'I spread the doubled bedsheet over the couch where I'll sit – I'll be working, I'll sweat.' Working? Well, yes. For soon, in these pages, Mr Rhodes becomes a part-time toiler in the sex-therapy business, ghostwriting a book called *ESO* (subtitles: 'The New Promise of Pleasure for Couples in Love' and 'How You and Your Lover Can Give Each Other Hours of Extended Sexual Orgasm') and acquiring the foolish and mischievous belief that 'sex is a skill like any other'.

Up until now Mr Rhodes has come across as something of a sweetheart in the sack, fanatically obliging and empathetic. The book's last and longest chapter chronicles his relationship with his current partner, 'G———', in the customary peeled-eyeball close-up. Their love life, embarrassingly good from the outset, reaches successive heights of rapture as they worship at the shrine of the Extended Orgasm. By this stage their sex sessions ('we showered for ESO training, the "sensual focus massage with verbal feedback"') are beginning to sound like some new form of transcendental traction. And one idly assumes that the undercharacterized G——— must be into it too.

Not so. Three pages from the end of the book we have G——— haggardly confessing that she doesn't *want* fourteen orgasms per afternoon. Mr Rhodes responds with rage ('I've never been angrier in my life') before predictably – though very hurriedly – calming himself down for the book's upbeat last paragraphs. 'You can't have all . . . Not all but enough, writes Leonard Shengold', whoever he may be. In conclusion Mr Rhodes perfunctorily attributes his own insidious sexual coercivenss to the abuse he suffered as a child.

He might have done better to attribute it to the how-to culture of which, in this reviewer's opinion, he remains a fuddled plaything, throughout the book. It is evident in his sprucely non-judgmental jargon: women who don't have orgasms are 'preorgasmic'; boy–boy sex in a no-girls environment is 'situational homosexuality'; taking a mistress becomes 'opening [a] marriage' – a marriage for whose foreseeable doom Mr Rhodes prepares himself by reading a book called *Uncoupling*. It is also evident, of course, in the way he tries to turn G—— into a G-spot, and in the misery of all 'ecstasy programmes' and go-for-it self-improvement manuals and no-problem personal-growth booklets, among which, if anywhere, *Making Love* confusedly and disconsolately belongs.

New York Times Book Review August 1992

Some English Prose

In Praise of Pritchett

*On the Edge of the Cliff; The Tale Bearers: Essays on English,
American and Other Writers* by V.S. Pritchett.

V.S. Pritchett's short stories are retrospective, provincial, formless and
feminine. His is an art that does not care how peripheral it sometimes
seems. There are no twists, payoffs, reverses, jackpots or epiphanies.
Pritchett never rubs life up the wrong way, and is happy to leave only
a faint shine on its fur. He uses the forms and addresses of minor art,
yet there is no one quite like him – no one alive or male, anyway.
'He is proof', Frank Kermode has argued, 'that an older tradition
could survive the importunities of the modernist Twenties and stay
modern, respond finely to the world as it is.' I am not sure how true
this is, or in what ways it might turn out to be true; but it is clearly
the central critical question posed by Pritchett's quietly extraordinary
way of looking at life. Of course, the answer to this question may in
the end not be very relevant or even interesting, assuming as it must
do that an art of such freakish fragility is pierceable by criticism in
the first place.

Luckily, Pritchett the explicator is on hand with a new collection
of essays to provide oblique guidance. All artist-critics are to some
extent secret proselytizers for their own work; they are all secret
agents. As Pritchett says of Graham Greene's *Collected Essays*, 'Let the
academics weigh up, be exhaustive, or build their superstructures –
the artist lives as much by his pride in his own emphases as by what he
ignores; humility is a disgrace.' Pritchett's judgments are emboldened
by this 'artist's necessity', but his professional fairmindedness always
keeps the picture steady. As in his stories, he has the curious ability to
let art shine through him, helplessly. Pritchett is a mirror, not a lamp.
He goes at criticism the old way, creeping up on a writer through

the life, the letters, the creative temperament on offer. When he interrupts a biographical account to put forward his own view ('I find this too simple: her religiosity was an assertion of pride'), he is not presenting a rival piece of evidence but merely exerting his artistic confidence. The New Critics tend to look at classic texts as if they were contemporary and anonymous; with Pritchett, criticism is always busily attentive to history, character and random human traffic.

Pritchett's fiction is like this too – inevitably. He does not feel at ease with the stylized and the exemplary. In his essay on Borges (reprinted in another recent collection, *The Myth Makers*) Pritchett responds finely to Borges's wit and elegance of mind, but is quickly dislocated by his panoptic coolness, the liberties Borges takes with the shape of life. As a result, Pritchett makes several fruitless attempts to humanize stories like 'Emma Zunz' and 'The Aleph', and simply misreads the irreducibly abstract fable 'The Circular Ruins'. If fiction is imagined as a globe, with realism at its equatorial belt, then Borges occupies a spectral citadel in the North Pole, while Pritchett sweats and smarts in the tropics. When one artist writes about another, the reader is doubly rewarded by this reverse-barometer effect. We enjoy Pritchett's culture shock – and note, too, the minor adjustments and time-lags he undergoes when he visits writers who live much nearer home.

'One often wishes he were less of a contriver and would let the characters show for themselves what their meaning is,' says Pritchett, rather testily, of Graham Greene. The reader reflects that this is exactly what Pritchett lets his own characters do. We hear the same double thunder when Pritchett approvingly observes that 'Kipling's characters are always thickly neighboured: the story exists in the minds of all who were there', or when he praises Flannery O'Connor's 'fidelity to the inner riot that may possess the lonely man or woman at some unwary moment in the hours of their day'. Now this is more like it, you can hear Pritchett saying to himself. The distinction he is secretly making throughout the book becomes explicit in his essay on Henry Green:

Some very fine artists impose themselves, but Henry Green belonged to those who masochistically seek to let their characters speak through them. In so speaking, they may expose more than they know: but don't we all stubbornly feel that . . . we are more than we know? There is a muddled justification for our existence. We are encrusted in something like a private culture.

It is clear from the construction of the first sentence that Pritchett aligns himself with the second kind of writer, with the masochist rather than the imposer. He doesn't go on to add – perhaps because he prefers epigrams to generalizations, with their suggestion of schools and 'modes' and whatnot – that the Moderns are all imposers, while the masochists belong to a quieter and more fitful tradition. One is tempted to make a third distinction here, which will become relevant later on. Male writers tend to be imposers, female writers masochists. Is it not remarkable that there is only one female Modern, Virginia Woolf? No wonder we're all so afraid of her.

Pritchett's fiction is suspended in place and time. *On the Edge of the Cliff* contains several stories set in present-day London, but the mild convulsions they describe could just as easily have taken place in, say, post-war Cheltenham. 'Look at that. Another bomb in Belfast,' murmurs Mrs Baum in 'The Worshippers'. When in the last Jeeves novel P.G. Wodehouse started dutifully noting the sit-ins and demos he saw in the London streets, the effect was disastrous, even blasphemous. As Evelyn Waugh observed, Wodehouse wrote of an unfading, green world, a world that simply wasn't equipped to admit such brisk topicalities. In Pritchett, these time-warps into the present have a different point: you're meant hardly to notice them. Ever-faithful to the landlocked egotisms of his characters, Pritchett is just reminding us how marginally the Belfast troubles really connect with people like Mrs Baum. She has far more important things to worry about: there is a man in her flat-block who bothers her, and someone has just spilt gin on her carpet. Similarly, when the seventy-year-old heroine of 'Tea with Mrs Bittell' starts noticing how London has changed in recent years – 'In the once quiet streets . . . there were empty bottles of whisky and brandy rolling in the gardens' – it is the fact that she has become aware of change that is important (as an expression of genteel anxiety), not the changes themselves. 'She noticed these things now because for three weeks Sidney had not been to church . . .' And when Sidney returns a fortnight later, Mrs Bittell stops noticing things again. She goes back to worrying about Sidney's friend Rupert, and about her feud with the doorman. So do we.

Pritchett's prose, too, is quirky and nostalgic in its devices. He continues to write in a style that has not noticed the regularizing, the tidying-up, that accompanied the concerted push towards naturalism in the middle of the century. His punctuation is tangled, hectic and Victorian. He sometimes uses semi-colons in the way Dickens did – as brackets; and he is a hardened exponent of the pause-for-breath comma that is being steadily driven out of English prose: 'As he wrote and re-wrote his sentences, a pencil drawing of Gant which he had found at a booksellers in Colchester, looked down . . .'; and from the essay on Beerbohm: 'If he had a secret it lay in his quite terrific will and the power to live as if he and the people he saw, were farcical objects.' He is equally capable of the condensed dangler ('This, knowing his skill and history, they [Rolfe's letters] may very well be') and the jumbled connective ('Ayesha is undoubtedly a disturbing figure and, I think, because she is a compendium'). Observe the cluttered confidence of the following constructions, all taken from *The Tale Bearers*:

> The amount of theatre criticism and essay writing he did as a young man, and the delightful trouble it stirred up among the respectable, is remarkable . . . That he was kidnapped as a baby in Ireland and taken to England by his nurse, with whom he lived for three years, is strange . . . The muddle he is in, his sense of victimisation, are valuable . . . The picture of Margaret thinking her pernickety way from the real-life character before her into the imaginary relations she is creating is good.

It is easy to imagine how a more self-conscious and workaday critic would settle down to transposing and tightening these sentences: 'It is remarkable . . .', 'How strange that . . .' and so on. But Pritchett's style answers to the shape and direction of his thoughts – and to their fertile swiftness.

In the stories also Pritchett's prose has little time for the guidelines of elegance. 'To heave this dead weight down the corridor from the old office was like lifting dead bodies'; and note the repeated 'even' here, with the word used in different senses, giving the reader a futile jolt: 'In the direct glare of Berenice's working lamp, Florence Cork looked even larger and even pregnant.' Pritchett must be aware of these verbal pile-ups, since elsewhere he shows himself to be an adept of deliberate, or controlled, repetition. Take the repeated 'little' here, which is delightfully resonant: 'once one has got used to the big wrongs of life, little ones wake up, with their mean little teeth.'

In the same way, most writers worry about internal rhymes and chimes in their prose to an almost comical degree. There is a marvellous joke about this in Nabokov's *Laughter in the Dark*, when Udo Conrad, the exiled highbrow novelist, inadvertently reveals to the pathetic Albinus that he is being savagely cuckolded by his mistress and his best friend. As Albinus reels away, Udo is left to muse on his *faux pas*: '"I wonder," muttered Conrad, "I wonder whether I haven't committed some blunder (. . . nasty rhyme, that! 'Was it, I *wonder*, a *la*, la la blunder?' Horrible!)."'

Sentences that resemble train-wrecks – 'The cook took a look at the book' etc. – are common enough in genre fiction, where simple inattention or mercenary haste must claim responsibility. And when, for instance, Anthony Powell writes a phrase like 'standing on the landing' you feel that it is the result of mandarin unconcern or high-handedness. Pritchett's prose is full of these jangles – 'Sitting behind the screen of the machine' is a random example – but the effect is entirely appropriate to his way of looking at life. Life *does* rhyme: it rhymes all the time. Life can often be pure doggerel. Pritchett's responsiveness to the quotidian is one of the reasons his stories seem formless, they are not comic, tragic, romantic, farcical, or like anything else that has a shape. Pritchett is locked into the kinks and rhythms of what he elsewhere calls the 'native ennui'.

This is surely a feminine style of apprehension. Pritchett himself would be unalarmed by the idea: in the essays, he reacts with

candid gusto to Leon Edel's hermaphroditic reading of Henry James.
Pritchett is no Jamesian dandy, and he is not a clever primitive like
Henry Green. He is an instinctivist who forgets all his reading as soon
as he starts to write. His fiction has the same freakish certitude as that
of Jean Rhys, Flannery O'Connor and Christina Stead. Pritchett's
curious inwardness when writing about women has often been
noticed:

> 'No,' he said and told her what he had told her a dozen times
> before. She liked her flat to have someone else's voice saying the
> same things again and again.

And:

> 'What an enormous tip.' In our heavy state this practical remark
> lightened us. And for me it had possessive overtones that were
> encouraging: she stood outside, waiting for me to bring the car
> with that air women have of pretending not to be there.

But Pritchett writes this way about men too. It is all part of a larger
habit of mind: the knack of looking at things the other way.

For Pritchett, the minutiae of the observed world are all ignited by
an emotional affect; the canvas is neutral and washy, but the details are
fluorescent. McDowell, in 'The Vice-Consul', has 'an unreasonable
chin and emotional knees'; Mr Ferney, in 'Tea with Mrs Bittell', has
'two reproachful chins and a loud flourishing voice'. It is almost a
perceptual tic of Pritchett's to register human objects in terms of an
emotional abstraction. A young maid is 'red as puberty in the face';
a woman at a wedding is 'dark haired and brimming with fat'; a
ditched wife's rings 'sparkle with sentiments'; in his club, a man is
'at home with his mysteries'; in her flat, an old woman sits 'among
the wrongs and relics of her seventy years'. Pritchett has always been
on fruitfully uneasy terms with the inanimate and domestic world.
His stories sometimes read like muffled and niggly versions of the
Dickensian cartoon: like Dickens, he has great trouble establishing
to what extent dead things are alive. A disused electric fire looks like

'a modern orphan'. Sofa cushions have 'red or green fringes, so that we seemed to be squatting on dyed beards'. In 'The Worshippers', Mrs Baum nostalgically contemplates the foyer of a once-fashionable hotel: 'They found themselves on the huge carpet of the hotel on which thousands of pairs of shoes without people in them might be treading.' What is the force of that 'might', exactly? 'In the village it is felt to be unnatural for a man of his size to be living alone . . .' Pritchett's method is in fact very simple, though vastly ambitious in its way: he tries to interpret the world through the romantic, nervous and mystical thoughts of his own characters, who are seldom remarkable except in their peculiar ordinariness. If one thing underlies his work it is the constantly dramatized proposition that ordinary people are really extraordinarily strange.

V.S. Pritchett is the same age as the twentieth century; he is at the height of his fame, and pretty well at the height of his powers. If none of the stories in *On the Edge of the Cliff* gives quite the concerted satisfaction of early masterpieces like 'Blind Love' and 'The Skeleton', this is because he is making fewer concessions to the usual demands of the form. His art is reaching its natural conclusion, slowly dispersing into odd flashes of intensity. The stories seem old-fashioned only in their insistence on the continued richness of life, whereas one of the pet dreads of the Moderns is that life might be losing its multiformity and superabundance. Pritchett is 'for life', but not in the Leavisite sense. Leavis had the notion that life was something he had to keep sticking up for – almost as if the rest of us had no time for the stuff. Actually, all writers are lovers of life, even the blackest of them; they all know that life has everything to be said for it. Few lovers are as generously inquisitive as Pritchett, and have such affection for vagaries and wrinkles – 'preserving especially', as he says of Saul Bellow, 'what is going on at the times when nothing is going on'.

London Review of Books May 1980

Kith of Death:
Angus Wilson

As If By Magic by Angus Wilson

Perhaps the most striking feature of Angus Wilson's work is the consistent horror and loathing with which he regards the family. From the sinister friskiness of the 'Crazy Crowd' (1949) – 'the Cockshotts had created their home alive, bright, happy-go-lucky, "crazy"' – to the bestial antics of Billy Pop and Countess Matthews in *No Laughing Matter* (1967) – 'That was the way they'd always lived, the kind of odd-job lot they'd always been' – we have had a constant stream of hair-raising households: the ruthlessly progressive Sonia and James in *Hemlock and After*, all moral hygiene and paperback discipline; the nauseating smugness of Marie Hélène's matriarchy in *Anglo-Saxon Attitudes*; the desirable 'Sycamores' residence in *Late Call*, with its duty-rosters and its 'we're-not-a-family-we're-just-good-friends'. For Wilson, the family unit not only guarantees the one-directional nature of middle-class psychology (the fact that the child is at the mercy of its parents and that no amount of humanistic self-appraisal will ever free it), but also provides those tiny resonances that make up the surface of his writing: the sickly whimsies, the exclusive codes, the desperate seriousness of coterie games, the malevolent secret jokes, the invidiousness he sees at the heart of all life.

Allied to this, of course, is the interest in homosexual relationships and the generalized 'nastiness' vulgarly associated with them – and with Wilson's novels. Not that Wilson goes out of his way to dispel the former misconception, if misconception it be; although we get a few durable 'marriages' (the most successful – Gordon and David in *The Middle Age of Mrs Eliot* – being, incidentally, the most platonic), Wilson is quite candid about the vulnerability of the homosexual to self-destructive guilt, rabid promiscuity, pleasureless bitching, vanity, greed and haemorrhoids. Nor do I find it hard to understand complaints about the nastiness of the novels themselves, even if in the end this is an extra-literary response to his work. One of the few things I would rather run a mile than do is have an Angus Wilson character over for the evening. His fictional world, as he himself seems to acknowledge via Margaret in *No Laughing Matter*, *is* a nasty world, but this doesn't stop him being a considerable novelist. No writer can determine what may appeal to his imagination and it is simply philistine to arraign him for the things he happens to write about best.

In this latest novel Wilson's twin preoccupations – the family and its alternative – are viewed separately, rather than in conflict, and this probably accounts for its lack of edge and intensity. Of the two main characters, Hamo Langmuir and his god-daughter Alexandra (A. Grant: she's a student), 'Hamo' is (small wonder) the homo. An agronomist, worker of rice-proliferating magic in the labs, Hamo is without 'the old magic' of the trustworthy erection – at least at the hands of anyone over twenty. It is with some enthusiasm, then, that he embarks on a working tour of the nubile East, and it is with increasingly little that we follow him on a long, diffuse, unfunny sexual picaresque. Meanwhile, pregnant Alexandra, organically scorning the 'conventionally bourgeois abortion', has escaped from her liberal-monster parents to make a hippie pilgrimage with her two boyfriends, who are characterized by Hamo (and no more searchingly by the author) as 'Beard' and 'Elegance'. Although Wilson doesn't regard the young with the obsequious respect of many elderly novelists (C.P. Snow, William Cooper), the hilarious inaccuracy of his observations renders this half of the book a more or less total write-off: 'Words . . . celebrations . . . like, y'know, shit,' is Beard's opening address to Ally's parents, while we later hear him chirping things like 'super' and 'Oh, Lor'!' The youngsters are extremely boring in their own right and this is the only part of them Wilson can bring alive.

The finale, quite unconvincing despite its huge predictability, brings Hamo and Ally together; they fall in love for ten minutes, then rush off to play their parts in a thematic scheme hardly less creaky than the plot. As in all but the last of Wilson's novels, the protagonists begin the action at a moral crisis-point and end it in triumphs of varying ambiguity: Hamo is worthily destroyed by an upsurge of confused altruism; Alexandra (according to the blurb 'ironically' – i.e., preposterously) is enabled to work her own modest magic through the acquisition of riches, resolving 'to betray the whole filthy system from inside' by leasing out accommodation at fairly cheap rents. Groggy readers might do well to attend to a hippie rebuke given at some smarmy Swami gathering: 'Oh! For God's sake! Who knows what positive etheric waves you're neutralizing with all that infantile defensive humour?' Search this reviewer. One would give Wilson the benefit of these grave doubts if it weren't for the scruffiness of much of the writing: 'his heart beat fast with randiness', 'only slightly shaking from a sobbing gulped down', Americans saying 'Noo York' and 'anyways', hippies using 'like' as if they were rustics, the word 'delicious' appearing seven times in as many pages, the whole book riddled with repetitions, unintentional rhymes, jangles, even solecisms. Naturally, one doesn't begrudge Wilson his Uproarious Jaunt, but one hopes that in future he will make better use of his travel diaries.

In a recent statement Wilson denied that he was a social realist and avowed an increasing interest in experimentation. Nothing in *As If By Magic* is experimental – except for routine eng-lit coltishness and a periodic uncertainty as to what the hell is going on – yet one suspects Wilson is using the tag merely to widen his pitying smile should anyone be gauche enough to raise questions of motivation and probability. Nobody is asking him to be subservient to realist conventions but his attempts to extend these do seem to work far better when he meddles with form (as in his last two novels) rather than content (as in *The Old Men at the Zoo*). The twinkly, walkabout exuberance of the present book isn't suited to Wilson's savagely direct talents, which lie firmly in the novel-of-manners tradition; like his beloved Jane Austen, he needs only a small vista for that rheumy but unblinking eye.

New Statesman June 1973

Diversity and Depth in Fiction by Angus Wilson.
Edited by Kerry McSweeney

'I think . . . I suspect . . . I imagine . . . I have no doubts . . . I am fairly sure . . . I believe, as I shall suggest . . . I think I would like to begin by simply saying . . .' And I think *I* would like to begin by simply saying that Angus Wilson's pot-pourri of critical writing is delightfully personal, impressively amateurish, and thrillingly unsystematic. It prompts the thought that the gurus and yogis of structuralism have done us all a great service. As criticism coagulates into a discipline in which only the academic lab-man feels at ease, a new and neglected subject looms imposingly in the foreground: 'It looks like literature. What a beautiful sight!' as John Updike observed in *Hugging the Shore*, a book that one places alongside other recent critical collections by Nabokov, V.S. Pritchett, and Philip Larkin. These are, of course, the artist-critics, and their authority has never seemed more natural and welcome.

Sir Angus's critical world, in particular, has a prelapsarian feel. 'Most of [Jane Austen's] defenders', he writes, from the sequestered innocence of 1962, 'belong to the upper middle class and have also gone on living in a country way.' We now know that most of Jane Austen's defenders belong to the academic industry and have started living in campus condominiums. David Lodge ably satirized the type in *Changing Places*: his hero, Morris Zapp, of Euphoria State University, has made a long career out of Miss Austen while privately admitting that he finds her 'a pain in the ass'. 'Eros and Agape in the later novels, wasn't it?' Zapp asks a baffled English student. 'What was the problem?' We have since moved Eros and Agape to hermeneutics and syntagmatics, to *lexia* and *irrealia*, and to other dialectical imperatives – political, sexual, and ethnic. One could attribute these fragmentations to the rise of the universities and their attempt to make the study of literature, if not as hard as philosophy or physics, then certainly a lot harder than geography. Or one could bluntly argue that the critical theorist (half high priest, half cultural janitor) fails to find literature very interesting, all by itself. It needs some gustier infusion.

Wilson has no head for theory and instinctively flouts it at every turn. It may be convenient for a critic to pretend that creative writing takes place *in vacuo*; but try telling a writer that. Wilson routinely commits the Biographical Fallacy, because he knows that the relationship between a writer's life and work, while not direct or unwavering, is there on the page, detectable in imagery as much as in content: what is Dickens without his blacking factory, or Kipling without his boardinghouse? Wilson intentionally commits the Intentional Fallacy, because he knows that a work of art, if it is alive, will lead the author down diversions to unscheduled stops: hence pretension, hence incongruity, hence failure. And Wilson proudly commits the Subjective or Affective Fallacy, because he knows (with Nabokov) that the sole end of art is 'aesthetic bliss', and that the critic's spinal cord is as vital as a tuning fork. Wilson also knows this from experience. Actually, we all know it. It is what we are thinking and feeling when we read.

Born in 1913, Wilson took up fiction and criticism relatively late in life. In his postwar evolution as a man of letters – a growth this book dramatizes – Wilson had two main influences to contend with and resist: on the one hand Bloomsbury, on the other F.R. Leavis. It is difficult for American readers to appreciate the power and ubiquity of Dr Leavis's Thought Police during this period. It is difficult for English readers, too, let it be said. Provincial, lofty, and fierce, the Leavisites sought to reduce literature to a moral audit, an elaborate way of determining whether individual readers were or were not mature and wholesome human beings. 'Literary values' were themselves illusory, Leavis asserted, because 'the judgements the literary critic is concerned with are judgements of life'. Thus the business of English studies was to whittle down the mass of literature into a hard core of mature and wholesome texts. As recently as 1970, you could walk into an undergraduate bedsitter and run your eye over the pitifully denuded bookcase of an aspiring Leavisite: the English poets (with Hopkins and Carew supplanting Shelley and Milton), Jane Austen (maybe), *Hard Times*, George Eliot, James, Conrad, Lawrence, plus one or two laughable latecomers like Ronald Bottrall and Elizabeth Myers. This was the Great Tradition – that is, the one okayed by Dr L.

It is fascinating, in the present book, to watch Wilson apparently flitting in and out of sympathy with the Leavisite doctrines. In his thrilling essay 'Evil in the English Novel', he uses various code words and phrases – 'felt life', 'anti-life', that 'great tradition' again – which seem to suggest a quiet affiliation with the cause. But one soon comes to realize that Leavis-speak was merely the prevailing literary jargon of the time. Whereas Wilson, as a liberal humanist, might have been attracted to Leavis's grimly secular creed, he was too much of a literary hedonist, a man of the pleasure principle, to linger with it long. Soon Wilson's apostasy is open and eloquent. It is disturbing, he writes,

> that the most suggestive and sincere literary criticism of our time should have to guard its moral health so desperately that it can find no place for the heterodoxy of Dickens's masterpieces. Perhaps the misuse of such brilliance may qualify him for the place of Lucifer – but a serious literary criticism should not be able to fall so easily into theological parody.

Literature is, among other things, a talent contest, and every reader must find his personal great tradition. Wilson's is eclectic, sometimes alarmingly so, but it is all his own.

The countervailing influence, one to which Wilson proved more lastingly susceptible, was that of Bloomsbury and its pre-eminent (perhaps its only) talent, Virginia Woolf. The ascendancy of Leavis himself might be seen as a reaction against the Bloomsbury establishment – against the snobbery, the leisure culture, the moneyed dilettantism of High Bohemia. A prosperous young aesthete (whose sexual tastes, incidentally, would have been deplored not only by Dr Leavis but also by the British Constitution), Wilson was naturally drawn to the 'feminine hypersensitivity' of Woolf rather than the 'hedgehog prickliness' of Leavis. To her he owes his conception of the novel, as both practitioner and pundit. The contexts, the great forms of the eighteenth- and nineteenth-century sagas, have been exhausted; realism and experimentation have come and gone without seeming to point to a way ahead. The contemporary writer, therefore, must combine these veins, calling on the strengths of the Victorian novel together with the alienations of post-modernism. Wilson's debt to Woolf is frequently acknowledged, and we see its full emotional charge when he dramatically records: 'I read in *The Times* of her suicide, and all the war of my intelligence work seemed as nothing. This was Hitler's triumph . . . the blackest moment of the war.'

That hint of preciosity reminds us, perhaps belatedly, that Bloomsbury was a narrow world, too, and that sensibility, as a credo, has its limitations. Consider these snippets, with their Woolfian airiness:

> Nancy Mitford and Angela Thirkell, who attempt to reconstruct the same scene with some of the childhood laughter that rang through the nursery in the old Hall in those far-off days . . .

> Like Firbank, [Henry Green] transformed his desperate tight-rope walk into a wonderful ballet of dancing words.

> Wafting from Cambridge and Bloomsbury, these seductive breezes blew across the England of the 1920s and early 1930s until they became the very atmosphere that the intelligentsia of the upper middle class breathed – a warm, enfolding air full of the breath of memories, sudden gaieties and strange little sadnesses.

The confidence of Bloomsbury lay in an assertion of taste – *taste*, with its eighteenth-century connotation of well-bred rectitude, of patrician right-thinking. Just as surely as in the Leavisite doctrine, the value judgment reflects on its espouser: on his or her background, fibre, cultural etiquette. When literary criticism began to be systematized (and thus democratized) in the Fifties, the value judgment was the first frippery to be outlawed; and the tendency shows no sign of being reversed, with the structuralists seeming equally happy filleting the minor or the major. If there ever was a middle ground – a still point somewhere between

the overaesthetic, the shrilly moral, and the pseudo-scientific –
Wilson never sought it. He had an artist's certainty, and trusted to
that.

So *Diversity and Depth in Fiction* completes a familiar and enjoyable
process. In the end, we learn more about the judge than the judged.
William Godwin's prose is 'at times unendurable'. Dostoevsky's ideas
are 'at times almost insane'. Thackeray's 'awful "sweet wisdom"' is
'nauseating', Gissing is often 'completely unreadable', indeed 'entirely
repellent'. 'It just does not do, I think,' Wilson decides, having
examined the dialogue in Isherwood's novel *The World in the Evening*.
For once he supports his view with adequate quotations. But the
tone? It just does not do, I think. The tone makes its appeal to a
lost consensus, a unanimity that might have existed in 'those far-off
days' but exists no longer.

Wilson's great tradition has a nostalgic or fossilized look about it,
too. Richardson's *Clarissa*, Austen, the major Victorians, Meredith
('the first great art novelist'), Huxley, Ivy Compton-Burnett ('a
great experimentalist'), and John Cowper Powys ('he will stand
with James, Lawrence, and Joyce'): there is a sense, not at all
uncongenial (and analogous to what one feels about Wilson's own
fiction), that this particular 'line' of English literature is losing its
hold on us, though perhaps it will one day revive. Similarly, when
Wilson offers his hot tips for future greatness (this is 1967), he arrives
at the following selection: John Berger, David Storey, Christine
Brooke-Rose, Randolph Stow, Chinua Achebe, Amos Tutuola, and
– at last – V.S. Naipaul.

Amateurism is not an unalloyed virtue, and it must be said that the
hobbyist brio of Wilson's prose is a constant distraction. He has a kind
of anti-talent for the rhyme, the repetition, the tongue-twister, the
ear-clouter: 'The admirable Admiral Croft', 'a revolting revolutionary
act', 'the last thing he would have been likely to do would have been
to . . .' Some passages are real so-and-sos: 'It is so over-used and
so often without a satisfactory content. So – this likeness between
Dostoevsky and Dickens, so frequently proclaimed . . .' And we
would need an editor far less torpid than Mr McSweeney to cope with
Wilson's random intensifiers: at one point we get 'very shocking',

'very disgusting', 'very possible', 'very difficult', 'very definite', and 'very important', all within half a page. Wilson lassoes himself into argument as if somebody else were constantly trying to thwart and bedevil him. But he is a man in love, after all, and one cheerfully grants him his excitements, his imprecisions, and his fertile swiftness of thought.

Atlantic Monthly May 1984

Iris and Love

The Black Prince by Iris Murdoch

Up to page 166 of Iris Murdoch's new novel its narrator, Bradley Pearson, seems a reliably emotionless, puritanical, Great-Book-pregnant littérateur, deliberate about everything he does ('I *think* I'm going to faint' – not my italics) and so fastidious that colloquialisms as raffish as 'sexy' and 'housewife' have him reaching for his inverted commas. Bradley's civilized existence is suddenly threatened by the arrival of his (deservedly) ditched sister, the reappearance of his ex-wife and her abject, sidling queer brother, the marital crises of the Baffins (respectively a spunkier, more successful novelist and his menopausal wife), and by the importuning of their twenty-year-old daughter, Julian, who wants Bradley to teach her Shakespeare. These untidy persons have variously to be coped with: the ex-wife shooed away, the sidling queer employed to tend the noisome sister; Bradley baits the novelist with talk about integrity and has a bedroom scuffle with his wife (a scuffle only, for Bradley can't command 'the anti-gravitational aspiration of the male organ' – and put like that it's a wonder anyone can). As Bradley comes and goes from the Baffin household, Julian is to be seen doing symbolic things with love-letters and balloons.

From page 167 of *The Black Prince*, after a chance hard-on in a shoe-shop and one *Hamlet* lesson with Julian, Bradley is behaving like a mawkish schoolboy: reeling, crooning, vomiting, weeping, and in love. Since he believes that 'there's a dignity and a power in silence' the reader suspects that he will be as reticent in life as he has been in art, happy to wince and gloat over all these emotions and experience them only via his usual footling *pensées* and *aperçus*. But Bradley movingly confesses his love and the impressionable Julian confesses that she reciprocates it. The couple escape to Bradley's hideaway and, once Julian gets the idea of dressing up as Hamlet (complete with skull), Bradley's erection problems are a thing of the past. Circumstances bring a typically melodramatic conclusion, which, whatever else it does, ensures that their relationship is nipped as it buds rather than as it wilts.

To summarize so unfeelingly is not to deride what Miss Murdoch would call the 'causality' of this intricate and fascinating novel. Patently, that was no ordinary *Hamlet* lesson: Bradley's rhapsody to the Swan's most elusive play is in every sense the heart of the book. *The Black Prince*, like Miss Murdoch's previous two novels, is an attempt to synthesize her earlier styles, the hang-dog existential shrugs of her work before *The Bell* and the somewhat contrived allegorizing of the work that followed it. On a naturalistic level, Bradley's love for Julian is no more than what Baffin sneeringly says it is: a flowery-minded man 'sowing some rather unsavoury wild oats at sixty'. If we step back, however, we see that it is also what Bradley says *Hamlet* is: the means to create a 'special rhetoric of consciousness', a self-purging in the glare of art; Bradley's book is Julian's 'deification', and so she becomes the *Hamlet* he never wrote.

But while Bradley presents his love as a liberation, an escape into life, he clearly remains 'a man who lives by words'. In the book's early pages he is confronted with two fat, miserable, ageing, halitosis-ridden women in need of reassurance, and his reaction to both is, simply, 'You're upsetting me.' Similarly, when Bradley's sister (who admittedly, by almost anyone's standards, would be better off dead) commits suicide, Bradley evades responsibility, and it is this act which precipitates his losing Julian. Bradley can recognize, in *pensée* form, that the human condition is pathetic and laughable, fundamentally ironic in shape, but love does not enable him physically to accept the messiness that has its place in art no less than in life – and Miss Murdoch has always wished for, if not prescribed, a certain congruence between the two.

Bradley's fastidiousness is abetted by Miss Murdoch's. The book, which is offered by its narrator as both a 'true story' and a 'work of art', is itself presented by an 'Editor' who in turn supplies 'Postscripts' from the other characters, all of which distort the story and accuse the story of distortion. When, at last, Julian speaks, when the reader is desperate to know *what happened* (*was it art or life?*), all we get is a feeble little essay on artistic theory from Julian and the 'Editor's' final scotching of the rumour that he and Bradley are 'the invention of a minor novelist'. Now you see her, now you don't. Elaborate track-covering does not heighten artifice, it exposes it. That 'minor' may turn out to be false modesty, but only if Miss Murdoch will refrain from washing her hands so clean of her own creations.

New Statesman February 1973

The Sacred and Profane Love Machine by Iris Murdoch

The most consistently provocative thing about Iris Murdoch's new novel is its title. Apart from being janglingly discursive in its own right, it extends a warm invitation to Miss Murdoch's decriers – to the satirical rogues who might claim that *The Sacred and Profane Love Machine* is just an upper-middlebrow version of the earthier *Love Machine* of Miss Jacqueline Susann, dignified in accordance with those two percussive epithets: the motivation orchestrated by someone of a rather more philosophical turn of mind, perhaps, the heartbreak less perfunctorily considered, people going to bed with each other for somewhat better-read reasons, but essentially the same sort of thing. And indeed the present book is particularly vulnerable to such a conceit; persons, symbols and ideas do their usual coming and going, are bound upon the Murdochian Ferris-wheel of fire, yet we seem to have only the title's ponderous word for it that they are doing so to much purpose.

In the sweaty, hunted life of Blaise Gavender there are two loves.

85

Harriet, his wife, sacredly tends their civilized Buckinghamshire home, blessing everything that falls beneath her damp, adoring gaze – the garden, the pets, the neighbours, and David, their lawful son. Emily, Blaise's secret mistress, profanely idles away her days in a Putney love-nest, the sluttish resort of delinquent friends, feckless protégées, and little Luke, the child of their shame. Between these hearths Blaise scrupulously divides his anxieties, tormented alike by the beaming serenity of his wife and the impish disgruntlement of his mistress. Whatever the prolixity of Miss Murdoch's scene-setting might lead one to believe, this can't go on for ever: Blaise's fool's purgatory ends; the secret is out, and he must choose.

And he goes on choosing. On the face of it Miss Murdoch seems to be doing little more than guiding the pens of a few Texan thesis-writers. Can she be saying merely that there are two sorts of love, that one gets boring while the other stays sexy, that it would be nice to have both and that it's a shame we can't? After a bit, though, one notices that the profane love has a habit of sounding a lot more highbrow than the sacred one. Blaise still goes to bed with Harriet and they enjoy a stately tenderness there, but his love for her is contingent, to do with decorum and self-preservation. Blaise's love for Emily, on the other hand, is mindless and absolute; they flop into bed drunk, then bicker halitotically until morning; he's glad to get away, desperate to return. It suits Miss Murdoch's peculiar type of romanticism to elevate the profane love to a quite disorientating degree: 'Intense mutual erotic love, love which involves with the flesh all the most refined sexual being of the spirit, which reveres and perhaps even *ex nihilo* creates spirit . . .' – this has a sacredness Miss Murdoch doesn't find among the soft vacillations and tooling whimsies of Buckinghamshire. This love is, above all, blindingly erotic, which for Miss Murdoch at once renders it amoral and, in that sense, transcendent. As soon as her typically melodramatic conclusion allows the profane union to be solemnized, it becomes dully 'sacred', losing its Promethean edge.

That title. It belatedly occurs to you that the epithets aren't meant to be antithetical but complementary – like *The Beautiful and Damned* rather than *The Naked and the Dead*. As Blaise ferries from one love to the other, both women are illuminated in turn by a queasy attraction they perforce lack when he has actually to be with them. Harriet's blandness becomes a sexy cool; Emily's clamorous presence becomes his true Lawrentian *locus*. Each gives him what the other can't supply – i.e., a change from the other one. Perhaps Miss Murdoch's concern is not an easy distinction between two varieties of love so much as a slant on their interdependence. The shabby Blaise exemplifies this unhappy tendency, but the other characters are subject to it also. A foxy novelist, although popular with the girls, clings to the shade of his rotten wife; a portly queer nurtures the one love that will degrade him most. For solipsists, suffering has its own glamour: it can't be shared.

Such an angle on the book gives a sense of unity which the experience of reading it is unlikely to reproduce. Miss Murdoch is, of course, endlessly acute and insatiably empathetic, and as notes towards a psychology of the upper-middle classes the book has plain uses. The ingredient it lacks – an ingredient that enriched its predecessor, *The Black Prince* – is a linguistic centre of gravity, and without it the book sprawls. Literature is, among other things, a pattern of words, and an author's more general procedures will always be reflected in its verbal surface. Just as Miss Murdoch's prose covers all the options, chucking in a dozen careless phrases where one careful word would do, she similarly attempts to evoke and dramatize by sheer accumulation. The book contains as many elegant paragraphs as slovenly ones and for somebody who writes so fast Miss Murdoch writes dismayingly well. But it is bloated and it sags.

I suspect that Miss Murdoch's huge productivity is, paradoxically, a form of self-defence or self-effacement: 300 pages a year disarm a lot of criticism. She can't, in the nature of things, revise much and probably she never re-reads; she just 'gets on with the next one'. Were she to slow down – were she to allow one of those ominous 'silences' to gather, silences such as more tight-lipped novelists periodically 'break' – she would be accepting a different kind of responsibility to her critics and to her own prodigious talents. She would, in short, begin to find out how good she is, that strange and fearful discovery.

New Statesman March 1974

Nuns and Soldiers by Iris Murdoch

Iris Murdoch is a believer: she believes in all kinds of things. She believes in magic, monsters, veridical visions, transcendent art, prophetic dreams, pagan spirits, God and the devil. But most centrally, of course, Miss Murdoch believes in love.

Her poor characters suffer and exult, groan and gloat – and with classic symptoms. They throw up and black out. They can't eat. They weep for joy. They pace the street, gazing up at forbidden windows. They live happily ever after. Sometimes the love is sacred, even courtly: instantaneous, infinite, unspoken, unrequited. Sometimes it is cheerfully profane: a sudden handclasp, and within seconds the paramours are making pigs of themselves in bed. No one is exempt; no one can resist. For better or for worse (and there are always some startling extremities on offer here), everyone must join the dance.

Love being the unironical thing it is, the outsider tends to look on with a keen sense of the ridiculous. *Nuns and Soldiers* begins with a long death scene. Guy Openshaw is succumbing to cancer, distractedly mourned by his wife Gertrude. Throughout the ordeal Gertrude is tenderly monitored by the Openshaw coterie, which features Manfred, an eligible banker, Peter, a laconic Pole known as the Count, Tim, a furtive and penniless young painter, and Anne, a recently lapsed nun. (Strangely, Miss Murdoch has renounced the transsexual cast-list she normally favours. Where are all the Blaises, the Francises, the Hartleys? I had hoped that this might be the Murdoch novel where, at last, the heroine was called Butch and the hero Maureen.)

Before he dies Guy tells Gertrude to marry the Count. After all, the Count has been 'in love with Gertrude for years'. Now, he is in 'a terrible frenzy': 'his love . . . filled every second with thrilling purpose'. But the Count also 'loved Guy'. He is diffident. So is Manfred, who probably loves Gertrude too. Gertrude cries for a month: she feels dead. Anne tends her. They swear eternal love.

Then gingery, indigent Tim approaches Gertrude to ask for money, egged on by his charmlessly foul-mouthed lover, Daisy. As a compromise Gertrude allows Tim to go and paint the Openshaw house in France. Tim travels to France, alone. He is 'mad with joy'. To escape her suitors Gertrude follows him there. They get on each other's nerves for a couple of days – then it happens. Tim feels it like 'a fast approaching comet which suddenly fills up the whole sky': 'some vast cosmic force' compels him. For her part, Gertrude feels that 'something uncanny is happening'. Tim kisses Gertrude's hand 'avidly hungrily' (a tautology, because 'avidly' already means 'greedily'). 'I love you,' he says. 'I think I love you too,' Gertrude replies. The next day they make love and do a morris-dance together in the meadow. They quaff the 'honey-joy', the 'honey-magic': Gertrude's body 'hums with a sacred love-awareness'. Suddenly Manfred shows up and they all go back to London.

Then Tim drops Daisy and moves in with Gertrude. Everyone is appalled. Anne moves out. The Count is in a 'frenzy' again, but one of 'grief and misery and rage'. Then Tim and Gertrude break up. Everyone is relieved. Tim goes back to Daisy. In a sense, Gertrude goes back to Guy, indulging 'this terrible love' for her lost husband. At the same time, it is 'as if she had fallen in love with the Count'.

Then Tim and Gertrude get married. (They meet again by chance. There is 'a celestial trumpet call' and 'no need of words'.) Tim redrops Daisy. Meanwhile Anne falls 'terribly terribly in love with the Count'. But the Count is still in a frenzy about Gertrude, living 'with black demons of jealousy'. Anne stays silent. Little does she know that Manfred is 'terribly in love' with her.

Then Gertrude drops Tim, believing (wrongly) that Tim hasn't dropped Daisy. Tim goes back to Daisy, 'in a phantasmagoria of misery'. Anne suffers. The Count exults, having decided that he now loves her 'more than he had ever loved her before'. Tim re-redrops Daisy. Gertrude, Anne and the Count go to France. Tim follows them, fearing a 'terrible terrible rejection' by Gertrude. He stands in the field where he and Gertrude once morris-danced so lyrically. Anne, still keen on the Count, observes his approach with 'a fierce wild almost cruel joy'. But Gertrude sees him too; 'Oh – Tim – darling – darling – thank God,' she says.

Then . . . Well, readers of this review are no doubt feeling sufficiently emotionally deprived as it is. Miss Murdoch's novels are tragi-comic, in the sense that about half her characters live happily ever after, while the nuns and soldiers soldier on alone. They all inhabit a suspended and eroticized world, removed from the anxieties of health and money – and the half-made feelings on which most of us subsist. It is the burden of this particular work that the least-deserving are often the luckiest in love, their talent for happiness undeflected by the scruples and habits of self-preservation. They believe, as Miss Murdoch believes, that 'love is their meaning'.

It will already be clear that this is not one of the major Murdochs. Her books now seem to alternate or zigzag: *The Black Prince* (excellent) was followed by *The Sacred and Profane Love Machine* (relatively footling); ditto with *A Word Child* and *Henry and Cato*; and now after *The Sea, The Sea*, perhaps her most delightful book to date, comes the minor entertainment *Nuns and Soldiers*. It is breathless, gushing, and hopelessly uneconomical – which perhaps suits its theme. Miss Murdoch is very addictive, however. As with *Nuns and Soldiers*, so with the condition of love: you want to know how it will turn out, but you certainly don't want it to end.

Observer September 1980

SOME ENGLISH PROSE

The Philosopher's Pupil by Iris Murdoch

Iris Murdoch's fiction is habit-forming, which is just as well, since her *oeuvre* now outbulks that of Tolstoy or George Eliot. You can see the Murdoch-addicts, with their enlarged, telltale irises, queueing like ghosts in the public libraries and bookshops. Another novel will, for a time, ease their craving . . . Well, the new book provides a chance to kick the habit. A diluted version of the real thing, softening the pain of outright withdrawal, *The Philosopher's Pupil* is a long course of methadone.

It would be futile to summarize the plot. Life is too short. The book is too long. But it is possible to offer a Murdochian paradigm, one that will serve, in fact, for all her fiction since *The Sacred and Profane Love Machine*. Imagine the teaching staff of a toytown university. The men all have names like Hilary and Julian. The women all have names like Julian and Hilary. Everyone is on permanent sabbatical, but they look in each day to sample the hallucinogenic love-potions available in the SCR.

The twenty-stone economist loves the nonagenarian philologist ('a nervous obsessive guilty angry craving'), who loves the alcoholic classicist ('a painful vertiginous thrilling urgent pressuring feeling'). The alcoholic classicist loves the deluded linguist ('a sudden piercing and obsessive jealous remorse'), who loves the schizophrenic sociologist ('feeling very very sorry for him, feeling oh so much protective possessive pity-love, a sort of desperate sorry-for affection'). Meanwhile, in the town, everyone talks in a strangely outdated slang ('I still play bridge, but that's not your scene!') while standing back in wonder as the campus hotheads do their stuff.

The Philosopher's Pupil is a tale told by one of Miss Murdoch's fastidious narrators. He is a rum sort of narrator, sometimes enjoying full authorial omniscience, sometimes operating as an ordinary member of the cast. Often he is helplessly reliant on rumour and speculation; often he dispenses hysterical interior monologues and seems to know

91

the thoughts of all the characters, even those of pet dogs and wild foxes. Like Bradley Pearson in *The Black Prince*, 'N', as he is called, uses quotation marks for such vulgarisms as 'sulks', 'commuters' and 'worthwhile activities', as well as for phrases like 'too good to be true', 'the wrong end of the stick' and 'keep in touch'. The reader reflects that a cliché or an approximation, wedged between inverted commas, is still a cliché or an approximation. Besides, you see how it would 'get on your nerves' if I were to 'go on' like this 'the whole time' . . .

Apart from a weakness for quotation marks, 'N' also has a weakness for ellipses, dashes, exclamations and italics, *especially* italics. Each page is corrugated by half a dozen underlinings, normally a sure sign of stylistic irresolution. A jangled, surreal (and much shorter) version of the book could be obtained by reading the italic type and omitting all the roman. It would go something like this:

> *deep, significant, awful, horrid, sickening, absolutely disgusting, guilt, accuse, secret, conspiracy, go to the cinema, go for a long walk, an entirely different matter, an entirely new way, become a historian, become a philosopher, never sing again, Stella, jealous, happy, cad, bloody fool, God, Christ, mad, crazy* . . .

The needless emphases and train-wreck adjectives are occasionally combined, as in 'the remarkable unique personal sense of *power*' and 'some terrible ghastly frightening *noise*'. These locutions – and locutions such as 'she was utterly utterly not English' or 'confronted by a thin thin blade' – remind you at first of excitable conversation. But the prose has no basis in the rhythms of the spoken language. It is utterly utterly not English. It is non-writing, unwriting, anti-writing.

'N' would probably diagnose 'loss of faith' or 'lack of conviction' as the poison in Miss Murdoch's prose. Why else the flailing repetitions and paranoid overkill? I think, though, that the answer lies the other way. Miss Murdoch's style was never elegant, but it was crisp and precise, capable of preserving her macabre and often beautiful perceptions. Here it is a hectic, ragged thing whose only function is to establish the dramatis personae and launch them on their amorous dance. Miss Murdoch believes in her characters – the good, the bad, the ugly – and it is a belief ignited by love. That love is palpable, inordinate, scarily intense. It is far too strong a force to tolerate the thwarting intercession of art.

Observer May 1983

J.G. Ballard

Crash by J.G. Ballard; *War* by J.M.G. le Clézio

'To be responsible for the happiness of the Universe', as W.H. Auden points out, 'is not a sinecure.' Equally, the apocalyptic-epiphanic mode in fiction is not for minor talents. It should be clear that the more superbly an author throws away the crutches of verisimilitude, the more heavily he must lean on his own style and wit. Experimental novels may have a habit of looking easy (certainly easier to write than to read), but their failure-rate is alarmingly high – approaching, I sometimes fear, 100 per cent.

J.G. Ballard's last 'collage' novel, *The Atrocity Exhibition*, had this to say on the subject of perversion: in our 'post-Warhol era', 'violence is the conceptualisation of pain . . . psychopathology is the conceptual system of sex'. Yes, perhaps, or not. *Crash* doesn't pontificate; here Ballard isn't out to rationalize but to actualize, to show us the perversion from the inside. And this particular perversion needs all the actualizing it can get: beside it, Joyce's penchant for excrement and Burroughs's interest in scaffolds seem sadly quaint.

At the start of the action the narrator has had a head-on car crash with a married couple: the husband was shovelled off the road, his widow and the narrator sensuously hospitalized before embarking on the inevitable affair. So far, so sexy – but it is not until the narrator meets, and falls for, the 'hoodlum scientist' Vaughan that he learns the true delights of impacted windscreens, dying chromium, wound-profiles, genital mutilations and optimum sex-deaths. Entirely, exclusively obsessed with the car crash, Vaughan's dream is to have a fatal collision with Elizabeth Taylor (Ballard has always shown an inordinate preoccupation with celebrities – see his restrained and sensitive short story 'Why I Want to Fuck Ronald Reagan'). As Vaughan trains for his sex-death by splatting dogs on pavements, lurching out of access roads for orgasmic prangs with female motorists, masturbating and taking snapshots at pile-ups, the narrator is led further into this tumescent heat-hazed car-scape to share Vaughan's vision of the 'whole world dying in a simultaneous automobile disaster, millions of vehicles hurled together in a terminal congress of spurting loins and engine coolant'.

Just how sexy is this? What is Ballard getting at? Well, consider the way your own reaction to car crashes can be distanced: they're blood-curdling in real life, but not bad at racetracks, and really very appealing on film. As Ballard keeps saying, the 'perverse' (used sixteen times) marriage of technology and flesh has a certain 'geometry' (twenty-one times) which may become increasingly 'stylised' (twenty-six times). Scar-contours and wound-orifices provide a fresh repertoire of sexual possibilities; injury gives one a new awareness of one's body; auto-perversion (the narrator reflects, fiddling with some leg-braces in a girl's cripple-car) can offer 'strange declensions of skin and musculature'.

I suppose that the improbability of such a deviation – like the nature of the author's personal problems – should be irrelevant to the reviewer. For the tone of the book is neither gloating nor priapic; the glazed monotony of its descriptions and the deadpan singlemindedness of its attitudes aren't designed to convert or excite the reader, merely to transmit the chilling isolation of the psychopath.* Granted this generous rationale, however, *Crash* remains heavily flawed: loose

---

* In which task *Crash* sensationally and scintillatingly succeeds. I came to Ballard through his hard science-fiction. (His SF novels are not hard SF, but something else instead, as we shall see. The SF short stories *are* hard SF, and they constitute the best hard-SF short stories ever written.) It took me a long time to get the hang of *Crash*, and of Ballard. My review, here, is so straitlaced that I hesitate to preserve it. But I do: readers should always be wrestling with the writers who feel intimate to them. I preserve the setting also, a two-book batch from the avant-garde. My first novel appeared towards the end of the same year. It was mildly and peripherally *post-modern*. Ballard, who with the novelist Emma Tennant ran or dominated an influential literary magazine called *Bananas*, was at this time *experimental*. A wing existed, in 1973. In literary terms I was a social democrat and Ballard was a marxist. At the end of this section we shall, in any case, return to *Crash*.

construction, a perfunctory way with minor characters, and a lot of risible overwriting make it hard not to see the book as just an exercise in vicious whimsy. True, the novelist must take from life what he can use rather than what he dares print; but Mr Ballard's obsessions are too one-colour and too solemnly redeployed to sustain a whole book. In science fiction Ballard had a tight framework for his unnerving ideas; out on the lunatic fringe, he can only flail and shout.

In the work of J.M.G. le Clézio you won't find anything so *outré* as an obsession – unless it be J.M.G. le Clézio, the marvellous boy of French letters. Persons still in two minds about the meaning of life would do well to study *War*. When le Clézio is not wandering about like an owlish Zulu or a fact-finding Martian (three pages on a department-store placard, four on a lightbulb) we're off on a guided tour of the cosmos, *pensée* after *pensée* on ecstatic materialism, para-Sartrean existentialism and *seizième* nihilism.

The level of interest is set by the opening words of the grumpily neurotic heroine, Bea B.: 'this girl blurted out, jokingly perhaps, or simply because it had suddenly become the truth: "I am nothing."' Now which? It isn't 'the truth'; nor is it funny. But le Clézio is indeed a *peut-être* novelist, forever gripped by these unlikely alternatives. Since he is all too clearly a stylist, why waste the excellent Simon Watson Taylor in an attempt to translate him? Without the verbal surface of the French, *War* is such a torment to read that one yearns for the kind of *nouveau-roman* pranking whereby (say) the final 150 pages are left blank in order to symbolize the void of late capitalism. Expectably, the hints of talent that here and there survive only confirm the elusiveness of their substance.

Observer July 1973

Concrete Island by J.G. Ballard

To anyone unfamiliar with J.G. Ballard's work, *Concrete Island* will seem ridiculously slight; for rather different reasons, it will seem ridiculously slight to *aficionados*, too. Motoring home from the office one afternoon, Robert Maitland crashes down through the roadside trestles of a 200-feet-long triangular concrete island, two of whose perimeters are formed by high banked walls. Barely hurt, he crawls back up the loose-soiled verge to the expressway. Four hours later he is still at the roadside, queasy with carbon-monoxide, waving and yelling as the automobiles zip past him. Dejectedly he boots a stray trestle into the road; it is glanced towards him by a speeding car, and Maitland is flung back on to the concrete island.

Where he stays. The rest of the book chronicles the injured Maitland's attempts not so much to escape from the island as to 'dominate' it. This involves marshalling its resources in the normal improvised-survival tradition and, more particularly, subjugating its two hidden occupants, a mad, dwarfish old tramp and a mad, whorish young girl. The improvised-survival stuff is about as good as it ever is when the hero wants water and remembers *the windshield-washer reservoir*, when the hero wants fire and remembers *the car cigarette lighter*, and so on. The interpersonal set-to is as preposterously remote as Ballard always is in his dealings with the human race: Maitland bests the dwarf by sexily urinating in his face, after which the girl says, 'We'll have some food and I'll fuck you,' after which, in turn, it isn't long before Maitland can call the island his own. A disastrously ambiguous last page sees an exhausted, triumphant Maitland resolving 'to plan his escape from the island' without showing any sign of wanting to do so; escape is now possible, but in Ballardian terms (one infers, pitching the book aside with a ragged yawn), the possibility no doubt renders the escape unnecessary, irrelevant.

And that's about it. There are inevitable resonances, of course. 'You were on an island long before you crashed here'; 'you're marooned here like Crusoe'; and (best) Maitland's husky 'I am the island': such keen observations assure one that significance is just round the corner. In fairness, the parallels aren't altogether as trite as these pointers suggest. However obliquely, Maitland's solitary explorations of the island do recapitulate the lone rambles of his childhood and the orderly heartlessness of his adult life. However predictably, the analogy with Crusoe, whose Rousseauesque exile has a certain wholesome domesticity, tellingly isolates the bleakly urban Maitland; whereas Crusoe is a stoical son-of-the-soil, Maitland is a ragged urchin of the city, picking his way through crushed cigarette packs, sweet wrappers, matchbook stubs, old newspapers and spent condoms to the endless drumming of the indifferent highways. And – however arcane the notion promises to be – Ballard is one of the few living writers who could get much out of his hero's half-delirious self-identification with the island, an adept as he is of the language of heightened, dislocated consciousness:

> As he crossed the island the grass weaved and turned behind him in endless waves. Its corridors opened and closed as if admitting a large and watchful creature to its green preserve.

> Night and silence settled over the motorway system. The sodium lights shone down on the high span of the overpass, rising into the air like some disused back entrance to the sky.

But despite these small felicities both the plot and the prose of *Concrete Island* are distanced by an oddly wilful negligence. One example of each. First, Maitland arrives on the island with £30 in his wallet; although he throughout defrays the cost of the wine the tramp buys from a local supermarket, he still has £30 in his wallet just before the end – a startling lapse in such a short, uncluttered book. Second, the slaggy girl, who is on-set for only twenty-odd pages, is 'strong': we get surer and surer about this because she is described as having 'strong hands' (four times), a 'strong body' (four times), a 'strong jaw' (twice), a 'strong head', 'strong shoulders', and 'strong arms'. Now it is true that all Ballard's novels are marked by similar inconsistencies and repetitions. Essentially, his fiction does not propound, it embodies; the prose is simply the rhetoric of an obsession, as dense, one-colour and arbitrary as the obsession requires it to be, and it's no use squaring such a writer with standard fictional procedures. *Concrete Island*, however, for reasons that will become clear, doesn't unnerve conventional criticism in this glamorous way.

Ballard's four early novels are ostensibly cataclysmic science-fiction stories in the routine Wyndham mode; gradually, though, as the texture of the prose thickens and Ballard's stare hardens on the bizarre landscape he has precipitated, the cataclysm ceases to be of much importance. In *The Crystal World*, for instance, the opulent refractions of the imagery become virtually self-generating, causing the end of the world to seem a rather footling affair by comparison. Although all these novels incorporate their own theoretical time-schemes – which are very complicated and (between ourselves) not very interesting – they are, broadly speaking, speculative and futuristic. More recently, Ballard has applied the imaginative habits of a lush, numinous fantasist to the present day, imposing an over-conceptualized, over-poeticized vision on the metal and concrete furniture of a technologized society. In the jangling, piecemeal *Atrocity Exhibition*, Ballard sets himself up as the apologist of deviance, breakdown and psychopathology. Its successor, *Crash*, a novel born of quite immeasurable perversity, posits an 'alternative sexuality', a sexuality emotionless, stylized and unerotic, which is offered as the appropriate response to a dehumanizing technoscape. Sample tumescents:

> Beside a casualty ward photograph of a bifurcated penis was an inset of a handbrake unit; above a close-up of a massively bruised vulva was a steering-wheel boss and its manufacturer's medallion. These unions of torn genitalia and sections of car body

and instrument panel formed a series of disturbing modules, units in a new currency of pain and desire.

I visualized the fantasies of contented paedophiliacs, hiring the deformed bodies of children injured in crashes, assuaging and irrigating their wounds with their own scarred genital organs, of elderly pederasts easing their tongues into the simulated anuses of colostomized juveniles.

While one is inevitably sickened and appalled by Ballard's glib whimsicality, *Crash* remains a mournful and hypnotic *tour de force*, possibly the most extreme example in modern fiction of how beautifully and lovingly someone can write 70,000 words of vicious nonsense.

For Ballard is the rarest kind of writer – an unselfconscious stylist: it is the measure of his creative narcissism that he has his eye on no audience. Equally, Ballard's characterization is hardly more than a gesture; his men are morose and fixated, his women spectral nonentities, his minor figures perfunctory grotesques. He has nothing coherent to 'say', and his plots are merely the gateways to exotic locales. *Concrete Island* is by far his most realistic novel to date and, patently, a writer with little nous, wit or concern for individuals has no business being realistic; the book is slight not because the obsession fails to engage us but because it demonstrably fails to engage Ballard. His *raison*, after all, is his awesome visual imagination and his complementary verbal intensity. Ballard's vision is, simply, too occult for the observable world; it needs some grand perversity to give it the altitude which good writing alone can sustain.

New Review May 1974

High-Rise by J.G. Ballard

Towards the end of Auden and Isherwood's *The Ascent of F6*, Ransom, the Oedipal, megalomaniac hero, is about to scale the last heights of the mountain when he is told that the local demon will be awaiting him on the summit. Ransom climbs on alone, and as he reaches the summit unharmed – his great moment of personal and public triumph – he sees a small hooded figure on the crest, facing away from him. He approaches the demon, it turns – and it is his mother. Folding on to the ground, Ransom feels his life begin to drain away, as the demon sings him a tender lullaby which is also his dirge. J.G. Ballard's *High-Rise* is a harsh and ingenious reworking of the *F6* theme, displaced (as one now expects from this author) into the steel-and-concrete landscapes of the modern city.

The high-rise, with its 1,000 overpriced apartments, its swimming pools and shopping concourses, is what Ballard calls 'the vertical city', and to begin with its residents observe conventional class and territorial demarcations ('upper', 'lower' and 'middle'), showing resentment, expediency and disdain for their fellow citizens in much the same way as life is run in the outside world. Soon, though, the enclosed nature of the building has encouraged and intensified these aggressions beyond any clear analogy with external society. After various piracies and beatings-up, the class system within the high-rise deteriorates as readily as the building itself, becoming a filthy warren of violent, apathetic or paranoid enclaves. Drunken gangs storm through the blacked-out corridors; women are found raped and murdered in defused elevators; disposal chutes are clogged with excrement, smashed furniture and half-eaten pets. Eventually the high-rise takes on that quality common to all Ballardian *loci*: it is suspended, no longer to do with the rest of the planet, screened off by its own surreal logic.

Ballard being Ballard, though, *High-Rise* explores no ordinary atavism. The mental journey undertaken by these colonists of the sky is not a return to 'nature'; it is a return to the denurtured state of childhood: 'for the first time since we were three years old what we do makes absolutely no difference,' enthuses one of the affluent anarchists. Ballard's stranded characters have always been more than half in love with their lethal and unnerving environments, and the delinquents of the high-rise are soon completely defined by their new psychopathological 'possibilities'. One of the most ghostly and poignant scenes in the book has a middle-echelon psychiatrist attempting to leave his barricaded slum and return to work at his medical college; he gets as far as the car park before the shrill clarity of the outdoors sends him running back to the affectless and soupy warmth of the high-rise, satisfied that he will never try to leave it again. In the closing pages, as hauntingly wayward as anything Ballard has written, the retrograde logic of the high-rise is fulfilled, when the passive, derelict women emerge as the final avengers.

I hope no one wastes their time worrying whether *High-Rise* is prescient, admonitory or sobering. For Ballard is neither believable nor unbelievable, just as his characterization is merely a matter of 'roles' and his situations merely a matter of 'context': he is *abstract*, at once totally humourless and entirely unserious. The point of his visions is to provide him with imagery, with opportunities to write well, and this seems to me to be the only intelligible way of getting the hang of his fiction. The prose of *High-Rise* may not have the baleful glare of that of *Crash* or *Vermilion Sands*, but the book is an intense and vivid bestiary, which lingers in the mind and chronically disquiets it.

New Statesman November 1975

Hello America by J.G. Ballard

J.G. Ballard's talent is one of the most mysterious and distempered in modern English fiction – and it is by far the hardest to classify. For the past two decades he has produced almost a book a year, without ever really making it clear what genre he belongs to, where he stands *vis-à-vis* realism and reality, or where (even in the vaguest terms) his fiction is heading. *Hello America* gives us no assistance on these points, unsurprisingly enough; so perhaps a brief Ballard retrospective is in order.

In the late 1950s Ballard was an exponent of hardcore science fiction. His early stories (about overpopulation, futuristic advertising, etc.) remain as good – as direct and logical – as anything by Fred Pohl or Arthur Clarke. Ballard's first novel, *The Wind from Nowhere* (1962), was so timorously conventional that the author has since disowned it. By the time of the book's appearance Ballard was already championing the 'New Wave' movement in SF, coining the phrase 'inner space' to delineate his own preoccupations within the genre.

His next three novels were variations on the cataclysm theme, imagining a world consumed by the peculiarly Ballardian elements of (respectively) water, crystal and sand. Crucially, these holocausts are seen not as fearful visitations; on the contrary, they are welcomed and embraced for the 'psychic possibilities' they disclose – the jewelled fantasies of *The Crystal World*, the deep-dreaming of *The Drowned World,* the atavistic rediscoveries of *The Drought.* The world's mutated panoramas are densely realized, and portrayed with livid beauty, full of wonder and anxiety.

The Atrocity Exhibition (1970) heralded Ballard's most problematical phase, his concrete-and-steel period. Training the electronic eye of the SF fantasist on the landscape of the present day, Ballard became the prose-poet of the tabloid headline, the operating theatre, and the motion sculpture of the highways. 'The Facelift of Princess Margaret' and 'Why I Want to Fuck Ronald Reagan' are two representative stories in this style, and they are as scurrilous, and as open to puzzled ridicule, as their titles suggest . . . Then, in 1973, came *Crash*.

This cult novel exclusively concerned itself with, of all things, the sexuality of the road accident. You'd think that a book with such a purview would turn out to be one of the shortest ever written – along with *Keats's Craftsmanship* and *The Vein of Humility in D.H. Lawrence*. In fact, when Ballard handed *Crash* in to Jonathan Cape, it was over 500 pages, and had to be cut by half for publication. Seemingly unaware of its own perversity, the novel is both obsessive and obsessed, with a numb, luminous quality that loiters in the mind. It is also, by virtue of the kind of paradox we expect from Ballard, his most mannered and literary book, its sprung rhythms and creamily varied vowel-sounds a conscious salute to Baudelaire, Rimbaud and Mallarmé. *Crash* seemed to bring Ballard near to the end of something in himself, and after two far milder experiments in the same style, *Concrete Island* and *High-Rise*, he found he had exhausted this cul-de-sac of his talent.

So we enter the present phase. In 1979, after a four-year silence, Ballard came up with *The Unlimited Dream Company*. A vision of death and deification, charged with sombre erotic ritual, it makes *Crash* look like *Sister Carrie*. Here as elsewhere, Ballard gives meaning to blurb phrases like 'hypnotic power', 'maniacal logic', and so on; with Ballard, fantasy takes on a vertiginous steepness, giving the reader a sense of near-depersonalization.

Hello America is recognizably a continuation of the same vein, though in terms of form it takes us back to Ballard's earliest mode, that of SF. In the twenty-second century an expeditionary force from Europe sets out to explore the wastes of post-industrial America. By means of the parenthetical SF style we piece together the past from stray details in the present: the Manhattan skyline, for instance, features 'the 200-storey OPEC Tower which dominated Wall Street, its neon sign pointing towards Mecca'. In the 1980s, apparently, energy depletion caused the evacuation of the continent; subsequent experiments in climate control have turned the eastern seaboard into a desert. As the party moves westwards it discovers a waterless Mississippi, a Death Valley transformed into an equatorial forest, and a Las Vegas half-submerged in a lake of rain-lashed water, its wheels stilled, the dying lights of its hotels reflected in the meadows of the drowned desert, a violent mirror reflecting all the failure and humiliation of America.

Initially we expect a mystic outward-bound course in the manner of *The Drowned World* or *The Drought*. 'Under the guise of crossing America . . . they were about to begin that far longer safari across the diameters of their own skulls,' promises Ballard; but in fact the psychic safari is never completed. The novel is more like a lightshow of the iconic past of pop America, and the characters are hardly more human than the laser projections of John Wayne and Gary Cooper, the androids of Frank Sinatra and John Kennedy that stalk through the action. In many respects *Hello America* is a simple adventure story, Buchan or Henty adrift in the time machine.

The bathos of the enterprise is perhaps attributable to the fact that Ballard's work is quite unprotected by irony. His eye for the comedy of human variety is non-existent, and this is why landscape naturally dominates his fiction. Only in the margins of the present novel is Ballard's real strength allowed any play: the ability to invest abstract vistas with intense and furtive life. In his last two books Ballard has been developing a free-floating style, something lax and capacious enough to accommodate his fevered images of sublimity and decay. *Hello America* doesn't in the end take him very far along this road, but the prospect still looks intriguing. In a way, though, it is futile to have expectations of Ballard: he will inevitably subvert them. All we know for certain is that the novels he will write could not be written, could not even be guessed at, by anyone else.

Observer June 1981

The Day of Creation by J.G. Ballard

Veteran Ballard fans were, I think, rather wrong-footed by *Empire of the Sun* – by the book and by its success. A heightened and 'mythicized' account of the author's childhood experiences as an internee in wartime China, *Empire* was autobiographical, but it wasn't characteristic. It was all about Ballard; but it wasn't Ballardian. The main corpus of his work had long been neglected by the general public. With *Empire of the Sun*, the one-off, left-field novel came along, and Ballard – but which Ballard? – was 'discovered'. When Ballard was the Booker favourite in 1984, his long-serving followers and addicts felt as if the street drug-pusher had been made chairman of Du Pont pharmaceuticals. This is just a way of saying that Ballard is – and, with fluctuations, will probably remain – a cult writer, the genuine article: extreme, exclusive, almost a one-man genre.

I don't know what post-*Empire* converts will make of his new novel; but I know what old Ballardeers will make of it. Dialogues like the following are easy to imagine (indeed I have shared in one or two myself): 'I've read the new Ballard.' 'And?' 'It's like the early stuff.' 'Really? What's the element?' 'Water.' 'Lagoons?' 'Some. Mainly a river.' 'What's the hero's name? Maitland? Melville?' 'Mallory.' 'Does Mallory go down the river?' 'No. Up.' 'Yes of course. Up. Does he hate the river or love it?' 'Both.' 'Is *he* the river?' 'Yes.' 'And does the novel begin: "Later . . ."?' 'Not quite.'

'An hour before dawn, as I slept in the trailer beside the drained lake, I was woken by the sounds of an immense waterway.' We begin, as usual, in aftermath, with the familiar cadences of exhaustion, of slow recuperation after some obscure psychic struggle, and in the familiar landscape, one from which vitality and human effort have at last absented themselves. 'The drained lake' is answered, in the first paragraph, by 'the abandoned town', 'the dry riverbed', 'the disused airfield'. Having established mood and setting (the two always identical in Ballard), he goes on to tell us how they got that way.

The author of *The Atrocity Exhibition*, *Crash* and *High-Rise* (which begins, 'Later, as he sat on his balcony eating the dog, Dr Robert Laing reflected on the unusual events . . .'), and our leading investigator of the effects of technology, pornography and television, Ballard often seems to be on the very crest of modernity. But there is something antique about him too, something prelapsarian. For all its ambition and Freudian grandeur, *The Day of Creation* is an adventure story, as was *Hello America*. Further paradoxes include the fact that despite his acuity and wit, his deep ironies, Ballard remains an essentially humourless writer. Humour is available to the man, but it is denied access to the page.

Set in Central Africa, near the borders of Chad and the Sudan, in 'the dead heart' of the continent, the novel assembles the expected cast: a wounded obsessive surrounded by self-sufficient egomaniacs. Everyone calls everyone else by their surnames and they are capable of saying things like 'Don't be a fool' and 'Little did I know' and 'You're still obsessed by this absurd dream.' The dialogue is 'stylized', as usual and of necessity, because Ballard has no ear for it, has no aural imagination: he is fixedly visual. And the prose itself is by no means free of *Boy's Own* intonations: 'A second shot rang out . . . Stunned by the blow . . . I was now a hunted animal . . . I was determined to press on . . .'

Another of Ballard's archaic mannerisms is a morbid fear of the common pronoun. Thus, instead of getting *it*, *him* or *her*, we get 'this harmless mass of water', 'this amiable imposter' or 'this distraught woman'. The cast can perhaps best be evoked by these elegant variations: Kagwa, the local capo ('this amiable but unpredictable police chief'); Miss Matsuoka, the oriental photographer ('this intense young Japanese'); Mrs Warrender, head of the nearby breeding-station ('this self-appointed guardian of the stream', 'this still numbed woman', 'this increasingly odd young widow'); Sanger, maker of soap documentaries ('this third-rate television producer', 'this likeable but sly opportunist'), and his colleague Mr Pal (known merely as 'the botanist'); and Noon, the pubescent desert woman ('this odd child', 'this disorientated child', 'this simple child of the waterways').

Most centrally, though, there is the river, the Mallory, the Third Nile which might irrigate the Southern Sahara and create a nature reserve ten times larger than the Serengeti – 'this strange waterway', 'this unique waterway', 'this mysterious creek', 'this immense mass of water', 'this vast channel', 'this impossible channel'. As is the way with the obsessional, everything stops mattering except the obsession. And here Ballard will always win out, because of the remorselessness of his imagination, which itself is strange, vast, unique – and impossible. In all senses the river is an original creation, beautiful and leprous, putrid and austere, and as feral as the mind from which it flows.

Like all obsessions, Ballard's novel is occasionally boring and frequently ridiculous. The invariance of its intensity is not something the reviewer can easily suggest. Ballard is quite unlike anyone else; indeed, he seems to address a different – a disused – part of the reader's brain. You finish the book with some bafflement and irritation. But this is only half the experience. You then sit around waiting for the novel to come and haunt you. And it does.

Observer September 1987

Crash by David Cronenberg

I reviewed *Crash* when it came out in 1973; and, as I remember, the critical community greeted Ballard's novel with a flurry of nervous dismay. But of course reviewers do not admit to nervous dismay. Nervous dismay is a response that never announces itself as such, and comes to the ball tricked out as Aesthetic Fastidiousness or Moral Outrage.

Crash provoked much fancy dress. Some reviewers reached for their thesauri and looked up 'repellent'; cooler hands claimed to find the novel 'boring'. I'm not sure if anyone else adopted the disguise I wore: sarcasm. Haughtily (and nervously), I sent *Crash* up. I was twenty-three. Later that year my first novel appeared, and, like Ballard, I stood accused of displaying a 'morbid sexuality'. In comparison, though, my sexuality – and my novel – were obsequiously conventional.

If you wanted to banish *Crash*, there was an obvious place to banish it to: a neo-Sixties avant-garde associated with confrontational theatre, conceptualist painting, installationist sculpture, experimental fiction, and the ICA. Originally a proponent of traditional SF (and, in this country, its brightest star),* Ballard was convulsing into maturity and freeing himself from the genre – was on his way, in fact, to becoming *sui generis*. *Crash* emerged from a background of surrealism, cultural activism, hyper-permissiveness and lysergic acid.

After its publication *Crash* settled down to being a cult classic. Ballard was in any case a cult author. And it was a cult I belonged to. Assembled votaries would spend whole evenings guiding one another round Ballard's beautiful, excessive, schematic and preposterously unsmiling universe. It is perhaps instructive, here, to distinguish the Ballard buff from the mere admirer. While sharing in the general reverence for *Empire of the Sun* (1984), the true cultist also felt minutely betrayed by it. Not because the novel won a wide audience and punctured the cult's closed circle. No: we felt betrayed because *Empire* showed us where Ballard's imagination had come from. The shaman had revealed the source of all his fever and magic.

It seemed to be an appropriately Ballardian development: *Crash* was being brought to the screen by the notoriously unsqueamish – and cultish – David Cronenberg, who made the equally unfilmable *Naked Lunch*. Cinematically, though, the Burroughs is full of exuberant possibilities, unlike the hard stare of *Crash*, which is about the

* I see I am quoting my father here. A vocal admirer of early Ballard, Kingsley was decisively turned off by *Crash*, on moral grounds, and on anti-experimentalist grounds too. And, once they had displeased him, he seldom gave novelists a second chance. To his son, incidentally, he gave three, *The Rachel Papers*, *Success* and *Time's Arrow*.

sexuality of road accidents and doesn't blink once in 225 pages.

The argument of the book gets going with a head-on collision between the narrator (called, uncompromisingly, James Ballard) and a woman doctor. The crash kills her husband. In the film, he goes out through one windscreen and comes in through the other; in the book he is content to die on the bonnet of Ballard's car. The two survivors stare at each other.

He encounters her again – at the hospital, at the police pound. Grief, guilt, aggression, the shared sensitivities and deadnesses of various contusions and scars: all this leads, with disquieting plausibility, to an affectless (and car-bound) love affair. Round about now the figure of Vaughan looms in on the novel – Vaughan, the 'nightmare angel of the expressways', his leathers reeking of 'semen and engine coolant'. At this point *Crash* bids farewell to plausibility and disquiet, and embraces unanimous obsession. Under the sway of a 'benevolent psychopathology', a 'new logic', the entire cast surges eagerly towards an autogeddon of wound-profiles and sex deaths.

Cronenberg had to take this vision and submit it to the literalism of film. He has also chosen to transport it through time: close to a quarter of a century. And it seems to me that all the film's dissonances arise from that shift. In 1973 the automobile could be seen as something erotic, conjuring up freedom and power. In 1996 the associations point the other way, towards banality: car pools, leadless fuel, and asthma. Nowadays the car conjures up nothing more than a frowsy stoicism. Cronenberg might as well have gone with tail-fins, flared trousers, mini-skirts and beehives, so remorselessly does the piece insist on its historical slot. The sex feels pre-AIDS; the work-shy sensualism feels pre-inflation; even the roads feel pre-gridlock. These cavils may seem pedestrian – but car culture feels pedestrian, too, as the millennium nears.

On the other hand it feels delightfully nostalgic, and triumphantly retro, to sit in a theatre watching an intelligent and unusual art movie. Cronenberg has somehow found the cinematic equivalent of Ballard's hypnotic gaze: the balefulness, the haggard fixity. By excluding all common sense (and therefore all humour), obsession invites comedy, and *Crash* is almost a very funny film. By a similar logic, the monomaniacal seem interestingly frail. Cronenberg's ending isn't there in the Ballard; it achieves a tragic modulation among all the gauntness and passivity.

Unlike the film, the novel is indifferent to the passage of time, and has lost nothing in twenty-five years. It is like a clinical case of chronic shock, confusedly welcomed by the sufferer. Prose remains the stronger medium for the glare of obsession. It's not so much what you can put in: it's what you can leave out. Ballard's rhythms control everything: the crowds, the weather, the motion sculpture of the highways. Only in the stories collected under the title of *Vermilion Sands* (1973) did he duplicate this glazed and melodious precision.

Independent on Sunday November 1996

Anthony Burgess:
Jack Be Quick

Abba Abba by Anthony Burgess

It was in *Joysprick* (1973), I think, that Anthony Burgess first made his grand-sounding distinction between the 'A' novelist and the 'B' novelist. The A novelist, apparently, writes in what we commonly regard as the mainstream: he is interested in character, motive and moral argument, and in how these reveal themselves through action (yes, oh dear me yes, the A novel tells a story). The spunkier and more subversive B novelist, however, is *quite* interested in these things but is at least as interested in other things too: namely, the autonomous play of wit, ideas and language (no, the B novel doesn't necessarily tell a story at all). Certainly, ambitious novelists tend to get more B and less A as they develop. *The Portrait of a Lady* is very A, whereas *The Ambassadors* is clearly hoping to be B. *Mary* is contentedly A, *Ada* haughtily otherwise. *A Portrait of the Artist* is already *fairly* B, and *Finnegans Wake* is about the most B novel we have. In *Joysprick* Burgess described himself as a 'minor B novelist'. He too, though, used to be happy enough being A. The Malayan trilogy, the Enderby books – these are all pretty A. *A Clockwork Orange* is definitely B-disposed, and the more recent *MF*, in which, for example, the protagonist's skin-colour (black) is revealed on the penultimate page, has nothing A about it whatever. *Abba Abba*, appropriately, mixes the two; it is at least as A as it is B.

And does the title refer to this division between the types? I don't see why not, since it refers to almost everything else you care to think of. Most specifically, of course, it refers to the rhyme-scheme of a Petrarchan sonnet octave (the first, and predominantly A, part of the novel stages a meeting in Rome between two sonneteers, Giuseppe

Gioacchino Belli and the dying Keats; the second, and predominantly B, part consists of Petrarchan sonnets, evidently from the pen of Belli and translated by an author surrogate). But Abba Abba means other things as well. It is Aramaic for 'father father'. It represents some sort of primal blurt about language (Keats dreams that Christ shouts the words from the cross) and about the way poetic form transcends it. Abba is a palindromic chant of the author's (pseudonymous) initials. It is, further, the name of a Scandinavian pop-group. There may be other references that I have missed.

Such speculation, and such facetiousness, properly belong to the B part of the novel. Some of the B bits, as is increasingly the case with Burgess, seem detachable from the body of the novel, just a gratifying bonus for punsters and polyglots. There is, in addition, a good deal of unrecycled literary criticism here − about the non-translatability of poetry, about the disinterestedness of creative effort. The seventy-odd Belli sonnets which end the book, and provide much of its cheek (did they come first, one wonders?), carry a lot of responsibility for the B-stream, attempting as they do to pick up themes touched on in the main text. It is a pity, then, that they are not more fun to read, despite Belli's much-plugged earthiness, scurrility, and so on. The rhymes, vital to the arresting monotony of the Petrarchan form, are impossibly lazy (begun/orison, skill/imbecile, fear/Maria, of/dove), and the roguish voice assumed for the poems is so uncertain of its real energy that almost every other sonnet ends in a yelp of mechanical obscenity. 'And waste 300 fucking cannon-balls', 'Would say: "I'd rather have a fucking hen"', and 'Don't leave a feather on their fucking backs' is how three consecutive sonnets draw to a close.

The A bits pose more familiar challenges. Keats is an especially delicate subject for fictionalization, and Burgess doesn't avoid many obvious traps. There are several near-crassnesses of the bio-pic variety ('Tomorrow I go north . . . I may see your friend Mr Shelley there'; 'Coleridge says something about the willing suspension of disbelief'), some startling indecorums of speech ('Your so-called Reformation cut you off from the family of Europe'; 'He ate the papacy for breakfast'), an awful, insistent 'lustiness' supposedly characteristic of the age ('Cats are the eternal truths, and the taste of noonday soup, and farting, and snot, and the itch on your back you can't quite reach to scratch'), and a tendency to present writers in general as unrelenting epigrammatists (Keats sometimes sounds like an amalgam of Beatrice and Benedick). But the book's principal gamble pays off – and very handsomely. The fact that Keats's death *already* has an almost unsurpassable poignancy does not make it easier to write poignantly about that death. The danger of blasphemy, indeed, is ever-present, and it is only by a new intensity in his prose that Burgess skirts it. Here is Keats's last fever:

> To put off the world outside – the children's cries, snatches of a song, a cheeping sparrow, the walls and the wallpaper and the chairs that thought they would outlast him but would not, the sunlight streaking the door – was not over-difficult. A bigger problem was to separate himself from his body – the hand worn to nothing, the lock of hair that fell into his eyes, even the brain that scurried with words and thoughts and images . . . He tried to give up breathing, to yield to the breathless gods, but his body, worn out as it was, would not have that . . .

Not all of this works, of course, but there is a sense of genuine transport here, as if the language were trying to find its own rhythms, independently of Burgess's often hectic orchestration.

Is intense writing B or can it be A too? Many A novelists have done extraordinary things with language and they didn't do them by accident. Burgess cares about his prose and works hard on it. Every sentence is sure to contain some oddity or other – frequently as a result of will, you feel, rather than of inspiration or even of appropriateness. Burgess starts a sentence, puts another clause in, ends it just like that, without the courtesy of an *and*. He is prone, also, to a kind of paraded muscularity, a needless vividness ('Seven came back . . . to gobble a hunk of yesterday's bread'; 'Belli grabbed his hat . . . and slammed it on his black locks') which is often quite at odds with the mood of the page – ditto his horribly Hopkinsian neologisms and 'kennings'. But the best paragraphs in the book show how the A novelist's material can be animated by the B novelist's preoccupations. Personally I've always believed in the indivisibility of form and content, and subscribe to the

Nabokovian view that there is only one type of writing – that of talent. Well-written A novels are always B novels too. *Abba Abba*, again, is a bit of both.

New Statesman June 1977

1985 by Anthony Burgess

London was certainly hard on the nerves in 1976 – the year, I'm sure, when Anthony Burgess's futuristic new fiction was conceived. During that equatorial summer England seemed to be boiling up, partly with crisis, partly with rage. The pound was pitiably weak: every time Callaghan sneezed the quid shed another dime ('Buddy, can you spare a pound?' ran the caption of a popular cartoon). The oil-state Arabs had begun their colonization of the capital; their desert costumes were to be seen everywhere in the streets – 'like the white gowns of a new and suddenly universal priesthood of pure money', in V.S. Naipaul's phrase. Inflation had cancelled out the Wilsonian prosperity of the working classes; the 'social contract', the Government's deal with the unions on wages, was being called the 'social con-trick'; strikes, claims, prices – everything seemed ready for the terminal lurch. It was in several senses a sweaty time for all of us here. It was class war: everyone felt it.

Burgess is a novelist who knows he is also a critic, and a critic who knows he is also a novelist. As critic, he knows that when a novelist writes about the future he is really writing about the recent past (the past being all there is to write about – the present is never around for long enough). As novelist, he knows too that when he sees the future, it will not work – he will automatically be creating a 'dystopia' (no one creates utopias any more: even the utopias of the past now look like dystopias). Pretty well inevitably, the speculative novelist becomes a satirist; he looks around, and he makes it worse.

Something in Burgess, however, and it is neither the novelist nor the critic, wants his projection to be a helpful, illuminating and, above all, accurate one. Well, how is he doing so far? Burgess encourages such literal-mindedness, and it is anyway tempting to wonder what the author thinks of England in 1978. I bet he is depressed by our recovery, however partial and temporary it turns out to be. I bet he wishes things were just a little more cataclysmic. The reading public would clearly be more sympathetically prepared for his book if the pound had now reached parity with the United States nickel, the police riot had just entered its second month, and mosques were being erected in Berkeley Square. It hasn't happened, though; 1985, and 1984, suddenly look quite close, and not very terrifying.

London wasn't easy on the nerves in 1948 either, and 1948 is what *1985* says *1984* is all about. *1985* is half fiction, half criticism. By this I do not mean that it is a mixture of the two like some of Burgess's recent novels, which try to tease and anticipate literary criticism in a sub-Nabokovian way. I mean that it is split down the middle. The first half is a critical launching-pad for the following fiction. It is an audacious scheme, involving many fresh dangers, and the book is an unexpected half-success. That is, the first half is reasonably good, the second half unconscionably poor.

People say 'It's like *1984*' when they see new airports. Actually, there's nothing science-fictional about the London of Airstrip One, or so Burgess argues, using his memory as well as his wit. Nearly everything in the London of *1984* had its counterpart in the London of 1948 – in the London of postwar depression. Everything was in decay, and nothing worked. Life was characterized by puritanism and inefficiency. The buildings were Victorian ruins; there were never any razor blades; cheap socks deliquesced beneath your feet. Orwell's intrusive 'telescreen' was an extrapolation from the arrival of ordinary television sets in middle-class homes (people used to switch them off when they got undressed). Even the ubiquity of the Big Brother posters had its precursor: The Bennet Correspondence

College, Burgess tells us, widely billboarded a sign saying, 'LET ME BE YOUR BIG BROTHER.' And 'Room 101' – the place where, in *1984*, the worst thing that can happen to you happens to you – was the room in the BBC where Orwell used to broadcast to India. Nothing too bad happened to Orwell in this room, so far as we know, but you get the idea, more or less.

Where is the idea taking us? It takes us as far as a self-evident satirical dictum (though it is one that leads Burgess into many baffling contradictions later on): 'Novels are made out of sense data, not ideas, and it's the sensuous impact that counts.' It then takes us, as the critical preface expands, into a capacious hold-all for the author's sociopolitical musings. With informality and inconoclasm, and a pleasant knack of engaging several cultural registers simultaneously, Burgess inspects, from various angles, the myth of perfectibility: he looks at the modern utopian tradition (Zamyatin's *We*, Huxley's *Brave New World*), derides the behaviourists B.F. Skinner and Arthur Koestler (who would burn out man's antisocial, non-perfectible drives), and gives a brief history of anarchism, with a funny, contemptuous account of its creaky reincarnation among the youth cultures. What is perfectible? Man isn't, but the speculative novel might be. Throughout Part One, the reader's appetite has been subtly sharpened for Part Two, where, the suggestion is, we will find a projection not only free of the literary flaws noted in others but also devastatingly humane, ameliorative, true.

The promise becomes explicit in Part One's final chapter, a curious item entitled 'The Death of Love'. Here Mr Burgess does what the logic and momentum of the whole section demand – though it still comes as a startling move. He 'rejects' *1984*. Orwell's novel, says Burgess sadly, is 'Not prophecy so much as a testimony of despair . . . a personal despair of being able to love.' Much as he tried, Orwell could not 'love the workers'; and he neglected to exalt sexual love as a passable alternative. It is 'a monstrous travesty of human possibility', Burgess decides, settling Orwell's hash with his closing line: '1984 is not going to be like that at all.'

Presumably, then, it's going to be like this, one thinks, turning the page to see the bold announcement: 'Part Two: 1985'. And suddenly one realizes the extent of Mr Burgess's nerve, or his nervelessness. There is nothing wrong – though there is plenty that is futile – about rejecting a proven classic; there is nothing wrong, I suppose, about rejecting the source of one's inspiration. But Burgess goes a stage further: the novelist in him rejects the critic. Orwell wasn't really 'forecasting the future', Mr Burgess has said at the outset; and art, anyway, 'is morally neutral, like the taste of an apple'. Some apples, of course, are more morally neutral than other apples. When the time comes to clear the decks for the fictional *1985*, Burgess dismisses *1984* for the very reasons that, as critic, he exalted it earlier on. He dismisses it for not forecasting the future and for not being morally neutral. Yet Burgess must know, whichever hat he happens to be wearing at the time, that novels do not fail for these reasons. They fail only when talent fails. 'Part Two' fails.

Burgess's *1985* is, unsurprisingly, a stoked-up 1976. 'Tucland' is nearing anarchy. Kumina gangs (that's Swahili for 'teenage') roam the streets, a-robbing and a-raping. Holistic syndicalism – whereby the firing of a supermarket cashier brings the Army out on strike – has strangled the economy. Thirteen-year-old girls masturbate indolently in front of television porno shows. London is dotted with teetotal hotels called the Al-Dorchester and Al-Klaridges, plus various Al-Hiltons and (steady) Al-Idayinns. People talk Worker's English ('you was', 'he weren't', etc.) and use unisex pronouns ('zer', 'heesh', etc.). Schools teach only trade-union history, and culture-starved punks rebel by seeking out learning at the Underground University. I can see it all now.

Though it is neither likely nor disturbing, there's no demonstrable reason why Burgess's projection fails to interest, let alone terrify. It could be argued that the utopian novel gains force and cohesion to the extent that the imagined society mirrors the human mind. In *The Republic*, for instance, we are told that the highly unattractive society envisaged by Plato is no more than an image of human wisdom: disciplined, hierarchical, rigidly selective about art. Similarly, the dystopia gains logic from its analogy to the pathological mind: Big Brother is the psychosis possessing Airstrip One, the Party merely the instrument of his paranoia, Winston Smith the weak, fluttering voice of sanity, quickly crushed. Burgess's *1985* is too chaotic to be a metaphor for anything but chaos – but, then again, this does not quite 'explain' its inertness. Alas, the failure is, (vexingly, boringly, ineffably) a failure of language.

Burgess's recent prose is characterized by professional haste and a desire to be a stylist. The result is a knotted, cadenced, bogus lustiness: every sentence, every phrase, is sure to contain some virile quirk or other: 'He scribbled something on a message pad, tore, folded, gave' and '"G-Gay?" puzzled Bev' are fair examples of Burgess's gimcrack contortions. And the dialogue is impossible. 'No need to tell me precisely where he sits on his revolving chair and watches the mineral fatness gush,' says Bev chattily of some oil-rich interloper. The workers, by the way, are presented throughout as the usual snarling, snivelling brutes, and Burgess recklessly admits in a postscript that he has been almost as unfair to them as Orwell was. So much for the failure of love. Where does this leave *1985* in relation to *1984*? Hanging on to its 'probability', I imagine, and looking sillier every month.

1985 contains a little apology to *1984*. In a facetious passage, Bev explains that Orwell was killed in the Spanish Civil War, just as he was about to write *Homage to Catalonia*. Thus Orwell never wrote *1984* and, without its lessons, 1985 is allowed to turn out as Burgess says it turns out. This makes amends of a kind, but points to a further fallacy. Novels don't care whether they come true or not, and Orwell has withstood the test of time in quite another sense. Still, it reminds you of a good reason for reading *1985*: it makes you reread *1984*.

New York Times Book Review November 1978

Earthly Powers by Anthony Burgess

There are two kinds of long novel. Long novels of the first kind are short novels that go on for a long time. Most long novels are this kind of long novel, particularly in America – where writers routinely devastate acres of woodland for their spy thrillers, space operas, family sagas, and so on. Long novels of the second kind, on the other hand, are long because they have to be, earning their amplitude by the complexity of the demands they make on writer and reader alike.

Earthly Powers is a long novel of the second kind, which makes it doubly remarkable. In Britain, the long novel was a fatal casualty of World War I; Anthony Burgess belongs to this culture, but he has always been a natural expatriate and nomad, spurning England not because of the usual constraints (i.e. sexual and fiscal) but because its artistic caution was uncongenial to his own talent. He has become a subversive interpreter of fictional conventions, developing freely under the lax and spacious influences of Europe. *Earthly Powers* also owes something to the neo-Victorian vigour of the modern American novel: it has the reckless scope of, say, Herman Wouk's *War and Remembrance* (note the bashful nods to Tolstoy and Proust) together with the tangled, page-by-page intelligence of Saul Bellow's *Herzog*, *Humboldt's Gift* and *Augie March*.

Even at 600 pages, however, the book feels crowded, bursting with manic erudition, garlicky puns, omnilingual jokes. The narrator of *Earthly Powers* is 81-year-old Kenneth Toomey, homosexual, Roman Catholic and bad novelist. In the course of this peripatetic and thickly peopled novel, which meshes the real and the personalized history of the twentieth century (more earnestly and intimately than E.L. Doctorow's *Ragtime* or Tom Stoppard's *Travesties*), Toomey visits Paris, Rome, New York, Los Angeles, Malta, Monaco, Malaya, Berlin, Barcelona and Algiers, and duly tangles with the likes of Hemingway and Hesse, Jim Joyce, Morgan Forster, Ruddy Kipling,

Tom Eliot, Willie Maugham and Plum Wodehouse. Typically, the young Toomey is seduced by George Russell (the writer 'AE') on the very day when, according to Joyce, Russell was meant to be playing his part in *Ulysses*.

As Toomey recounts the story of his life, we notice that terrible things keep happening to him – or near him, anyway. His brother-in-law is chopped up by Chicago gangsters; his closest friend is wasted by the voodoo of a Malayan warlock; his nephew is the victim of the bitter pill in a Jonestown-style massacre. Toomey inspects the elaborate severity of nature, experiences the neuroses and hysterias of his various host nations (censorship, Prohibition, the rise of Mussolini), staggers through liberated Buchenwald – 'what was the smell? All too human . . . it was the smell of myself, of all humanity.' The ultimate moral, or theological – or theodicean – irony (whereby divine intervention preserves the life of the future cultist mass-murder) is stark and ferocious; it is the kind of challenge that the literary Catholic enjoys throwing out to the world, as if to testify to the macho perversity of his faith. Graham Greene did it in *Brighton Rock*, Evelyn Waugh in *A Handful of Dust*; but Burgess is more vehement than either.

To compound his difficulties, Toomey is a homosexual, and he sees this sinful state as one of entrapment, a denial of free will. Toomey, so to speak, does not like what he likes, and he resents God for his condition. The various thieving, foul-mouthed catamites with whom Toomey tarries will no doubt offend many sectors of homosexual orthodoxy. Accustomed to police persecution for his shame, Toomey lives to see a homosexual marriage blessed by an archbishop; but very little hope is held out for man plus man. (After all, to quote the Rev. Jerry Falwell, leader of the Moral Majority: 'God created Adam and Eve in that garden – not Adam and Steve.') His one satisfactory love affair is entirely platonic, and quickly aborted by the powers of evil. 'The only way out of homosexuality is incest,' Havelock Ellis tells Toomey. Sure enough, and inevitably, Toomey's chaste but erotic relationship with his sister Hortense is the only bond that survives the novel.

What affirmation is possible, in Toomey's determinist world?

Burgess sees artistic creation as man's only god-like act, which is appropriate in a book whose twin themes are art and evil. Toomey, of course, is the most sterile kind of artist – pretentious and pitifully transparent – and Burgess has great parodic fun with his efforts: lush period epics, doomed libretti, catchy doggerel for stage musicals, a sentimental homosexual rewrite of the creation myth, even a theological work on the nature of evil (written in collusion with his relative Carlo Campanati, a Vatican high-up who later 'makes Pope'). As Toomey begins the act of creation, he experiences a divine confidence; as the work takes shape, he feels himself already falling short, as earthly compromise and contingency closes in on the pristine dream. What is intended as radical and pure becomes tainted and familiar.

In a sense, though, *Earthly Powers* belongs to Toomey as well as to Burgess. It is a considerable achievement, spacious and intricate in design, wonderfully sustained in its execution, and full of a weary generosity for the errant world it recreates. As a form, the long novel is inevitably flawed and approximate; and this book contains plenty of hollow places beneath its busy verbal surface. But whatever its human limits it shows an author who has reached the height of his earthly powers.

New York Times Book Review December 1980

Little Wilson and Big God: Being the First Part of the Confessions of Anthony Burgess

Not many people know this, but on top of writing regularly for every known newspaper and magazine, Anthony Burgess writes regularly for every unknown one, too. Pick up a Hungarian quarterly or a Portuguese tabloid – and there is Burgess, discoursing on goulash or test-driving the new Fiat 500. 'Wedged as we are between two eternities of idleness, there is no excuse for being idle now.' Even today, at seventy, and still producing book after book, Burgess spends half his time writing music. He additionally claims to do all the housework.

The first volume of the Burgess autobiography is only 450 pages long. Accordingly one would expect it to end when the author is about five. In fact, we follow him to the halfway mark, to early middle age, just as his writing career was getting into its gallop. Between then and now he has produced a further fifty-odd books. He was born Jack Wilson; Anthony Burgess is a *nom de plume* – probably one of many.

We begin to get the hang of things when Burgess reveals that he first read *Don Quixote* at the age of ten: 'I have read it four times, the second time in Spanish.' When it came to scholarships, 'I won them all.' At eleven he was published in the *Manchester Guardian* (a drawing) and in the *Daily Express* children's corner (an essay); but these ventures, like his passion for chemistry and the stage, were just exploratory sidelines. At thirteen 'I decided that I was to be a great composer'. Although he liked the 'simple tonalities' of Handel and early Beethoven, he 'rather despised these diatonic harmonies as all too easy to anticipate'. *His* music 'was to be "modern", like Stravinsky or Schoenberg'.

Not that the thirteen-year-old modernist fell too far behind in his reading, coolly tackling Ibsen and Schopenhauer:

> I also knew the Faust legend, because of Gounod and Busoni, and could read Cyrillic, having studied . . . the original score of *Sacre du Printemps* . . . In school essays I would refer to the Mozartian limpidity of Addison's prose or the Wagnerian rashness of Thomas de Quincey's, always to find these similitudes questioned by the teacher and derided by the class.

Derided? One is surprised that he remained unlynched.

But little Jack's eye-catching precocities must be seen against a background of deep terror and isolation. In early 1919 Wilson Sr, not yet demobbed, came on a furlough to Carisbrook Street, Manchester, to find his infant son gurgling in his cot – and his wife and daughter lying dead in the same room.

The Spanish influenza pandemic had struck Harpurbey. There was no doubt of the existence of a God: only the supreme being could contrive so brilliant an afterpiece to four years of unprecedented suffering and devastation.

Jack grew up 'weak and unmuscular through having no proper mother', 'persecuted or ignored', 'a lone walker-home' from school, 'a mere household animal', with a distant stepmother and 'a mostly absent drunk who called himself a father'. Burgess claims to 'resent nothing' and to 'feel no self-pity', but there is an intelligible bitterness in his iterations. The key moment, perhaps, comes very early on, with recurring nightmares that were never adequately comforted, never assuaged. 'After so much public horror, what was a mere child's nightmare?'

The childhood, then, was emotionally sparse or lopsided, yet it was also crammed with anarchical life. Twenties Manchester, as evoked in these early pages, is even more exotic than Fifties Malaya and Brunei (where the book ends). This is the world of Mrs Winslow's Soothing Syrup, and tobacco 'called Baby's Bottom (smooth as a)', the world of five-course breakfasts, tenpenny bottles of Médoc, forty-year courtships and everyday incest, rape and murder.

Throughout his education Jack Wilson was always wondering what to do with his impossible intelligence, his impossible energy and will. Huge autodidactic projects are routinely undertaken in the ragged margins of daily life. As a private in the army he boldly encounters many a thug and brute, and somehow manages to avoid getting his head kicked off – perhaps because his bedside copy of Finnegans Wake was 'generally supposed to be a codebook'. 'I had composed one Sunday, in the intervals of reading Hemingway's

Fiesta in German, a setting of a song by Lorca . . .' The reader is himself reduced to the status of a scowling squaddy, as Burgess swans imperturbably on, with his panoptic suavity, his chuckling insouciance, his word-perfect putdowns. Even fist-fights (frequent occurrences, one imagines) 'bored' him, what with his mind being on higher things. This is autobiography of the total-recall school; and Burgess's war, while reasonably soft, was unbelievably long.

All work and no play would have made Jack a dull boy. But Jack played hard too: an epic drinker, 'an eighty-a-day man' on the snout, and, it would seem, a remorseless puller of the women. In this last activity he was assisted by a seigneurial attitude towards domestics, traditional female generosity in wartime, a first wife who espoused and practised free love, and a typically recondite ploy for delaying climax: 'it was a matter of reciting Milton inly – "High on a throne of royal state . . ." (*Paradise Lost*, Book Two).'

One would hesitate to connect Burgess's erotic prowess with his literary heft, but the two appear to be intimately linked. When he goes out to teach at 'the Eton of the East', he busily compares the bedroom skills of the Chinese as against the Malayans; but his insatiability, here as elsewhere, is an attempt at synthesis, at topology. His women are pillow dictionaries. And in between sessions he is composing his *Sinfoni Melayu* ('which tried to combine the musical elements of the country into a synthetic language which called on native drums and xylophones') or translating Eliot ('*Bulan April ia-lah bulan yang dzalim sa-kali*'). Burgess may swank exasperatingly at times, but his book's only real boast is in its subtitle, with its hi to Rousseau. Even this might be allowed as a necessary elevation in an age when the autobiography, as a form, has become little more than the pension-book of politicians and actors.

Jack Wilson's greatest project was Anthony Burgess. Like all writers he had to systematize a self; he had to cobble something together out of his admitted shortcomings (coldness, coarseness, sharp appetites) as well as his manifest and superabundant natural gifts. The man who emerges is a composite glued together by energy – or 'holding energy', as physicists say. His eyesight has always been rocky ('I once entered a bank in Stratford-on-Avon and ordered a drink'); his grip on Newtonian reality has always been contingent ('occasionally I see the impossibility of walking and have to stumble to a bench'); and his spiritual dreads have been lifelong and omnipresent. But he has built many mansions with this peculiar house of cards:

> I am poised till I die between fear of the cardboard darkness of the stockroom and the terror of space. I wanted the free limitations of my own skull and a world I could build with a pencil. I have not changed much since 1925.

Observer February 1987

Shorter Shrift

The Malcontents by C.P. Snow

Authors ought generally to be praised for writing about people who are remote from their own lives. Such transsexual novels as Angus Wilson's *Late Call* and Iris Murdoch's *Under the Net*, for instance, show us what the imagination can do without the corroboration of experience. The factual-autobiographical basis of C.P. Snow's eleven-book sequence, *Strangers and Brothers*, has long been recognized, and it is often hinted – sometimes petulantly – that this must tend to make the work less literary, more historical. In his latest novel, however, Snow has gone and written about the young – the dissident, *relevant* young – and without Lewis Eliot's helpfully conjunctivitic eyes to see them through.

The story is brisk enough, and Snow tells it in his effortful but competent style. Seven provincial subversives, who call themselves the 'core', manage to frame a Shadow Minister via a local case of Rachmanism. But there's a leak (a traitor in their midst, etc.), one of them dies misadventurously, prosecution looms, their plans and aspirations disintegrate.

This is all very well, and doubtless *The Malcontents* will be noticed quite generously by reviewers as old, or nearly as old, or possibly even older, than Snow himself. But the younger reader is sure to be embarrassed by Snow's cluelessness. This is not invidious. Any teenager who wrote a supposedly naturalistic novel about an old-people's home that had jukeboxes and pinball machines flanking its aisles would also have to steel himself for a fairly cool press.

For example: when the core convenes there are 'Greetings, hallo and hi: some used the American style by now.' In all fairness, 'now' is January 1970, so Snow isn't more than a couple of decades out. Nor is it just a question of surface; the pacing gets tripped up, too. During a party in which LSD is being doled out, one of the boys, Bernard, wanders out of a fifth-floor window. The protagonists spend a lot of time musing about whether someone might have spiked his beer with acid (thus perhaps giving Bernard the impression that he could fly), but finally dismiss the idea as too fantastic to be true. Unless they had spent their university lives entirely behind drawn blinds they'd have dismissed it instantly as far, far too *corny* to be true. If the publicity were anything to go by, you would barely be able to step into the street nowadays without seeing some drug-crazed youngster being hosed off the pavement.

Two of the core are girls; one is caricatured, the other idealized. Also, there's Neil, the very personification of a class-embittered Angry; Lance, the very personification of a druggy, foppish dabbler in revolt; and poor Bernard, the very personification of an austere Jewish intellectual. Snow's main concern, though, is with Stephen and Mark, especially Stephen. (These young gentlemen, of course, are not at the local university, but on vac from Cambridge.) They're not interested in demonstrations and unworkable ideologies so much as in trying genuinely to improve the quality of life – not unlike the young Snow, one imagines. As people they are about as real as the polo-necked smoothies who pout at you from the book's cover, but it must be said that through them Snow manages to locate and examine a suggestive assortment of motives and dialectic.

Mark describes Stephen's social concern as follows: 'It's a kind of love.' Probably, Snow's portrait of Stephen is based on the raffish view that no decent social democrat wasn't a bit of a revolutionary in his youth. Towards the end, however, when Stephen realizes that he has been saved from prosecution by the very worst aspects of the system and has to choose whether to reincriminate himself by giving evidence for the victimized Neil – then rationalizes his motives for doing so – all this is compassionately and intelligently observed. And, despite the howlers, one can only continue to admire Snow's tolerance and honesty, and his eloquence when writing about the possibilities of doing good and the difficulties of behaving well.

The book ends up telling us more about growing old than it

tells us about being young. 'Neither he nor the others could project themselves into their middle age. They couldn't predict the nostalgias, the regressions, even the pathos, that might be waiting for them.' This is well said, and it is a pity when the projection doesn't work the other way either.

Observer July 1972

The *Malacia Tapestry* by Brian Aldiss

Established science-fiction writers have a habit of getting bored with their genre – sometimes out of frank debility, more often out of ambition and a sense of critical neglect. One defector, Kurt Vonnegut, says that until critics learn to differentiate between SF and a WC he 'wants out'. Brian Aldiss has been wanting out for some years now: apart from his priapic autobiographical sequence (*The Hand-Reared Boy* and *A Soldier Erect* – with more to come), he has recently produced a critical history of SF (*Billion-Year Spree*) and two uneasily upmarket fantasies, *Frankenstein Unbound* and *The 80-Minute Hour*. *The Malacia Tapestry* is Aldiss's longest watertread in the mainstream to date, and by now, I'm afraid, the lifeguards are getting nervous.

Malacia is a Byzantine city-state in a suspended, never-never pre-Renaissance resembling in flavour – with its mountebanks, hucksters and soothsayers – the Venice of Jonson's *Volpone*. Mind you, it is not an historical world but an alternate one, certain SF aspects being ornamentally retained in the form of fabulous beasts and nude girls who can fly about in the air. All this, strictly, is lumber, since everything 'new' in the book could simply be retranslated into standard historical-novel terms: calling elephants 'mangonels', for instance, is not that much eerier than calling them elephants. The only things about Malacian society that turn out to matter to the action are its repressiveness and its decadence, which, as well as dramatizing 'the conflicts and contradictions of our own day' (true, O blurb), allows Mr Aldiss to offer what he wouldn't dare conventionally attempt: not just an historical romance but a *romantic* historical romance.

Stripped of its intermittently vivid background, the book is a sentimental study of the education of its hero, Perian de Chirolo – and, if I may lean on Perian's punning style, *The Malacia Tapestry* could unfussily be retitled *Tom Cojones* and left at that. De Chirolo, a raffish scaramouche, is a terrible 'one' for the girls; and, although morals are quite exacting in Malacia, his battery of racy quibbles, oniony innuendoes, lugubrious quatrains ('Dear Bedalar, of all the girls I have laid, Yours is the music . . .', etc.) and energetic feelings-up seldom misses.

Perian's tragedy, however, is that he subscribes to such modern ills as the double standard, socio-sexual self-betterment, male chauvinism and indifference to the plight of the working-class sex object. On these points Mr Aldiss sorts Perian out as thoroughly as his fondness for the character will permit, and we leave the young actor in an adulterous embrace, as he resolves to join the 'Progressive' movement *mañana*.

Bewilderingly trite though all this is, the book might have been rescued by some non-trite prose – something to which Mr Aldiss is not a stranger. But you don't evoke a sense of other-worldliness by having people say 'mayhap' every so often, or by such exotic remarks as Perian's 'I was without a single denario to my name.' Similarly, the book's nagging bawdy is not sensitized by phrases like 'reaching for the scrumptious mounds of her breasts' and 'my eyes stood out like her nipples'. Genre fiction is, very broadly, idea fiction, and what distinguishes it from the mainstream is for the most part a question of pace. To make the switch you must, first of all, *slow down*. Mr Aldiss did not slow down for *The Malacia Tapestry*. It shows.

Observer July 1976

The Rock Pool by Cyril Connolly

Cyril Connolly had powerful disqualifications for writing a good novel. A bored hedonist, francophile in his literary tastes, Latinate in his style (a seeker of wisdom, a brooder on greatness): here was a man, you would think, who had every incentive to stick to book chat, belles-lettres and Sunday journalism. And yet *The Rock Pool* (1936), Connolly's first book and his one and only novel, is full of low human comedy and pretty well free of pretension. More remarkably still, it has not dated. Genially aware of his own infirmities, Connolly cast himself in an anti-heroic mould, and made his aspirations the stuff of weary, regretful satire.

Edgar Naylor, 26, with a tiny private income, snobbish, defensive and cautiously lustful, arrives in Trou-sur-Mer, a low-bohemian shanty town on the Côte d'Azur peopled by drunken *artistes manqués*, rapacious caterers and cosmopolitan lesbians with names like Toni, Dicky and Duff. Cruising into town with an air of anthropological detachment, Naylor gradually and helplessly finds his own level in Trou's murky rock pool.

During the early pages, Connolly is doing what all novelists have to do: he is finding a voice, and a way to interpret the voices of other people. Still, it is a shaky start by any standards, with many a reflexive cliché ('moody silence', 'a grip of iron') and factotum adjective ('charming', 'pleasant'). Connolly also reveals what appears to be an anti-knack for catching human speech. Americans say 'gee' and 'swell' all the time. 'Did yu raow? Did you reide?' asks an English poseur. And to render Naylor's nervous pomposity Connolly hits upon the laborious trick of stringing his words together, like so: 'it's oneoftherudestthingsthat'severhappenedtomeinmylife'. This mannerism is abandoned more or less for good after the first chapter; it is evidence, perhaps, of Connolly's well-attested indolence that he never went back and tidied up. From here on, following Naylor's first hangover, the novel steadies, and goes on to chart with grisly verve Naylor's thoroughly merited decline. Connolly says at the outset that his hero is 'neither very intelligent nor especially likeable' – a dud, in fact, who might pass himself off as a 'character' in Trou. It is a precise irony, well caught by Connolly, that communities of this kind, supposedly full of outrageous dropouts and bohos, are packed with variegated bores who show nothing but a fierce and brilliant talent for self-preservation.

Yet Naylor fails to shine even here. Rooked, duped and dumped, he finds that his unattractiveness, like his Englishness, hangs on him like damp clothing: 'Sonia took one look at his long empty face. She felt for the first time the proximity of some ancient enemy of youth and spirit, and moved quietly away.' His popularity – his pitiable notoriety, even – lasts as long as his money. Thereafter Naylor teams up with the only comparably unattractive personage in Trou – Ruby, a deluded American drunk of exemplary squalor. In the last pages, trying to make friends over a free drink, Naylor is taken for 'just another' English bum. But then he was that all along.

The Rock Pool is a short, slight, funny novel, altogether an agreeable surprise. Connolly's rather cumbrous erudition is held in check most of the time, with only occasional signs of strain: feathery reeds are as 'sad and insubstantial as a Chinese poem', Nice is 'dowdy and romantic, like Offenbach', a girl has the pagan aura of 'a verse of Meleager' – and so on. These perceptions are half-attributed to Naylor, but there are many passages which are too elaborate, too aphoristic, too *good* to be shrugged off in this way. *The Rock Pool* was originally intended as part of a triptych, three studies of English snobbery and hopelessness, and this might account for the odd twinge of ironic imbalance.

Why only the one novel? What was the enemy of Connolly's promise? Peter Quennell, in his introduction, echoes Connolly's apprehension that he was ruined by too much fiction-reviewing: he knew all the larks, and he knew them all too well. Such truth as there is in this theory relates only to Connolly's limited store of intellectual energy or creative brashness. Pointed nearer the truth, I think, is the precept that a novelist needs to be unsophisticated, childish, even rather obtuse and naïve. Connolly was, in his criticism, in his tremulous *pensées*, in his editorializing for *Horizon*, often transparent, foppish and vague. But no one could have accused him of innocence.

Observer November 1981

Words of Advice by Fay Weldon

Success is well known to be a risky business for writers: sometimes the mere fact of social mobility is enough to maroon a talent. In America, of course, acclaimed novelists can repair to fortresses girdled by moats and electric fences. In England, they don't have the cash – but they get to know people who do. Fay Weldon's novels have so far moved pretty confidently up the social scale. From the girls-together scruffiness of *The Fat Woman's Joke* and *Down Among the Women*, she has progressed via the TV-executive and career-person stratum of *Female Friends* to the stockbroker suburbia of *Remember Me*. In this, her fifth novel, Miss Weldon finally strikes it rich, and is ushered into the presence of her first millionaire.

Her first millionairess, too, naturally. Miss Weldon's world has always been assertively, almost parodistically, matriarchal; she writes as if *men* had the pretty little heads: when things happen, you may be sure that the women are the puppeteers. Hamish is our puppet millionaire: an aged plant-tub tycoon, ensconced in a country house of sprawling vulgarity, he remains the befuddled pawn of his wife, Gemma, a sterile but artful empress who has long been crippled by psychosomatic paraplegia. Their principal houseguest is handsome, forty-ish Victor. A go-getting antique dealer, he too remains the venal, guilt-soaked plaything of his abandoned wife on the one hand and, on the other, of his buxom ingenue mistress, eighteen-year-old

Elsa, who accompanies him on his acquisitive visit to the Hamish mansion. As is the case with most fictional millionaire's houseparties, the weekend features a good deal of intrigue, social humiliation and exhaustive sexual interplay. Everyone, more or less, insults, betrays and sleeps with everyone else.

Gemma is the chief puppeteer. She is also the chief monologist in this generally rather voluble novel, punctuating the manoeuvres with a detailed account of her formative years. (You feel, during these speeches, that Weldon is writing flat-out for Gemma: they certainly share a taste for didacticism and the epic simile.) Gemma's history is directed at the long-suffering ear of Elsa, whose socio-sexual prospects it is clearly meant to allegorize and, ultimately, to define. Yes, the Weldon woman still carries the same albatross: the Weldon man. He will either be a solvent cuckold (who will at least look after you, and defray your infidelities) or an arty maverick (who will awaken you, then break your heart and very possibly your back too). 'Sex', says Weldon, who has plainly mused thoroughly on this topic, 'is not for procreation; it is for the sharing out of privilege.'

What, then, has privilege done to Miss Weldon's world? Most obviously, it has stylized it. Miss Weldon has never been much of a socially 'concerned' writer, and although her eye for the hardware of status remains unblinking, she is not particularly interested in the moral meaning of wealth. Rather, she sees the moneyed life as being *suspended*. It is, as they say, no accident that the most naturalistic scene in the book is a glimpse of Victor's abandoned wife, chugging enjoyably along in middle-class obliviousness – a milieu much closer, one suspects, to Miss Weldon's natural habitat. As a result of this spry distancing, anyway, *Words of Advice* is a raffish, open-ended novel, in which all kinds of cockeyed notions, crooked parallels and unassimilated themes can be harmlessly let out to play. The impression is abetted by the tricky disjunctions of the book's layout, though in this innovation Miss Weldon has unluckily failed to secure the full co-operation of her typesetters.

Stylization, however, inevitably puts style under the limelight, and Weldon's prose – normally a crisp and functional performer –

makes a somewhat bashful leading lady. As she aspires more and more identifiably to the wise, otherworldly manner of Muriel Spark, it becomes clear that Miss Weldon's intention is to let language reflect the dutifully trite ponderings of her characters. But whose clichés are they? Love, for instance, strikes 'like a shaft of sudden light from heaven', reassembling the 'very roots' (or alternatively, seventeen pages later, the 'very particles') of 'your being'; the sexual act, in addition, makes you 'cry out aloud from fear and joy, pain and pleasure mixed'. Naïve people often have naïve thoughts – but aren't they often vividly naïve? I suppose Miss Weldon should know, since she is ever-ready to dispense timely adages whenever the action pauses to catch its breath: 'The good we do lives after us . . . what are good times without the bad? . . . from generation to generation . . . back and back through generations . . . So men have spoken to women from the beginning . . . Sexual passion requited invigorates the parties concerned . . .' – though with a bit of pain and pleasure mixed, perhaps. These strides towards the lectern are curiously out of place among Miss Weldon's devil-may-care ironies, and point to larger flaws.

Cliché spreads inwards from the language of the book to its heart. Cliché always does. Miss Weldon may have climbed the social scale, but she now seems absurdly remote from its lowlier representatives. Even when it is your intention to show people pathetically conditioned by their experience, you can't have dumb secretaries saying things like 'I'll look it up under "superstitions" in *Occult Weekly*' and 'Everything can be filed. It said so in Lesson Six, Office Routine.' Unsurprisingly, when Miss Weldon chooses to gouge some 'real' emotion out of these mock-ups, she starkly announces that this is what she is doing – we get 'real sorrow' and 'real affection' within a few lines. Similarly, in a novel where the heroine is a psychosomatic cripple (all she has to do is 'want' to talk, etc.) the last thing you expect, outside pulp fiction, is that she will actually get up and *walk*. But that's what Gemma actually does – in an attempt to join Elsa in the customary dash from the men-folk which supplies Miss Weldon with her codas. '"Run!" cries Gemma . . . "You must! You must run for me and all of us."' Social mobility should, of course, be available to all; but, as we've seen, it remains a risky business.

New York Times Book Review October 1977

Mantissa by John Fowles

It would be inaccurate to say that John Fowles is a middlebrow writer who sometimes hopes he is a highbrow: it has never occurred to him to believe otherwise. There is a difference, morally.

Mantissa gives us certain scenes from a marriage – the marriage between the author and his muse. It is set inside the author's head. The muse, who is called Erato, turns up in various guises and goes through various routines with the author, who is called Miles. They have lots of rows and sex. Both wield supernatural powers: hers are mythical, his authorial, so they even out in the end. Thus the novel seeks to explore the nature of reality and creativity, the alienations of art, the evolution of literature to its present self-conscious phase, the relationship between men and women, and much more.

But never mind about all that for now. Let us swim back to the surface and inspect the quality of the performance on offer. Seldom in his fiction has Fowles played host to humour, gaiety or brio. Here, alas, he lets his hair down. *Mantissa* is serious all right, but it permits itself to be 'deliciously irreverent' too. There are conundrums for the erudite, but there is also honey for the bears.

Most of the book is in dialogue. The dialogue is terrible. 'I'm not just an idiot pair of nymphs in some fancy Frog poet's afternoon off,' warns Erato. 'You may be quite a good-looking goddess as goddesses go. Or go-go,' cracks Miles. Or again: 'I don't think you'd recognise an olive-branch if you were sitting in a whole orchard of the things.' No room for improvement there? Not even 'grove' instead of 'orchard', to begin at the very beginning? But the surrounding prose features many a line, and many a witticism, in comparably poor shape.

'He glares up at her, with all the revulsion of a lifelong teetotaller being offered a magnum of malt whisky.' Now, would the teetotaller be *that* revolted? How revolted, exactly, is he meant to be? Would it be funny if Fowles had piled it on even thicker – say, 'a whole case of 100-year-old Highland malt whisky'? No. The sentence just lies there, pining for another visit to the drawing-board.

Apart from a few set-pieces (one or two of them not bad either), the prose has no other function but to pad the dialogue. In one scene, Miles is getting dressed as he talks. He is tying his tie. We become surer and surer about this:

He stands, and picks up the tie from the back of the chair. He leaves the tie hanging untied round his neck . . . He starts tying his tie . . . He ties his tie . . . He realizes something has gone wrong with the tying of his tie; and rather irritatedly pulls it apart, then starts tying again . . . [He] gives the better knot of the second tying a last little tightening.

How fervently the reader hopes that the second tying will be the last! Such are the dazzling word-tapestries that Fowles the magician spins!

'That's a perfect example of your asinine female logic.' 'Look, I'm not going to pursue this totally irrelevant red herring.' It has a familiar ring, doesn't it? 'He managed a wan smile.' 'She gives him a sarcastic little smile, and looks away.' 'God you're so naïve.' Take away the quotes from Descartes, Marivaux and Lemprière, the embarrassing jive-talk about Aristophanes and Mnemosyne, subtract the patina of learning, the callow pedantry, and you are left with a writer toiling away with the materials of substandard art – what Fowles might call the low-mimetic mode: farces, sitcoms, buxom novels.

Although *Mantissa* is Fowles's first work of fiction for several years, in another sense it is hardly a bolt out of the blue. The first half of *The Collector* is excellent; quite a lot of *The French Lieutenant's*

Woman is interesting. The other novels and stories are Georgian, silver-age efforts; and they are crammed with clichés. Fowles's success, particularly in America, has something to do with making culture palatable – with giving people the impression that culture is what they are getting. He sweetens the pill: but the pill was saccharine all along.

A writer cannot do this cynically, in bad faith. Fowles is genuine, and *Mantissa* remains a genuine curiosity. Stripped of the usual scaffolding (Fowles's considerable gifts as a middlebrow story-teller, the protective glaze of his pedagogy), such talent as survives stands there naked and trembling in the cold. Few writers have ever blown the whistle on themselves so piercingly.

Observer October 1982

The D.M. Thomas Phenomenon

Ararat by D.M. Thomas

It looked like the perfect success story – and still does, in many ways. Already it has acquired the tranquil glow of fairy tale. D.M. Thomas was once an unregarded novelist and a steady, unexceptional, mildly insouciant poet. He was a Cornishman (a specific thing to be, like a balladeering hillbilly – but with Celtic, messianic associations), exiled to humble Hereford, in the marshlands of England, where he taught at a rude and lowly training college. His most recent novel, a little offering called *The White Hotel*, had tiptoed through the review pages of the London press and had sold the usual 500 copies. In America, Thomas's publisher seemed to have higher hopes for the book. Perhaps Thomas might even buy himself a new typewriter, or take the family off for a weekend in Anglesey.

The rest we know. The American reviews maintained a note of tearful, inconsolable gratitude; the book started to sell like *Garp* T-shirts. When Thomas's agent called him in Hereford and rattled off the polysyllables of the paperback sale, Thomas was still so poor that he had to celebrate with a bottle of cooking sherry. In England, embarrassed reviewers began to take a second look. *The White Hotel* became a bestseller in the Cornishman's native land. He was runner-up for the Booker Prize. Glamorously, he went AWOL while being lionized at an American university. In the gossip columns, his name was linked – however erroneously, however excitably – with that of the popular novelist and official reviser of the *Oxford Companion to English Literature*, Margaret Drabble . . . It may not sound like much; but for a Brit these things definitely count.

And everyone was pleased – or 'genuinely' pleased, as they say. Thomas was working in such a depopulated area (not Hereford, but the genre of the sexual surreal) that even his fellow writers were only mildly distressed. There was also the consoling thought that *The White Hotel* had gained its American lift-off for peculiarly American reasons. In a country so obsessed by the Holocaust that even a flapping, gobbling, squawking turkey like William Styron's *Sophie's Choice* (that thesaurus of florid commonplaces) enjoyed universal acclaim, *The White Hotel* had a lot going for it. Styron offered sex and the Final Solution; Thomas had all this and psychoanalysis too – the full triumvirate of national fixations. Finally, though, and more important, Thomas had written an interesting novel; overrated, perhaps, but fresh, freakish, and solitary.

The predictable undertow that followed the book's success did at least take a surprising form. Vigilant readers discovered that the Babi Yar section of *The White Hotel* had been laboriously transcribed from *Babi Yar*, by Anatoli Kuznetsov. True, the copyright page acknowledged 'use of material' from Kuznetsov, and in his apologia Thomas persuasively stressed the need for the impersonal voice of history, of testimony, at this stage in the narrative. Analogous accusations then greeted *The Bronze Horseman*, his verse translations of Pushkin. Thomas's counter-argument was forceful and immediate: case dismissed. The borrowings from *Babi Yar*, however, remained an anomaly. It wasn't a case of plagiarism; but it was clearly a case of something. When the reviewers spoke of the transports and crackups they weathered as they checked out of *The White Hotel* ('I walked out into the garden and could not speak', and so on), it was *Babi Yar* that had assailed them. The testimony is unbearably powerful; it is the climax of the novel; it is, in plain terms, the best bit – and Thomas didn't write it.

In publishing, success creates a centrifugal process: the big book spins off spinoffs. The popularity of *The White Hotel* ironically gave rise to a reissue of *Babi Yar*. It also gave rise to a reissue – in England, recently – of *Birthstone*, Thomas's long-remaindered second novel. Now just how ironic is this?

I didn't know which to be most shocked by – the violation, the sadism, the kleptomania or the exhibitionism. As if suspicion of terrorism wasn't enough. I could be in the dock for shop-lifting and indecency. I had a picture of me haemorrhaging on to a rubber sheet while two policemen took statements.

Birthstone has many things in common with *The White Hotel*, including frequent descents to a flat, tinkertoy, children's-book prose style. In addition, they both feature androgynism, meteoric disturbances, Freudian scatology, dreams, poems, and a rampant sexuality. The sex is particularly hard to get away from. It is like pornography in that it escalates fantastically with new permutations and perversities. It is unlike pornography in that its concerns are dourly anti-erotic – except for readers who harbour very specialized tastes: rubber, enemas, gerontophilia, and a denunciatory attitude towards pantyhose. *Birthstone* is an embarrassment; it spreads unease; it makes you wonder whether the author's effects – murky, cosy, risible, banal – are the result of calculation or of a fanatical tastelessness. *The Flute-Player*, Thomas's first novel, might help to clarify the matter; no doubt it awaits its own vampiric resuscitation.

So, with all kinds of disquiet, one opens *Ararat*. There are signs of authorial disquiet also. The text is preceded by half a page of acknowledgments and disclaimers: 'the author's invention . . . translated by the author . . . from the Armenian poet Nareg . . . principal source . . . factual details.' We confront the prologue and the slinky decadence of its opening: 'Sergei Rozanov had made an unnecessary journey from Moscow to Gorky, simply in order to sleep with a young blind woman.' On the third page, one brief paragraph contains, by my count, five exuberant clichés: 'through to the bitter end'; 'the oblivion of sleep'; 'torrential rain lashed the window'; 'the autumn trees stripped bare'; 'make the most of every moment'. We creep on. The poet Rozanov sleeps with the blind woman. 'Olga's love-making was acrobatic but lacking in finesse.' Olga asks Rozanov to tell her a story. The first section, 'Night', begins. 'Why are you so obsessed with sex?' the woman doctor asks Surkov, another poet. The reader leans forward. No answer. They sleep together; there is a further attack on pantyhose, an *ubi sunt* lament for stockings and garter-belts. Surkov takes an ocean cruise on his doctor's advice. He sleeps with a virgin gymnast. An old fellow passenger, Finn (a superb comic-sinister creation), turns out to be a multiple war-criminal. Within a few pages we encounter the Armenian genocide, Babi Yar, the 'Devouring' of the Gypsies, the purge of the kulaks, the Gulag Archipelago, Yezhov, Beria, Stalin, and Hitler. It seems to be Thomas's world: poems, dreams, a supercharged and eroticized landscape – sex and violence, on the cosmic scale.

And so the book proceeds, by turns fascinating, repellent, funny; owlish, ingenious, and shallow. *Ararat* is a novel of five poets, from Pushkin to Yevtushenko; it is a novel about Russianness. It is a series of improvisations on the theme of improvisation – its very method, sentence by sentence, is improvisatory, as all dreams are, as all fantasy is. Thomas can often sustain a note of charming inconsequentiality, of free-fall, an intoxicating liberty from the world of cause and effect. During these moments one may gain much slothful pleasure from following the skittish fantasist, who has no imperative other than to seem striking.

Thomas's use of cliché is so insistent, and so remote from his poetry and discursive prose, that it can only be aiming at a kind of back-door subtlety – a Tolstoyan transparency, perhaps, or a Pushkinian purity. Chekhov and Nabokov used cliché, particularly in interior monologue, to suggest the reduced and bounded lives of their characters. In Solzhenitsyn, the cliché expresses a hearty stoicism. D.M. Thomas, who is thoroughly Russian in many of his predilections – 'making strange', the delights of decadence and vulgarity, the alienations of the 'superfluous' man – is clearly in pursuit of an artful simplicity. But the style has its dangers. Take the descriptions of formal womanly beauty:

> . . . the golden coils of her hair, her full lips, her voluptuous figure, her lustrous eyes . . . her face, with its high cheekbones, was a perfect oval. Her black eyes flashed provocation . . . Her red lips were inviting – full and exquisitely curved. Her bosom swelled over the décolletage of her white dress . . .

Reading this, you fear that the writer's face is about to flop on to the typewriter keys; the sentences conjure nothing but an exhausted imagination. Similarly, much of the verse incorporated into the story is so 'free' that it is scandalized by its own line breaks: 'Turning in bed / restlessly, you urge me / not to smoke so much, / recalling someone dear / to you who died / of lung cancer . . .' For long stretches Thomas seems to do no more than wallow in stock response. Elsewhere, he achieves a weird weightlessness, an effect perfectly attuned to the marshlight of this misty romance.

Quite possibly, *Ararat* will reproduce the success, if not the *succès*, of *The White Hotel*. That success is inordinate, of course, by definition, but I don't think Thomas will be distracted by its unreality. (He will be distracted by further controversy, however: the version of Pushkin's *Egyptian Nights* that he incorporates – supposedly 'a translation by the author' – uses chunks of a translation by Gillon R. Aitken, word for word.) But for all his reputation as a magpie, he is an original; to my knowledge, the only novelist whom he even remotely resembles is the underrated J.G. Ballard. Although Ballard is more of a stylist than Thomas, their prose has the same glassy fragility and dazzle, and the same susceptibility to quirkiness and excess. To appraise his achievement in the most generous terms, Thomas may be the first writer who has been able to translate the poet's world (with all its chaotic, shadowy, and fugitive elements) to the more accessible arena of the novel. Nowadays the great literary successes are nearly always democratizing in tendency. The converts are honoured and flattered by their invitation to the pantheon – or, more appropriately in Thomas's case, their summons to the pandemonium.

Atlantic Monthly April 1983

Philip Larkin

The Beginning:
Larval Larkin

A Girl in Winter by Philip Larkin

At the age of twenty-four, with three books already behind him, Philip Larkin looked all set to become a novelist. He had produced one fragile, half-forgotten collection of verse, *The North Ship*, and two vigorous full-length novels – *Jill* and *A Girl in Winter*. That was thirty years ago. Since then he has published a slender volume of poetry every decade, and he is slowing down all the time (averaging, nowadays, about a poem a year). The fiction, however, stopped dead. As Larkin has ruefully explained, he waited for more fiction to come – but it never did.

Why? Well, the two novels we have provide what clues there are. In this respect *Jill* (1946) is the less significant book. It is less significant because anyone could have written it – or, to put the point more exactly, it needn't have been written by Philip Larkin. Blending fantasy and self-absorption in the usual first-novel style, it recounts the gaucheries of a furtive, owlish working-class boy during his first term at Oxford: the hero's queasy sense of social inferiority, his emulation of a dissolute roommate, and his own graceless erotic yearnings combine to bring about his tragi-comic humiliation. *Jill* is a funny, confused, likeable and quite undisconcerting book.

A Girl in Winter, published in England in 1947, is something else again: it is Larkinesque. At first it looks like a similar novel – indeed, the *same* novel, except that it is told from the woman's point of view. Katherine is a European schoolgirl, invited over for a vacation *en famille* with her English penpal, Robin. Robin is as boring as his letters suggest, but he is personable enough, and, as with the Jill figure in the previous book, he soon becomes the bland receptacle of Katherine's overheated longings (one sudden, sweaty kiss is all she has to show for her turbulent four-week visit). A girl in summer, perhaps.

Years later, during the war, Katherine finds herself in England; she is working in frozen squalor at a public library somewhere in the North, and trying, one feels, to discover strength in her misery rather than any plausible escape from it. In response to a casual letter, Robin suddenly appears. It is clear that he has come along with no more complicated aim than to go to bed with her, and then go away again. Now *he* is the gawky one, petulant and charmless, unmatured (the implication is) by the pangs of loneliness and regret. Entirely unmoved by Robin's resentful overtures, Katherine none the less complies: it is the easiest way of forgetting him. The novel ends on a note of tremulous optimism, as wintry solitude gathers once more.

It is a far more enigmatic book than *Jill*; and it is also, somehow, far less of a *novel*. Haltingly paced and erratically written, *Jill* is at least integrally thought out – its minor characters are assimilated, its questions resolved, its themes dispatched. In *A Girl in Winter* the fictional accessories melt to nothing in the glare of the heroine's solipsism. The minor figures are, strictly, mere walk-ons, liable to be shrugged off as soon as they cease to stimulate Katherine's introspection; and the moral oppositions of the novel loom and flicker with similar caprice. But these aren't criticisms – they are clues. The answer is, of course, that Larkin is already becoming less of a novelist and more of a poet.

The process of distillation, of reduction to essences, shows itself in a number of ways, some of them poignant, some of them effortful. Larkin is prepared, for instance, to write an impossibly flat sentence ('It was very solacing to be alone'; 'The truth was, she had not been facing facts') if an abrupt mood-swing requires it. Then, too, he will fasten consecutive scenes on some tritely effusive image – there's a symbolic snail, a flock of symbolic pigeons, even a symbolic frog – and almost every other chapter fades out in a kind of neon wistfulness: 'She dropped the dead flowers into the wastepaper basket', and the like. Correspondingly, though, *A Girl in Winter* gives us a unique insight into the origins of a remarkable talent. Here we see Larkin getting ready to use his special genius: his ability to make landscape and townscape answer to human emotions. The snow, the shopfront, the rivers, the blacked-out streets – each gives its own expression to the intense seclusion at the heart of the book.

This is the larval Larkin, displayed more transparently here than in even his earliest verse. If you turn to *The North Ship* (1945) for some lines appropriate to *A Girl in Winter*, you will find only a remote evocation:

> To pull the curtains back
> And see the clouds flying –
> How strange it is
> For the heart to be loveless, and as cold as these.

If you turn to *High Windows* (1974), however, you will find the essence of the same story, retold in poem after poem:

> The way the moon dashes through clouds that blow
> Loosely as cannon-smoke . . .
> Is a reminder of the strength and pain
> Of being young; that it can't come again,
> But is for others undiminished somewhere.

New York Times Book Review December 1976

The Ending: Don Juan in Hull

When poets die, there is usually a rush to judgment: a revaluation, a retaliation – a reaction, anyway. We know how these things go, with the poets. He who was praised and popular is suddenly found to be facile and frictionless. He who was mocked and much-remaindered is suddenly found to be 'strangely' neglected. In 1985, the year of his death, Philip Larkin was unquestionably England's unofficial laureate, our best-loved poet since the war: better loved, *qua* poet, than John Betjeman, who was loved also for his charm, his famous giggle, his patrician bohemianism, and his televisual charisma, all of which Larkin notably lacked. Now, in 1993, Larkin is something like a pariah, or an untouchable. He who was beautiful is suddenly found to be ugly.

The word 'Larkinesque' used to evoke the wistful, the provincial, the crepuscular, the sad, the unloved; now it evokes the scabrous and the supremacist. The word 'Larkinism' used to stand for a certain sort of staid, decent, wary Englishness; now it refers to the articulate far right. In the early Eighties, the common mind imagined Larkin as a reclusive yet twinkly drudge – bald, bespectacled, bicycle-clipped, slumped in a shabby library gaslit against the dusk. In the early Nineties, we see a fuddled Scrooge and bigot, his singlet-clad form barely visible through a mephitis of alcohol, anality, and spank magazines. The reaction against Larkin has been unprecedentedly violent, as well as unprecedentedly hypocritical, tendentious, and smug. Its energy does not – could not – derive from literature: it derives from ideology, or from the vaguer promptings of a new ethos. In a sense, none of this matters, because only the poems matter. But the spectacle holds the attention. This is critical revisionism in an eye-catching new outfit. The reaction, like most reactions, is just an overreaction. To get an overreaction, you need plenty of overreactors. Somebody has to do it. And here they all are, busy overreacting.

There are those who believe that the trouble began with the *Collected Poems*, in 1988. Its editor, Anthony Thwaite, who has also edited Larkin's *Selected Letters*, decided not to segregate the published poems from the unpublished. So instead of the three volumes of clearly finished work – *The Less Deceived* (1955), *The Whitsun Weddings* (1964), and *High Windows* (1974) – with all the other stuff tucked away at the back, we get a looser and more promiscuous corpus, containing squibs and snippets, rambling failures later abandoned, lecherous doggerel, and confessional curiosities like the frightening late poem 'Love Again':

> Love again: wanking at ten past three
> (Surely he's taken her home by now?),
> The bedroom hot as a bakery,
> The drink gone dead, without showing how
> To meet tomorrow, and afterwards,
> And the usual pain, like dysentery.
>
> Someone else feeling her breasts and cunt,
> Someone else drowned in that lash-wide stare . . .

You could say that the editorial decision had a clouding effect on the poems. You could even argue that it went against Larkin's spirit. Larkin left a lot of good things out. His oeuvre (like his taste) was narrow, but it was crystallized; he could circle around a poem for years, in drafts, before completing or rejecting it. In any event, Larkin the man had started to look a little stranger. The *Collected Poems* didn't open him to attack. But it might have softened him up.

The frontal assault began in the autumn of 1992, with the English publication of the *Selected Letters*. The charge was led by Tom Paulin, an ageing turk, who is well known, in the UK, for his literary criticism, his poetry, his controversialism, and his small-screen losses of temper. In the correspondence columns of *The Times Literary Supplement* (and on television) Paulin articulated the case against. It centred on accusations of 'race hatred': 'racism, misogyny and quasi-fascist views'. He suggested that the editor, Thwaite, had doctored the letters with ellipses to suppress even more 'violently racist' passages than those he was prepared to include. Paulin summarized: 'For the present, this selection stands as a distressing and in many ways revolting compilation which imperfectly reveals and conceals the sewer under the national monument Larkin became.'

I remember thinking, when I saw the fiery Paulin's opening shot: we're not really going to do this, are we? But the new ethos was already emplaced – and, yes, we really were going to do this. On Paulin's terms, too: his language set the tone for the final assault, and mop-up, which came this spring with the publication of Andrew Motion's *Philip Larkin: A Writer's Life. Revolting, sewer:* such language is essentially unstable; it calls for a contest of the passions, and hopes that the fight will get dirty. (Blake Morrison, another poet, welcomed Paulin's intervention, with its summoning of the cloacal and the diseased, as – of all things – 'salutary'. Look that word up.) Thus the reception of the *Life* was marked by the quivering nostril, and by frequent recourse to the pomaded hanky, the smelling salts, and the sick bag. Writing in *The Times*, Peter Ackroyd attributed 'a rancid and insidious philistinism' to the 'foul-mouthed bigot'. Similarly, Bryan Appleyard saw, or nosed, 'a repellent, smelly, inadequate masculinity' in 'this provincial grotesque'. ('To the objective eye he seems to have been almost wholly repulsive.') A.N. Wilson, in a piece graciously entitled 'Larkin: the old friend I never liked', said that 'Larks' was a 'really rather nasty, prematurely aged man', and 'really a kind of petty-bourgeois fascist', and 'really a nutcase'.

We get an idea of the breadth of the debate when we see that it extended to the normally tranquil pages of the Library Association *Record*, alongside headlines like 'New approach to DNH PL review' and 'Funding blow to NVQ Lead Body'. Here an unnamed columnist called the Commoner compared Larkin to David Irving (the historian who keeps discovering that the Holocaust never happened, and who, whether by accident or design, looks more like Hitler every year); the Commoner also said, in conclusion, that Larkin's books 'should be banned'. The more senior commentators in the mainstream press are, of course, not so impetuous. But offended senses rouse the will; and the will looks around for something to do about it. They can't ban – or burn – Larkin's books. What they can embark on is the more genteel process of literary disposal. A third alternative would be to group Larkin with the multitude of other major writers who harboured undemocratic (or predemocratic) opinions: but they're too stirred up for that – the offence is too rank and too immediate. So: 'a sporadically excellent minor poet who has been raised to an undeserved monumentality' (Appleyard); 'essentially a minor poet who, for purely local and temporary reasons, acquired a large reputation' (Ackroyd); 'he seems to me more and more minor . . . [The poems] are good – yes – but not *that* good, for Christ's sake' (Wilson).

In late April, when the smoke was clearing after the appearance of the biography, Andrew Motion reviewed the controversy in his column in the *Observer*. Sadder and wiser – not shocked, just disappointed – Motion identified several regrettable tendencies in the anti-Larkin crusade: the lack of sociohistorical context (Larkin, 'alas', was pretty typical of his time and place); the failure to distinguish private from public utterance ('We need to remind ourselves that we are dealing with Dr Larkin here, not Dr Goebbels'); 'the evidence of people struggling in the straitjacket of political correctness'; and the naïve 'conflation of life and art'. Such a conflation, he went on:

> rest[s] on the assumption that art is merely a convulsive expression of personality. Sometimes in its purest lyric moments, it may be. More generally, it is a suppression of personality . . . an adaptation, an enlargement. It's intensely disappointing to read literary commentators who write as if they don't understand that art exists at a crucial distance from its creator.

Which sounds – and is – very sensible. But what we can also hear is the whirr of bicycle spokes: for the *Observer* piece is in fact a Tour de France of back-pedalling. Unstridently, often rather hesitantly, and even sensitively, Motion's book commits all the sins that he is now wryly shaking his head over. It is not a position so much as an attitude, or just a tone. *Philip Larkin: A Writer's Life* is confidently managed, and chasteningly thorough; it is also an anthology of the contemporary tendencies toward the literal, the conformist, and the amnesiac. Future historians of taste wishing to study the Larkin fluctuation will not have to look very much further.

The book – the life – is rich in the authentic poetry of dowdiness and deprivation, although Motion hears it faintly or not at all. Hardly anything in Larkin's letters is as thrillingly grim as the little clump of words and numerals in their top right-hand corners: Flat 13, 30 Elmwood Avenue, Belfast; 200 Hallgate, Cottingham, East Yorkshire; 192A Hallgate, Cottingham, Yorks; 172 London Road, Leicestershire ('I am established in an attic with a small window, a bed, an armchair, a basket chair, a carpet, a reading lamp THAT DOESN'T WORK, a small electric fire THAT DOESN'T WORK, and a few books'); Glentworth, King St, Wellington, Salop. Even his holiday spots sound far from festive: for example, Dixcart Hotel, Sark. No, the place-names don't help. 'I envy you your visit to Sledmere,' he writes to an intrepid acquaintance. When his girlfriend's mother gets her fatal heart attack, she does so 'at her home in Stourport-on-Severn'. Watch the sap rising as Larkin contemplates his summer break:

> My holidays loom like fearful obstacle-races: Mallaig–Weymouth with no sleeper (probably) & no reserve seats: they reserve seats, it seems, only on days when there will be enough to go around. On July 25 & Aug. 1 – two busiest days in the year – *they don't*. I'M TRAVELLING ON BOTH.

One significant address was 73 Coten End, Warwick. This was the house that contained Larkin's parents, Sydney and Eva. Motion is quietly persuasive about the feel of the household, with its airlessness and constraint. Nor does he make too much of various sexy discoveries about Sydney Larkin's pro-German – even pro-Nazi – bent. It seems that Sydney attended several Nuremberg rallies in the Thirties; bizarrely, he kept some sort of mechanical statue of Hitler on his mantelpiece, 'which at the touch of a button leapt into a Nazi salute'. Even a Nazi might have found that mannequin a little too kitsch, and insufficiently serious. Old Sydney, a city treasurer, sounds like a miserably typical eccentric of the prewar English provinces: a mood tyrant, a man who set the emotional barometer, and set it low, for everyone around him. In an unpublished autobiographical fragment cited by Motion, Larkin wrote, 'When I try to tune into my childhood, the dominant emotions I pick up are, overwhelmingly, fear and boredom . . . I never left the house without the sense of walking into a cooler, cleaner, saner and pleasanter atmosphere.' Sydney died in 1948, when Larkin was in his mid-twenties; and Eva then began a widowhood that was to last almost as long as her marriage. During those twenty-nine years, Larkin wrote to her several times a week. None of these letters appears in the *Letters* (there are presumably many thousands of them), but from Motion's quotes we see that they were candid and detailed, and were not dashed off in a couple of minutes. Her letters to him are almost artistic in their flair for the trivial. Here is an especially lively extract:

> I do hope you achieved some warmth after loading all your apparel upon the bed like that. Of course you ought not to have changed those pants – remember that I thought it very unwise at the time.

Larkin's life, Motion writes in his introduction, was not 'much diversified by event'. This is one way of putting it. What he gives us, then, is chronic inactivity in an epic frame (570 pages in the British edition). This is one way of doing it. Larkin grew up, studied at Oxford, had a series of jobs as a librarian (and as nothing else), grew fat, grew frail, and died. War, travel, marriage, children: none of this ever happened to him. The poverty of event is best illustrated by the kinds of nonevent that Motion finds himself including. When Larkin attends a wedding or a musical ('he took Monica to London to see *The Boy Friend*'), when he involves himself in the expansion of the Hull University Library ('The existing plans consisted of two stages – Stage 1 and Stage 2 – the first of which envisaged a central administrative three-storey block with a two-storey wing of the same height joined to it on the south side'), when in the course of his duties he is sent on a short tour of northern universities to study 'issue desk layouts', we get to hear about it. No, nothing happened. Larkin worked nine to five, then wrote, then drank; he coped with his mother, he corresponded with his friends, and he had perhaps half a dozen love affairs. And that was all.

The attics-digs-lodgings period lasted from 1943, when Larkin left home, to 1955, when he arrived at Hull (where he would dourly remain). It was in 1955 that he commemorated those years in 'Mr Bleaney':

'This was Mr Bleaney's room . . .'
So it happens that I lie
Where Mr Bleaney lay, and stub my fags
On the same saucer-souvenir, and try

Stuffing my ears with cotton-wool, to drown
The jabbering set he egged her on to buy.
I know his habits – what time he came down,
His preference for sauce to gravy, why

He kept on plugging at the four aways –
Likewise their yearly frame: the Frinton folk
Who put him up for summer holidays,
And Christmas at his sister's house in Stoke.

But if he stood and watched the frigid wind
Tousling the clouds, lay on the fusty bed
Telling himself that this was home, and grinned,
And shivered, without shaking off the dread

That how we live measures our own nature,
And at his age having no more to show
Than one hired box should make him pretty sure
He warranted no better, I don't know.

In such habitats, Larkin's nature was being measured. And his sexuality was fermenting, or congealing. Earlier, at Oxford, he had briefly kept a dream journal. This is Motion:

Dreams in which he is in bed with men (friends in St John's, a 'negro') outnumber dreams in which he is trying to seduce a woman, but the world in which these encounters occur is uniformly drab and disagreeable. Nazis, black dogs, excrement and underground rooms appear time and time again, and so do the figures of parents, aloof but omnipresent.

Which sure looks like a mess. He had also devoted a ridiculous amount of time and energy to the composition, under the pseudonym Brunette Coleman, of prose fictions about schoolgirls ('As Pam finally pulled Marie's tunic down over her black stockinged legs, Miss Holden, pausing only to snatch a cane from the cupboard . . .'). Along the way, he was developing a set of sexual attitudes as an obvious and understandable defence against his shyness (bad stammer), his unattractiveness ('My baldness seems to be keeping its end up well': he was twenty-six), and his fear of failure and of unrequited expense (he was always psychopathically cheap). Thus: 'Women . . . repel me inconceivably. They are shits.' Or 'All women are stupid beings.' To his old childhood friend J.B. Sutton he confessed to feelings of anxiety and cowardliness (he worried that he 'had been "doctored" in some way'), but to his own peer group he liked to sound defiant:

> Don't you think it's ABSOLUTELY SHAMEFUL that men have to pay for women without BEING ALLOWED TO SHAG the women afterwards AS A MATTER OF COURSE? I do: simply DISGUSTING. It makes me ANGRY. Everything about the ree-lay-shun-ship between men and women makes me *angry*. It's all a fucking balls up. It might have been planned by the army, or the Ministry of Food.

On another occasion, he confided, 'I *don't* want to take a girl out, and spend *circa* £5 when I can toss off in five minutes, free, and have the rest of the evening to myself.'

Those five minutes, it seems, would normally be spent under the auspices of pornography, or what passed for pornography at the time. Once, loitering around a sex shop in London, Larkin was approached by the owner, who quietly asked, 'Was it bondage, sir?' Actually it *was* bondage: bondage, spanking, intertwined schoolgirls. He was mightily gratified when he first got his hands on a copy of a magazine called *Swish*. 'Jolly good stuff, *Swish*,' wrote Larkin in his thank-you letter to the friend who had sent it to him. ('Also I wanted to know if the head master stuck his cock up her bum or up her cunt but no doubt I shall go to the grave unsatisfied.') This area of fantasy is referred to in the correspondence when Larkin complains about the kind of letter he *isn't* getting. Extracts from Larkin's dream mail:

Dear Mr Larkin, I expect you think it's jolly cheeky for a schoolgirl to –

Dear Dr Larkin, My freind [*sic*] and I had an argument as to which of us has the biggest breasts and we wondered if you would act as –

My youngest, she's fourteen and quite absurdly stuck on your poems – but then she's advanced in all ways – refuses to wear a –

Today, we all know how we feel, or how we're supposed to feel, about such 'attitudes' or 'mind-sets', especially when we have shorn them of individuality and self-mockery. Motion duly reaches for the nearest words: 'misogyny', which at least in theory describes a real condition, and the still more problematic 'sexism'. He spots 'a masturbatory impulse' behind several of Larkin's poems: 'Wild Oats', 'Sunny Prestatyn', 'The Large Cool Store', and, he writes, 'even "An Arundel Tomb"'. ('Even' is certainly the mot juste.) Of 'Lines on a Young Lady's Photograph Album' Motion says, 'The poem connects with the other pictures Larkin liked to gaze at: the photographs in pornographic magazines. The sex life they entail – solitary, exploitative – is a crude version of the pleasure he takes in the album.' 'Exploitative' is the key word here. It suggests that, while you are free to be as sexually miserable as you like, the moment you exchange hard cash for a copy of *Playboy* you are in the pornography-perpetuation business and your misery becomes political. The truth is that pornography is just a sad affair all round (and its industrial dimensions are an inescapable modern theme). It is there because men – in their hundreds of millions – want it to be there. Killing pornography is like killing the messenger. The extent to which Larkin was 'dependent' on it should be a measure of our pity, or even our sympathy. But Motion hears the beep of his political pager, and he stands to attention. The two poems he specifically convicts of sexism were written in 1965, at which point 'sexism' had no currency and no meaning. This is a mild enough incidence, but one wonders how the literary revisionists and canon-cleansers can bear to take the money. Imagine a school of sixteenth-century art criticism that spent its time contentedly jeering at the past for not knowing about perspective.

Applied to the individual, 'sexism' has always been a non-clarifier. Unlike the relationship between the races ('racism' describes a much simpler hostility), the relationship between the sexes is based on biological interdependency, which takes complex forms. Still, the biological imperative was something Larkin never felt. A virgin himself until the age of twenty-three, he was excited by virginity in women. His first love, Ruth Bowman, was not much more than a girl when he took up with her, and in appearance remained avian-childlike into middle age. (In a marvellously depressing coda to their relationship, Larkin offered Ruth 'some money to help pay for a hip-replacement operation'.) His other – comparatively – great romantic love, Maeve Brennan, was principled and religious and took many years to wear down. Larkin's thing with Maeve was accommodated within, and balanced against, a steadier relationship with his long-term companion, Monica Jones. The two women knew about each other: Larkin expended a lot of effort managing to hang on to both.

Thus the reader is almost as scandalized as Andrew Motion when, after so much temporizing, after so many survived ultimatums, Larkin starts an affair (significantly, soon after Maeve's surrender) with a *third* woman: Betty Mackereth, his secretary.

Now, you might perhaps feel that having one girlfriend is happenstance, having two girlfriends is coincidence, but having three girlfriends is enemy action. After registering his astonishment at this latest turn, Motion quickly decides that 'it is all of a piece with [Larkin's] previous behaviour'. There is selfishness and duplicity; there is even a touch of seigneurism. One can almost hear Motion begging Larkin to seek professional help. Why can't he be more . . . sensible, caring, normal? But, of course, Larkin, at fifty-two, didn't have three women: he had four. He had Eva Larkin, who just went on and on living. 'My mother,' he wrote in 1977, 'not content with being motionless, deaf and speechless, is now going blind. That's what you get for not dying, you see.' It has been pointed out that of the score or so major reviews of the biography none was written by a woman. (Were the literary editors feeling protective? Stand back, my dear: this won't be a pretty sight.) The job was left to the hardy menfolk, with their insecurities, their contemporary *amour propre*. It occurs to you that women may be less inclined to be baffled or repelled by Larkin's peculiar chaos, and less inclined to reach for the buzzwords of the hour. Just as a 'philistine' does not, on the whole, devote his life to his art (however clumsily), so a 'misogynist' does not devote his inner life to women (however messily). Larkin's men friends devolved into pen-pals. Such intimacies as he shared he shared with women.

Before moving on to the charge of racial hatred, it will be necessary to answer to younger readers (those under about seventy) the following question: What is a correspondence? Younger readers know what a phone message is, and what a fax is. They probably know what a letter is. But they don't know what a correspondence is. Words are not deeds. In published poems (we think first of Eliot's Jew), words edge closer to deeds. In Céline's anti-Semitic textbooks, words get as close to deeds as words can well get. Blood libels scrawled on front doors *are* deeds. In a correspondence, words are hardly even words. They are soundless cries and whispers; 'gouts of bile', as Larkin characterized his political opinions; ways of saying 'Gloomy old sod, aren't I?' or, more simply, 'Grrr.' Correspondences are self-dramatizations. Above all, a word in a letter is never your *last* word on any subject. Although in Larkin's writings on jazz (collected in *All What Jazz*) admiration and nostalgia for black musicians are sometimes tinged with condescension, there is no public side to Larkin's prejudices, and nothing that could be construed as a racist act.

The racial hatred – and fear – in the *Selected Letters* is insistent; and very ugly it often looks to the contemporary eye. '"Sidney Keyes is already outstanding" says Stephen Spender ... So is the rock of Gibraltar & a negro's cock' (Larkin at nineteen). 'This Cambridge Guide looks pretty bad to me: explaining Scott's plots for niggers' (at sixty). 'Too many fucking niggers about' and 'I can hear fat Caribbean germs pattering after me in the Underground' – such remarks are pitched to what each correspondent is felt likely to indulge. Colin Gunner, an old school friend, brings out the worst in him: 'And as for those black scum kicking up a din on the boundary – a squad of South African police would have sorted them out to my satisfaction.' In this case, words are *about* deeds. (Still, there is some justice here. Gunner ended up in a house trailer: this is not much of a destiny.) For Motion, the rambling rubbish of Larkin's prejudice comes under the heading of 'racism'; he even has a little subentry on it under 'Larkin' in his (brilliant) index: 'racism 65, 309, 400, 409–10'. The word suggests a system of thought, rather than an absence of thought, which would be closer to the reality – closer to the jolts and twitches of stock response. Like mood-clichés, Larkin's racial snarls were inherited propositions, shamefully unexamined, humiliatingly average. These were his 'spots of commonness', in George Eliot's sense. He failed to shed them.

'Politically correct' is a better designation than '*bien pensant*': both bespeak a strong commitment to the herd instinct, but P.C. suggests the necessary regimentation. Although it is French in its philosophical origins, P.C. begins with the very American – and attractive and honourable – idea that no one should feel ashamed of what he was born as, of what he is. Of what he does, of what he says, yes; but not ashamed of what he is. Viewed at its grandest, P.C. is an attempt to accelerate evolution. To speak truthfully, while that's still okay, everybody is 'racist', or has racial prejudices. This is because human beings tend to like the similar, the familiar, the familial. I am a racist; I am not as racist as my parents; my children will not be as racist as I am. (Larkin was less racist than his parents; his children would have been less racist than he.) Freedom from racial prejudice is what we hope for, down the line. Impatient with this hope, this process, P.C. seeks to get the thing done right now – in a generation. To achieve this, it will need a busy executive wing, and much invigilation. What it will actually entrain is another ton of false consciousness, to add to the megatons of false consciousness already aboard, and then a backlash. Still. Here it is.

In Andrew Motion's book we have the constant sense that Larkin is somehow falling short of the cloudless emotional health enjoyed by (for instance) Andrew Motion. Also the sense, as Motion invokes his like-minded contemporaries, that Larkin is being judged by a newer, cleaner, braver, saner world. In the 1968 poem 'Posterity' Larkin envisages 'Jake Balokowsky, my biographer'. 'I'm stuck with this old fart at least a year,' says Jake, not bothering 'to hide / Some slight impatience with his destiny'. 'What's he like? / Christ, I just told you . . . One of those old-type *natural* fouled-up guys.' Jake, then, is hardly ideal for the job; but in the space of a few lines he gets further than Motion gets. He is asking himself the right questions, and neutrally: what is the difference between being like him and being like me? What is the difference between living then and living now? Motion maintains the tone of an overworked psychotherapist dealing with a hidebound depressive who, exasperatingly, keeps failing to respond to the latest modern treatments. There is nothing visceral in it. The mood of the book is one of impatience: mounting impatience.

It sometimes seems that the basis of the vexation is that Larkin was born in 1922, rather than more recently. Not only is he not well adjusted; he *doesn't want to do anything about it.* There are no serious shots at self-improvement, at personal growth. Larkin left it too late to 'change his ways'. Even when he spots the difficulty, he 'gives little sign of wanting to make analysis part of a process of change'. He doesn't show a healthy enjoyment of positive experiences like sex and travel. Of Larkin's first love: 'The best he could do in the way of celebrating physical tenderness was to say "Her hands intend no harm."' Of a late (and rare) trip abroad: 'The best he could manage was a grudging admission that he had "*survived*".' With women generally, Larkin morbidly refuses to be caring and upfront: he is 'deceitful', a 'self-tormenting liar', and his affairs are characterized by 'indecisions, lies and contradictions'. After a while, the book starts to feel like some kind of *folie à deux*: Motion is extremely irritated by Larkin's extreme irritability; he is always complaining that Larkin is always complaining. One thinks of a remark in the *Letters* when Larkin is commiserating with (and complaining to) a woman friend about the inconveniences of Christmas: 'Yours is the harder course, I can see. On the other hand, mine is happening to me.' Motion is only *writing* the *Life*. Larkin had to live it.

Towards the end, even Larkin's fear of death – so central, so formative, so remorseless – has come to strike Motion as just another skein of unsalubrious egotism. After seeing the *Times* obituary for Bruce Montgomery, 'a really close friend', Larkin said in a letter that 'it makes it all sort of realler'. Motion continues: 'Larkin aired the same sorrowful but self-interested feelings in a letter to Robert Conquest. "Funeral was today," he reported. "All very sad, and makes the world seem very temporary."' Since when are intimations of mortality, at a friend's graveside, 'self-interested'? But perhaps all such thoughts, and perhaps mortality itself, are now suspect. Don't dwell on death. It's anti-life.

Motion is so shamanistically sensitive to self-interest that you wonder whether this is a personal quirk or whether it somehow fits in with the new-ethos picture. Sober materialism and machine careerism, in response to the incontinence of the Eighties? In any event, you have to warp your mind into novel contortions as Motion monitors Larkin's 'self-interest', and identifies this or that apparently straightforward remark as a 'pretence' or a 'tactic'. The friendship with Kingsley Amis, for example, was not as warm as it seemed to 'the wide world', for 'both men went to some lengths to publicize it as a way of consolidating their literary reputations'. My filial reluctance to make much of this (it might look like a 'tactic') disappeared thirty-odd pages later, when Motion repeats his depressing strophe with regard to John Betjeman: their friendship was 'affectionate but not . . . intimate'; for Larkin there was 'something self-protective' in it. ('By extolling Betjeman's virtues he helped to create the taste by which he wished his own work to be judged.') And he played the same angle, according to Motion, when he edited the *Oxford Book of Twentieth-Century English Verse* (a seven-year job): 'Larkin used the

Oxford book to define and promote the taste by which he wished to be relished.' Even the friendship with Barbara Pym, which comes across in the *Letters* as a jewel of delicacy and disinterestedness (in fact, Larkin did more than anyone to help resuscitate Pym's ailing career), is mysteriously found wanting: despite 'a genuine warmth', Larkin 'nevertheless addressed her as if he knew an audience was listening'; he 'projects', he 'parades'. Motion says, 'To the extent that Larkin ever shouldered Pym's worries, he did so knowing he would never be crushed by them.' What test is Larkin failing here? It is a pity that Pym never held out to him the promise of a free hardback or a bottle of milk, so that Motion could call the friendship 'self-interested'. O brave new superego world, where you shoulder each other's worries, where men never lie to women, where people will, of course, be marvellous when they are old and dying, where everyone is so incredibly interested in self-interest.

Biography, besides being a lowly trade, may also be attritional. Perhaps Motion (who knew Larkin, who knew Hull, and who is a poet) had his empathic powers blunted rather than sharpened by the years of (dedicated) research and (workmanlike) composition. Certainly his perspectives become fatally erratic. In his *Observer* piece, which contained more about-faces than a battalion parade ground, Motion spoke of the relationship between art and life: 'All good biographers insist on separation, as well as connection.' No, what they do, or what they end up doing, is insist on connection. And Motion connects *ad nauseam*: 'obviously the spur', 'the message for Ruth in these poems', 'put these fears into the mouth of', 'the precise source . . . is easy to trace', 'arising from the continuing wrangle', 'prompted by Maeve', 'released the rage he had been storing', 'feeding off his suppressed rage with Eva', 'the only begetters of many of his poems', and so on. Only begetters, however, are a romantic convention: poems don't have only begetters. At one point, Motion says that the influence of one of Larkin's women friends 'extended beyond the poems in which she appears' – appears, just as Marla Maples appears in *The Will Rogers Follies*. Biographers may claim separation, but what they helplessly insist on is connection. They have to. Or what are they about? What the hell are they doing day after day, year after year (gossiping? ringing changes in the Zeitgeist?), if the life doesn't somehow account for the art?

'You know I was never a child,' wrote Larkin, at the age of fifty-seven. 'I really feel somewhat at the last gasp. Carry me from the spot, Time, with thy all forgiving wave,' he wrote at the age of twenty-seven. Arriving in Hull, aged thirty-two, he wrote to his mother, 'Oh dear, the future now seems very bleak and difficult.' It is in the word 'difficult' that we hear the authentic quaver of the valetudinarian. 'I'm so finished,' he wrote to a woman friend when the end really was getting closer. When it was closer still, he told Monica, with 'a fascinated horror', that he was 'spiralling down towards extinction'. His last words were spoken to a woman – to the nurse who was holding his hand. Perhaps we all have the last words ready when we go into the last room. Perhaps the thing about last words is not how good they are but whether you can get them out. What Larkin said (faintly) was 'I am going to the inevitable.'

Inevitable in the sense that death could never be avoided – as a fate, and as a fixation. 'I don't want to write anything at present. In fact, thinking it over, I want to die. I am very impressed by this sort of unrealised deathwish of mine,' Larkin wrote at eighteen. They probably have a name for it now, something like Early Death-Awareness Syndrome. What we get at forty or forty-five he had all along. He never did anything about it (you didn't, then); he seemed to nurture this adolescent lassitude; he made it his own patch of melancholy, and tried to write the poetry that belonged there. Humanly, it turned him into an old woman – like his mother. 'I bought a pair of shoes and they don't even *try* to keep the water out.' 'I have an insensate prejudice against people who go abroad AT ANY TIME OF THE YEAR, but PARTICULARLY at Easter & Christmas.' Given his opportunities for variety and expansion, he makes Mr Woodhouse, in *Emma*, look like Evel Knievel. 'This is a hell of a week. Must get a haircut. Wanted to get another dark sweater from M and S' – Marks & Spencer – 'but doubt if there'll be time or if they'll have one.' He was so worried about his weight that he took his bathroom scales on holiday. 'I've just returned from Hamburg,' he wrote in 1976 (it was his first trip abroad in twenty-four years). 'They were all very kind, but oh the strain! The best thing was a little "mini-bar", a kind of locked drink-cupboard in my hotel room.' Colloquialisms like 'news', 'deal', 'make my bed', 'deep freeze', and 'embarrassing' similarly had him reaching for his inverted commas. 'How very bold of you to buy an electric typewriter,' he wrote to a friend in 1985.

What redeems and monumentalizes this slow drizzle – what makes the *Letters* a literary experience and the *Life* just one thing after another – is the comedy of candour. Here melancholy still hurts, but it embodies its own comic relief; and dignity is not needed. 'The US edition of [*High Windows*] is out, with a photograph of me that cries out for the caption "FAITH HEALER OR HEARTLESS FRAUD?"' 'And then my sagging face, an egg sculpted in lard, with goggles on.' 'None of my clothes fit either: when I sit down my tongue comes out.' A Life is one kind of biography, and the *Letters* are another kind of Life; but the internal story, the true story, is in the *Collected Poems*. The recent attempts, by Motion and others, to pass judgment on Larkin look awfully green and pale compared with the self-examinations of the poetry. They think they judge him? No. He judges them. His indivisibility judges their hedging and trimming. His honesty judges their watchfulness:

If my darling were once to decide
Not to stop at my eyes,
But to jump, like Alice, with floating skirt into my head . . .

She would find herself looped with the creep of varying light,
Monkey-brown, fish-grey, a string of infected circles
Loitering like bullies, about to coagulate . . .

– 'If, My Darling'

For something sufficiently toad-like
Squats in me, too;
Its hunkers are heavy as hard luck,
And cold as snow . . .

– 'Toads'

169

Larkin the man is separated from us, historically, by changes in the self. For his generation, you were what you were, and that was that. It made you unswervable and adamantine. My father has this quality. I don't. None of us does. There are too many forces at work on us. There are too many fronts to cover. In the age of self-improvement, the self is inexorably self-conscious. Still, a price has to be paid for not caring what others think of you, and Larkin paid it. He couldn't change the cards he was dealt ('What poor hands we hold, / When we face each other honestly!'). His poems insist on this helplessness:

> And I meet full face on dark mornings
> The bestial visor, bent in
> By the blows of what happened to happen.
> — 'Send No Money'

> Most things are never meant.
> — 'Going, Going'

> The unbeatable slow machine
> That brings what you'll get.
> — 'The Life with a Hole in It'

> Life is first boredom, then fear.
> Whether or not we use it, it goes,
> And leaves what something hidden from
> us chose,
> And age, and then the only end of age.
> — 'Dockery and Son'

My most enduring memory of Larkin is a composite one, formed from the many visits he paid to the series of flats and houses where I spent my first ten years, in Swansea, South Wales. My elder brother was Larkin's godson and namesake, and Larkin's visits were doubly welcome: it was the custom then for godfathers to give money to their godsons (and to their godsons' brothers); in our family we called it 'tipping the boys'. *My* godfather was Bruce Montgomery, who makes frequent – and decreasingly jovial – appearances in both the biography and the letters (thin talent; alcohol). When I was a child, Bruce was always jovial, and ridiculously generous. There was one occasion – it was Bonfire Night, in perhaps 1955 – when Bruce gave my brother and me the usual florin or half crown, plus a *ten-shilling note*: for fireworks. We couldn't believe it. We were like the brides' fathers in 'The Whitsun Weddings', never having known 'Success so huge and wholly farcical'.

It was different with Larkin. We were told that Larkin 'didn't really like children' ('children / With their shallow violent eyes'), and we tended to stay out of his way. When it came time for him to tip the boys, we would stand there with our palms outturned, quite flattered to think of ourselves as representatives of a menacing subgroup: children. The tip, always in the form of big, black old pennies, would be doled out in priestly silence. Threepence for Martin, fourpence for Philip (a year my senior). Later, sixpence for me, ninepence for him. The money still meant a lot to us, because we intuited what it had cost Larkin to part with it. (He was, by the way, a genuine miser. In his last weeks, he lived off 'cheap red wine and Complan'. He left over a quarter of a million pounds.) No, Larkin did not come out and gambol with us in the garden. (Neither, to be sure, did Bruce.) He did not tell us magical bedtime stories. But when I readdress my eager, timid, childish feelings in his presence, I find solidity as well as oddity, and tolerant humour (held in reserve, in case it was needed) as well as the given melancholy. 'When will it get dark? When will it get dark?' I kept asking, that Bonfire Night. The answer in Swansea, in that vanished world, was three o'clock in the afternoon – even earlier than in Hull, where 'the lights come on at four / At the end of another year'. And it was always raining, whatever the season. I remember Larkin coming in from the rain, or preparing to go out in it: slightly fussy, cumbrous, long-suffering.

Rain, as an element and an ambience, provides a backdrop to the life and to this very English story. 'On 13 November Larkin travelled through heavy rain to Wellington for his interview, clutching his green-bound copy of *The Public Library System of Great Britain*.' 'Heavy rain', 'driving rain', 'torrential rain'. Under the heading 'FIVE DON'TS

FOR OLD CREATURES' Larkin wrote to his mother: '4. Don't waste time worrying about *rain*. This is a wettish country. Lots of it falls. It always has done, and always will.' What was Hull? Hull was as dull as rain. Rain was what Larkin felt marriages turned into; rain was what love and desire eventually became. 'The Whitsun Weddings' describes a rail journey to London in which the poet witnesses the aftermaths of wedding parties as, at every stop, the train fills up with 'fresh couples' about to begin their honeymoons and the rest of their lives. London approaches:

> and it was nearly done, this frail
> Travelling coincidence; and what it held
> Stood ready to be loosed with all the power
> That being changed can give. We slowed again,
> And as the tightened brakes took hold, there swelled
> A sense of falling, like an arrow-shower
> Sent out of sight, somewhere becoming rain.

Everybody knows 'They fuck you up, your mum and dad' and the thrilled finality of that poem's closing stanza ('This Be the Verse'):

> Man hands on misery to man.
> It deepens like a coastal shelf.
> Get out as early as you can,
> And don't have any kids yourself.

But there is always a sense of romantic balance in Larkin, however reluctant, however thwarted. 'This Be the Verse' has a sister poem, called 'The Trees'. After finishing it, Larkin wrote 'Bloody awful tripe' at the foot of the manuscript. But the last lines stand:

> Yet still the unresting castles thresh
> In fullgrown thickness every May.
> Last year is dead, they seem to say,
> Begin afresh, afresh, afresh.

New Yorker July 1993

From the Canon

Coleridge's Beautiful Diseases

Coleridge: Poet and Revolutionary, 1772–1804
by John Cornwell

The critical biography has several claims to being a dead genre. The main aim of criticism, nowadays, is to provide intellectual stimulation; the main aim of biography (or so it seems to this reviewer) is to amuse the over-sixties. A knowledge of a writer's life may give the odd insight into his work, but you don't have to be a structuralist to see the dangers of studying them in tandem. What does the poet's critical biographer do with the poems? Well, he's indulgently knowing about the juvenilia, inclined to tick the author off for being 'effusive', 'derivative', etc. Then he cheers on the youthful work, pleased to see signs of 'real development', though he'll still have a thing or two to tell him about 'control' and 'self-discipline'. Next comes applause for the first 'mature' or 'major' verse, and for the rest the biographer will reckon to plant his feet so firmly in the facts of the poet's life that he'll be able to lever up his oeuvre on a biographical crowbar: this poem 'reflects' these events, that poem 'lays bare' those tensions – and the work has become a stupefied outpouring on the life. No biographer known to me can put on a fresh suit of clothes for the poetry, so perhaps it ought to be left alone and we should simply be told where the genuine criticism is to be found.

Inside John Cornwell's 400-page critical biography of Coleridge there is a 200-page uncritical one trying not nearly hard enough to get out. Unlike his predecessors, Mr Cornwell looks at Coleridge's life (up to 1804) with patience and sympathy – qualities very much in demand when one contemplates the rumpus-room of delusion and credulity that form Coleridge's early years. He ran away from Cambridge, enlisted in the Dragoons under a zany pseudonym (which Mr

Cornwell, in the grand tradition of Coleridge biography, gets wrong
– see Grigg's edition of the *Letters*, I, 66), and was, understandably,
discharged as insane. He hiked around England pretending to be
a revolutionary, sneering at 'WORLDLY PRUDENCE!' and sponging
off his friends. He dumped the 'Pantisocracy' scheme (whereby
twelve couples were to live as intellectual subsistence-farmers in
Pennsylvania) when Southey proposed taking servants along, but
tried to revive it later, suggesting a West Indian plantation as
venue and Negroes as home-helps. He took up the Shrewsbury
Unitarian ministership one Saturday in January 1798 and dropped
it the following Wednesday, by which time he had wangled an
annuity out of his patrons. He jeered at Southey for considering a
civic post; the book ends with him sailing to Malta to be secretary
to the governor. Despite its unscholarly randomness, this part of Mr
Cornwell's book is successful; in particular, Coleridge's wretched
marriage, his opium habit and his illnesses are treated with consistent
lucidity and intelligence.

But what does the rest of the book think it's doing? Mr
Cornwell expounds that amorphous leviathan affectionately known
as 'Coleridge's thought' in a way that will merely bore and confuse
the uninformed reader; and, more seriously, he whips back and forth
from the discursive to the creative writings as if there were some
kind of reliable equation between the two. It 'may be very wild
philosophy', said Coleridge of a theory of Fénelon's, 'but it is very
intelligible poetry'. Regard poetry as autonomous, said Coleridge;
don't go beyond it 'in order by means of some *other* thing analogous to
understand the former'. Mr Cornwell quotes both these remarks, with
apparent approval, but without seeming to realize that this is precisely
his own method. Unsurprisingly, when he comes to the three poems
which clearly resist biographical or philosophical underpinning, he
flounders. 'Christabel' is ignored. *The Ancient Mariner* gets a string of
pedestrianisms plus a toiling analysis of its rhythms and vowel-sounds.
And 'Kubla Khan' is reinterpreted so zestlessly that Mr Cornwell is
forced to conclude that 'whatever else one might say about "Kubla
Khan", it seems to be expressing in metaphorical form Coleridge's
consistent preoccupation with the tension and reconciliation of

polarities'. An offer: 50p for every poem of Coleridge's (or anyone else's) about which this could *not* be said. Possibly Mr Cornwell has something of interest to say about the verse, but the requirements of the conventional biography keep his hands well tied here.

The book might have gained in coherence if it had stuck to the blurb's purview: 'The early decline of Coleridge's poetic powers is one of the more poignant episodes in the history of literature.' In fact, the issue detains Mr Cornwell for only a few paragraphs, and the usual reasons are given: Coleridge spread himself too thin intellectually, unhappy home life, overshadowed by Wordsworth, opium, sickness, anxiety. On this last point Mr Cornwell says, 'he knew only too well that to realise his true potential he must be free of anxiety'. And here he shows a fundamental lack of empathy. If the anxiety were not there, nothing else in Coleridge would be there: the vicious-circle psycho-somatic illnesses, 'compleat Self-knowledge, so mixed with intellectual complacency', hypochondria coupled with appalling self-neglect, and, in the poems, the rootless apocalyptic fear of the *Mariner*, 'Pains of Sleep' and 'The Wanderings of Cain'. The paradox was never more fetchingly (if obliquely) stated than by Coleridge himself:

> It is a theory of mine that Virtue & Genius are Diseases of the Hypochondrical & Scrofulus Genus . . . – analogous to the beautiful Diseases, that colour & variegate certain Trees.

Witness how Coleridge set about his genitals when he developed an endocele. Rather than consult a doctor he applied 'fumigations of Vinegar', 'Sal ammonica dissolved in verjuice', 'three leaches', 'hot cloaths' and poultices 'of bread grated & mixed up with a strong solution of Lead'. Net gain? Five 'angry ulcers'. Coleridge was the sort of man who would always come up with something to get him down.

His biographers generally give Coleridge a hard time, and with Norman Fruman's recent sniping at the work (*Coleridge, the Damaged Archangel*) it seemed that Coleridge was due for one of those ominous (and pointless) 'reassessments'. But William Empson's compassionate essay, introducing his and David Pirie's selection of the verse, should restore stability to the critical stock-exchange; and now we have a sympathetic, if uninspiring, view of the life. Is it worth asking how much of Coleridge is likely to survive? His philosophy has had some influence, though largely in America; the criticism has given us nothing we could not have done without (the famous Fancy/Imagination distinction, for example, is just another pretence that we can officially separate the excellent from the less excellent). And what is left of the verse? The Conversation Poems do what little they do well; there are a few incidental successes, already mentioned; 'Dejection: A Letter' is too personal and 'Dejection: An Ode' too formal to repay close study. Only the obvious three remain, while writers with more good poems somehow stay decidedly less great. Perhaps Coleridge's status is not threatened by this, or any, paring-down simply because of the age at which we first come to him. If Keats is the poet of adolescence, Coleridge is the poet of childhood; his world of lonesome roads, flashing eyes and demon lovers settles in the mind too early to be exposed by the sober light of adulthood.

New Statesman March 1973

Coleridge's Verse: A Selection edited by William Empson and David Pirie*

The 'intentional fallacy' has been irking editors ever since W.K. Wimsatt's discovery of it in 1946. William Empson, in his 100-page

* This piece appeared in *The Times Literary Supplement*, where I worked on the staff as a Trainee Editorial Assistant. I was twenty-three. William Empson, author of *Seven Types of Ambiguity* and *Milton's God*, was one of my outright heroes (as a poet as well as a critic). When his devastating letter to the editor came in, I not only feared for my job; I felt like a starstruck clapperboy who has just been terminated by Arnold Schwarzenegger (see below). In those days, fortunately, all *TLS* reviews were unsigned.

introduction to this new selection of Coleridge's verse, quickly shrugs off these restraints. The editor, he says, *has* to make a guess at the author's intention so that he can intercept the poem before it has been mucked up – after all, poets regularly get anxious and self-conscious about their work and tamper with it when it has gone dead on them; the editor, therefore, must gather the evidence and make an informed speculation about what the poet 'really meant'. The editor, in other words, picks the bits that he thinks make the best poem. (Another 'fallacy' could be invoked in Professor Empson's defence here; the editor is at least as likely as the author to know what the best poem is.) Professor Empson's empiricism does lead him to see the creative process as far more furtive and equivocal than most of us would be willing to accept, but, as always, he is learned, lively, and often most stimulating when he is wrong.

Professor Empson and David Pirie select all the good poems Coleridge wrote – no great number – including passages from prolix failures like 'Religious Musings'. The main effort, however, has gone into *The Ancient Mariner*, which Coleridge never tired of worsening and which therefore poses the most serious editorial challenge. The result is an eclectic text which effectively rescues the pantheist poem of 1800 from the Christian one of 1817. The 1817 prose gloss – Professor Empson describes it at one point as 'leering' and at another as trying to put over a 'greasy injustice' – is omitted completely. The gloss is a distraction, certainly, and often a misleading distraction; but it has its moments of beauty, and, since all students and most curious readers will want to consult Coleridge's later commentary, it might have been as well to include it in an appendix. As the text stands, without the gloss and without Coleridge's nervous emendations, the *Rime* is a darker and more worrying poem.

Unsurprisingly, Professor Empson claims that *The Ancient Mariner*, not altogether unlike *Paradise Lost*, is a covert indictment of the Christian God. Coleridge's intention was, so to speak, to 'bore from within', an aspect of the poem we no longer appreciate for the simple reason that it has been so successful – we would be pretty startled nowadays to hear anyone suggest that the Mariner actually *deserves* his punishment. It might be said that the 1817 version carries this meaning, too, if less candidly. At the end of the poem the Mariner, for all his sacramental torments, is still condemned to traipse round the country scaring people with his tale, and the poem's chirpy *sententia*, 'He prayeth best, who loveth best / All things both great and small', does not actually say that praying and loving are going to do you any good. Professor Empson rightly takes the *Rime* as the work of a man who sees the universe as devoid of moral order, and his analysis of the poem as being fundamentally about 'neurotic guilt' is more or less unanswerable.

What *is* answerable, though, is Professor Empson's suggestion that the *Rime* is, among other things, an 'adventure story', partly concerned with 'maritime expansion', and including a 'horror of the Slave Trade'. Professor Empson thus identifies Life-in-Death's skeletal bark as standing for a slave ship. Because the slaves' body-heat customarily rotted off the ships' planks after five to ten voyages, Professor Empson deduces that 'while mulling over the first edition Coleridge felt' (Professor Empson makes great play with phrases like 'Coleridge would have thought', 'Coleridge must here have felt') 'that this point might not be obvious to everyone, so he wrote in the margin another verse, saying that the hulk was "plankless"'. Surely, no matter what Coleridge felt, and no matter how much he mulled, the insertion of 'plankless' hardly makes the point 'obvious' to *everyone*. Perhaps Coleridge just thought it was a good image.

Professor Empson is equally coltish on the 'adventure story' line. With endearing, Boys' Own eagerness he follows up what would have happened if the Mariner had been pulled in by the local authorities at the end of his voyage: 'The accusing spirits . . . would next impose slanderous dreams on the magistrates at the court of inquiry . . . So the mariner would be driven into exile, probably on suspicion of having eaten the rest of the crew.' John Carey once accused C.S. Lewis of writing about *Paradise Lost* as if it were taking place in North Oxford; Professor Empson here writes about *The Ancient Mariner* as if it were an eighteenth-century piratical skirmish on the River Don.

The more general remarks about Coleridge are so luminous that one wishes there were more of them. Professor Empson's criticism has always depended on the intensity of his response not only to the work but also to the author, and he here shows a moving sympathy with Coleridge which – were all critics so intelligent – would make us want to lose the intentional fallacy for good. The more one studies Coleridge, it seems, the less one likes him, as the alarmed fastidiousness of Norman Fruman's recent biography shows. Professor Empson is more patient. He is not slow to point out that Coleridge wrote very few good poems and he is very eloquent on the guilts and anxieties that inhibited him. And his throwaway conclusion – that 'In [Coleridge's] heart, I suppose, he always blamed himself for writing good poetry because it was showing off' (i.e., it was a mere excrescence) – has a sad and inescapable truth.*

The Times Literary Supplement December 1972

★ What I did was: I read the book, then sold it, then reviewed it. This partly accounts for my vulnerability to Empson's first point, which ran as follows: 'The reviewer says that the glosses to *The Ancient Mariner*, if removed from the text of the poem, had better have been given in an appendix. On pages 212–13 they are given in full, with line references, and on page 48, after the first discussion of them, the reader is told twice where they can be found.' Here, with an elision or two, is my squirming reply:

> Our reviewer writes: (1) Apologies are due to Professor Empson on his first point – a bad lapse. (2) I did not 'assert' that Mr Pirie and Professor Empson 'say an editor should "pick out the bits that he thinks make the best poem"', only that this is what these editors end up doing. (3) I think a disinterested reader, as opposed to a cross author, would agree on the 'boring from within' point, and also that the Christian position on 'cruelty to animals' is peripheral to the moral scheme of the poem. Neither Coleridge nor, surely, Professor Empson, would want to rest his case there. (4) When I referred to Professor Empson's 'Boys' Own eagerness' I was referring not to his 'style' but to his eagerness, on a different point, which he does not question here. So far as I am concerned, Professor Empson always writes like an angel.

Tinkering with Jane

Sandition: A novel by Jane Austen and Another Lady

All Jane Austen's novels are comedies – i.e., they are about nice young couples eventually getting married. Hero and heroine will both be supplied with a foil or distraction, someone whom they are mistakenly beguiled by for a time, and there will invariably be some pressure and interference from obstructive oldsters to be duly overcome. Further in the background, there will be a more vivaciously imagined cast of frumps, fools and snobs, whose structural relevance will generally be minor.

Presented with what appears to be a standard formula, someone was bound to come along and complete Jane Austen's uncompleted novel, *Sanditon*, which she abandoned shortly before her death in 1817. The extant 20,000 words certainly contain most of the ingredients: a modest and impressionable heroine, a rich and witty offstage hero, one old tyrant, one endearing hobby-horseman, one young bitch, one sickly heiress, two flirts and three hypochondriacs. Plenty, it seems, to be going on with.

Jane Austen's coyly anonymous collaborator is clearly a very 'professional' writer – a rather more contemplative Barbara Cartland, one imagines – and she develops the plot and characterization with a good deal of resource. More surprisingly, the Austen prose is fairly creditably sustained. Of course, Jane's prose is not nearly as inimitable as Janeites will lead you to believe, and the Collaborator is able to reproduce the tart periodicity of her sentences in a blithe, unselfconscious way – with a minimum of toe-stubbing, though without much of the panache and asperity of her original. If *Sanditon* had come down to us in this form, I think it would be regarded as a mildly embarrassing piece of senilia rather than an obvious fake.

But what does the completed novel attempt to be about? The original *Sanditon* is not only a fragment, it is also a first draft, the only one that Jane Austen, a most assiduous reworker, didn't have the chance to destroy. As a result, it is both sketchy and bald, offering few thematic starting-points to spur the would-be co-author. From what one can infer, *Sanditon* was to include some light literary satire, in the way that the first three novels satirized Mrs Radclife's *Udolpho* and Fanny Burney's *Evelina*. Burney's *Camilla* is lingeringly mentioned early on – appropriately, since it's about a high romance developing alongside a subcast of buffoons and hysterics – and the rich-wit hero is a strident literary poseur, an admirer of Richardson and his more vulgar copyists. But apart from this thread, and some preliminary guying of fashionability, the Collaborator undertakes a journey without maps.

Which needn't slow her chariot, of course. Broadly, Jane Austen's novels are about good behaviour, and her subsidiary themes ('ordination' in *Mansfield Park*, for instance) are really only ways of re-examining more or less static verities. The progress towards the Austen marriage tends to be one of self-improvement rather than self-discovery: each protagonist has to turn into the sort of person whom the other deserves to marry, and you're meant to feel that the need for correction will continue long after the symbolic final kiss. This may seem to abet the view that Miss Austen is concerned merely with questions of propriety. But I would argue that all the pathos and eloquence of the novels derive from the characters' subservience to convention: the reticence and constraint allow for a quiet undertow of emotion which it is impossible to simulate in more uncorseted fiction.

Take away the conventions, and little remains – as the *Sanditon* Collaborator here amply proves. Barely halfway through the novel, the hero's 'teasing gleam' has become 'quite irresistible' to the heroine, and she gets 'a flutter of singing, exclaiming, joyful spirits' when he saunters by. But then, too, the object of this trashy pash would be well down the minor-villain league in the normal Austen canon. A liar and a trifler, he also masterminds his friend's elopement (which would damn him irretrievably in Miss Austen's eyes); and at one point the heroine forgives him his whoppers and his flirtiness because, after all, he was only furthering this noble end. Similarly, when the heroine herself is actually *abducted* by the crazed dandy, she regards the incident with the mildest amusement. 'Bless my soul!' muses her father when she tells him of her escape. Given such an easy-going world, one wonders what was stopping the hero from getting his leg over in the early chapters.

I suppose it all depends on what you go to Jane Austen for. The Collaborator, in her very pertinent 'Apology' to the reader, claims that 'we turn to her for relaxation on plane journeys, in family crises and after the sheer physical exhaustion of a servantless world'. Well, 1975 is the bicentenary of Jane Austen's birth – an appropriate time to suggest that her appeal must be rather broader than that.

Observer July 1975

Sticking up for Milton

The Life of John Milton by A.N. Wilson

The Milton multinational is now so far-flung that one must always query any addition to its holdings. A monograph on Milton's ostler bills or ministerial memos might be in order – but another Life? A.N. Wilson's biography is not a scholarly biography; it isn't popular either, or semiotic or psychohistorical. It is not a critical biography. It is, rather, an uncritical biography. You expect something unusual when a youngish novelist tackles an icon. But *The Life of John Milton* is, by any standards, remarkably headstrong, beleaguered and quaint.

It transpires that an attempt at rehabilitation is on offer here, rehabilitation of the man rather than the work. Milton's vicissitudes at the hands of twentieth-century taste – Eliot's about-turn, Leavis's full-frontal assault ('we dislike his verse'), Christopher Ricks's rear-guard action in *Milton's Grand Style* – interest Wilson not at all. His concern is for Milton's personal image, which, he feels, has been tarnished by a vulgar modernity.

When Wilson refers to 'Milton's enemies', he doesn't mean Royalists, Catholics and Frenchmen. He means unsympathetic readers and commentators – people who don't like him. We are warned about 'the papist bias' of the Yale *Complete Prose*, the 'malicious and crude pen' wielded by Robert Graves in *Wife to Mr Milton*, the cheap jibes of Dr Johnson. Milton's enemies are those who persist in regarding him as a misogynistic, authoritarian relict, when in fact, Wilson argues, he was really much nicer than that.

The author goes to bizarre lengths, early on, to establish his subject as a charmer, a looker, a wag. Milton was 'an infinitely intelligent and very beautiful youth', such a vision, indeed, that 'no engraver could hope to convey the delicacy of the complexion, or the beautifully textured auburn hair'. 'An accomplished swordsman', with his 'wit, his good looks' and his 'young, laughing face', Milton, we learn, was 'quite a lady's man'. (I think he means 'ladies' man', but the slip may be instructive: Milton's contancy is often praised.) It was for his exquisiteness that the undergraduate Milton was nicknamed 'The Lady of Christ's College', not for any effeminacy or skittishness, or so Mr Wilson believes.

A desire to correct such common and hostile misapprehensions provides the main thread of this *Milton*. True, Milton was unpopular at Cambridge, but he was exasperated by 'the silly, boyish chatter' and 'the crushing boredom of the dons'. It does seem frivolous of Cambridge not to have interested Milton more. No, Milton did not mistreat or estrange his first wife, Mary Powell, who left him: her behaviour was 'silly and superficial', or else she was 'kidnapped' by her family. He wasn't particularly nasty to his daughters either: they were thieves and gadabouts, and he was right to disinherit them.

So, too, on the public stage. Mr Wilson sees the difficulties but always contrives, with the air of a fond schoolmaster, to give his star pupil the benefit of the doubt. Milton's championship of divorce was not self-interested, although it seemed at the time that his wife had deserted him for ever: 'we have the testimony of "Defensio Secunda", says Wilson trustingly, 'that he genuinely had the public good in mind'. An erstwhile foe of censorship, Milton performed a certain amount of 'piffling' censorship work for Cromwell – 'unpleasant perhaps for the author of *Areopagitica*'. Similarly, the scurrility of Milton's pamphleteering, considered scabrous enough even by contemporaries, was no more than 'a delight in the rough and tumble', the cut and thrust, of ecclesiastical controversy.

These exculpations involve Mr Wilson in a fair amount of generous conjecture. His book must set some kind of record as a thesaurus of speculation: it is conceivable, it is tempting to suspect, it seems more than likely, I rather doubt whether, it is not fanciful to think, if I rightly guess, presumably, surely, doubtless. At one point in his attack on the 71-year-old Mary Powell, Wilson quotes Milton's first biographer: 'her friends, possibly incited by her own desire, made earnest suit . . . to have her company'. Wilson slips in with a forensic 'Notice that "possibly".' We do. We also notice that, a thousand words earlier, Wilson has used 'rather improbable', 'no reason to suppose', 'probably', 'almost undoubtedly', 'probably', 'perhaps', 'very probably', 'probably', 'almost certainly' and 'perhaps' in the space of a single page.

The selectivity, then, is rampant, and is abetted throughout by the vagaries of Wilson's biographical style. Carriages 'creak northward', autumn leaves 'rustle thickly', Milton 'paces' or 'wanders heedlessly'. 'Thither, early each morning, Milton would squelch his way through the pigeon-droppings and the [etc., etc.].' As is the case with Mr Wilson's capricious use of the interior monologue, these flights of fancy have an unpredictable bearing on the arrangement of facts and sympathies.

Sometimes A.N. Wilson sounds like A.L. Rowse ('What a contrast with the reality Milton knew at home! And yet, compared with Italy, how abundantly true!'), sometimes like Gina Lollobrigida ('What sort of Church was it, this Church of England in which Milton was destined to serve as a priest?'). When one considers his octogenarian references to the 'electric train' and 'the motor-car', his glimpse of Milton in his 'three-and-twentieth' year or as a child already 'drunk with that Castalian wine' (i.e., relishing the classics), it is hard not to think of Wilson as Milton's marooned contemporary, shielding his old friend from the depravities of 'modern' biographers. His descriptions of church interiors – 'a somewhat baroque late seventeenth-century reredos with (apparently) Flemish communion rails' – and his love of doctrinal contention are also impressively anachronistic, and do much to establish the book's antique and antic charm.

Although it has been often enough discussed, the crux of Milton's life is still hard to grasp. His existence was spent waiting to become the author of an epic poem. Hence the conventionality of Milton's minor work; hence his often-dramatized dread of premature action. Wilson sees this of course, but he does not accept its implications. 'We must remember always, when dealing with Milton's egotism, that he had something to be egotistical about.' He had *Paradise Lost*, as it turned out. But the poem cannot serve as a retroactive justification. In its light, however, Wilson is remorselessly indulgent to Milton, and correspondingly uncharitable to everyone else.

Does it matter, finally, whether Milton was a good man? Wilson finds a great deal of helpless self-revelation in the verse ('Samson', for instance, 'is in exactly the position of Milton at the time of the Restoration'), and this perhaps inclines him to seek a moral identity of the work and the man. He may also have spiritual imperatives not fully disclosed here. Yet the major poets are not an especially scrupulous or affable band. Nor are the minor ones. Milton produced the central English poem; it is of great interest, though of no great moment, to calculate the human cost of writing it.

Observer January 1983

The Darker Dickens

The Violent Effigy: A Study of Dickens' Imagination by John Carey

While assured of his status as a great writer, Dickens is still uncertain of his status as a serious one. He insists on being romantic, melodramatic, unrepresentational (like his trashier contemporaries) and will not be adult, introspective, mimetic (like the major Victorians). Criticism is traditionally nervous about such discrepancies and, accordingly, most of the recent work on Dickens has urged him back into what we invidiously imagine to be 'the tradition' – i.e., the social-realist tradition. Robert Garis's *The Dickens Theatre*, stressing Dickens's gift for 'social prophecy', explained that he's unrealistic because he is shrewdly deploying theatrical conventions. John Lucas's *The Melancholy Man*, stressing Dickens's social criticism and symbolic structures, explained that he's unrealistic because society is too. The Leavises' *Dickens the Novelist*, stressing Dickens's moral intelligence, erudition, and likenesses to James, Conrad and George Eliot, explained that he's realistic. When asked about the large stretches of implausibility, mawkishness and exaggeration to be found throughout his work, these critics tend to reply that Dickens put them in to beguile his Victorian public.

John Carey is equally willing to chuck out something like half of Dickens, but it is not quite the same half. With no fuss at all the frowning reflective Dickens is dispatched and the comic, ebullient Dickens as cheerfully embraced. The heavier critics usually start in earnest at *Dombey and Son* and salvage what they can from its successors; Dr Carey is more interested in local effects, in 'imaginative habits', and so can afford to give more space to *The Old Curiosity Shop*, the current whipping-boy, than to *Little Dorrit*, the current front-runner. For 'we could scrap all the solemn parts of Dickens's novels without impairing his status as a writer'. And scrap them Dr Carey does. Not surprisingly, *The Violent Effigy* is a splendid *jeu d'esprit*, a brilliant *tour de force*; not surprisingly, too, it is wildly over-corrective.

Right then. Out goes Dickens the social thinker, the visionary. As Dr Carey eagerly reminds us, Dickens was a champion of capital punishment, applauded the cannonballing of mutinous sepoys, thought Negro suffrage preposterous, recommended imprisonment for bad language, and flogging for bigamy, and was a convinced and passionate sexist. In the novels themselves, Dr Carey finds most of the social criticism either laughably inconsistent, weakly argued or pallidly retrospective. Dickens 'did not want to provoke . . . reform so much as to retain a large and lucrative audience'. Perhaps a salute to Orwell isn't a bad thing at this stage, but how easily we could have done without its concomitant, a string of tweedy egalitarianisms whenever Dickens offends the modern liberal taste: the working-class Toodle children in *Dombey* are smilingly presented so that 'the middle classes may sleep soundly in their beds'; Gamfield, the chimney-boy in *Oliver Twist*, 'suddenly' gets less funny once the author has researched the plight of the Victorian sweep – and so on. First, as Dr Carey well knows, Dickens is not unegalitarian or anti-egalitarian, but pre-egalitarian, at least in the way we understand it. Second, as Dr Carey well knows (and elsewhere demonstrates), nothing is immune from humour: in the Preface to *Joseph Andrews* Fielding says that 'The only source of the true Ridiculous . . . is affectation', and twelve pages into the text he has us sniggering about Mrs Slipslop's club foot. Third, as it suits Dr Carey to forget, social issues should have only a conditional bearing on what we generally regard as works of the fancy.

Next, out goes Dickens the symbol-tout. Critics devoted to the unearthing of these commodities, says Dr Carey, seldom come up with anything more than a hackneyed adage or dispensable catchphrase; they boil down *Little Dorrit* to 'the world's a prison', or *Our Mutual Friend* to 'money is dust'. 'Why', Dr Carey asks, 'should one want to read a novel, to enter into possession of something so trite?' Nor is this merely a case of critics' excitability – Dickens can be found 'endorsing similar trite formulations himself', as when Carker gloats over his Edith Dombey-surrogate caged bird, or when Louisa Gradgrind, cuffing her bosom, so tellingly exclaims: 'O father, what have you done, with the garden that should have bloomed once, in this great wilderness here!' Dr Carey's firm preference is for the recurring emblems and images that loom into significance without depending on any facile equation: the reechy atmospheres, the crumbling buildings, the effigies and cadavers, the ramshackle furniture of his urban landscape. Again Dr Carey underestimates his enemy (is the 'money-equals-excrement' idea, for instance, really so over Dickens's head when one considers the symbolic names of Merdle and Murdstone?), but this is one of his more salutary chapters; if nothing else it should put a few PhD theses quietly out of their misery.

With particular alacrity, out goes Dickens the humanist sage, the mature investigator of relationships and personalities. His heroes and heroines are faceless, indeed bodiless, automatons. His villains, all either improbably converted or cornily punished, are without moral significance. Excepting David Copperfield and Pip, his children are mini-adults designed to solace the oldsters, dwarves who 'have close affinities with the modern garden gnome'. His women are frumps, haughty termagants or simpering little housewives. The plots are all creaking lumber. Dickens was prepared to sermonize, patronize, sentimentalize; 'with his eye on sales', he embraced every possible opportunity to write nonsense. And yet, somehow, 'the triumphs of his art stick out like islands, and there is no difficulty about distinguishing them'. What Dr Carey finally distinguishes in Dickens is a talented fool and a collection of good passages.

In his wittily subversive book on Milton, Dr Carey concluded: 'a study of how Milton uses words makes him look more of a poet than what he uses them for. He is, massively, a moral phenomenon.' In his wittily subversive essay on 'D.H. Lawrence's Doctrine', Dr Carey concluded: 'the final paradox of Lawrence's thought is that, separated from his . . . wonderfully articulate being, it becomes the philosophy of any thug or moron'. A similar last-minute rescue-job is attempted on Dickens (his 'imagination transforms the world;

his laughter controls it' – the two being interdependent), but only a streakily vivid humorist remains. Given the adaptability of Dr Carey's critical predilections it is disappointing that sympathy is so determinedly withdrawn from Dickens, who gets a much more effective initial response from Dr Carey than Milton or Lawrence ever could. As a result *The Violent Effigy* is always pointing beyond itself without ever seeming to want to get to where it points; one goes through the book much as Dr Carey goes through Dickens, with periodic delight and a strong sense of futility.

Although Dr Carey doesn't appear to have read Northrop Frye's essay 'Dickens and the Comedy of Humours', a good deal of his book reads like an annotation of its insights, only without Frye's accompanying sense of their coherence. Briefly, Frye sees the structure of a Dickens novel as a conflict between two social groups, the family-orientated 'congenial' society (normally based round a quite young, and quite boring, couple) and the institutionalized 'obstructing' society (normally old, hide-bound and corrupt). True to the Plautus–Terence New Comedy tradition, grotesque implausibility is considered a small price to pay for bringing about the triumph of youth and the inevitable festive conclusion. The congenial society, apart from the odd fool or wag, is mostly featureless and uniform; the obstructing society is far more exuberantly imagined, peopled not so much by caricatures as by humours – of hypocrisy, parasitism, pedantry. Up to Jane Austen the structure is used fairly conventionally but becomes steadily debased (its chief modern representative is the Disney cartoon, with its plastic goodies, vivaciously absurd or sinister baddies, semi-magical twists, etc.). In the more vulgarly romantic context of Dickens the opposed societies taper off into hidden, elemental worlds of Good and Bad, or rhetoric and melodrama, dream and death, placidity and obsession, cosy arcadias and chaotic hinterlands, where nice girls become angels and nasty men become puppet-like demons. According to Frye, the unique energy of Dickens derives from these extremes; although one can protest all one wants about their stiltedness and unreality, it is doubtful whether there would be much left of Dickens without them.

Like a lot of Frye's criticism the placing of Dickens is both rather schematized and rather woolly. Nevertheless, alone among critiques of Dickens, it manages to see him all at once, unhampered by a desire to square him with the modern and the commonsensical. Dr Carey also responds to the black and anarchical area of Dickens, an area which embarrasses more austere critics, and his book is a consistently enjoyable counter to those who wish to clean Dickens up. But the other side of Dickens, the unctuous fairytale side, won't go away either, for all our twentieth-century fastidiousness. It is just as closely connected to his 'intransigence', his refusal, in Dr Carey's phrase, to accept 'that what's normally thought to be seen is what he sees'.

New Statesman November 1973

Donne the Apostate

John Donne: Life, Mind and Art by John Carey

To begin with, it looks as though John Donne is going to be given a pretty rough ride by John Carey. Dr Donne had his faults, after all, and Professor Carey – stern enough as an essayist and reviewer – is always particularly hard on the authors he elects to write whole books about. Quite what Carey has against these characters isn't entirely clear. For all its brilliance of address, Carey's criticism is unusually vehement, idiosyncratic and low on charity. His *Milton* presented us with a deluded and humourless tyrant, his *Dickens* with a retarded sentimentalist, his *Thackeray* with a smug and venal philistine.

True, Carey's hostility towards his chosen writers is amused and sardonic in tone, and doesn't decisively prejudice him against their work. You sense that he is simply too levelheaded, too modern and liberal to have much sympathy for the essential messiness of the creative temperament. It seems that Carey can't get over feeling cleverer and above all more practical than those chaotic charlatans, who are thrashing about in history and their own disordered lives, while laying their claims to enduring art.

So how will Carey hit it off with Jack Donne, the Dean of St Paul's, the Monarch of Wit? None too well, one suspects – though there are surprises in store. 'The first thing to remember about Donne is that he was a Catholic,' Carey begins; 'the second, that he betrayed his faith.' Descended on his mother's side from Sir Thomas More, Donne was born into the pre-Armada, anti-Catholic terror of the 1570s. His mother was active in the recusant underworld; his brother was an unwilling martyr, dying of plague after a spell in prison for harbouring a priest . . . The main spur behind Donne's apostasy, Carey tells us, was worldly ambition. He could not prosper as a Catholic, so in his mid-twenties he changed camps, becoming a vocal and militant Anglican, 'willing to abuse, in public', as Carey notes, 'those valiant Catholics who had gone to the scaffold for their Faith'.

Donne then threw himself into the humiliating business of sponging a living from the Anglican bigwigs of the day. Presenting himself as a 'poore worme' and 'clodd of clay', he toadied to the 'rabble of idlers, confidence men and pederasts' at court, accumulating patrons with begging letters and written-to-order verse epistles. He attracted the attention of the Earl of Essex, whose 'gallantry, youth and courage', in Carey's novelettish formulation, 'dazzled all eyes', and joined him on a couple of expeditions to Spain and the Azores.

In 1601 Donne secretly contracted what he hoped was a brilliant marriage to the daughter of a Surrey landowner. He was instantly disgraced. For years the embittered courtier lived in a damp cottage in Mitcham, where his wife churned out children so monotonously that when one of the daughters died, Donne 'did not stoop to give details' in letters to friends. By this time he was back to his fawning ways. When James I became entangled in the controversy about the Oath of Allegiance, Donne put together an anti-Catholic treatise and 'hurried down to Royston, where the King was staying, expressly to present him with a copy'. In the end the ploy backfired: it was under direct regal pressure that Donne was ordained in 1615, reluctantly abandoning the court for the Church.

Carey clicks his tongue here and there, as the quotations show, but for the most part he is unwontedly generous, even forgiving about Donne's throughgoing frailty. It seems that Carey senses a rare congruence between Donne's life and his poetry which retroactively cleanses Donne of his worldly sins. The two main themes of his career, spiritual guilt and secular frustration, are held to be triumphantly nutritious to his verse. Neatly, Donne's 'spiritual life' is 'preserved for us in the "Holy Sonnets"', while the songs and satires 'may be seen as a reaction against the constriction and dependence that actuality imposed'.

Although one searches Carey's work in vain for any consistent literary theory, it appears that the art he likes best is the art that corresponds most faithfully to life. This at any rate is how he repeatedly signals his preferences. Exceptionally responsive to Donne's poems, Carey is obliged to claim that they bear 'the stamp of self more deeply than those of any other English poet'. This desperate remark — unverifiable, and anyway meaningless — frees Carey to treat the poems as if they were confidential memos to Donne's confessor or marriage-counsellor, or to some spectral Jacobean psychiatrist. He talks of Donne 'relapsing' into his fixations; he detects 'an almost confessional relevance' in one poem and identifies the 'motives' that 'underlie' another.

The analysis of Holy Sonnet XVII ('Since she whom I lov'd hath payd her last debt') is fairly typical of his method. The sestet, Carey says, 'sounds like someone making a superhuman effort to put a brave face on things'. But 'after the sixth line, the effort collapses, and Donne's distressed feelings come pouring out'. We imagine the grim-faced poet heroically completing the sestet, then cracking up on line seven, until the final couplet comes 'pouring out' through his sobs. Or, rather, we don't imagine it; instead we remember the old distinction between real sincerity and literary sincerity: when told of his wife's death, the poet can burst into tears, but he cannot burst into song. 'S. Lucies Day', which rhymes and scans, is described as 'suicidal'. Suicides write notes, not elegies.

The New Critics, who already seem a bit old-fashioned, like to regard all poems as contemporary and anonymous-hermetic, in a word. Carey's method, here and elsewhere, is to feel his way outwards from the details and imaginative habits of a writer's work, and see them in terms of his life, time and thought. Often, of course, it comes off. Lively and learned in equal measure, Carey produces many stirring commentaries on Donne's evasive, sophistical and entangling verse. However, his sympathy for Donne the man intensifies but also confuses his receptivity to Donne the poet, with odd results for his book. Carey is moved to narrow the gap between life and art. Such proximity, though, is undercut by the very fact of literary form. Life doesn't scan, after all, and the poet must get his weeping done with before he goes in search of his rhymes.

Observer May 1981

Waugh's Mag. Op.;
Wodehouse's Sunset

Brideshead Revisited by Evelyn Waugh

This busty new paperback of *Brideshead Revisited* recommends itself on the cover as Evelyn Waugh's best-loved novel. The claim may be accurate; but *Brideshead* is Waugh's most hated novel too. Equally enthralling and distasteful, it is a problem comedy, like *Mansfield Park* – worrying, inordinate, self-conscious, a book that steps out of genre and never really looks at home with its putative author. Snobbery is the charge most often levelled against *Brideshead*; and, at first glance, it is also the least damaging. Modern critics have by now accused practically every pre-modern novelist of pacifism, or collaboration, in the class war. Such objections are often simply anachronistic, telling us more about present-day liberal anxieties than about anything else. But this line won't quite work for *Brideshead*, which squarely identifies egalitarianism as its foe and proceeds to rubbish it accordingly.

Of course, the modern world, 'the age of Hooper', has now arrived, and even the most well-adjusted vandal – the most helpless product of junk food, adult videos and mangled cityscapes – must find plenty that is cheerless in his new surroundings. Yet the present age will be lamented in its turn, like the last. The good is gone, the bad is all to come: this theme is as old as literature. What a writer does with it is simply a matter of style and tone.

The novel is littered with countless, often laughable asides on the Great Falling-Off. One thinks of such moments as the passage on the decline of the English bathroom (where the chrome tap? where the carpet?); the escape from Lady Marchmain's cluttered parlour into the main rooms of Brideshead and 'the august, masculine atmosphere of a better age', under 'that high and insolent dome'; the painful meal with know-all, know-nothing Rex Mottram in Paris, where 'the burgundy seemed a reminder that the world was an older and better place than Rex knew, that mankind in its long passion had learned another wisdom than his'. Ryder must be a simple soul, by God, to be so elaborately solaced by a glass of wine.

These are minor follies, perhaps, pitiable but innocuous. Try this, though, for authentic hatred of the common age: 'These men [Lady Marchmain's brothers] must die to make a world for Hooper . . . so that things might be safe for the travelling salesman, with his polygonal *pince nez*, his fat wet handshake, his grinning dentures.' Or this, after the disclosure that Rex is a divorcee: 'Round the argument circled and swooped like a gull, now out to sea . . . now right on the patch where the offal floated.' Offal, eh? But then Rex (or 'people of Rex's sort') is someone 'that only this ghastly age could produce', in Julia Mottram's ringing phrase.

Waugh's snobbery is revealed here as a failure of imagination, an artistic failure; it is stock-response, like sentimentality. This brings us to the second main objection to the book, one that is closely connected, in my view, with the vulgarly romantic version of Catholicism which Waugh chooses to celebrate. There is something barefaced, even aggressive, in the programmatic way that the novel arranges for its three most unregenerate characters – Sebastian, Lord Marchmain and Julia – to claim the highest spiritual honours. Sebastian, whose life has been impartially dedicated to shiftlessness, whimsy and drink, becomes a holy fool, shuffling among lepers and sleeping in his 'monk's cell'. Lord Marchmain, who likewise has done nothing in his seventy years but follow his own hackneyed inclinations, snatches salvation in the last seconds of his existence. 'I've known worse cases make beautiful deaths,' says the priest, rubbing his hands after Marchmain has jeered him from the sick room. And Julia . . .

For the first two-thirds of the book, Julia doesn't constitute much of a departure from the standard vamp/heartbreaker/scatterbrain of Waugh's fictional women, who are presented as embodiments of philistinism, will and appetite, cynical *in the heart*, above all. Quite what qualifies Julia for her moral jackpot in Book 3 remains unclear.

Her rollcall of worldly infamies is unflinchingly stressed – she has her 'vicious' escapade in New York, she 'lives in sin' with Ryder. And yet here is her curious epiphany, a two-page 'tumult of sorrow!' complete with semi-colons and telltale adjectives:

> . . . never the cool sepulchre and the grave cloths spread on the stone slab, never the oil and spices in the dark cave; always the midday sun and the dice clicking for the seamless coat.

Ryder's love for the Marchmains, it would seem, is aroused not only by their noble blood but by their congenital holiness. Whether the reader feels much uplift during Julia's voluble trance is more open to doubt. What the reader senses, I suspect, is the fat wet handshake and grinning dentures of bad art.

Bad art is of course a major theme in *Brideshead Revisited*. The book would be without much of its staying power if Waugh hadn't hedged his bets in this way. Ryder's artistic talent is seen in terms of his infatuation with Brideshead itself – in terms of connoisseurship, of English 'charm'. 'It was an aesthetic education to live within those walls,' says Ryder. 'This was my conversion to the Baroque.' It was Waugh's conversion too, but to the Baroque in its decadent, bastardized literary form. 'I have been here before': the opening refrain is from Rossetti, and much of the novel reads like a golden treasury of neo-classical clichés: phantoms, soft airs, enchanted gardens, winged hosts – the liturgical rhythms, the epic similes, the wooziness. Waugh's conversion was a temporary one, and never again did he attempt the grand style. Certainly the prose sits oddly with the coldness and contempt at the heart of the novel, and contributes crucially to its central imbalance.

'Most of the reviews have been adulatory except where they were embittered by class resentment,' said Waugh in his *Diaries* (written while drunk). In his *Letters* (written while hungover), Waugh refers to *Brideshead* repeatedly as his 'magnum opus' – 'a very beautiful book', 'my first important book'. In a touching letter to his wife Waugh tenderly scolds Laura for not taking the 'Mag. Op.' seriously enough; it is almost a whimper of neglect. Later he confessed himself 'greatly shaken by its popularity in USA'. 'I re-read

Brideshead Revisited,' he wrote to Graham Greene in 1950, 'and was appalled.'

Perhaps Waugh would regard *this* review as a product of class resentment, the complaint of a Hooper who doesn't know which fork to use, and who says 'Rightyoh' and 'Okeydoke'. I think it unlikely. Waugh wrote *Brideshead* with great speed, unfamiliar excitement, and a deep conviction of its excellence. Lasting schlock, the really good bad book, cannot be written otherwise. 'The languor of Youth . . . How quickly, how irrevocably lost!' The novel had its origins in this regret, the more keenly and confusedly felt by someone 'beginning to be old'. But then all this had somehow to be turned into art, that is where the real trouble started.

Observer October 1981

Sunset at Blandings by P.G. Wodehouse. With Notes and Appendices by Richard Usborne

P.G. Wodehouse was the exponent of a form that no intelligent writer has been able to take seriously for several hundred years: the comic pastoral. You would have to go back to the enchanted forests of Shakespearean comedy to find even a fleeting analogy with his fiction – to the suspended green worlds of Arden and Illyria, where love-knots are festively disentangled, parentage mysteries advantageously resolved and fortunes miraculously accumulated, all without pain. And when we note that Wodehouse's green world tolerantly includes twentieth-century London and New York, as well as the forgiving lawns of rural England, we begin to see his true cloudlessness as an author.

It is a world devoid of all the baser energies. The greatest terrors its denizens face are mild social embarrassment, the pecuniary delinquencies of friends, the occasional unrequited crush and the prospect of being bullied by an aunt into marrying a bossy cousin. The fact that these pitfalls, when translated to the burly contingencies of real life, can cause genuine hurts and fears merely strengthens the glow of innocuousness. Wodehouse loved to play on the genial insensitivity to suffering that centuries of thoughtless privilege produce. The only moment of anomie I can recall in his fiction occurs in an early short story, when Jeeves, prompt as ever, brings Bertie Wooster his usual whisky-and-soda at six o'clock. 'It's the bally monotony of it all', complains the alienated Bertie, 'that makes everything seem so perfectly bally.' *Bally*, by the way, is a public-school diminutive of 'bloody'. Even here, you see, things aren't *that* desperate.

I quote from memory – something that will doubtless oblige Richard Usborne, our premier Wodehouse scholar, to reach for his index cards. Mr Usborne spearheads the clique of British belletrists who, in the pantheon of world literature, would place Wodehouse somewhere between Homer and Dante. In editing this uncompleted novel for publication (the title, incidentally, is the handiwork of the British publisher), Mr Usborne has managed to give full vent to his fanaticism: the 100-odd pages of Wodehouse text are bulked out with sixty pages of the author's drafts and scribblings, Mr Usborne's footlingly digressive textual notes, a topology of Blandings Castle (with sketch-maps), a breakdown of the rail service between Paddington and Market Blandings (with timetables), and such like. Clearly this enthusiasm is not to do with literature. It must then, I assume, be to do with something else. Together with the clip-clop of the hobbyhorse, one senses a kind of innocent, wistful snobbery – as if the Wodehouse world were really locatable in time and space. Anthony Powell, who also chronicles the upper crust, is the only other modern writer to win this unfathomably obsessive treatment. One awaits equivalent studies of the Nottingham of Alan Sillitoe, the Northern Slums of Stan Barstow. It won't happen.

The rescue operation itself, however, was well worth undertaking, and the quality of the Wodehouse text makes additional

MARTIN AMIS

nonsense of Mr Usborne's twinkly rubrics. As with all the best
Wodehouse, the pleasures of the Blandings books are totally reliable
and undisconcerting. There are the usual bust-ups, alarms, duplicities
and misapprehensions, but even a newcomer to Wodehouse would
quickly see that this world is quite static and accessible, its arms ever
open to receive its guests. There is almost something sub-literary in
the derisory demands Wodehouse makes on his audience; his ghost
hovers over the book like the solicitous Jeeves, only wishing he could
turn the pages for you. It is quite unlike any other sort of writing. But
then Wodehouse was unique in every way: he had boundless comic
genius and a laughably limited range.

He only made it *look* easy, though. It appears from the worksheets
appended to the novel that Wodehouse had some ticklish difficulties
in the plotting of *Sunset at Blandings*. That tiny, tortured hand
experiments with dozens of variations before fixing the one presented
to us here (the most frequent scribble is an introductory 'Try this';
'Fix', 'Okay', 'Good', '*Very Good*' and '*Very Good XX*' are also
popular). The hesitance is surprising. Whereas Wodehouse's prose
was obviously the result of fond and obsessive labour, his plotting
always seemed the most perfunctory thing about his work: the
Blandings novels, including this one, are all permutations of the
peaceable oldster / troublesome aunt / lovelorn youngster setup,
with the usual machinery of letters, thefts, coincidence and dramatic
irony. Mr Usborne explains that Wodehouse lost some of his impetus
as he grew older; he found the business of moving action forward
increasingly irksome. When he died, P.G. Wodehouse had been
Sir Pelham Wodehouse for forty-six days. He was ninety-three and
had a sunny farce still warm on his typewriter. Right to the end, that
green world of his never began to lose its vernal brilliance.

New York Times Book Review December 1978

Lowry: In the Volcano

Pursued by Furies: A Life of Malcolm Lowry by Gordon Bowker

Dipsomaniacs are either born that way, or they just end up that way. Vastly distinguished in the sphere of dipsomania, Malcolm Lowry, it seems, actually planned to be that way, from childhood. The gift was not inherited. In an early short story the narrator records his (Methodist) father's disapproval of a local lawyer, who lacked 'self-discipline'. 'He did not know', Lowry wrote, 'that secretly I had decided that I would be a drunkard when I grew up.' While most schoolboys dreamt of becoming engine-drivers or cattle-punchers, little Malcolm dreamt of becoming an alcoholic. And the dream came true. Excluding a few dry-outs, in hospitals and prisons, and the very occasional self-imposed prohibition, Malcolm Lowry was shitfaced for thirty-five years.

How much do we need to know about a writer, personally? The answer is that it doesn't matter. Nothing or everything is equally satisfactory. Who cares, in the end? As Northrop Frye has said, the only evidence we have of Shakespeare's existence, apart from the poems and plays, is the portrait of a man who was clearly an idiot. Biography is there for the curious; and curiosity gives out where boredom begins. Certainly we think that scholarly investigation has gone too far when it starts offering us monographs on, say, the laundry lists of Shackerley Marmion or the tram tickets of Lascelles Abercrombie. But the author of *Under the Volcano* is a special case. His addiction becomes our addiction. Anyway, The Bar Tabs of Malcolm Lowry would tell most of the story, and it would be no shorter than Gordon Bowker's 600 pages. The biography is thorough, and thoroughly engaged; it is both gripped and gripping. It won't have to be done again.

To make a real success of being an alcoholic, to go all the way with it, you need to be other things too: shifty, unfastidious, solipsistic, insecure and indefatigable. Lowry was additionally equipped with an extra-small penis, which really seemed to help. He was of course a prodigious self-mythologizer, or a braggart and a liar, if you prefer. A playground scar on his knee he passed off as a bullet-wound sustained in crossfire during the Chinese Civil War. Jailed for one of his solo riots in Mexico, he listed his torments in a letter to a friend: 'They tried to castrate me too, one fine night, unsuccessfully I regret (sometimes) to report.' That hardy 'one fine night' acts as a kind of semaphore of mendacity. In 1939 he used the outbreak of war, and his own entirely hollow vow of immediate enlistment, in a number of self-interested ways, including this bold strophe in a letter to his sweetheart: 'If you truly love me as I love you greet me as one come back from a long journey & who must go again, as I must.' That last heroic cadence bespeaks both congenital insincerity and a delighted self-loathing. Lowry was a world-class liar. Even his commas and colons were lies.

Like Isherwood and others, Lowry was the kind of Englishman who had to get out of England, and sooner rather than later. His parents were ordinary products of their time and place but it was their very ovinity that haunted him. When imagination comes up against no-imagination, then no-imagination wins every time. So you have to get out. At seventeen he sailed east to China, as a deckhand; a year later he sailed west to America, as a passenger, on a literary pilgrimage. North and south, though, turned out to be the significant points on his personal compass. The south meant Mexico, the scene of his most shameful rampages. The north started out meaning Scandinavia but ended up meaning Vancouver and a two-room shack in the frozen wilds; here, and here only, he could write; everywhere else he just went on word-binges, or word-blinders. Lowry was the kind of man the Russians call a walrus: he responded to the asceticism of long winters, sub-zero swims, the cobalt-blue skies. He tried very hard, but he couldn't make it as one of nature's geckoes, able to wallow in the ooze and booze beneath Popocatepetl.

Before his long exile could begin (nothing would tempt him back to England except free health care) Lowry had to lurch and barf his way through university and then spend a couple of years crashing around Fitzrovia with a succession of manqué poets and brawling book-reviewers. His erotic interests, like his literary interests, were vital to his sense of himself – to the internal romance – but nothing deflected him from his dedication to alcohol. Of a make-out session with a famous Cambridge vamp, Lowry wrote: 'Charlotte . . . has offered me her body . . . I drank a lot of whisky . . . and was nearly sick into her mouth when I was kissing her. She says she loves me.'

His talent was a precocious one: even in his early twenties, not content with the usual debauches and disappearances, he was already experimenting with paranoid hallucinations involving salamanders and male nurses. By the time he got to Mexico (aged twenty-six) he was downing any liquid that came his way on the off-chance that it might contain alcohol: he once drank 'a whole bottle of olive oil thinking it was hair tonic'.

So the years of Lowry's maturity unfold: binnings, bannings, arrests, ejections, screams in the night, expired visas and lost passports, together with a lengthening rap sheet of domestic arson, larceny and GBH. In 1938 his first wife Jan 'rationed' him to a quart of liquor a day, but he hoarded his allowance to buy 'fortified wines costing only fifty cents a gallon'. In 1947 his second wife, Margerie, noticed that Lowry, after a period of abstinence, had started enjoying a cocktail before lunch – 'and pre-dinner cocktails started as early as 3pm'. In 1949 he was averaging three litres of red wine per day topped up by two litres of rum. His varicose veins stretched from groin to ankle. One morning he collapsed and started 'vomiting black blood'. We then duly witness the straitjacket, the padded cell, and the serious discussion, with wife and doctors present, on the pros and cons of lobotomy.

Towards the end, even Lowry's freak accidents and cluster catastrophes are assuming an air of the dankest monotony. An average hour, it seems, would include a jeroboam of Windowlene or Optrex, a sanguinary mishap with a chainsaw or a cement-mixer, and a routinely bungled attempt to guillotine his wife.

Around Malcolm and Margerie, everything that could go wrong would go wrong. He falls in the bath and breaks a blood-vessel: 'She tried calling the hospital but the phone was out of order; she rushed out into the elevator and got stuck between floors.' He falls on a country path and shatters his leg: she runs to the local store and is 'severely mauled' by the neighbour's dog. Certain friends of theirs always kept packed suitcases by the front door so that they could claim to be off on vacation if the Lowrys horribly appeared, hoping to stay. Her psychology was one of self-immolation in the dread face of genius ('I feared he'd hurt me badly and feel so awful the next day'). As for Malcolm, he was plain incorrigible, resolved – unto death – on making the same old mistakes.

The biographical context, as usual, turns out to be the least congenial setting for any consideration of the work. Of course we learn a thing or two about Lowry's 'working habits', which included habitual plagiarism on a surprising scale. Plagiarism is the perfect crime for the masochist: dross can change hands freely, but anything worth stealing carries its own guarantee of detection and exposure. Lowry was exposed, many times. The book is called *Pursued by Furies*, but Lowry's path, in fact, was smoothed by mercies: a small private income, devoted women, talent. It was all laid out before him. Nevertheless you would not wish for a sharpening of Mr Bowker's appalled, but generally lenient, tone. The furies were internal. There was nothing to be done about them.

What of the fiction – i.e., what of *Under the Volcano*, which is pretty well all it amounted to? Writing both compelled and mortified Lowry. Peering back through the viscous shards of his life, you wonder how he ever wrote anything – how he ever signed a cheque or left a note for the milkman. The only thing that worked was the shack on the water, and its extreme simplicities. Drunkenness recollected in sobriety: surrounded by the celestial clarity of the north, he could recreate the sweat and corruption of the south. I remember *Under the Volcano* as chaotically confessional, as a torrent of consciousness. Now it feels formal, literary, even mandarin in its intonations (the word 'pub' is daintily sequestered by inverted commas). It is what Lowry could never be: it is lucid and logical; it is well-behaved.

Independent on Sunday December 1993

Popularity Contest

Chandler Prolonged

Perchance to Dream by Robert B. Parker

If Raymond Chandler had written like Robert B. Parker, he wouldn't have been Raymond Chandler. He would have been Robert B. Parker, a rather less-exalted presence. The posthumous pseudo-sequel never amounts to more than a nostalgic curiosity, and it is no great surprise that *Perchance to Dream* isn't much good. The great surprise (for this reviewer) is that *The Big Sleep* isn't much good either; it seems to have aged dramatically since I last looked at it. Still, *The Big Sleep* has its qualities, and they include originality and a tremendous title – two departments in which *Perchance to Dream* is conspicuously shaky. Would *Maybe to Dream* have been any better? Or *To Dream (Maybe)*? Or how about *The Bigger Sleep*? Or *Sleep Bigger*? Come to think of it, this exploratory, drawing-board stage might have been the right point to abandon the project. But Mr Parker didn't abandon it until it was finished. And here it is.

1   'The sunshine was as empty as a headwaiter's smile.'
2   'His grin had all the warmth of a pawnbroker examining yr mother's diamond.'
3   'She approached me with enough sex appeal to stampede a businessmen's lunch.'
4   'The room was as charming as a heap of coffee grounds.'

Quotes 1 and 3 are Chandler; 2 and 4 are Mr Parker. True, these are among Mr Parker's best shots, while the Chandlerisms aren't much more than routine; but I see no yawning gulf in class. I remembered Chandler's prose as being hypnotic and frictionless, without false quantities. It isn't like that; it is full of stubbed toes and barked shins.

In this area Mr Parker can match and easily outstrip his mentor. Hardly any of Chandler's sentences, after all, are outright catastrophes, as Mr Parker's often are: 'I looked at the lock and tried a key that looked like it would match from the key ring I'd taken from the Mex', for instance, or 'She was in . . . a bell-sleeved silk top with a plunging neckline and wide floppy silk pants that hid the great legs but hinted to you that if you got a look they would indeed be great.'

Sexually, Chandler is constrained and ambiguous, whereas Mr Parker is candidly puerile: 'She leaned forward toward me, showing me a white lace bra and a good deal of breast as well.' Chandler's Marlowe may be a snoop, but he's no peeper (and he would never say 'bra'). Then again, Mr Parker's Philip Marlowe has much rounder heels than the original, who, although irresistible to all women ('My God, you big dark handsome brute!'), is an old hand at just saying no. Indeed, degraded female sexuality is *The Big Sleep*'s heart of darkness: drugs, dirty pictures ('indescribable filth'), drooling nymphomaniacs. It sounds both tame and creepy to the modern ear, as do the persistent – and related – snarls about homosexuality ('A pansy has no iron in his bones', and so on). Revisiting the scenes of the first murder, Marlowe senses 'a stealthy nastiness, like a fag party.' Well, 'a fag party' no longer sends shivers up the spine. But it's less laughable, I suppose, than *Perchance to Dream*'s climactic depravity, where the sicko billionaire and the zonked heiress are surprised in the act: 'She stood over Simpson, giggling her giggle and spanking him with a gold-inlaid ivory hairbrush.' Which is certainly no average hairbrush. Sin, it would seem, has come a long way since 1939.

So has profanity, and the general style of crime. The underworld advances more quickly, and dates faster, than the overworld. As a result, Chandler's heavies just aren't heavy; his mean streets are clean streets – they are positively Arcadian. Thus, in *The Big Sleep*, he substitutes a dash when the sneering murderer tells Marlowe what he can go do to himself, and the hissing, frothing murderess is reduced to calling him 'a filthy name'. Verbally, Chandler is as chaste as the *New York Times*. Mr Parker has plainly made an effort to transport himself to this more innocent era. But he remains a man of the Nineties. He lets Marlowe swear, and can't resist allotting him a (highly unsuitable) amourette, and stands by while he fraternizes with a known pimp, which *The Big Sleep*'s Marlowe, with his pipe and his 'six-mover' chess problems, is far too literary for. One definite gain is the restoration of 'Okay' in place of the ridiculous and distracting 'Okey'. (Reading *The Big Sleep*, you keep stressing 'Okey' on the first syllable, and then fruitlessly picture a resident of rural Oklahoma.) Apart from a telltale mention of 'abusive treatment', meaning cruel rather than insulting, Mr Parker avoids specific anachronisms. He manages to get through the novel without having Marlowe fasten his seat belt or lose sleep over global warming.

One might expect Mr Parker to make up some ground on the plot, because Chandler is far too glazed and existential for efficient storytelling. *The Big Sleep*'s premise (the dying General, the two wild daughters, the vanished son-in-law) is elegant, but the murder-trail stuff is repetitive, implausible and hard to follow. Every few pages, it seems, there's a knock on the door and another new gun barrel for the reader to peer into. Mr Parker starts strongly, and for a while *Perchance to Dream* trundles along with more uncomplicated thrust than Chandler ever cared to generate. Marlowe is furnished with an impregnable adversary and long odds against. But the denouement is a chaos of tawdry short cuts. The impregnable villain confesses instantly, and his main sidekick disappears 'in the scuffle', paving the way, perhaps, for *Ay, There's the Rub*, the pseudo-pseudo-sequel of a thriller-writer yet unborn.

Most seriously, the character of Marlowe collapses. Raymond Chandler created a figure who hovered somewhere between cult and myth: he is both hot and cool, both virile and sterile. He pays a price for his freedom from venality; he is untouchable in all senses; he cannot be corrupted, not by women, not by money, not by America. The 'big dark handsome brute' makes an interesting contrast with the photo on the back of my green Penguin edition: spectacles, receding hairline, lips so thin they seem to be licked away. Finding the rich nympho in his bed ('You're cute'), *Sleep*'s Marlowe tells her to leave before he throws her out 'by force. Just the way you are, naked.' When she goes, having called him that filthy name, Marlowe airs the room, drinks his drink and stares down at the imprint of her 'small corrupt body' on the sheets. 'I put my empty glass down,' the chapter ends, 'and tore the bed to pieces savagely.'

Mr Parker's Marlowe, more modernly, would have given her a soft drink and a long talk about her substance problem. He has no turbulent soul, no inner complication to keep in check. Mr Parker neither understands nor respects Marlowe's inhibitions; he fritters them away, unconsciously questing for some contemporary ideal of gruff likeability. By the end of the book, Marlowe has become an affable goon. This guy grins and preens and jollies things along. This guy talks too much.

New York Times Book Review January 1991

Park II

The Lost World by Michael Crichton

When the dino colouring-books have at last been put aside, and
they've cleaned their teeth with dino brushes and dino paste, and
they're lying there in dino pyjamas, under dino duvets, what do
children want to talk about? Dinosaurs. Dinosaurs as brought to them,
vivified and literalized, by the dream team of Michael Crichton (the
novel) and Steven Spielberg (the film). And for two years now my
sons and I have been tossing the scenarios back and forth. What would
they give us, what would we be looking at, in Park II?

Discussions with my pre-teens were, as Crichton might put it,
dogged by controversy. But we were sure we knew where the sequel
would have to begin: with that steel cylinder full of dino embryos
dropped by fatso computer dweeb Dennis Nedry, just before he got
smeared by the dilophosaurus. One or other pre-teen would then go
on to remind the company that dilophosaurs didn't spit. And they
didn't have that mad-granny frill around their necks. Modern parents
hover at about A-level standard on prehistoric fauna. Children are all
PhDs. Anyway, that embryo cylinder had to be the germ of Park II.
That can had Park II written all over it.

Not that speculation ended there. John Hammond, the megalomaniac geneticist, or megalomaniac fundraiser, who created the dino
park, was killed off by Crichton in the novel, pecked to death by
a gaggle of 'compys' (compsognathus: a carnivorous dino fowl). But
Spielberg spared him. Maybe Crichton would clone us up a new
Hammond, or provide a like-minded twin brother. Towards the
end of the novel, raptors start escaping from the island, stealing rides
on ferry boats. Would they hit the mainland? Would the monsters
take Manhattan, or at least Miami?

219

On one point we all languidly agreed: there would be an array of new dinosaurs. Avians, for instance, which were deftly yet briefly introduced by Crichton but ignored, for now, by Spielberg. Conversely, how could the creator of *Jaws* fail to steer Crichton towards the dino cousins of the deep? Imagine it: the beach party, the blonde skinny-dipper, the looming plesiosaur or mosasaur or ichthyosaur . . . Half of all known dinosaurs have been discovered in the last twenty years: they find a new one every seven weeks. So what about a role for the utahraptor, officially named and described in 1993? This beauty resembled a velociraptor but was three times its size. A twenty-foot kickboxer with a fifteen-inch 'slasher' claw on each foot, utahraptor was hailed by palaeontologist James Kirkland as 'the most vicious of all dinosaurs, as well as one of the most intelligent'. It seemed that the fossil record was jumping with fresh talent.

Here comes *The Lost World*, and here come the answers. No embryo cylinder, no Hammond, no mainland incursion, no dilophosaurs, no giant predators of the oceans or the skies. And only one new monster. Let us quickly deal with the new monster, which shows promise. It is a carnotaurus, a light-heavyweight with horns, and the possessor, according to Crichton, of near-magical chameleonic powers. 'Diet: Meat', as my dinosaur encyclopaedia bluntly assures us. This is good. In the Jurassic era, as in our own, vegetarians are a drag. Meateaters get around more, and have more energy. I welcome carnotaurus, and only wish it had been given somebody to savage. By the time it appears we're down to the two kids and a skeleton staff of goodies. The villains have all been used up. And no kid is going to buy it in a mere PG.

On with Crichton's tale! After 131 remarkably leaden pages we find ourselves on an island very like and certainly very near the island in *Jurassic Park*. But that island was Isla Nublar (since shut down). This island, Isla Sorna, we learn, was 'Hammond's dirty little secret. It's the dark side of the park.' Hammond's cloning lab and dino hatchery were just window-dressing. With any new manufacturing technology, 'initial yields are low'. To get the good specimens for his park, Hammond must have been churning out embryos on an industrial scale. Where? On the mist-shrouded isle of Sorna . . .

The reader's heart soars like a pterodactyl. Isla Sorna, it seems fair to expect, is a kind of dinosaur borstal, where all the real hardcases are confined: the lowlifes, the hopeless recidivists. Or maybe it's a holding pen for mutant dinosaurs: half-breeds, hybrids, mongrels. Then, too, we would tolerantly settle for diseased dinosaurs: pathopods, toxoraptors, carcinosaurs. Whatever way Crichton spins it, the stage is set for escalation. We expect nastier dinosaurs. But what we get, on the whole, is *nicer* dinosaurs.

Fossils are static things, but they are elastic in our imaginations and we shape them to our needs. As Crichton explains, in one of the mini-lectures slotted shamelessly into his text, our image of the dinosaurs has undergone clear changes since their discovery 150 years ago. It seemed to suit the upwardly mobile Victorians to regard the dinosaurs as contemptibly retrograde: slow, dumb, torpid and blundering towards extinction. 'Dinosaur' became a synonym for something that didn't deserve to be around. The twentieth century saw the beginning of a long course of rehabilitation. Gradually the dinosaurs' blood temperature rose; their movements quickened; their brains expanded. Nowadays, or so Crichton has it, they have been enveloped by a kind of Disneyfication: anthropomorphized, euphemized, sentimentalized. The filthily careening gas-guzzlers have all been traded in for two-door saloons, running on unleaded fuel – and, yes, with a bumper sticker saying Baby On Board.

Crichton is neither mawkish nor censorious. What he wants to emphasize is the weakness of our grip on a world of vanished complexity. Still, the artist in him (a diminutive personage, true, but a definite presence) insists on test-driving the two rival models. Thus dinosaur herds now practise 'inter-species symbiosis': the powerful and myopic apatosaurs hang out with the smaller, sharp-eyed parasaurs, forming a united front against predators. Triceratops are drilled in 'group defensive behavior'. Maiasaurs engage in 'complex nesting and parenting'. There are rituals of courtship and display. These animals sleep together and stick together. They even go to the bathroom in packs.

The unlikeliest beneficiaries of the new-look ecosystem are the tyrannosaurs. Mr and Mrs Rex, as here portrayed, are outstanding citizens, 'cautious, almost timid animals' with 'an extended parenting role'. It is the velociraptors, fortunately, who buck the trend. For reasons not altogether clear, they have gone downhill in the last five years, and now form the island's underclass. Their nest is a disgrace – even Crichton is scandalized: 'the eggshells crushed; the broken mounds stepped on . . . the youngsters looked thin, undernourished'. In the earlier book the velociraptors were a crack platoon; here they're a mob of squealing squaddies. Unsurprisingly, perhaps, they are a delight. These glittering yahoos steal *The Lost World*, just as they stole *Jurassic Park*, both book and film. If Hammond was Nublar's Prospero, then the velociraptors are Sorna's Calibans.

At his best Crichton is a blend of Stephen Jay Gould and Agatha Christie. He emplaces a series of zoological mysteries which are far more arresting than the conveyor-belt jeopardies of his plot. Animals – especially, if not quite exclusively, velociraptors – are what he is good at. People are what he is bad at. People, and prose.

When you open *The Lost World* you enter a strange terrain of one-page chapters, one-sentence paragraphs and one-word sentences. You will gaze through the thick canopy of authorial padding. It's a jungle out there, and jungles are 'hot' sometimes 'very hot'. 'Malcolm wiped his forehead. "It's hot up here."' Levine agrees: '"Yes, it's hot."' Thirty pages later it's still hot. '"Jeez, it's hot up here," Eddie said.' And Levine agrees again: '"Yes," Levine said, shrugging.' Out there, beyond the foliage, you see herds of clichés, roaming free. You will listen in 'stunned silence' to an 'unearthly cry' or a 'deafening roar'. Raptors are 'rapacious'. Reptiles are 'reptilian'. Pain is 'searing'.

The job of characterization has been delegated to two or three thrashed and downtrodden adverbs. 'Dodgson shook his head irritably'; '"Handle what?" Dodgson said irritably.' So Dodgson is irritable. But '"I tell you it's fine," Levine said irritably.' 'Levine got up irritably.' So Levine is irritable too. 'Malcolm stared forward gloomily.' '"We shouldn't have the kids here," said Malcolm gloomily.' Malcolm seems to own 'gloomily'; but then you irritably notice that Rossiter is behaving 'gloomily' too, and gloomily discover that Malcolm is behaving 'irritably'. Forget about 'tensely' and 'grimly' for now. And don't get me started on 'thoughtfully'.

After a while you come to realize that this is prose from another medium:

Levine removed the black anodised Lindstradt pistol in its holster, and buckled it around his waist. He removed the pistol, checked the safety twice, and put it back in the holster. Levine got to his feet, gestured for Diego to follow him. Diego zipped up the backpack, and shouldered it again.

Recast those sentences in the present tense and you see them for what they are: stage directions. I certainly hope that that's what this book is: a creative-input memo to Steven Spielberg. Crichton has an anti-talent for dramatic speech ('Brace yourself, Sarah!', 'There's no time to waste', 'There's something funny about this island, Ian'), but many of his scenes are blueprints for something vivid: a mysterious carcass torched by flamethrowers on a volcanic beach; a velociraptor feeding-frenzy glimpsed through an electric storm. Reading these passages, why, you can almost hear the cinematographer unscrewing his lens cap; you can almost see the rewrite team activating their laptops.

Never mind. Crichton has pushed dinosaurs yet deeper into our psyches. And we seem to enjoy having them there. Dinosaurs remind us that our planet is as exotic as any other we can imagine. In essence, *The Lost World* is a children's book. Like all good bad stuff, it is conjured with eagerness and passion.

Sunday Times October 1995

Maintaining on Elmore Leonard

Riding the Rap by Elmore Leonard

Let us attempt to narrow it down. Elmore Leonard is a literary genius who writes re-readable thrillers. He belongs, then, not to the mainstream but to the genres (before he wrote thrillers, he wrote westerns). Whereas genre fiction, on the whole, heavily relies on plot, mainstream fiction, famously, has only about a dozen plots to recombinate (boy meets girl, good beats bad, and so on). But Mr Leonard has only one plot. All his thrillers are *Pardoner's Tales*, in which Death roams the land – usually Miami or Detroit – disguised as money.

Nevertheless, Mr Leonard possesses gifts – of ear and eye, of timing and phrasing – that even the most snobbish masters of the mainstream must vigorously covet. And the question is: how does he allow these gifts play, in his efficient, unpretentious and (delightfully) similar yarns about semiliterate hustlers, mobsters, go-go dancers, cocktail waitresses, loan sharks, bounty hunters, blackmailers and syndicate executioners? My answer may sound reductive, but here goes: the essence of Elmore is to be found in his use of the present participle.

What this means, in effect, is that he has discovered a way of slowing down and suspending the English sentence – or let's say the American sentence, because Mr Leonard is as American as jazz. Instead of writing 'Warren Ganz III lived up in Manalapan, Palm Beach County', Mr Leonard writes: 'Warren Ganz III, living up in Manalapan, Palm Beach County.' He writes, 'Bobby saying', and then opens quotes. He writes, 'Dawn saying', and then opens quotes. We are not in the imperfect tense (Dawn was saying) or the present

(Dawn says) or the historic present (Dawn said). We are in a kind of marijuana tense (Dawn saying), creamy, wandering, weak-verbed. Such sentences seem to open up a lag in time, through which Mr Leonard easily slides, gaining entry to his players' hidden minds. He doesn't just show you what these people say and do. He shows you where they breathe.

'Dutch' Leonard is as American as jazz, and jazz is in origin a naïve form. Yet he is no Louis Armstrong. He can do melody, but he is also as harshly sophisticated as late-period Coleman Hawkins. He understands the post-modern world – the world of wised-up rabble and zero authenticity. His characters are equipped not with obligingly suggestive childhoods or case-histories, but with a cranial jukebox of situation comedies and talk shows and advertising jingles, their dreams and dreads all mediated and secondhand. They are not lost souls or dead souls. Terrible and pitiable (and often downright endearing), they are simply junk souls: quarter-pounders, with cheese.

In *Riding the Rap*, Chip Ganz, ageing pretty boy, parasite and predator, plans to commit the crime of the century. Not this century: the next. His crime will be a new crime. 'Burning herb', 'maintaining on reefer', the marijuana-sotted Chip has picked up various odds and ends about the hostages in Beirut – 'seen them on TV when they were released, read a book one of them wrote'. His idea is to take rich Miamians hostage. 'You talking about kidnapping?' asks his associate, Louis Lewis. No. You don't demand a ransom. You don't call his family. You wait, and then you ask the victim how much his life is worth.

> Starting out, Chip had pictured a damp basement full of spiders and roaches crawling around, pipes dripping, his hostages huddled against the wall in chains. He wanted it to be as bad as any of the places in Beirut he'd read about.
>
> He told Louis and Louis said, 'Where we gonna find a basement in Florida?'

So the malefactors have to catch as catch can. The hostage they take is not a politician or a diplomat; he is a mob bookie called Harry

Arno. The muscle they hire is not a Shia terrorist but a Puerto Rican debt-collector called Bobby Deogracias. (Leonard's names: he once had a woman called LaDonna team up with a man called DeLeon.) The dungeon they use is not a fetid cellar but a spare bedroom in an oceanfront residence in Palm Beach owned by Chip's mother. The diet they put their hostage on consists not of bread and water but of frozen dinners and Jell-O. 'Louis said the Shia fixed their hostages rice and shit but no doubt would have given them TV dinners if they had any.'

Of course the scheme unravels into a peculiarly American havoc. Crime, Mr Leonard insistently informs us, is always half-baked, and always goes off half-cocked. Death (or life, behind bars) comes in the form of the fast buck, or its promise. Ranged against these seedy blunderers is United States Marshal Raylan Givens (a welcome carry-over, like Harry Arno, from the previous novel, *Pronto*). Raylan is perhaps the cleanest character in the entire oeuvre, dead straight and 'all business', a genuine enforcer, unlike the grey-area skip-tracers and writ-servers who, in Mr Leonard's work, usually represent the law-and-order industry. Raylan isn't post-modern; he is an anachronism from out of town. And he is fascinating, because he shows you what Mr Leonard actually holds dear – the values he can summon in a different kind of prose, in different American rhythms, those of Robert Frost, or even Mark Twain:

He could cut official corners to call a man out . . . but couldn't walk in a man's house unless invited, or else with a warrant and bust down the door.

It was the way he was raised, to have good manners . . . back when they were living in a coal camp and the miners struck at Duke Power: Raylan walking a picket line most of the year, his dad in the house dying of black lung, and company gun thugs came looking for Raylan's uncle . . . They came across the street, five of them, a couple with pick handles, and up the walk to where his mother stood on the porch . . . The gun thugs said they wanted to speak to her brother . . . She told them, 'You don't walk in a person's home 'less you're invited. Even you people must believe that. You have homes, don't you? Wives and mothers keeping house?' . . . They shoved her aside and hit Raylan with the pick handles to put him down . . .

Her words hadn't stopped them. No, what they did was stick in Raylan's mind – her words, her quiet tone of voice – and stop him, more than twenty years later, from breaking into this man's house.

I first read *Riding the Rap* in mid-January. In mid-March I read it again. The reviewer curling up with the present participle. Re-reading Elmore Leonard in the morning, and saying it was work. The experience, like the book, was wicked and irresistible. This was post-modern decadence. This was bliss.

New York Times Book Review May 1995

Half Wolfe

A Man in Full by Tom Wolfe

This book will be a good friend to you. Maybe the best you ever had – or so it will sometimes seem. I read *A Man in Full* during a week of lone travel, and it was always there for me: nestling in my lap on planes and trains, enlivening many a solitary meal, and faithfully waiting in my hotel room when I returned, last thing. Like its predecessor, *The Bonfire of the Vanities*, Tom Wolfe's new novel is fiercely and instantly addictive. It is intrinsically and generically disappointing, too, bringing with it an unavoidable hangover. But a generously mild one, really, considering the time you had.

We begin with the bovine figure of Charlie Croker, out shooting quail on his vast South Georgia plantation with an old-money Atlanta pal, Inman Armholster. Although Croker is a semi-literate redneck from 'below the gnat line', he has amassed a volatile real-estate fortune that now rivals Armholster's. But retributive justice – known hereabouts as capitalism – stands ready in the wings. Croker's empire is haemorrhaging money on a 'dead elephant' called Croker Concourse: 'You could take somebody into the lobby and the sheer "curb flash" would bowl him over . . . the Henry Moore sculpture out front, the marble arch over the doorway . . . the Belgian tapestries, the piano player in a tuxedo playing classical music from 7:30 a.m. . . .' As always, Wolfe is very good at evoking the unreality and weird onerousness of colossal expenditure. It brings out the sadist in him. Croker, like Sherman in *Bonfire*, is about to be hideously stripped.

Now we switch to a spiffy black lawyer, Roger White, as he drives to an urgent appointment with Buck McNutter, coach to the local football team. McNutter, a Mississippi cracker with a neck that seems to be 'unit-welded' to his shoulders, has a problem in the person of his star player, Fareek Fanon, an ex-ghetto boy who now wears a gold chain 'so chunky you could have used it to pull an Isuzu pickup out of a red clay ditch'. Fareek has just been accused of raping the eighteen-year-old daughter of a white Atlanta bigwig – Croker's old buddy, Inman Armholster . . .

The next chapter, mysteriously entitled 'The Saddlebags', is the best thing in the book. Croker has been summoned to a breakfast meeting with the 'workout team' at PlannersBanc, where he owes half a billion dollars. The stage has been lovingly set. Croker is seated facing the unbearable glare of the early sun, with a paper mug of coffee smelling of 'incinerated PVC cables' and a 'huge, cold, sticky, cheesy, cowpie-like cinnamon-Cheddar coffee bun that struck terror in the heart of every man in the room who had ever read an article about arterial plaque or free radicals'. For the 'orientation' of the workout team is now 'post-goodwill'; and Croker, once so eagerly wined and dined, has descended to the status of 'shithead': 'Shithead was the actual term used at the bank and throughout the industry. Bank officers said "shithead" in the same matter-of-fact way they said "mortgagee," "co-signer," or "debtor," which was the polite form of "shithead," since no borrower was referred to as a debtor until he defaulted.' As the grilling continues ('This here's the morning after, bro'), we approach the moment devoutly anticipated by the whole team. It comes when the two patches of sweat from the shithead's armpits finally converge on his sternum, and his breasts look like saddlebags.

With the appearance, now, of the black Mayor, we seem ready for a most welcome reheat of *Bonfire*: a smug nabob will crash and burn across the racial fault line. But here the novel lurches off in an unexpected direction – and it depresses me to have to report, for instance, that the mouthwatering duo of McNutter and Fareek will absent itself for 500 pages. Instead we meet Conrad Hensley, an entirely (and entirely improbably) wholesome young man employed as a 'product humper' or 'freezer picker' at a Croker meat-warehouse near Oakland, Calif. Charlie Croker's snap decision – 15 per cent layoffs – sets the wronged Conrad on a course that will lead him, over several chapters, to one of the greatest anti-epiphanies that American life can offer. Imagine: you're in the 'reeking lizard cage' of Santa Rita Rehab Centre, and the big ponytailed shot-caller named Rotto comes strolling across the pod room to ask you for a date. And not nicely.

All the prison stuff is so harrowing and comic and above all thorough that you feel that Wolfe, going about his famous 'research', must have voluntarily served at least a five-year term. Still, the fight with the excellent Rotto is effectively the novel's climax. Hereafter *A Man in Full* is afflicted by a strange *tristesse*. As almost invariably happens in the Big Picture narrative, the second half becomes a zestless hireling of the first. Our author has so many structural chores to get done (like the transfer of Conrad from Santa Rita to Croker's house in Buckland, Atlanta: real product-humping, this) that there's little room or energy for the incidental pleasures of Wolfe's satire. And besides, for all the scaffolding he throws up and for all the grunting menials he sets to work on it, the plot just doesn't stay standing. The destiny cobbled together for Croker is both implausible and sympathy-forfeiting. And Conrad, the other half of 'the man in full', is a 2D, for-younger-readers creation, and one sentimentally conceived.

You also have the leisure, around now, to inspect Wolfe's dependency on mannerism and iteration. 'Sullenly, sulkily, surlily, Roger sank back . . .'; 'he had suffered a dreadful, shameful, humiliating defeat'; within half-a-dozen lines a dancing girl is described as 'salacious', 'lubricious' and 'concupiscent'. Well, they're all in my thesaurus too. Later on, it occurs to Wolfe that a crowded party is like a sea; so, in ten pages, we get a 'regular Typhoon', a 'roaring sea', a 'shrieking sea', a 'roaring swell' and a 'boiling social sea' (complete with 'boiling teeth' – a steal from *Bonfire*). There would also appear to be something wrong with Wolfe's typewriter: a faulty repeater-key, perhaps. Or maybe he meant to write 'Ooooooooooo' and 'Ahhhhhhhhh' and 'Nahhhhhhhh' and 'Hmmmmmmmmmmmmm'.

In an oft-quoted manifesto for the 'new social novel' Wolfe advised writers to go easy on the inspiration and buckle down to some real 'research'. The great stories were out *there*, not in *here*; and the future of the novel lay with 'a highly detailed realism' based on journalism. Journalists, obviously, were much taken with this notion, and still use it as ammunition against more 'literary' efforts. It seems to me equally obvious, indeed tautologous, that if you take a journalistic approach then you will write a journalistic novel. In other words, local ephemera will tend to deuniversalize your prose. Tom Wolfe, with his bright architectural eye, writes so well about institutions that he forces you to compare him to his beloved Dickens. Dickens was a great visitor of institutions and no doubt he 'researched' his Marshalsea Prison, his Chancery, and so on. But he also dreamt them up, and reshaped them in the image of his own psyche, his own comic logic. That is perhaps why they have lasted and why Wolfe's edifices look more trapped in time.

Guardian November 1998

Bob Sneed Broke
the Silence

Hannibal **by Thomas Harris**

Mason Verger, the villain of Thomas Harris's *Hannibal*, is an incredibly
evil guy. Here's a thing he likes to do: he likes to get hold of one of the
'African-American children' – preferably orphans – he keeps around the
place and tell the kid horrible things. Your foster-mother doesn't love
you because your skin is too dark. Your pet, Kitty Cat, is going to hurt
and die. When the child cries, a nurse wipes the tears away and puts
'the wet swatches in Mason's martini glass, chilling in the playroom's
refrigerator beside the orange juice and Cokes'. What a terrible guy.
And what a terrible martini. To Mason Verger, though, the tears of
an African-American orphan are as sweet, and as drunk-making, at the
finest Tanqueray. That's how incredibly evil this guy is.

So ends page 66. With another 420 to come. A Harris fan from
way back, I got through the thing in the end, with many a weary
exhalation, with much dropping of the head and rolling of the
eyes, and with considerable fanning of the armpits. In evaluating a
novel with a lot of pig interest (man-eating hogs, bred for savagery)
it seems apt to bellow the assurance that *Hannibal* is, on all levels, a
snorting, rooting, oinking porker, complete with twinkling trotters
and twirlaround tail.

Try telling that to the Gadarene swine. The publication of
Hannibal back in June cut the ribbon on a festival of stupidity. In
the US the critical consensus was no more than disgracefully lenient.
In the UK, though, the reviews comprised a veritable dunciad. There
were exceptions, most of them (significantly, I think) written by
women. Elsewhere the book pages all rolled over for Dr Lecter. I

sat around reading long lists of what *Hannibal* isn't ('a great popular novel', for instance), long lists of what it doesn't do, long lists of what it never gets close to pulling off or getting away with. The eager gullibility felt sinisterly unanimous. Is this the next thing? Philistine hip? The New Inanity?

There's really not much you can say to the miserable idiots who were 'skewered' to their seats by this harpoon of unqualified kitsch. And I found I could sit still while pundits talked about Harris's 'real moral impact', how 'every line . . . is suffused with the sense of a titanic struggle with evil in its blackest form' despite the clear fact that the novel is helplessly *voulu*, sentimental, and corrupt. But when I see *Hannibal* enlisted as literature ('a plausible candidate for the Pulitzer Prize', 'a momentous achievement'), then my pen is obliged to flash from its scabbard.

At this point, Lecters I and II – *Red Dragon* (1981) and *The Silence of the Lambs* (1988) – cry out for reinspection. And they effortlessly withstand it. In these books Harris has done what all popular writers hope to do: he has created a parallel world, a terrible antiterra, airless and arcane but internally coherent. It is the world of the human raptor in the American setting (with his equipment, his weapons, his mobility), and of those who would hunt him down. Harris's subject is predacity – serial murder – but his intelligent eye is alert to its quieter manifestations. Look at this apparently incidental passage, in *Red Dragon*, which describes the career of a tabloid reporter. It has the cold satirical swing of Kurt Vonnegut:

> He started as Cancer Editor at a salary nearly double what he had earned before. Management was impressed with his attitude . . .
> Marketing surveys showed that a bold 'New Cure for Cancer' or 'Cancer Miracle Drug' cover line boosted supermarket sales of any [*National*] *Tattler* issue by 22.3 percent. There was a six-percentile drop in those sales when the story ran on page one beneath the cover line, as the reader had time to scan the empty text while the groceries were being totaled.

Marketing experts discovered it was better to have the big cover line in color on the front and play the story in the middle pages, where it was difficult to hold the paper open and manage a purse and grocery cart at the same time.

The standard story featured an optimistic five paragraphs in ten point type, then a drop to eight point, then to six point before mentioning that the 'miracle drug' was unavailable . . .

Now consider this pivotal modulation from *The Silence of the Lambs*. The scene is a rustic funeral home in the town of Potter, West Virginia, and young Clarice Starling is about to unzip a body bag containing a scalped and half-flayed 'floater' – the waterlogged corpse of a girl with waxed legs and glitter polish on her fingernails. In a few moments Clarice will get her first apprehension of the nature of the killer she hunts ('sometimes the family of a man produces, behind a human face, a mind whose pleasure is what lay on the porcelain table'). But first she must clear the room of a crowd of mumbling deputies and state troopers, asserting her slender authority. Notice how the author binds us to the victim, allowing us, through Clarice ('let me take care of her'), to mourn for the girl on the slab:

Starling took off her scarf and tied it over her hair like a mountain midwife. She took a pair of surgical gloves out of her kit. When she opened her mouth for the first time in Potter, her voice had more than its normal twang and the force of it brought Crawford to the door to listen. 'Gentlemen. Gentlemen! You officers and gentlemen! Listen here a minute. Please. Now let me take care of her.' She held her hands before their faces as she pulled on the gloves. 'There's things we need to do for her. You brought her this far, and I know her folks would thank you if they could. Now please go on out and let me take care of her.'

Hannibal Lecter, as we are often told, does what he does 'for fun' – or, more accurately, he does what he does for the hell of it. Needless to say, the books would fall apart in an instant if we thought the same were true of his creator. Lecters I and II are thrillers, procedurals of pain and panic, and they involve the reader in various simplifications and unrealities (particularly towards the endings, with all their ritual satisfactions). This is generic decorum. But Harris maintains human decorum, too. His prose is hard and sober and decently sad as he takes us to the place where the dragon bears down on the lambs.

The author's original title for *Hannibal* was, apparently, *The Morbidity of the Soul*. Well, somebody must have had a word with him about that, and they whittled it down (probably via stuff like *Hannibal and the Soul's Morbidity* and *Morbidity, the Soul and Hannibal*) to *Hannibal*, under the cover strap line (in the English edition), THE RETURN OF HANNIBAL LECTER. Now, it was an appealing notion that the serial-killer subculture – that fraternity of sweating mutes and blood-spattered inverts – should boast a lone highbrow: Hannibal, the rogue shrink, the Camus of carnage, who, I repeat, rips people up for the hell of it. But there has been a reckless reconfiguration here. A minor character in *Red Dragon* and an ensemble player in *The Silence of the Lambs*, Hannibal owns *Hannibal*. And the consequences, of which Harris seems only dimly aware, are seismic. They force our fuddled novelist into a change of tone, a change of style, and a change of genre.

As *Hannibal* opens Lecter is at large, and we catch up with him in Florence, where, ridiculously (and also boringly, therefore), he is 'translator and curator of the Capponi Library'. And shouldn't that 'of' be 'at'? Or does Lecter translate the library as well as look after it? It's possible: although Lecter created the vacancy by murdering the incumbent, 'once the way was clear he won the job fairly, demonstrating to the Belle Arti Committee an extraordinary linguistic capability, sight-translating medieval Italian and Latin from the densest Gothic black-letter manuscripts'. We see him wowing an audience of world-class scholars with a lecture that has taken him 'a little more than three minutes to organize'. Sample brilliancy: 'Avarice and hanging, then, linked since antiquity, the image appearing again and again in art.' The infallible Hannibal, by the way, thinks that the plural of 'imago' is 'imagi'. He's only human. Or is he? Meanwhile, with much heaving and clanking, the plot is preparing Lecter's 'reception committee' (the man-eating hogs) on the island of Sardinia. Drunk on the tears of African-American orphans, and bent on revenge for an earlier maiming at Lecter's hands, Mason Verger will want 'a ringside seat' when Hannibal is thrown to the reception committee.

Back in Florence, Hannibal goes about his business. You might glimpse him in the Teatro Piccolomini ('a baroque jewel box of gilt and plush'), looking down 'from a high box, alone, immaculate in white tie, his face and shirtfront seeming to float in the dark box framed by gilt baroque carving'. At home, wearing 'a quilted silk dressing gown', 'elegant, straight-backed', he sits at an 'ornate clavier': 'He plays with his eyes closed. He has no need of the sheet music.' The melody 'vibrates to silence in the great room'. 'Crossing the great hall he has no need of light. A puff of air as Dr Hannibal Lecter passes us. The great door creaks . . .' The Capponi Library's unique collection of ancient documents gives Lecter the chance to investigate his genealogy; noted forebears include Bevisangue and Machiavelli. 'While he had a certain abstract curiosity about the matter, it was not ego-related.' Everyone else's ego, of course, is measurable by conventional means, but Lecter's 'ego, like his intelligence quota, and the degree of his rationality; is not measurable by conventional means'.

A couple of murders later, the plot puts Lecter on a jumbo jet to Detroit. Harris draws our attention to the poor quality of airline food – particularly bad in economy, where our felon is compelled to ride. Lecter cannot and will not eat 'this sorry fare', 'this airline swill'. From beneath the seat in front of him he produces a lunchbox acquired from Fauchon, the Paris caterers, containing 'wonderfully aromatic truffled pâté de foie gras, and Anatolian figs still weeping from their severed stems'. He also has 'a half-bottle of a St Estephe he favors. The silk bow yields with a whisper . . .' After landing in Detroit, Lecter heads south and promptly equips himself with a nice house, a black Jag, a gourmet pantry, an arsenal, and a late-eighteenth-century Flemish harpsichord. We can tell he is settling in: 'Late in the night, his lips stained by the red Château Pétrus, a small crystal glass of honey-colored Château d'Yquem on his candle stand, Dr Lecter plays Bach.'

By now, I think, it should be clear that Lecter is of that stratospheric breed of men to whom the world is but a gout of pulp, infinitely pliable to their wants and whims. He is (in other words) that awesome presence, a European aristocrat. Supercapable, he has 'no need' of this and 'no need' of that. In fact, he has no need of 'need': Given the choice, he – and Harris – prefer to say 'require'. Dr Lecter doesn't really care how aristocratic he is because 'Dr Lecter does not require conventional reinforcement'. Out buying weapons – or rather, out 'purchasing' weapons – he tells the knife salesman, 'I only require one.' Why, I haven't felt such a frisson of sheer class since I last heard room service say 'How may I assist you?' And when Lecter is guilty of forgetfulness he says 'Bother!' – not 'Shit' or 'Fuck' like the rest of us. It's all in the details.

Lecter's pedigree is unscrolled about halfway through. His mother, although 'highborn' (Italian, 'a Visconti'), belongs to a line that sprang out of nowhere in the twelfth century. But Lecter's father was a Lithuanian count, 'title dating from the tenth century'. That's 900 and something: only a millennium ago. Why not the third century? Why not the tenth century BC? In any case the back story turns out to be a useful prop-shifter in Harris's morality play. 'Nothing happened to me, Officer Starling. I happened,' Lecter told Clarice, bracingly, in *The Silence of the Lambs*: 'You can't reduce me to a set of influences.' Clarice can't – but Harris can. Lecter, it transpires, was traumatized as a child. German panzers retreating from Russia shelled the Lecter estate, killing 'both parents and most of the servants'. Then young Hannibal's sibling, Mischa, was dragged off by starving soldiers. That will cut you some slack, won't it, having your little sister eaten by Nazis? And Harris craves our indulgence for this troubled blueblood, killer (by my reckoning) of eighteen, in his journey from villain to hero. Lecter, after all, has to deserve to get the girl.

The bloating of the Lecter figure entails, or is at any rate accompanied by, the shrivelling of Clarice Starling. Throughout, Harris writes about her without the faintest quickening of authorial love; having gone gay for Hannibal, the author has palpably wearied of Clarice, whose main function in this novel is one of humble plot-furtherance. Look at the chores he gives her ('A chrome padlock and chain secured the gate. No sweat there. Starling looked up and down the road. Nobody coming. *A little illegal entry here*'), look at the perceptions he coarsely saddles her with ('[The woman's] cornsilk hair had receded enough to make Starling wonder if she took steroids and had to tape her clitoris down'), look at the jokes he has her crack ('*Paul*, I have to tell you, the Apostle *Paul* . . . hated women too. He should have been named *Appal*'). Following the riot of paceless implausibilities that serves as the book's climax, Hannibal and Clarice ecstatically elide. What is the more incredible, at this point: that Clarice should actually go off with the murdering bastard or that Hannibal would cross the street for such a charmless little rube? (It's hard to think what woman would be capable of diverting Hannibal for more than five seconds. Mata Hari? Baroness Orczy? Catherine the Great?) By exchanging a few platitudes, the two orphans succeed in 'curing' each other. Then comes the moment with the firelight 'dancing in the golden wine' – and the sub-Faulkner high style of a strong man quaking over his ThinkPad. Let's see if I can bear to type this out (note, towards the end, the Joycean word-ordering)

'Hannibal Lecter, did your mother feed you at her breast?' . . . Clarice Starling reached her cupped hand into the deep neckline of her gown and freed her breast, quickly peaky in the open air. 'You don't have to give up this one,' she said. Looking always into his eyes with her trigger finger she took warm Château d'Yquem from her mouth and a thick sweet drop suspended from her nipple like a golden cabochon [some kind of gem] and trembled with her breathing.

He came swiftly from his chair to her, went on a knee before her chair, and bent to her coral and cream in the firelight his dark sleek head.

We last glimpse the 'handsome couple' three years later, in Buenos Aires. Handel's *Tamerlane* is playing at the Teatro Colón. Jewels 'winked'. A Mercedes Maybach 'whispered to the curb'. You'll have to stop minding about the tenses here, because Harris switches freely from past to present, sometimes in the same paragraph. During intermission in their 'ornate box', 'the gentleman took a champagne flute from a waiter's tray and handed it to the lady . . .' And after the show the Mercedes 'purrs' off and 'disappears into the courtyard of an exquisite Beaux Arts building near the French Embassy'. How does it go for them – for Count and Countess Lecter? Us scum, of course, are given only a few tantalizing glimpses. Clarice often talks Italian at mealtimes ('She finds a curious freedom in the visual nuances of the language'). Hannibal is committed to the daily 'penetration of Clarice Starling, which she avidly welcomes and encourages'. Ah, but now Harris tastefully withdraws, murmuring in gnomic valediction, 'We can only learn so much and live.' In *The Silence of the Lambs*, when Clarice began her interviews with the caged cannibal, the *National Tattler*, that vicious slur-sheet, called her the 'BRIDE OF FRANKENSTEIN!!' It is a symmetry, of a sort, that Harris should work himself around to giving that headline flesh.

'Beautifully written . . . the webs of imagery that Harris has so carefully woven . . . contains writing of which our best writers would be proud . . . there is not a single ugly or dead sentence . . .' – or so sang the critics. *Hannibal* is a genre novel, and all genre novels contain dead sentences – unless you feel the throb of life in such periods as 'Tommaso put the lid back on the cooler' or 'Eric Pickford answered' or 'Pazzi worked like a man possessed' or 'Margot laughed in spite of herself' or 'Bob Sneed broke the silence'. What these commentators and literary editors must be thinking of, I suppose, are the bits when Harris goes all blubbery and portentous (every other phrase a spare tyre), or when, with a fugitive poeticism, he swoons us into a dying fall: 'Starling looked for a moment through the wall, past the wall, out to forever and composed herself . . .' 'It seemed forever ago . . .' 'He looked deep, deep into her eyes . . .' 'His dark eyes held her whole . . .' Needless to say, Harris has become a serial murderer of English sentences, and *Hannibal* is a necropolis of prose.

With the change of genre, from procedural thriller to gothic fantasy, all internal coherence is lost. That this loss has been widely indulged and even welcomed by the critics is perhaps not very surprising, because vanished coherence is also a feature of the world of the literary middleman. There is a levelling impulse at work. To put it simply, the book-chat mediocrities have had it with the hierarchy of the talents. In promoting the genre novelist (Tom Wolfe is another candidate, though a much worthier one), they demote his mainstream counterpart, and doing this has long been their pleasure and solace. Meanwhile, the general reader can I think be trusted to tire of the new Lecter and sense the tawdriness of the snobbo sadist with his smoking jacket, his ascot, and his sneer of cold command.

It is additionally intriguing to see Harris touted as a populist, championing the honest demand for a good read. Because in *Hannibal* he severs himself from the commonalty, and it is precisely this severance that has demolished his talent. Moving through the crowd, Lecter 'presses a scented handkerchief to his face', and so, these days, does Harris. Lecter squirms in the purgatory of the 747, and so does Harris, grossed out by the snarling tourist, the whining child, the reeking baby. 'Look at this crowd,' he writes (the scene is 'The Mid-Atlantic Regional Gun and Knife Show'): 'scruffy, squinty, angry, egg-bound, truly of the resinous heart'. (Vintage Harris: what does 'of the resinous heart' mean, truly, and what does 'egg-bound' even think it means?) The author of *Red Dragon* and *The Silence of the Lambs* would have looked at that crowd and told us interesting things about it. Harris has relinquished the connection – the line that connects him and us and Clarice Starling and the girl on the porcelain slab. So maybe it all works out in the end. Only by turning his back on the vulgar could Thomas Harris write a novel of such profound and virtuoso vulgarity.

Talk September 1999

Vladimir Nabokov

Life

Nabokov: His Life in Part by Andrew Field

Writers are now accorded their biographies whether or not anything ever happened to them, on the principle – and surely it is a long-exploded one – that such studies help explain why they wrote what they wrote. E.M. Forster, for instance, whose ninety-one years were chiefly remarkable for being utterly devoid of incident, is the current beneficiary of a two-volume life – and a life that will no doubt be rewritten many times.

But things *did* happen to Vladimir Nabokov, and this fact is among the pleasing eccentricities of the present book. His was a life of quixotic, almost novelettish, glamour, often farcical, often tragic, often (and this is a genre more appropriate to his fiction) sublime. Nabokov, of course, regarded cliché as the key to bad art, yet it is an attractive irony that bad art is what his life so frequently resembles. His first biographer frequently abets this impression – though the bad art Mr Field aspires to is not the cheap romance so much as the expensive psychological 'dialogue'.

Nabokov's family was one of the most opulent in pre-revolutnary Russia: wealthy, ancient, aristocratic (Mr Field goes on at surreal length about all this), and so talented that anything short of national celebrity would have classified any Nabokov as a dunce and a sluggard. The author's grandfather was Minister of Justice under tsars Alexander II and III. His household was cultured, serious, enlightened: 'it was French at the table, English in the nursery, and Russian elsewhere'. Nabokov's father, a prominent liberal in the Provisional Government (and especially disliked by Trotsky), was so 'European' that he sent his shirts to London to be laundered.

Count Tolstoy tousled the young Vladimir's hair. Mandelstam

gave readings at his school. While in his teens, Nabokov inherited an independent fortune of one million roubles. He had some poems privately printed and began to chase girls, becoming something of a man about St Petersburg. His older hussar-poet friends were already eagerly getting killed in the White Army.

Bolshevik troops fired at the boat in which Nabokov and family fled the Crimea in 1919. They never returned. From the affluence of unfallen Russia, the Nabokovs uncomplainingly accepted the trite privations of exile. Vladimir had three years, and several more romances, at Trinity College, Cambridge (Mr Field is desperately uncertain of his tone in this chapter), before leaving for the *émigré* mecca, Berlin. It was here that Nabokov's father was shot dead at a meeting, as he attempted to shield his political rival from an anarchist's bullet.

Here, too, Nabokov set about writing his Russian novels, earning a living as a tutor: his subjects, characteristically, were English, French, boxing, tennis and prosody. He married a Russian Jewess, Véra Evseevna, the dedicatee of all his novels, who now survives him in Montreux. They lived as quietly as one could in Weimar Germany (the world of Herr Issyvoo *et al.* Nabokov describes as 'the acme of vulgarity'). Jews were being terrorized and beaten up in the streets by the time the Nabokovs moved on, in disgust and some fear, to Paris in 1937. Nabokov's brother Sergei, a homosexual, later died in a Nazi concentration camp.

In Paris Nabokov's reputation started to grow beyond *émigré* cliques, which were anyway dispersing by this time. There was much insecurity and bickering, and if people behaved badly Nabokov tended to challenge them to duels. Joyce heard him give a talk, and they had an inconclusive meeting. The *Wehrmacht*, however, had followed them from Germany. It was only an unsolicited 'loan' from Rachmaninov that allowed the Nabokovs to flee, yet again, as France fell. They sailed to America on the last Jewish-organized relief ship; the name of Nabokov's father (he was a famous foe of anti-Semitism) probably secured their berths. In America, the *émigrés* became mere immigrants, and they struggled. Academic and literary success accrued gradually. After the somewhat hesitant appearance of *Lolita* (its English publication was evidently discussed in

Cabinet), the Nabokovs repaired to their luxurious twilight in a hotel on Lac Léman – where the book ends.

It begins there too, for this is no tamely sequential biography. Mr Field opens with a longish, first-hand evocation of the aged Nabokovs ensconced in their Montreux hotel. The sketch is raffishly new-journalistic in style, tricked out in bold type, with Field trying hard to be elliptical and sly and generally Nabokovian. But the chapter has a genuine if fortuitous charm. Nabokov himself comes over engagingly enough – affectionate, mercurial, a compulsive tipper of the hotel staff, powerfully anxious about 'how things will look' in Mr Field's probing opus.

The real fun, though, resides in the spectacle of Field being shoved round the board by the old Grandmaster. Every now and then Field realizes Nabokov is twitting him, and sulkily admits that he sulked about it at the time. On other occasions, however, he is simply the chronicler of his own obtuseness. My favourite example involves the discussion of a rumour (later discredited in the text) that Nabokov's father was the product of a grand-maternal fling with Tsar Alexander II. 'Yes, sometimes I feel the blood of Peter the Great in me,' says Nabokov, as the biographer's Grundig whirrs credulously on.

'Do you know this man now?' Field asks in his cute 'Conclusion'. No, not really. But it's a start: you certainly get more of the man from Mr Field's pages than you get from *Speak, Memory*, Nabokov's deliberately oblique and stylized autobiography. At one point in Chapter 1 Nabokov mildly insults Mr Field over some aspect of his procedure. Field then observes: 'There are ways (and I am not thinking now of his many virtues and attributes) in which I am too much like Vladimir Nabokov to judge him.' Perhaps it's just as well that Nabokov had this brooding, self-satisfied presence as the receptacle for his official confidences. Anyone else would have been a nervous wreck within half an hour. *Nabokov: His Life in Part* performs a service, if only as a pre-emptive strike. It is bold and enthusiastic, and, despite Field's best efforts, seldom very boring.

Observer August 1977

Lectures

Lectures on Literature by Vladimir Nabokov.
Edited by Fredson Bowers

Reading is a skill: you have to be taught how to do it. Here is some fatherly Nabokovian advice.

You must not 'identify' with Stephen Dedalus or Fanny Price; you must not regard *Madame Bovary* as a denunciation of the bourgeoisie or *Bleak House* as an attack on the legal system; you must not ransack novels in search of those bloated topicalities, 'ideas'. The only things that a good reader needs are imagination, memory, a dictionary and some artistic sense. At this point the good teacher will lean forward and remind his students that he is using the word *reader* very loosely. 'Curiously enough, one cannot read a book: one can only reread it.'

Reading is an art, and Vladimir Nabokov did it to perfection. Collected here are roughly half the lectures which Nabokov delivered to his fortunate students at Wellesley and Cornell from 1941 to 1958. They have been cobbled together by Fredson Bowers – a task calling for fanatical meticulousness, if the reproductions of Nabokov's frenzied lecture notes are anything to go by. Professor Bowers also reproduces such enjoyable teaching aids as Nabokov's groundplan of Mansfield Park, his map of Joyce's Dublin, and his drawing of Charles Bovary's layered cap ('a pathetic and tasteless affair'). The present volume contains two general pieces and seven long discourses on masterworks of European fiction; a subsequent volume, it is hoped, will show how Nabokov tackled the Russians. In every sense, the project is a delightful monument to literary rediscovery.

One would call Nabokov's teaching method idiosyncratic if

it weren't so unswervingly true to its models. Not surprisingly, Nabokov treats with contempt the schools-and-movements, myth-decoding, fallacy-mongering constructs of the Eng-Lit racket. He negotiates his chosen books with the confidence, coolness and superlegitimacy of the fellow practitioner. The professorial impulse is to pontificate or generalize. Nabokov never does this. He is, above all, robustly unacademic.

At first, Nabokov's approach seems crude and old-fashioned, even perfunctory. He certainly had a patronizing way with him, no doubt for sound reasons. According to John Updike's introduction, which does much to establish the air of pedagogic raillery that wafts through the lectures, Nabokov would open his course with the words: 'All satisfied with their seats? Okay. No talking, no smoking, no knitting, no newspaper reading, no sleeping, and for God's sake take notes.' He would then proceed to startle and goad the earnest and morose, briskly crushing their fashionable and half-baked preconceptions. Similarly, his end-of-term exam-questions merely prompt the pupils to regurgitate the master's ideas ('Discuss Flaubert's use of the word "and"').

As an explicator, Nabokov used the Granville-Barker method – i.e., the most dramatic and least sophisticated. It is the linear approach. Nabokov marches us through the text, often doing no more than telling us the story, quoting at great length, sometimes haring off on strange errands, asides, whimsies. 'Jefferson in this country had just passed the Embargo Act . . . (If you read *embargo* backwards, you get "O grab me").' Or, in his essay on *Swann's Way*: 'Incidentally, the first homosexuals in modern literature are described in *Anna Karenina*, namely in chapter nineteen, part two.' The manner is relaxed, amused, coltish – and apparently very narrow. There is no standing back from the novels under discussion.

One comes to realize, however, that Nabokov's plot-summaries, with their emphasis on patterning and local effects, have in their way an immaculate decorum: they perfectly recreate the tone and ironic distance of the original. Nabokov is hilariously damning about Homais in *Madame Bovary*, humouringly protective about sickly Fanny in *Mansfield Park*; his summary of Kafka's *Metamorphosis* is

250

almost unbearably inward, with Nabokov the lepidopterist indulging a special tenderness for the tranformed Gregor:

> Curiously enough, Gregor the beetle never found out that he had wings under the hard covering of his back ... Gregor, though now a very sick beettle – the apple wound is festering, and he is starving – finds some beetle pleasure in crawling among all that dusty rubbish.

Nabokov makes the same kind of pure and unfastidious response when he defends the death scene of Jo the Roadsweeper in *Bleak House* against the charge of sentimentality: 'I want to submit that people who denounce the sentimental are generally unaware of what sentiment is.' As Nabokov has explained earlier, the fit reader does not read with his brain or his heart but with his back, waiting for 'the telltale tingle between the shoulder-blades'.

Most literary criticism tends to point beyond literature towards something else. It points towards marxism, or sociology, or philosophy, or semiotics – or even life, that curious commodity to which Dr Leavis always stressed his commitment. Nabokov points to the thing itself, the art itself, trying to make us 'share not the emotions of the people in the book but the emotions of its author'. He wanted to teach people how to read. In addition, and perhaps unconsciously, he attempted to instil a love of literature by the simple means of revealing his own love. Nabokov's remark about Emma Bovary's reading habits has the right cadence of grateful solemnity:

> Flaubert uses the same artistic trick when listing Homais's vulgarities. The subject may be crude and repulsive. Its expression is artistically modulated and balanced. This is style. This is art. This is the only thing that really matters in books.

Observer January 1981

Plays

The Man from the USSR and Other Plays by Vladimir Nabokov.
Translated and introduced by Dmitri Nabokov

> I detest the theatre as being a primitive and putrid form, historically
> speaking; a form that smacks of stone-age rites and communal
> nonsense despite those individual injections of genius, such as, say,
> Elizabethan poetry, which a closeted reader automatically pumps
> out of the stuff.

This is not Nabokov speaking: it is Humbert Humbert, in *Lolita*,
and Humbert has special reasons for despising the drama. His young
girlfriend wants to perform in the school play (*The Enchanted Hunters*),
thus bringing her into close contact with boys her own age, an
activity classed by Humbert as 'absolutely forbidden' as opposed
to 'reluctantly allowed'. And, of course, it is the author of *The
Enchanted Hunters*, Clare Quilty, who deprives Humbert of his own
enchantress, little Lo. Humbert, then, is a special case. But I think
that he would have despised the drama anyway – with Nabokov's
unqualified approval.

The Man from the USSR is essentially a collection of fascinating
juvenilia, or rather marginalia. Like the childish home-carpentry of
a major sculptor, the book shows an artist dabbling in an inferior and
limited form, before going on to find his proper niche elsewhere.
Satisfyingly, the volume closes with two fierce and brilliant essays on
the paltriness of dramatic art, written around 1940 (i.e., fifteen years
before *Lolita*). At this stage, Nabokov's contempt for the theatre is
coming along very healthily.

Of the four plays collected here, the title piece is by far the most
successful, partly because it is set in a living milieu: *émigré* Berlin in the

Twenties, a world of crummy boarding-houses, straitened gentility, of titled barmen and landowners turned pub landlords. Through the action saunters Kuznetsoff, the man from the USSR, a splendidly unattractive creation. Ugly, brusque, mean and charmless, a man without qualities, he is none the less mystically revered by the entire *dramatis personae*, cowing the men and causing hot flushes of arousal in the women.

Why? Because the featureless, cheerfully blaspheming Kuznetsoff is an Evolved Being, a man of the twentieth century, while the huddled *émigrés* – with all their emotion and delicacy – feel themselves to be meaningless remnants of a vanished age. Kuznetsoff's position vis-à-vis the new regime is ambiguous, but he has certainly come to terms with the faceless USSR, and is free to return to it when he pleases. The pining exiles in Berlin would give anything to set foot on Russian soil, if only to dig their own graves there. Kuznetsoff is their Messiah – a false one, needless to say. 'I am a very busy man,' as he characteristically points out. 'To tell you the truth, I don't even have the time to say I am a busy man.'

'The Man from the USSR' is suggestive and neatly arranged, and impressively coolly handled by a writer still in his twenties. That said, the only bit of *writing* in the entire play appears in the stage directions. 'To the left . . . a wide passageway crowded with movie props, creating an effect reminiscent simultaneously of a photographer's waiting room, the jumble of an amusement-park booth, and the motley corner of a futurist's canvas.' The reader suddenly thinks: now you're writing. Now you're writing *prose*. Nabokov is indeed a loving set-dresser, but only at moments such as this can he dress the page with literature.

Two of the other three pieces are fragmentary attempts to escape, by traditional means, the pokiness and gloom of the prose drama: they are verse dramas, one an elegy for Scott's quest in the Antarctic, one a tranced fable set in post-revolutionary France, in which an aristocrat encounters his thwarted guillotinist. These are 'adjective' plays as opposed to 'verb' plays (in the terminology with which Nabokov later acquaints us), florid-static as opposed to slender-mobile. They proceed restfully enough, and show the dormant traces of later themes

– as Dmitri Nabokov notes in his typically affectionate yet rigorous introduction. But they are cloudy trophies, with little real affect. After all, we have Eliot's example to prove that a play's unplayability is no guarantee that it will be any fun to read.

The longest and proportionately least enjoyable effort is called 'The Event' and is strictly speaking a non-event, since the villain never appears. But it's a very verbal affair none the less, in the coming-and-going, fetching-and-carrying sense that passes for dramatic action. Nabokov composed or at any rate completed 'The Event' rather later on, in 1938, by which time he had such masterful novels as *The Defence* and *Laughter in the Dark* well behind him. It is pretty much his last entanglement with the drama; in its cacophony and chaos we see his final exhaustion with – and of – the theatrical form.

In a spirit of shared relief, then, we come to the two essays that round off the book. Here Nabokov flatly states the obvious truth: 'The most popular plays of yesterday are on the level of the worst novels of yesterday. The best plays of today are on the level of magazine stories and fat bestsellers.' And the reasons for this are obvious too – the fatigue and artificiality of dramatic conventions, together with the insidious reliance on market forces (and just *look* at those market forces, out on Broadway and Shaftesbury Avenue). Kicking off with Aeschylus, Nabokov conducts a murderous parade from which very few individuals escape summary court martial. Chekhov, Gogol maybe, some Shaw, a little Ibsen, and that's about it.

Oh yes. And Shakespeare. The fact that Shakespeare should have been, of all things, a *dramatist* is one of the great cosmic jokes of all time – as if Mozart has spent his entire career as second wash-board or string-twanger in some Salzburg skiffle group. (It is also a deft confirmation that Shakespeare is an exception to every conceivable rule.) The bottom line, as impresarios say, is as follows. In submitting a play for production or publication the writer relinquishes his artefact in the equivalent of note form. All he has done is finished the dialogue; and, as any novelist knows, compared to the other exertions of fiction, the demands of dialogue are negligible. The drama duly failed to detain Nabokov for more than a fraction of his creative life. He had better things to do: dreaming up Humbert Humbert, for example, and all his sound and strong opinions.

Observer 24 February 1985

Letters

Vladimir Nabokov: Selected Letters 1940–1977
edited by Dmitri Nabokov and Matthew J. Bruccoli

I assume we all have more or less shameful fantasies about our best-loved writers. We meet them, in our heads – and everything works out fine. Indeed, we become our favourites' favourites. These mental thank-you notes are, of course, composed entirely of clichés. For instance, the sightless eyes of Borges brim with tears as we entrance him with our readings from Kipling; we out-drink Joyce in the bars of Paris; after an hour with us, J.D. Salinger is rueing his reclusive ways. The dream day with Vladimir Nabokov would include successful butterfly-hunts and doughty tussles at the chessboard, and so on. But here, even fantasy quails. Even in the daydream, we are speechless with humility and nerves. For the snorting wizard of Montreux is perhaps the most personally intimidating of our modern masters. As a distinguished Jewish writer said of V.S. Naipaul: 'One glance from him, and I reckoned I could skip Yom Kippur.'

It is clear from this delightful book that Nabokov was a delightful man: loyal, generous, affectionate, and wonderfully funny. I am obliged to claim, however, that this was clear already, and not only from the three earlier books in which he addresses us without the formal indirection of art. *Speak, Memory*, the volume of autobiography, is in fact the least revealing, because the most artistic: it traces the formation of the talent, not the personality. In *Strong Opinions*, the collection of interviews and utterances, Nabokov is often at home but seldom out of uniform: the full-dress iconoclast. Vivid intimacy begins with *The Nabokov–Wilson Letters, 1940–1971*, a two-handed tragi-comedy in which Vladimir steadily outsoars the limited, custodial and fatally envious Edmund.

The new *Selected Letters* brings depth and detail to the human picture. Those who are generally unsympathetic to the Nabokovian voice will succeed in finding plenty to be unsympathetic to here: some preciosity, some ferocity, much superbity, awkward political views, and cordial relations with *Playboy*. He was proud, and proudly private; the getting-to-know-him period was evidently lengthy, and he relied on family, not friendship. But the true fan will experience this book as a massive and triumphant confirmation: a confirmation of the virtues and powers that shine through every page Nabokov wrote. Every page, even the most devastating, the cruellest, the saddest.

As in *Nabokov–Wilson*, the narrative begins with the family's dazed arrival in America. After the panic and lawlessness of Europe, 'Our normal everyday existence, in contrast, seems the height of luxury, like some millionaire's coarse dream . . . it is embarrassing to repose – as I do now – on a blanket in a meadow amid tall grass and flowers . . .' Memories of Europe – where, for example, Nabokov lost his brother Sergei ('Poor, poor Seryozha . . . !') – must be left to ferment, as this very distinguished and entirely anonymous re-*émigré* sets about assembling a second career, in a second language. The process proved to be far from effortless.

The second language, of course, advanced with thrilling rapidity. Even its exoticisms seem apropos: 'involve me into difficulties', 'understand in what a ridiculous position I am', 'I do not have the gift of gab'. But the second career just kept on not coming. He was 'absolutely pennyless [*sic*]' in 1957, after seventeen years of fanatical labour. Although quite free of self-pity, or complaint, the letters give the odd hint of dissimulated desperation: 'Have you tried to get any of the so-called "book clubs" interested . . . ? I am told one can make quite a bit of money that way.' Those groping inverted commas might as well have gone around the word 'money'. Colossal, health-sapping expenditures of energy were repaid in dribs and drabs. Nabokov often – and brilliantly – compared his labour to a mother's trials. After finishing *Gogol*: 'I would like to see the Englishman who could write a book on Shakespeare in Russian. I am very weak, smiling a weak smile, as I lie in my private maternity ward, and expect roses.' After finishing *Bend Sinister*: 'I repose like a brand-new mother bathed in lace, with slightly damp skin, so tender and pale that all the freckles show, with a baby in a cradle beside me, his face the colour of an inner tube.'

Nabokov's critical, pivotal years came in the mid-1950s. *Lolita*, first mentioned here in 1951 (and to Wilson in 1947), seemed to be unpublishable; so did *Pnin* (perhaps his most accessible masterpiece); and so did his massive *Eugene Onegin*. He was still teaching, reviewing, translating (Lermontov into English, *Speak, Memory* into Russian). And he owed his bank $800. The vindication, when it came, was sudden and lasting. By 1959 he had given up academic life (and was exchanging telegrams with Stanley Kubrick); by 1961 he was a permanent resident of Switzerland and more particularly of the Montreux-Palace Hotel. 'But all this ought to have happened thirty years ago,' he notes, sparely. Nabokov was now liberated – for more focused labour. In 1975 he was, as always, 'overwhelmed with work', and remained ecstatically productive until his death. Intransigent dedication: this was his mission and his meaning. He gave it – and he gave us – everything he had.

In these *Letters* too: the book contains hardly a sentence that isn't droll, delicate, precise and alerting. Even the chores and quotidiana of the literary life are freshly painted by Nabokov's unwearying responsiveness. He comes across a publisher ('an American millionaire with a splendid boil on his nape'), a literary agent ('a short, fearsome, bandy-legged woman, her hair dyed an indecent red'), an ingrate biographer ('Dear Mr Field, Your ignoble letter of July 9 . . .'), an inept illustrator ('the title-page butterfly . . . is as meaningless . . . as would be a picture of a tuna fish on the jacket of *Moby Dick*'), an editor angling for a puff: 'Let me thank you, or not thank you, for Harry Matthews' *The Conversions*. It is a shapeless little heap of pretentious nonsense.' Mr Matthews is at least in good (and numerous) company, along with the 'big fakes' Thomas Mann ('that quack') and T.S. Eliot ('disgusting and second-rate'), Pound ('a venerable fraud'), Paul Bowles ('devoid of talent') and Saul Bellow ('a miserable mediocrity').

Edmund Wilson thought Nabokov had a weakness for 'malicious humor'. Later, in *Upstate*, the accusation hardened into one of

'Schadenfreude'. Nabokov was calmly aware of the tendency. As he wrote to an editor: 'The "unpleasant" quality of Chapter 2 is a special trait of my work in general; you just did not notice in Chapter 1 the same nastiness, the same "realism," and the same pathos.' These qualities are part of a unifying intensity and extravagance: an absolute trust in style ('For me "style" is matter'). To his absent wife Véra: 'The eastern side of every minute of mine is already colored by the light of our impending meeting. All the rest is dark, boring, you-less.' To his sister Elena (the theme here is parental love, and how children seem to stay the same even as they grow): 'See – you must grab and hold in the fist of your soul everything about Zhikochka today: that way it will all shine through him, too, for a long time.'

This book is bound by parental love: the love between its author and its co-editor and part-translator, Dmitri Nabokov – Mitya, or Mityusha, or Mityenka, or Mityushenka, or Dmitrichko. Their love is very full and very open, and very Russian to our Western ears. Dmitri evolves from 'the little one', with his 'forty-degree' fevers, into a preposterously capable adult (racing driver, mountaineer, opera singer), but he is always the cause of patient concern: 'It is very unhealthy for us to worry like this (we are 120 years old), and we simply cannot understand why you don't understand this.' Nabokov's life, with its double exile, its obsessiveness, its integrity, has a romantic coloration to it, and there is something cleanly artistic in its shape. It is harrowingly appropriate, then, that the book should conclude with his last letter to his son, which begins 'My dearest', and itself concludes: 'I hug you, I'm proud of you, be well, my beloved.'

Independent on Sunday February 1990

Lolita's Little Sister

The Enchanter by Vladimir Nabokov.
Translated by Dmitri Nabokov

Nabokov variously referred to *Volshebnik* (*The Enchanter*) as 'a proto-type' of *Lolita*, 'a kind of pre-*Lolita* novella', 'a dead scrap' and 'a beautiful piece of Russian prose'. The long short story had to wait twenty years before it fulminated into the famous novel, and another thirty before its triumphant resuscitation. *The Enchanter* is quite a discovery. After this, 1987 will be all downhill.*

What exactly do the two works share? Elements of the same obsession, one or two crucial joists in the plotting, a verbal surface of the highest tautness and burnish. But as reading experiences they remain sharply distinct. You read *Lolita* sprawling limply in your chair, ravished, overcome, nodding scandalized assent. You read *The Enchanter* on the edge of your seat, squirming with fearful admiration and constant resistance; you are always saying no, no, no. *Lolita* is comedy, subversive yet divine: somehow, it describes an ascent. Whereas *The Enchanter* is a moral horror story, the last twching of a dead soul.

The man is fortyish, like Humbert. He is a jeweller: 'There were numbers here, and colors, and entire crystal systems.' At the outset, some pathos accrues to his shadowy presence – an inert haunter of public parks, dodging little thunderbolts, as the girls play: 'and tomorrow a different one would flash by, and thus, in a succession of disappearances, his life would pass'.

Like Lolita, the girl is twelve. Her effect on him is immediate:

---

* This review appeared on 4 January. See, in due course, the essay on *Lolita*, pp. 471–90.

'suddenly you are traveling through the dust on your back, banging the back of your head, on your way to being strung up by your insides'. But it is not passion that emboldens him, only circumstance, a glimpse of the possible laxity of future events. The world will have to let it happen. He befriends the girl's mother (a widow), who is promisingly sickly and may have only a year to live. He forms a plan, or he lets it form, or it forms itself.

In *Lolita*, however inadvertently, Lolita is the enchantress. Here, the ravisher assumes that role — or he tries. In fact he enchants nobody except himself. For all its lucidity, the world of *The Enchanter* is affectless, morally dead. The main characters are nameless (though this is done so artfully that you scarcely notice); the settings of time and place (the Thirties, Paris and Provence) are unimportant, indeed drearily incidental. *Lolita* is, among other things, a landscape novel, satirically fixed in its period. The turpitude of *The Enchanter*, it seems, can happen anywhere, at any time. Unlike Humbert, with his crooner's mug, his 'ad-eyebrows', his 'striking if somewhat brutal good looks', the enchanter is quite faceless, except when he leers; he is just subtly sub-human. And the girl has nothing but her ordinary innocence, her freshness, her brandnewness.

Grimly the enchanter courts the girl's ailing mother. He listens 'to the epic of her malady'; he makes 'mooing sounds of consolation' and false tenderness; he 'wordlessly compresses or applies to his tense jowl her ominously obedient hand'. Ironically, in the fairytale scheme of the story, she is the 'monster', with her hairless wart, her cold brow, her surgeons' scars, seemingly pregnant 'with her own death'. On their wedding night, the enchanter bluffs and stalls; yet 'in the middle of his farewell speeches about his migraine' he suddenly finds himself next to 'the corpse of the miraculously vanquished giantess'. The successful copulation, with its dire presentiment, occurs only once. Soon, the wife is dead for real, and the enchanter is heading south for the union with his little princess.

Only at this point does he fully immerse himself in his sexual plans for the girl. 'The lone wolf was getting ready to don Granny's nightcap.' These four pages of drooling reverie — and they have a radiant ghastliness — constitute the enchanter's inexpiable moral trespass: salacious, savage and *sentimental*. And it is for this, rather than for the actual molestation, that the enchanter is so roundly punished. The sexual spasm is still cooling on his mackintosh when he receives his spectacular and sanguinary retribution. Thrice-orphaned, the girl is left behind, as she was always left behind, humanly unregarded.

Many readers may find the moral starkness of *The Enchanter* somewhat Russian Orthodox, when set against the decadent complexity of *Lolita*. Certainly it belongs to Nabokov's Berlin period, more specifically to the line of antic cruelty which runs from *King, Queen, Knave* to *Despair*. In any event it is a little masterpiece, witheringly precise and genuinely shocking. Special praise must go to the translator. It may be that Nabokov's death has paradoxically liberated his sometime collaborator, for *The Enchanter* is seamlessly Nabokovian.

The evident persistence of the nympholepsy theme is striking, but only because the theme is striking. It is no more persistent than Nabokov's interest in doubles, mirrors, chess, paranoia – and much less persistent than his interest in the *artiste manqué*, with which, however, it is importantly connected. *Lolita* has a redemptive shape. As narrator, Humbert gives us something, in propitiation: he gives us the damned book. He also gives us the full moral accounting of this sombre theme. The crime is great; the invoice of guilt is detailed; and it took the later, 'older' book to make a final balance of the figures. As in an American hospital, every tear-stained pillowslip, every scrap of soiled paper tissue, has eventually to be answered for.

Observer January 1987

Some American Prose

Mailer's Lows and Highs

The Essential Mailer by Norman Mailer

Norman Mailer's new book bears all the signs – all the watermarks, all the heraldry – of a writer faced with an alimony bill of $500,000 a year. Two separate and elderly chunks of Mailer's oeuvre have been whittled down and stuck together, then entrusted to NEL, one of our less-exalted hardback dealerships. The book incorporates stories, essays, verse translations, letters (to and from the author), reviews (by and of same), interviews, speeches, extracts, oddments, and lots of misprints. The front cover features the second-worst photograph of Mailer ever published: in a V-necked singlet, Mailer stares sweatily out over the top rope of a boxing ring. The worst photograph of Mailer ever published appeared on the front cover of the American edition of *Why Are We in Vietnam?* (1967): it showed Mailer sporting a big black eye.

Certainly, Mailer can be made to look ridiculous without recourse to visual aids – and without recourse to his busy history of high-profile fiasco (his sponsorship of the murderer and wordsmith Jack Henry Abbott is the latest in a long line). No one in the history of the written word, not even William MacGonagall or Spike Milligan or D.H. Lawrence, is so wide open to damaging quotation. Try this, more or less at random: 'A murderer in the moment of his murder could feel a sense of beauty and perfection as complete as the transport of a saint.' Or this: '*Film is a phenomenon whose resemblance to death has been ignored for too long.*' His italics.

On every page Mailer will come up with a formulation both grandiose and crass. This is expected of him. It is also expected of the reviewer to introduce a lingering 'yet' or 'however' at some point, and say that 'somehow' Mailer's 'fearless honesty' redeems his notorious excesses. He isn't frightened of sounding outrageous;

he isn't frightened of making a fool of himself; and, above all, he isn't frightened of being boring. Well, fear has its uses. Perhaps he ought to be a little less frightened of being frightened.

Mailer thinks on his feet and writes off the top of his head. His prose is dotted with gear-changes, premise-shifts, rallying-cries from the ringside: no, yes, okay, strike it like this, see here, look further, good, wrong, say it better. If every writer has a private mental thesaurus, a slim volume of key word-clusters, then Mailer's would read as follows: ego, bitch, blood, obscenity, psyche, hip, soul, tears, risk, dare, danger, death. Especially death. Film reminds Mailer of death because everything reminds Mailer of death, danger, dare, etc. 'One kissed the devil indeed,' says Mailer. What is he writing about? Prizefighting? Crossing the road? 'Brutal-coarse, intimate, snide, grasping, groping, slavering . . .' It turns out that Mailer is writing about book-reviewing. But then he does tend to take things personally.

He writes scathingly about the New York theatre, and the average Broadway audience: 'This liberal complacent materialistic greedy pill-ridden anxiety-laden bored miserable and powerless jumble of suburban couples . . . dying to be manipulated.' There is some rough justice in this snarl; but really Mailer is in a vengeful frazzle about his own play, *The Deer Park*, which is busy failing downtown. (His *movie* 'evolved into the foulest-mouthed movie ever made, and is thus vastly contemporary and profoundly underground'.)

It is the same with poetry. It is the same with politics, and everything else our 'Renaissance man' dabbles in. The devastating paradox of Mailer's life and work is that this pampered superbrat, this primal-scream specialist and tantrum expert, this brawler, loudmouth and much-televised headline-grabber, suffers from a piercing sense of *neglect*. When running for mayor of New York in the late Sixties (on a platform resembling a gallows, or a stocks), Mailer contended that 'literary men . . . would know how to talk to the people – they would be forced to govern by the fine art of the voice'. On the next page we are offered one of Mailer's mayoralty speeches, an example of the lulling accents of suasion:

You're not my friend if you interrupt me when I am talking 'cause
it just breaks into the mood in my mind. So fuck you, too. All right,

I said you're all a bunch of spoiled kids . . . I'll tell you that, I'll tell you that. You've been sittin' around jerkin' off, havin' your jokes for twenty-two years. Yeah!

And he still can't understand why he came nowhere in the race.

'For every lion of our human species there is . . . a trough of pigs, and the pigs root up everything good.' Or, in 'verse': 'You pic the bull back / far back along his spine . . . You will saw the horns off / and murmur / . . . ah, the bulls are not / what once they were.' The lone lion, the wounded, goaded bull – why should the aged eagle stretch its wings? In a *Playboy* interview featured here, Mailer is invited to give his views on God: 'I can see Him as someone who is like other men except more noble, more tortured, more desirous of a good that He wishes to receive and give to others – a tortuous ethical activity at which He may fail.' Now wait a minute: doesn't He remind you of somebody?

One's interest naturally focuses on the essays, the 'Existential Errands' which have crossed the Atlantic for the first time; but it should be stressed that *The Essential Mailer* contains a generous selection of the author's short fiction. Mailer, astonishingly, declines to make high claims for his stories (some of the work is practically juvenilia). Here, though, Mailer's strengths are constantly visible: raw nerves and peeled senses, an intense identification with every form of physical extremity, above all an ear that precisely renders the wistfulness and humour of ordinary American voices. It is an exceptional talent. What became of it?

Mailer has published no fiction for fifteen years. During that time he has apparently been searching for 'the biggest mine of them all'. There have been plenty of rumours about Mailer's magnum opus; promises have been made, advances eaten up. It is, at least in outline, an omniscient, architectonic 3,000-pager: part one is set in the ancient world, part two traces an American family from Independence to the present day, and part three is set on a spaceship.* Bits have been read out by the author to select gatherings in New York. People say it is

* *Ancient Evenings* (see below).

stunning, magical, divine. Perhaps that book will give us the essential Mailer. Or perhaps not. Let us pray.

Observer August 1982

Tough Guys Don't Dance by Norman Mailer

Just over halfway through *Tough Guys Don't Dance* narrator Tim Madden is jumped by a pair of cut-throats off a back road on Cape Cod. They wield a knife and a tyre iron, yet Tim has good reason to show what he's made of: 'I had the heads of two blonde ladies to guard in the trunk of my car.' That's right: not one but two severed heads, two slain vamps. Tim's dog takes out one attacker, while Tim himself handles the other, felling his man with a 'thunder-bolt' of a right. 'Then I made the mistake of kicking him in the head,' the narrator growls. 'That broke my big toe.'

At times like these the reader's reaction (in my case one of spontaneous laughter) quietens into something more circumspect. Is this just exorbitance, or is it caricature? Certainly, from the title onwards, the book seems to flirt pretty heavily with lampoon. Tim Madden, ex-con, stalled writer, alcoholic and blackout-artist; his wife Patty Lareine, sneering blonde, half angel, half witch; Bolo, her big black ex-boxer boyfriend; Regency, the well-hung psychocop; Meeks Wardley Hiby III, the snivelling Wasp faggot: all are caught up in a seething and sanguinary thriller written very fast by Mr Mailer for a well-known reason. When, oh when, will all the kids grow up, all the wives remarry?

Still, Mailer may be capable of mischief, flippancy and haste, but he is not capable of broad comic design. For all his wit, irony and high

270

spirits he is essentially humourless: laughs in Mailer derive from the close observation of things that are, so to speak, funny already. The humour can never turn inward. Besides, one smile in the mirror at this stage in his career and the whole corpus would corpse. Self-parody is not Mailer's style. What is Mailer's style?

The new novel has clear affinities with *An American Dream*, also written fast, also concerning itself with murdered wives, pistol-whipping cops, forensic subtleties, daredevil steeplejacking. The earlier book, however, was composed on a genuine high (some of it chemically induced), emboldened by various Lawrentian/Sartrean ideas about the fundamental purity of very bad behaviour. Despite its subject-matter, *Tough Guys* is a return to a more hesitant and delicate mode, that of *Barbary Shore* and *The Deer Park*. Those two novels followed *The Naked and the Dead*, preceding *Advertisements for Myself* and the process of mythologization which that book inaugurated.

His voice is sadder and wiser than it once was. Here is someone (you're meant to feel) who has taken his share of beatings, torments, skunk hours; someone who has pondered deeply on the workings of the world; someone, above all, who understands the ways of a man with a woman. Yet the style is often awkward, self-conscious – and stilted. It relishes pallid qualifiers ('barely', 'hardly', 'somewhat'), bookish archaisms ('of other ilk', 'wont to do', 'drear', 'bodeful') and fastidious double-negatives ('not unlike', 'not unanalogous to' and – my personal favourite – 'not wholly un-macho'). Mulling over his own prose, Tim makes 'small sounds of appreciation at some felicity of syntax': a fancifully 'writerly' notion if ever there was one, like savouring a subjunctive. None the less, for all the squalor and gore, felicities of syntax are what the book aspires to be full of.

It is, then, a highly contorted performance, containing much trapped energy. Perhaps *Tough Guys* is simply a brief and lurid vacation after the great girdings and flexings of its predecessor. One admires the ambition of *Ancient Evenings* because that's all there is to admire. That's all the book is: 700 pages of ambition. The new book settles for talent rather than genius, and brings homelier pleasures: a natural sensitivity to place and to weather, and an eloquent awareness of the human vicissitudes, the raw edges of even the most ordinary day.

As indicated earlier, some readers will find *Tough Guys* merely preposterous, and others will find it bracingly comic. In the end the humour arises from the humourlessness, the vitreous fixity, the loyalty to the old obsessions and drives. These now seem impossibly dated: all that butch spiritual anarchism, solemnly endorsed, all the booze, the brawls, and the bull. The ideal of manhood is seen as a weird union of, say, Søren Kierkegaard and Oliver Reed. The ideal of womanhood is even stranger: the bitch-goddess, an object of terror and desire who must, even so, be given her sentimental due. Since the bitch-goddess is invariably engaged on bitch-goddess activities (taunting, pouting, packing pistols, fellating strangers, and whatnot), the author is obliged to attempt the most unlikely feats of lyrical transcendence: 'as tender as the stem of honeysuckle on a child's mouth', 'emotions that were close to sunlight', 'the velvets of her loving heart'. Tough guys don't dance. But they're not afraid to cry.

Mailer's chief addendum to the Hemingway tradition he loyally follows is the element of paranoia. The Hemingway hero saw what dangers faced him and recognized them for what they were. The Mailer hero is fuzzier on the whole question of threat, less sure of its provenance. Is it real? Is it self-projected? (The spectre of latent homosexuality is directly faced in *Tough Guys*, perhaps giving weight to the notion of *unconscious* self-parody.) But paranoia excites Mailer and makes him write well:

> ... he had the ability of many a big powerful man to stow whole packets of unrest in various parts of his body. He could sit unmoving like a big beast in a chair, but if he had a tail, it would have been whipping the rungs.

Mailer's presence on the page has something of this quality – compelling, uncomfortable, on bad terms with its own sexuality. The presence fills you with disquiet; but then you have to find the nerve to get up and leave the room.

Observer October 1984

Oswald's Tale: An American Mystery by Norman Mailer

On page 1,288 of *Harlot's Ghost*, Norman Mailer's prodigious – and prodigiously underrated – novel about the CIA, the author takes us up to the seventh floor of Agency HQ on the afternoon of 22 November 1963. The grandmasters of national security, the men who had sought to become 'the mind of America', are gathering in the director's meeting room. 'And we sat there,' one of these mandarins recalls, on page 1,288, after 600,000 words of exponential intrigue, of second-guessing, double-lifing, triple-dealing:

> And we sat there . . . It's the only time in all these years I saw
> so many brilliant, ambitious, resourceful men – just sitting there.
> Finally [Agent] McCone said, 'Who is this Oswald?' And there
> was a World Series *silence*. The sort you hear when the visiting
> team has scored *eight runs* in the first inning.

Oswald's Tale attempts to fill that silence. Many million man-hours have been spent 'following the bullet trajectories backwards' from the President's bespattered limousine 'to the lives that occupy the shadows', as Don DeLillo put it in *Libra* (1988), his dauntingly brilliant novel about Oswald. But the facts of the assassination will always be partly subsumed by Mailer's subtitle. What have we got? The *where* and the *when* are totemically established. We have the *who*, if not the *how* or the *who with*. We have means and opportunity; we lack motive. *Oswald's Tale* is non-fiction, but Mailer can rely on the novelist's forensic talents: he knows that the *who*, properly considered, will give us the *why*. And then, perhaps, meaning will be glimpsed in this wilderness of mirrors.

During the winter of 1959, Lee Harvey Oswald went and did something interesting. After a lonely and fatherless childhood, a morosely politicized adolescence, and a stint in the Marines (where his nicknames were Mrs Oswald, Oswaldskovich and 'Shit-bird'), Oswald defected to the USSR. As he probably saw it, the Soviet Union stood up for the little guy – and Oswald was certainly little. It worked out, too, in a way. Fortuitously, ominously and instantly, he elevated himself from mediocrity to exotic. He was 'a real American, and unmarried', one of his minders observed: 'Young women even came to the hotel and said, "How do we meet this guy?"' Being American had never cut so much ice in New Orleans or the Bronx.

The authorities – the 'Organs' – soon got him out of Moscow and parked him in Minsk, a city he had never heard of. They gave him a flat and a job and light surveillance: Oswald would have been mortified to learn that his KGB handler regarded him as 'primitive – a basic case', of 'zero' political value. And yet he blundered along, dependably feisty, incurious and obtuse. One morning at seven, he was roused by election workers (it was the day of some obligatory vote) 'and Lee wouldn't open up. He kept yelling, "This is a free country."' He fell for a girl called Ella, and was spurned. He married a girl called Marina ('to hurt Ella', according to his diary), and soon settled into a husbandly regime of bickering, fist-flexing, and premature ejaculation. He liked the Russian summers but he didn't like the Russian winters. Ever since Ella he had been trying to wheedle his way back to America (he did have the knack of outwitting, or outlasting, titanic bureaucracies). With his wife and daughter he sailed for New York in the summer of 1962, and then made for Texas. He flunked a series of cheesy jobs. He bought a cockroach spraygun. He acquired a rifle. He had a year to go.

Of course, the literature on Oswald, official and freelance, is by now biblically vast. DeLillo imagines the Warren Report as 'the megaton novel Joyce would have written if he'd moved to Iowa City and lived to be a hundred'; and Warren, like Joyce, has spawned an industry. Mailer was emboldened to add his book to the stack when he was offered 'an Oklahoma land-grab' of fresh material: the KGB dossier on Oswald, and the chance to interview his comrades and controllers in Moscow and Minsk. Whereas the American Oswaldiana is porous and bloated from constant exposure, the Russian material has been hermetically sealed. It is thirty-five years old, but it is pristine. In these cogent and artistic pages Oswald is no longer the spectral, hangdog examinee of various hearings and post-mortems. He comes alive. And he looks horribly familiar. From a KGB transcript of a bugging ('for Object LHO-2983'):

> LHO: Shut up. Take your baby (*baby is crying*) . . .
> WIFE: (sobbing) Don't look at me that way – nobody is afraid of you. Go to hell, you bastard!
> LHO: You're very good.
> WIFE: You can go to your America without me, and I hope you die on the way.

Oswald did indeed go back to his America. And at Dealey Plaza he duly ruptured its history in 6.9 seconds.

What we seem to be contemplating, then, is a tale of egregious disproportion. Simply put, the most potent and promise-crammed figure on earth had his brains blown out by a malevolent Charlie Chaplin with a wonky rifle and a couple of Big Ideas. Now, everything in Mailer rebels against this reading. If Oswald was a nonentity, acting alone, all we are left with is absurdity – more garbage, more randomness and rot. Clearly, there are only two ways out of the bind. Either Oswald wasn't acting alone – or he wasn't a nonentity. He was complex, tortured; he was tinged by the 'tragic'.

To our initial surprises, Mailer rejects conspiracy. According to Oliver Stone's feverish movie, *JFK*, the assassination involved practically 50 per cent of the American populace. The unlikelihood of a pan-national cover-up would seem to outweigh the more local lacunae – Oswald's marksmanship, the 'magic bullet', Jack Ruby – which are merely 'evidentiary', and subject to the ping-pong of rival advocacies. More crucially, all conspiracies founder on the crags of Oswald's character, as here established. No concerted effort, however harebrained, could have placed Oswald at its leading edge. Even as a patsy he was unemployable.

This clincher appears to preclude any attempt to upgrade Oswald from the ranks of lumpen inadequacy and delusion. But Mailer persists, cautiously, candidly (nothing is fudged), until he can descry a 'young intellectual', however stunted, with a 'vision', however warped. Thus Mailer takes the admitted 'liberty' of cosmeticizing Oswald's dyslexia. He had a genuine handicap, after all, and wasn't just another tub-thumping illiterate. To show him 'at his best', quotations from Oswald's writings 'have been corrected here for spelling and punctuation'. Well, Oswald's prose was pure alphabet soup: he could spell *Ukrainian* 'Urakranion' and 'Urakrinuien' in the same sub-clause. To regularize his spelling seems merely humane; but to regularize his punctuation (in an age when the semi-colon, say, is a profound public mystery) catapults him into the cultural elite. Besides, inarticulacy is the key to Oswald's thwartedness. He was a wife-beater; and what else is a wife-beater but a man who runs out of words – who keeps coming up empty on the words? In his essay on life in Minsk, Oswald included a section called 'About the Author'. The death of his father, he wrote, 'left a far mean streak of indepence brought on by negleck'. Here is Oswald captured in a poem one word long: Negleck . . .

Mailer has written some pretty crazy books in his time, but this isn't one of them. Like its predecessor, *Harlot's Ghost*, it is the performance of an author relishing the force and reach of his own acuity. Recalling his championship of the unreformed convict Jack Henry Abbott, we see that he still has the old weakness for any killer who has puzzled his way through a few pages of Marx. But Mailer does have real feeling for frustrated and effaced existences. And his portrait here of Khrushchev's Russia reproduces the fluid empathy of his other non-fiction monument, *The Executioner's Song*. In late-period Mailer, deep resources are being marshalled. With DeLillo's *Libra*, *Oswald's Tale* presides over the Dallas mausoleum. Mailer provides the broad architecture, DeLillo the gloating gargoyles. In a sense, the two books constitute Oswald's most coherent achievements and the only valuables in his legacy.

To return to the subtitle: *An American Mystery*. Mailer remarks that he might have opted for *An American Tragedy* if Theodore Dreiser hadn't pre-empted him. As it turns out, Mailer comes close to solving the mystery, but he never establishes the tragedy. Dreiser's tale was tragic and American because it happened every day. Oswald made only one notch on the calendar. It was meaningless; he just renamed an airport, violently. His tale was American in its inclusiveness: he connects Hugh Auchincloss, the Washington socialite, with Brenda Jean Sensibaugh, the stripper employed by Jack Ruby who was found hanging by her toreador pants in an Oklahoma jail in 1965.

Oswald's life was not a cry of pain so much as a squawk for attention. He achieved geopolitical significance by the shortest possible route. He was not an example of post-modern absurdity but one of its messiahs: an inspiration to the glazed loner. He killed Kennedy not to impress Jodie Foster. He killed Kennedy to impress Clio – the muse of history.

Although he never makes it into tragedy, Oswald deserved the tragic attendants of irony and pathos. This is Oswald's mother, the devouring Marguerite (and by now we have seen Oswald crying many, many times), as she describes her son's corpse:

Marina went first. She opened his eyelids . . . This is a very, very strong girl, that she can open a dead man's eyelids, and she says, 'He cry. He eye wet.' To the doctor. And the doctor says, 'Yes.'

It was a hectic struggle to find a minister and a grave. They buried him under his last and least-dignified pseudonym, William Bobo. His eye was wet. He was twenty-four.

Sunday Times September 1995

Vidal's Mirror

Palimpsest by Gore Vidal

Gore Vidal's *Palimpsest* is a tale of the unexpected. Contemplating its arty, finicky title (pronounced 'Pelimpsest', perhaps, with full Sitwellian delicacy), its handsomely 'integrated' photographs (grand houses, Caligulan profiles), its bulk, its celebrity-infested index, one gears oneself for predictable pleasures. Namely, the invigoratingly high-plumed cynicism of Vidal's discursive prose, plus plenty of gossip.

I thought I was wise to all his moves. I knew Vidal would have me frowning and nodding and smiling and smirking – with admiration, and exasperation, and scandalized dissent. I never dreamed Vidal would have me piping my eyes, and staring wanly out of the window, and emitting strange sighs (many of them frail and elderly in timbre). Approaching seventy, Vidal now takes cognisance of the human heart, and reveals that he has one. *Palimpsest* is a tremendous read from start to finish. It is also a proud and serious and truthful book.

First, though, the familiar diversions, and the familiar humour which, frequently and typically, tends towardsthe unintentional. How can this be? Is it that Vidal, like Lear, has ever but slenderly known himself? Or is it that he just wants it both ways – all ways? The latter, I believe. Vidal is determined to be a) in the thick of things, and b) above the fray. He knows everybody and doesn't want to know anybody. He has had lovers by the thousand while doing 'nothing – deliberately, at least – to please the other'. Publicly despairing of the American political system, he runs for Congress (and, later in the life than this book takes us, for president). The ambivalence follows Vidal through all spheres and orbits, and involves him in many decorative contradictions.

Gossip, particularly sexual gossip, is viewed as the sworn enemy of truth; and truthfulness, for Vidal, remains the prince of the natural virtues. Yet gossip-fans will find much to gossip about in *Palimpsest*. On page seven, Jackie Kennedy is already hoiking up her gown to show Vidal's half-sister Nini 'how to douche post-sex'. Elsewhere, we are told that Marlon Brando had 'two abortionists on retainer'. 'Look at that ass,' says Tennessee Williams 'thoughtfully', as he follows Jack Kennedy through a doorway. Then there are Nureyev's dreamy insinuations about *Bobby*. Promiscuity was 'perfectly normal . . . in the high-powered world', as Jackie knew. Gore himself got about a bit: 'Jack raised his head from the pillow to look at me over his left shoulder.' But relax. This isn't Jack Kennedy. It's only Jack Kerouac.

Towards the end of the book, Vidal confides that he dislikes social gatherings. Still, this hater of parties clearly went to several thousand of them, perhaps just to make sure. Vidal never had to go looking for all these parties, unlike Truman Capote, say, whom Vidal keeps running into at all these parties, along with Williams, Kerouac, Isherwood, *et al.* ('Avoid writers,' Vidal cautions us, more than once.) 'Celebrities are invariably celebrity-mad,' he wearily notes, having charted another 'season' spent among the white trash (up to and including the Duke of Windsor and Princess Margaret). Vidal isn't namedropping. Who else *is* there? A galaxy of luminaries has always clustered itself around this literary quasar and his huge gravitational pull. The bloke in the next office is Federico Fellini ('Fred, as I called him'). The current flatmates are Paul Newman and Joanne Woodward. In these pages, ordinary people are the true exotics – such as Howard Austen, who has written no operas, ruled no countries, and inherited no fortunes, and with whom Vidal has chastely dwelt for more than forty years.

These days, Vidal is resignedly aware that he has somehow gained a reputation for physical vanity. It seems inexplicable, because he never boasts about his looks. He may remark on the 'astonishingly handsome' figure cut by his father, and may mention the 'flaring Gore nostrils' that he has inherited, as has the current Vice President (a dim cousin). But that's all he'll say on the matter. Others can say what they like, and Vidal is of course free to adduce their testimonies, in print.

Harold Acton found him 'aggressively handsome'. Cecilia Sternberg thought his face 'curiously of the antique world, like a Greek mask'. 'Just the sight of Gore', wrote Elaine Dundy, 'had the effect of instantly cleansing my palate – like some tart lemon sorbet' ('He is handsome, yet'). Having seen 'the picture of him that adorns his latest opus', William Burroughs urgently wanted to know: 'Is Gore Vidal queer or not?'

To which the answer is a strangely qualified *yes*. Vidal *is* queer, sort of: but in Vidal's world so is everybody else. There's Capote, Williams, Isherwood, Kerouac, Baldwin, E.M. Forster, and so on. But even the fanatical skirt-chasers – Marlon, Jack, Bobby – betray certain leanings. Greta Garbo had 'an eye for girls'; in Hollywood, so did 'just about every star or star's wife'. Ken Tynan, too, was 'one of nature's innate and unalterable lesbians'. During the war, in Vidal's all-gay army, 'most of the boys' embraced the chance 'to do what they were designed to do with each other'. Earlier, in Vidal's all-gay school, boys 'thought that kissing had been invented by girls . . . it was not always pleasant for us when the increased estrogen flow made their salivas taste unpleasant.' No, unpleasant things are not always pleasant. But I have never before heard a word of complaint about that oestrogen flow, or indeed any mention of it. Maybe the boys I know are differently 'designed'. As elsewhere in his writing, Vidal gives the impression of believing that the entire heterosexual edifice – registry offices, *Romeo and Juliet*, the disposable diaper – is just a sorry story of self-hypnosis and mass hysteria: a hoax, a racket, or sheer propaganda.

Sexually – and here we approach the heart and truth of the book – Vidal is a fabulous beast. A unicorn, perhaps, or a satyr with a strict set of rules. 'I never go to bed with friends,' he writes. A hyperactive cruiser, Vidal has never had a love affair. Indeed, 'since I don't really know what other people mean by *love*, I avoid the word'. But he knows what *he* means by it, and in the end the word can't be avoided. For once and once only he 'moved far beyond sex or eroticism and on to the wilder shores of love, and shipwreck'.

In general, novelists are intimately repelled by the business of psychoanalysis. Nabokov could probably have written an extra book or two in the time he sat around loathing Freud. The self – that holding operation between the mind's various factions – is what novelists feel they are obliged to grope their way around: they don't want to see the *A to Z*. Vidal is, of course, painfully reluctant to view himself as a clear-cut case. But he has the courage to let the pattern emerge, in all its embarrassing symmetry.

Two relationships appear to have decided everything, and they are established early on in the life, and in these pages, with passionate force. 'Never have children, only grandchildren,' Vidal was told by his grandfather, T.P. Gore. Having lost his sight in two different accidents, one for each eye, and then gone on to become the first senator from the state of Oklahoma, T.P. was an inspirational figure for the whole nation. In his grandson (and sometime ward), Senator Gore found a vital resource: little Gore would read to him, eagerly, for hour after hour – an indefatigable falsetto. After such a childhood, after such an example, Vidal was destined for stoicism. Any weakness can be worked into a strength, he writes, in the book's steeliest phrase, by 'those who mean to prevail'.

The second formative figure is the vanished young man called Jimmie Trimble. Vidal's first and only love is insistently summoned in terms of a lost duality: 'What I was not, he was, and the other way around'; 'Jimmie, of course, was something else – me'; 'He was the other half of me that never lived to grow up.' Jimmie was killed on Iwo Jima in 1945. He never grew up, and never grew old, and never relinquished his pristine burnish. *Palimpsest* thus shyly invites us to see Vidal as a version of Narcissus, in the classical mould, struggling with illusion, with despair, with death. It is a lot to ask – but this reader assented willingly enough. When he died, Narcissus was transformed into the flower that bears his name. Vidal wanted a different fate: he wanted to survive and prevail.

With its elaborate double-time scheme, its cunning rearrangements and realignments of the past, its blend of impetuous candour and decent reticence, *Palimpsest* is a work of considerable artistry. And Jimmie, the hidden other, illuminates its core. As a character, as a creation, he seems to shine through unassisted, all by himself; but this is an effect wrought by great authorial guile. He becomes universal

– like the German soldier in Wilfred Owen's 'Strange Meeting' ('I am the enemy you killed, my friend'). Of course, Jimmie was an American. In a late letter to his mother, he signed off as follows: 'All my love to the swellest Mom in all the world.' It was very intelligent of Vidal to quote another letter, from another marine on Iwo Jima, whose ingenuous repetition ('he was a joy') give the right sense of there being nothing more to say:

> We were all real proud of Jim Trimble, and everybody else was.
> He was a joy to be around. He had a good personality. He was
> always joking. I know he wanted to go back and go to school and
> play professional baseball. He was just a joy to be around.

Sunday Times October 1995

Philip Roth and the Self

My Life As a Man by Philip Roth

Although Philip Roth's novels have got steadily sillier since *Portnoy's Complaint* (1969), the quality of his prose has continued to improve. Indeed, the panache with which Roth recreated the soft fantasies of *The Great American Novel* (1973) makes even the most impressive pages of *Goodbye, Columbus* (1959) seem rather pietistic by comparison. *My Life As a Man*, Roth's miraculous mess of a new novel, marks a return to the heartache-in-the-humanities circuit of the early books – most obviously that of *Letting Go* (1962) – but in other respects it keeps up the recent tradition: however lazy, fanciful or lugubrious he gets, Roth's sentences are dapper and sonorous, always eventful, never congested.

We still have problems, though. *My Life As a Man* begins with two autobiographical short stories, presented as the autobiographical work of an autobiographical novelist, about a young autobiographical writer. The rest of the book is a first-person account of the autobiographical novelist's attempt to write a new autobiographical novel and his final abandonment of it in favour of unadorned autobiography. Intimations of the confessional are not, then, easy to pooh-pooh, and I had to resist the temptation to get the dirt on Roth before starting to write this review. In fact, there's enough internal evidence to settle the matter. There always is. One could even have forgone the po-faced disclosure on the title-page that parts of the book have appeared, 'in somewhat different form', in periodicals as various as the *New York Times*, *Modern Occasions* and (best) *Marriage and Divorce*.

The resulting patchwork tells of the suicidal alliance of a young Jewish novelist, Peter Tarnopol, and a world-class predator called Maureen, their separation, his protracted analysis with Dr Spielvogel (another refugee from *Portnoy*), his subsequent affair with a WASP non-predator, and his attempts to exorcize Maureen, even after her violent death, in literary form. Along the way we encounter the standard Roth preoccupations. The perils of having an over-literary mind – perils which *The Breast* (1972) so unenlighteningly dramatized – are once more examined; Tarnopol marries Maureen because it's the sort of thing people in tortured novels do, and then tries, in turn, to make a tortured novel out of her: 'Literature got me into this,' he writes, 'and literature is gonna have to get me out.' Allied to that complaint is the old *Portnoy* one about the temperamental inability to get 'on good terms with pleasure', a syndrome that persuades you to ditch girls for being too sexy and intelligent and then to give yourself a nightly stroke in an attempt to bring unintelligent and sexless bedpartners to orgasm. As for experimentation, the province of Roth's last three books, we get only the odd gentle-reader interlude (an improvement, admittedly, on the thick-lout reader, scum-of-the-earth reader asides of *The Breast*) and some routine confusion between Lit Crit and literature. And then there's the Jewish blues, too, of course.

Now either these events and concerns are the stuff of self-revelation or *My Life As a Man* is a museum of perversity. The solipsism takes two main forms. First, it shows itself in Roth's neurotic deference to his neuroses. (The only dead section of the book is the Spielvogel chapter, and some of the duller anecdotes read like experiences recollected in analysis.) Psychological accuracy, after all, is not the same as literary shape. One thing shrinks don't do is shrink. As with lawyers and other social parasites, it is in their interests tediously to augment; and artistically Roth would be better employed baying at the moon once or twice a week. The second giveaway has to do with the novel's surface. *My Life As a Man* sags with the minutiae that belong to life and not to art; it displays a wooden fidelity to the inconsequential, a scrupulousness about detail which isn't significant, merely true.

And yet the book is alive. I read it twice with constant disapproval and no loss of interest and pleasure. As a valediction, however, one might remind Roth that there is a lot of fictional terrain between what happened to you yesterday and Richard Nixon's attempts to coax votes out of foetuses (*Our Gang*), between bitching about your wife and turning into a mammary gland, between your psychiatrist's couch and a hinterland of baseball: I mean the terrain he glimpsed in *When She Was Good* (1967). There are, in short, people in the world other than middle-class Jewish Professors of English Literature: to paraphrase Moe Tarnopol, one of the superbly compact cameos in this ragged knapsack of a book – *enough with them already*.

New Statesman November 1974

Zuckerman Unbound by Philip Roth

This is a new kind of autobiographical novel. It is an autobiographical novel about what it is like to write autobiographical novels . . . The question is: do we *need* this new kind of autobiographical novel? We all seemed to be getting by without it.

The hero of the book is Nathan Zuckerman. This is Nathan's third consecutive outing as Philip Roth's fictional *alter ego*. Roth has used other, more fictional *alter egos* in the past – Peter Tarnopol, for instance, in *My Life As a Man*, who differs from Roth in at least one or two bold particulars. But there is nothing very *alter* about Nathan Zuckerman. He is more of an *ipse ego*. To all intents and purposes – and it is still not clear what these are – Zuckerman and Roth would *seem* to be the same guy. A curious side-effect of autobiographical fiction is that it puts the reader in a state of salacious curiosity about the author's private life. I was minding my own business before this book came along.

In *Zuckerman Unbound* Nathan has just published *Carnovsky*, an

287

autobiographical novel about his youth and early manhood, featuring a predatory Jewish mother, an enervated Jewish father, and many a haggard handjob in the bathroom of the family apartment in Newark. The year is 1969, which, of course, is the year that Roth published *Portnoy's Complaint*, an autobiographical novel about his youth and early manhood, featuring a predatory Jewish etc., etc. Both books enjoy uncontrollable success. Nathan and Philip wake up to find they are headliners, millionaires, and self-trumpeted satyrs.

'Hey, you do all that stuff in that book? With all those chicks? You are something else, man,' the meter-reader tells Zuckerman. The *meter*-reader ... New York is a good place for this type of generalized paranoia, a place where everyone likes to involve themselves in the huff-and-puff of celebrity. 'Those cover stories were enough of a trial for a writer's writer friends, let alone for a semi-literate psychopath who might not know about all the good deeds he did at the PEN club.' Nathan duly tangles with the wackos and crazoids of Manhattan, the self-elected *alter egos* of the streets, and garners his share of the fan-mail and hate-mail, the anonymous telephone calls, and the lurid speculations in the gossip columns.

Roth has written about this period of his life before, non-fictionally, in *Reading Myself and Others*. The essay is baffled and rueful in tone. After the publication of *Portnoy*, Roth's name was linked with that of Barbra Streisand; he read newspaper reports of his own nervous breakdown (all that masturbation catching up on him); the pulp novelist Jacqueline Susann said on a chat-show that she would like to meet Philip Roth but wouldn't like to shake his hand. 'She, of all people,' wrote Roth in the authentic accent of wounded pride – not personal pride so much as pride on behalf of his art. 'They had mistaken impersonation for confession,' says Zuckerman, 'and were calling out to a character who lived in a book.' Well, that might have been true of *Portnoy*. But in what sense can it be true of *Zuckerman*?

The main ethical and emotional burden of the novel concerns Zuckerman's parents: though they may not be directly traduced in *Carnovsky*, the world certainly thinks they are. Mr and Mrs Zuckerman suffer; and Nathan, again for reasons of literary *amour propre*, is slow to believe in their pain. He manages to patch things up with his mother (as, you feel, Roth is doing: it's a new-deal Mrs Portnoy in this book – she's a sweetheart), but his father dies with the word 'Bastard' on his lips. 'You selfish bastard,' echoes Zuckerman's kid brother towards the end. 'You can't believe that what you write about people has *real consequences*.' Now this is meant to be challenging stuff. And yet – what about *this* novel, and *its* consequences? The title, and the ending, suggest a new freedom, a throwing-off of the merely personal, the merely local. However, the promise is not realized here. Nathan is still shackled to his rock, and the vulture is still lunching on his liver.

'Literature got me into this,' says the wretched Tarnopol in *My Life as a Man*, 'and literature is gonna have to get me out.' It remains a good slogan. For all the self-immersion on view, *Zuckerman Unbound* is a frictionless read: indeed, it's over before you know it. In the age of the how-to book, the case-history and the agony column, this sort of thing has an inordinate appeal; everyone who can read has by now cultivated the habit of reading their own lives. A talent the size of Philip Roth's will always confer a touch of universality. Reading about his life has satisfactions analogous to reading about one's own. Ah, life: *Zuckerman Unbound* is life all right. But is it literature?

Observer August 1981

The Counterlife by Philip Roth

Philip Roth's new novel is so formidably good, and so perversely surprising, that it prompts a question: how did he get here? How did he wind up with *this*? Over the space of ten books and almost twenty years Roth has endured an odd kind of impatience from his public, an impatience resembling pique or obscurely hurt feelings. The reason for this seems to me quite straightforward. Roth is a comic genius, and there are never enough comic geniuses – there are never enough to go around. In 1969 he published *Portnoy's Complaint*. It was his fourth work of fiction; the dutiful tyro stuff was out of the way; he had found his voice. We sat back, asking for more. And he gave us less.

What *did* he give us? First a trio of formal satires, if you please: *Our Gang*, *The Breast*, and *The Great American Novel*. These were comic in shape, but contrary to our wishes, only glancingly comic in execution. Looking on with expressions of strained indulgence, we allowed Roth this holiday, and calmly waited for the comic genius to resume his obligations. Next came *My Life as a Man* and *The Professor of Desire*, two novels that, it was widely felt, were not funny enough. And where did Roth get off, not being funny enough? No, *My Life* and *The Prof* erred on the side of bookishness, introspection, and anguish. We wanted the old get up and go. For our pains we were zapped by the Zuckerman quartet, perhaps the most cramped and stubborn exercise in self-examination known to modern letters. As its title suggests, *The Counterlife* marks a parting of the ways, which, though, lead in unexpected directions. Zuckerman is still there; Zuckerman is still in solitary. But Roth is back on the streets.

There aren't supposed to be degrees or intensities of uniqueness, and yet Roth is somehow inordinately unique. He is bloodymindedly himself, himself, himself. The trouble with Zuckerman, the trouble with the self as a literary idea, is that *there is no subject*. Ironically, it is Zuckerman whom we thank for this elusive truth, at the end of *The Counterlife*, 1,000 pages having gone by since the experiment began. Hence the desperate thinness, the unbearable lightness of much of the earlier Zuckerman work. How it yearned for escape into the concrete, how it sobbed and pleaded for sub-stance. One felt that Roth couldn't possibly go further – that, indeed, there was nowhere further to go. But on he went, with typical and (it now seems) heroic pertinacity. Like a dying star, Roth hovered on the point of catastrophic collapse. With *The*

Counterlife, however, the supernova has arrived, and it almost hurts the eye.

The agent, the catalyst, is unquestionably Israel. Here is a subject all right, and it may even be that Roth has spent half his life readying himself to take it on. He went there before, carrying Portnoy's passport, and the place defeated him: the Israel section was the only major weakness of *Portnoy's Complaint*, and that is a measure of how far we have come. Set against *The Counterlife*, the earlier book looks regressive and dead-ended; for all its savage splendours, *Portnoy* was a farewell to youth, and Roth *had* to say goodbye to all that. Yet Jewishness in one form or another – and the more obsessive the better – has always been the real goad to his eloquence. One could even half-frivolously accuse the earlier, weaker Zuckermans of being assimilationist in tendency, doomed tryouts of inauthentic lives: the celebrity hobnobber of *Zuckerman Unbound*, the flailing penitent of *The Anatomy Lesson*, the cultural cosmopolitan of *The Prague Orgy*. In any event, Roth has now come home, artistically. 'Jews Jews', 'Jew-engrossed, Jew-engorged', 'JewJewJew': this is the front line of the talent.

His Israel chapters, 'Judea' and 'Aloft' (aboard an El Al jet), are choric songs for vying voices, successions of dramatic monologues marshalled by the man with the golden ear. 'The Bible is their *bible*,' Zuckerman incredulously notes. Yes, and it is also their *babel*. Shuki Elchanan, a liberal Tel Aviv journalist: 'This place has become the American-Jewish Australia. Now who we get is the Oriental Jew and the Russian Jew and . . . roughnecks in yarmulkes from Brooklyn.' Shuki's father: 'See that bird? That's a Jewish bird. See, up there? A Jewish cloud . . . We are living in a Jewish theater and you are living in a Jewish museum!' Mordecai Lippman, a West Bank frontiersman: 'They are throwing stones at *Jews. Every stone is an anti-Semitic stone.*' An El Al security guard: 'The weak little shnook Jew was fine, the Jewish hick with his tractor and his short pants, who could he trick, who could he screw? But suddenly . . . *Real Jewish might!*'

Zuckerman seems to steer his way through the cacophony with flawless scepticism. Shuki says that in Israel 'it's enough to live – you don't have to do anything else and you go to bed exhausted', yet

Zuckerman shrewdly reasons that here 'everything comes bursting out of everyone all the time, and so probably means half as much as you think'. In a brush with a wailer at the Wailing Wall, Zuckerman confesses that all four of his wives have been shiksas. 'Why, mister?' 'That's the sort of Jew I am, Mac.' He is contentedly assimilated, contentedly 'decadent'. When, in Judaea, Zuckerman is informed that 'what Hitler couldn't achieve with Auschwitz, American Jews are doing to themselves in the bedroom', he shrugs and keeps his counsel, fondly anticipating his return to London, to his pregnant Maria, his new intermarriage, his new life in 'Christendom'. But it doesn't work out; it never does in Roth's world. A radical epiphany, an uncovenanted conversion, is at hand. Maria's baby is a boy. On Dizengoff Street, Zuckerman has told Shuki that circumcision, like every other biblical injunction, 'was probably irrelevant to my "I"'. Practically the next day his entire existence is hingeing on that one question, circumcision, the mark of the Jewish reality, 'this old, old stuff'.

To engineer such an about-turn it is additionally necessary for Zuckerman to apprehend anti-Semitism in England, 'deep, insidious Establishment anti-Semitism', and to apprehend it, moreover, in the space of a single evening. Writing in my capacity as an Englishman, I am both ashamed and surprised to say that Roth pulls it off – he makes this murky thing happen on the page. The picture is slanted, and confessedly slanted, relying on 'a madwoman of a fucked-up sister [of Maria's]' (not to mention an old bitch of a mother-in-law, called, of all things, Mrs Freshfield); but Roth detects a phenomenon that is really there. It is peculiarly and powerfully repellent, something like a dirty habit of privilege. It is also largely clandestine, and in retreat. Roth did well to hear it, to catch it; but that is how he interprets the world – he *listens* to it.

There is a good deal else going on in *The Counterlife*. It is, for instance, a rare addition to the body of successful – one could almost say readable – fiction of the strenuously post-modern type. Here Roth is audacious, grimly playful, almost Parisian (but the Paris of exile – Milan Kundera, say). He takes a dilemma and runs it past two different lives, that of Zuckerman and that of his 'uninteresting' brother, Henry. How brothers 'know each other, in my experience, is as a kind of deformation of themselves'; by crosshatching their realities, Roth can undertake his characteristic search for 'the real wisdom of the predicament'. The predicament has to do with impotence and its opposite, death and its opposite, with the longing to escape inherited identities, and with the prostrated addiction to a supposed authenticity, the hamming-up of a self that barely exists outside the perceptions of others. 'All I can tell you with certainty is that I, for one, have no self,' Roth concludes, not profoundly but with maximum appositeness, 'and that I am unwilling or unable to perpetuate upon myself the joke of a self. It certainly does strike me as a joke about *my* self. What I have instead is a variety of impersonations I can do . . .' The joke of a self: it is a bad joke, too, not a funny one.

The book convocates in the theme of Israel, but loosely, not too schematically, not too *teachably*, above all. One of the things that can't be thematically squared, it seems to me, is Roth's entirely personal bedevilment by the ramifications of autobiographical fiction. For what must be historical reasons, modern fiction is unprecedentedly close to the authors' peculiar realities: the idea of the freely gambolling fancy doesn't appear to cut much mustard any more. Roth has never looked at these questions historically, only personally. How does this fit in with Israel? In its tendency to exploit and gobble up half-formed lives? Well, here I think we are stretching it; and there is no need or inclination to stretch it elsewhere. One equation feels particularly satisfying: that between Israel and Philip Roth. In *Ulysses* Joyce calls Judaea 'the grey sunken cunt of the world'. I wouldn't like to say what Roth does to the place, or with what mixture of emotions; but the union is explosive. Like Israel, he exhausts you, he unsettles you, he galvanizes your responses. In this book (wonderfully sharp, worryingly tense) he is an electrifier.

Atlantic Monthly February 1987

MARTIN AMIS

Sabbath's Theater by Philip Roth

Pondering *Sabbath's Theater*, and sitting around recovering from it, I found myself reaching for the new seminar buzzword, performative. Performative literature, the idea is, coerces the reader into a personal enactment of its themes. Thus *Paradise Lost*, read performatively, tempts you to sympathize with Satan, with Adam, with Eve; it tempts you to doubt God's wisdom and God's justice; it tempts you to stray, to sin, to fall. What *Sabbath's Theater* involves you in is a 450-page spasm of hysteria. It is an hysterical novel about the hysteria of an hysterical man, and it leaves you feeling hysterical.

Philip Roth has always been a rich but miserly comic genius. Comedy is hoarded, and Roth receives his compound interest in the form of more sophisticated perversities and contortions. Well, *Sabbath's Theater* isn't funny. That gulping and cackling you hear coming off the page may sound like laughter, but hysteria is never funny. As a spectacle, hysteria is embarrassing, then alarming, then depersonalizing. All hysteria does is sustain itself until it exhausts itself. In this novel Roth conducts an amazing tantrum: a tantrum directed at that tragi-comic duo, sex and death. Halfway through the book you begin to think: yes, this is what morbid erotomania must really feel like. It's an itch in the brain: a cerebral nettlerash.

Sabbath's Theater is an upheaval novel, a crisis novel, a howl novel. Its authentic power is not in doubt, but one quickly starts questioning its universality. How general is the fate that befalls Mickey Sabbath? Can we all start pencilling it in? Talking of another casualty, an acquaintance of Mickey's comments: 'Some shock just undoes them around sixty, the plates shift and the earth starts shaking and all the pictures fall off the wall.' Sabbath has felt this seismic stirring throughout his adult life. What triggers his personal Big One is the death of his mistress,

294

Drenka, 'the erotic light of his life', as Roth puts it, unusually mildly.

I am writing in a family newspaper, but *Sabbath's Theater* can hardly inspire a family book-review. It is not a family novel; it is an anti-family novel, in several senses. It is also unbelievably dirty. Drenka is that rare find, 'a conventional woman who would do anything': 'Inside this woman was someone who thought like a man.' Carnal bliss, as we shall see, is more or less impossible to evoke. Humble plot summary, therefore, must serve as Drenka's tribute. In one of his routine visits to the cemetery, where he intends to masturbate on Drenka's grave, Sabbath finds that his spot has been taken by another lover. On his next try, Sabbath finds that his spot has been taken by *another* lover. There is practically a queue up there, or a circle jerk. That's how good Drenka was.

The dangers of writing concertedly about sex are numerous, and Roth skirts none of them. To his left, the Scylla of schlock; to his right, the Charybdis of pornography. So we are bounced from 'the breasts whose soft fullness had never ceased to captivate him' to the Cro-Magnon gurgle of 'Ohhhh. Ohhhh. Ohhhh' and 'There! No there! Right . . . there! There! There! There! Yes! There!' and 'Oh! Oh! Oh! Mickey! Oh, my God! Ahh! Ahh! Ahh!' Roth even *combines* schlock and pornography, as in Drenka's response to her first taste of Mickey's belt on her backside ('It's tenderness going wild!'), or in the soaring hymn to sexual urination which constitutes the novel's climax. Erotic prose is either pallidly general or unviewably specialized. Universality crumbles into a litter of quirks. After a while it provokes in the reader only one desire: the desire to skip. You toil on, looking for the clean bits.

And what are *they* about? Despite its deliberate barbarities, *Sabbath's Theater* is not a primitive work. Old Mickey was once a street-showman type, a puppeteer; and the standard range of puppet motifs – inertness, manipulation – is predictably collocated. Similarly, for all his hostility to therapeutic nostrums (twelve-step programmes, 'Courage to Heal', and so on), Roth presents Mickey as an intelligible case. The awful agitation of his lusting and rutting is seen as a response to the immanence and imminence of death. Mickey blunders through a veritable necropolis of funeral parlours, cadavers, cemeteries, centenarians, hospitals, deathbeds. Of course he behaves badly: 'If you can still do something, then you must do it!' It wasn't Mickey's fault. Death did it.

Perhaps the most significant page of any novel comes early on and is normally headed 'By the Same Author'. Contemplating this sturdy pillar of high achievement, you realize that the vapours and humours that becloud *Sabbath's Theater* have always been present in Roth's work: the unapologetic cynicism, the scarily illusionless intelligence, the reductive sexuality, the sociopathic laughter. These transgressive tendencies were given balance by a series of opposing preoccupations. In the very early novels, the culture of academic earnestness; rather later, a cluster of concerns about Jewish identity which eventually found their focus in the question of Israel; the interplay, or interface, between fiction and autobiography; finally, a passionate dedication to literary form. *The Counterlife* was a work of such luminous formal perfection that it more or less retired post-modern fiction, and may well have proved to be a heavy trophy for its author. Maybe *Sabbath's Theater* is the counternovel. Roth has always been a divided self. But this is the first time that Mr Hyde has been given the floor.

Simplifying Tolstoy, Sabbath suggests that all marriages are unhappy marriages. All couples are terrible couples. Thus, infidelity becomes a sacrament; and even death can look good if you regard it as an instant divorce. Like his creator, Sabbath is childless: he is resolutely childless. He may be married, but he's not *completely* stupid. There is much undeclared emotion here, you suspect. Famed for his crucifixion of the Jewish Mother, Roth is an unfailingly gentle memoirist of his own parents: see, particularly, *Patrimony* (1991). *Sabbath's Theater* offers us a freakshow of fearsome fathers, 'an alcoholic suicide who terrified [his daughter]', 'a bullying, vulgar businessman', 'an even more bullying and vulgar businessman', 'an overbearing bastard'. The Roth male may be miserable, but he won't hand on misery. Well, people have children for a big reason, if not a good one. Whatever else they may get up to, children prolong your story. They escort you from the biological desert, where all you hear are the jabberings of sex and death. And sex and death, of course, are the most terrible couple of all.

Sunday Times September 1995

The Name Is
William Burroughs

The Wild Boys: A Book of the Dead by William S. Burroughs

If a weak baboon is attacked by a strong baboon it has two means of escape: it can offer up its awful plum-hued rear for passive intercourse or it can mastermind and lead an attack on an even weaker baboon. Thus, in *The Naked Lunch*, Dr Benway moralizes: 'Baboons always attack the weakest party in an altercation. Quite right too. We must never forget our glorious simian heritage.' William Burroughs's characters are rarely in danger of doing that. They are the ironist's version of nature without nurture, like Swift's Yahoos – filthy, treacherous, dreamy, vicious and lustful.

The 'wild boys' are an army of jock-strapped Arab terrorists dedicated to mindless violence (they make hashish pouches out of their enemies' scrotums) and pensively ritualized male orgies. Financed by the harmless practical joker A.J. – who is so rich that his annual parties collapse currencies – the boys finally defeat the military and begin destroying civilization. In the last sentence they are glimpsed smiling for the first time as the 'stars are blowing away across a gleaming empty sky', having subverted, it seems, the entire universe. But that's only the plot.

Most of the book, like most of Burroughs, is a *tour de force* of delirious erotic imagery, clipped and spliced like a stream-of-consciousness shooting-script. Heterosexuality is strictly eschewed: 'two translucent salamanders in slow sodomy golden eyes glinting enigmatic lust . . . Lesbian electric eels squirm' – and so on. Halfway through there's forty solid pages of rectal mucus, rainbow ejaculations, craning phalloi and scoured tubs of Vaseline – all written with devout lyricism, and of only academic interest to the heterosexual reader. The intensity and the verbal contortions are still there, but one feels that Burroughs is losing some of the unselfconsciousness, the *artlessness*, that made his earlier novels so horrific and so hilarious.

The blurb calls *The Wild Boys* science fiction and explains to you how 'prophetic' Burroughs is being in it. But this is precisely how not to read him. SF always tries to be realistic. Burroughs never does. Some critics are confused by his lack of realism and get depressed because they feel that the world is a rather more decent and wholesome place than he would have us believe. But the only time an educated and well-balanced person has any business being depressed by a book is when its author is simply a bore. (One wearily instances the possibility represented by *King Lear*, at once the most harrowing and uplifting work in the language.) Art can be illustrative, where it's the subject-matter that is important, or it can rely on the play of words, ideas and wit. Burroughs doesn't want to convert or convince us; he wants only to write well, and very often does.

Observer June 1972

Cities of the Red Night by William S. Burroughs

To begin with, *Cities of the Red Night* reads like a new departure for William Burroughs: it has a plot, it has characters, and you can just about tell what's going on. This is daring stuff indeed, coming from the zap-poet of drug-highs and sex-deaths, the militant Beat, the author of *The Naked Lunch* and six further experiments in hallucinatory chaos.

The novel opens with a series of historical – and futuristic – vignettes. Health Officer Farnsworth is marooned at a remote colonial outpost, *circa* 1920. In the speculative present, military scientists look for new angles in virus warfare. Captain Strobe, the utopian pirate, sails the seas, tangling with the Spanish in Central America, *circa* 1700. These chapters are, for Burroughs, bafflingly straightforward – and deliberately clichéd ('grinding poverty', 'oppressive heat', 'searing pain'). Often we are not far from the gentle pastiche of, say, Golding's *Rites of Passage*.

Chopped in with the narratives is a stylistically antithetical tale set in the near future. The voice behind this story-line, however, is much more familiar: 'The name is Clem Snide. I am a private asshole' (as opposed, presumably, to a private dick). In relaxed, slangy, Chandleresque prose, Clem tells of his investigation into a sex-murder in Greece – 'A real messy love death.' The mystery even has elements of suspense, a commodity quite unknown in Burroughs's previous work. All this naturalism – it seems terribly unnatural. What is happening? Is Burroughs going straight?

Not really. The alert and wary reader will have noticed that all the narrative lines have been increasingly threatened by the usual convulsions of Burroughs's anarchic impulses. There have been blackouts and crackups, time warps and fear probes. The bizarre obsession with body transference starts to make frequent intrusions: 'Something familiar about Adam, Audrey thinks. Why . . . it's me!' '"No! No!" Audrey screams without a throat, without a tongue.' Characters switch from one narrative and show up in another. The genres began to mangle too: there are snippets of science fiction, westerns, fairy tales. Before long, and with a surge of previously checked energy, we are back in the known Burroughs world, the world of spectral rhetoric, drug withdrawal, urban breakdown, rampant vandalism, and no women. So in the cities of the red night the DNA Police quell the ID riots. The Chameleon Kids and Carrion Boys maraud among the cathouses and ghostly penny arcades. Dream Killers writhe to the drug-induced Black Hate Fever.

The Dog Catchers will seize any youths they encounter in the Fair Game areas and sell them off to hanging studios and sperm brokers . . . The boys sprint around the bodies and turn into an alley . . . The days seem to flash by like a speeded-up chase scene . . . Shatter Day always closer . . .

Experienced readers of Burroughs will know this sort of stuff pretty well by now. Tyros, on the other hand, will feel like the passer-by to whom a street-arab 'makes a gesture that is unmistakably obscene and at the same time incomprehensible'. The confusion is a legitimate one. Does Burroughs 'add up'? Is he anything more than a gloating litanist of turmoil?

There will always be people who think so. The academic machine is busy decoding him, dispensing a symbol here, a structure there. For instance Eric Mottram, in his long and humourless monograph *The Algebra of Need*, claims that Burroughs's obsession with the sexual hanging of young boys (and there must be more than a hundred gallows scenes in the new novel) merely constitutes a symbol of 'critical anarchism'. Well, you said it. The truth is that for all his sophistication Burroughs remains a primitive, extreme, almost psychotic artist. His work is in many respects impenetrably clandestine, and frighteningly personal.

Those who persist with Burroughs do so for the accidental delights of his style. It is muscular, musical and profane. His ear for the vernacular is marvellously sharp; he has an evidently limitless talent for parodying contemporary voices. It is perhaps inevitable that, despite his recent excursions into narrative, his prose should helplessly fragment into the same street scenes, the same blasphemous fantasies, the same sense of ubiquitous collapse. How long can Burroughs's writing follow this trail without impacting altogether? Shatter Day feels always closer.

Observer March 1981

Queer by William Burroughs

Shocking the world all over again, William Burroughs has written a thoughtful and sensitive study of unrequited love. Mind you, he wrote

it a long time ago – in the early Fifties, between the documentary
Junky and the hallucinatory *Naked Lunch*. The author explains, in
an agonized introduction, why the manuscript was for so long an
object of untouchable distress. 'The book is motivated and formed
by an event which is never mentioned . . . the accidental shooting
death of my wife, Joan' (by his own hand). So *Queer* is oddly snared
in Burroughs's personal voodoo; it is like him, and not like him;
surprisingly lucid and touching, recognizably antic and feral.

The unrequited love is of course homosexual. William Lee (an
often-used surrogate) is lying low in Mexico City in a halfway house
full of American dropouts and bail-beaters, all hectically gratifying
their 'uh, proclivities'. '"Maurice is as queer as I am," Joe belched.
"Excuse me. If not queerer . . . As a matter of fact, he's so queer I've
lost interest in him."' Intransigently Lee yearns for what is presented
as an impossibility: homosexual love, the real thing. It never works,
but Lee 'had never resigned himself'. By a process of elimination he
settles on Eugene Allerton, a man without qualities (he isn't even
queer), an appropriate recipient for unrequitable love.

One of the obstacles appears to be money, in that homosexual sex
is always bought sex, sooner or later. Lee, who is rich, seduces Allerton
through money and then loses him through money. After a while he
wins him back through money. An 'arrangement': rostered sex in
return for a free adventure holiday. They go to South America,
in search of an 'altering' drug which, Lee jokes, will make Lee less
queer or Allerton queerer. More impossibilities. The book ends
with a horrifying dream in which Lee comes to haunt Allerton, to
reclaim his loan. '"I wonder if you know just what '*or else*' means,
Gene?"'

How do things work, anyway, when a male desires maleness? Is
it something to do with wanting to *become* the other person? 'I want
myself the same way I want others . . . I can't use my own body for some
reason.' Disembodiment is a constant theme here, as it is in all Burroughs.
Earlier, Lee daydreams that he is in the body of a young boy.

Now he was in a bamboo tenement. An oil lamp lit a woman's
body. Lee could feel desire for the woman through the other's

body. 'I'm not queer,' he thought. 'I'm disembodied.'

Perhaps, then, we do glimpse the dead wife, the marriage, the other impossibility.

Allerton is featureless but everything about Lee is inordinate. His need for love has a tearing avidity that is in itself repellent. Lee is impossible, and he knows it. The lovers squabble about separate beds: '"Wouldn't it be booful if we should juth run together into one gweat bib blob? . . . Am I giving you the horrors?" "Indeed you are."' Lee releases tension through what he calls 'the Routine', fantastic monologues that are deliberately embarrassing, scabrous, pathological. They point the way, as do many local effects ('pathic dismay', 'so nasty', 'another angle is malaria', 'like music down a windy street'), to that great extended Routine, *The Naked Lunch*: 'I am a ghost wanting what every ghost wants – a body.'

Retroactively the book humanizes Burroughs's work. An impossibility to which one never resigns onself: this is as good a reason for writing as any. *Queer* also helps account for the particular slant of Burroughs's humour, the comic valuelessness of his despair. In the jungle:

'Gene, I hear something squawking over there. I'm going to try and shoot it.'
    'What is it?'
    'How should I know? It's alive, isn't it?'

Observer April 1986

Kurt's Cosmos

Galapagos by Kurt Vonnegut

This is far and away Kurt Vonnegut's best novel since *Slaughterhouse 5*. However, that's not saying very much, in itself – especially if you look at Kurt Vonnegut's novels *before Slaughterhouse 5*. These include a beautifully intricate space-fantasy, *The Sirens of Titan*, a coruscating satire on human destructiveness, *Cat's Cradle* (usually referred to by fans as 'the ice-nine book' or simply 'Ice Nine'), and a work of moral and comic near-perfection, *Mother Night*. *Mother Night* remains to my knowledge the only funny book about the Third Reich ever written, or indeed ever attempted. It is perhaps appropriate that such a novel should have been produced, not by a Jew, but by a German, a German-American who fought the Nazis in World War II.

Galapagos begins brilliantly with a description of a Vonnegut villain. Nobody writes about villains the way Vonnegut writes about villains (as *Mother Night* proves): he makes them look like lab rats, stupidly pursuing their projects and programmes, quite deaf to the disgusted laughter up there in Rat Control. James Wait, for example, first seen at the bar of the Hotel El Dorado in Guayaquil, Ecuador, presents himself as entirely unexceptional, 'drab and friendless', tamed by deep sorrow. 'He was pudgy, and his color was bad, like the crust of a pie in a cheap cafeteria.' In fact, Wait is a one-time homosexual prostitute who has made a million in the 'confidence' business, marrying and ruining rich old widows. Vonnegut views human infamy as, in the end, a condition of chronic indifference:

> It was . . . hotter than the hinges of hell outside. There was no
> breeze outside, but he did not care, since he was inside, and the

hotel was air conditioned, and he would soon be away from there anyway.

James Wait is fresh off the plane from New York. 'He had just pauperized and deserted his seventeenth wife.'

Wait has come to Ecuador to embark on 'the Nature Cruise of the Century', a luxury excursion to the Galapagos Archipelago. Joining him on the trip are a familiar bunch of megalomaniacs and nobodies, each of them in thrall to laughable or mischievous non-value-systems: big business, blind scientific advance, the myth of American innocence (an offstage character, a sprightly wreck called Bobby King, memorably embodies the non-values of public relations). It will not alarm Vonnegut fans to learn that the narrator is a ghost, an immortal soul who tells his story from the viewpoint of a million years in the future. This is a necessary distance, if your subject is evolution.

Vonnegut is not embarrassed by the Darwinian perspective, since he has always gazed down on Earthling confusions as if from some cosmic vantage of space and time. A million years hence, according to Leon Trout (1946–1,001,986), human beings will be no more intelligent than the blue-footed booby. In evolutionary terms, man went wrong when his brain outgrew his soul. 'In this era of big brains, anything which can be done will be done – so hunker down.'

The first half of the book teems with the kind of odd connections and telling metaphors that we reverently associate with early, pre-*Slaughterhouse* Vonnegut. The organized exposure of various animals to the effects of nuclear blasts was, in the disturbed mind of a Bikini veteran, 'the exact reverse of Noah's ark'. Killing people is here called 'outsurviving' them (an armed madman rampages, hoping 'to find more enemies to outsurvive'). All evils, for the purposes of this satire, come from ideas, from big brains. The Galapagos Archipelago was insignificant until Darwin found it instructive: 'Darwin did not change the islands, but only people's opinion of them.' Similarly:

From the violence people were doing to themselves and each other, and to all other living things . . . a visitor from another planet might have assumed that the environment had gone haywire, and that the people were in such a frenzy because Nature was about to kill them all.

But the planet a million years ago was as moist and nourishing as it is today . . . All that had changed was people's opinion of the place.

The second half of *Galapagos* we reluctantly associate with late, post-*Slaughterhouse* Vonnegut: it tends towards the formless, the random, the diffuse, the anecdotal. Always tempted by the delights of playful inconsequentiality, Vonnegut grows too attached to his pet grotesques and loses sight of their structural function. Perhaps this is a vestige of another weakness of the late phase, namely sentimentality. But it is only a vestige, and *Galapagos* is his most tough-minded book since *Mother Night*.

One of the purest delights of early Vonnegut was the phrasing. As with Elmore Leonard (in this respect, at least, a comparable popular artist), you can read for hours without hearing a single false quantity. *Galapagos* kicks off with that relaxed musicality and swing. It makes the reader sweat with pleasure, but also with suspense. And if in the end the novel doesn't quite come good, it makes some marvellous noises along the way.

Observer November 1985

Truman's Remembrance

Answered Prayers by Truman Capote

A long novel 'about the Very Rich', this was to be Capote's master-work, or so Capote used to claim. Recycling the author's baubled past, incorporating twenty years' worth of terrifyingly intimate letters and diaries, trumpeting the sleepy confidences of maudlin hostesses and blabbing billionaires, it was going to be a *tour de force* of vicious scandal that would, withal, aspire to the architectonic superbity of Proust. Or so Capote used to claim.

The Very Rich thought that Capote was their mascot or lapdog. In fact he was their unblinking chronicler. The soft-voiced sweetie on the *chaise-longue* or at the end of the bed was really a pitiless satirist, biding his time. 'What did they expect?' said Capote. 'I'm a *writer*.'

But what did *Capote* expect, exactly? When four sections of the novel appeared in *Esquire* in 1975 and 1976, the Very Rich dropped Capote. And, instead of not minding, instead of going on being a *writer*, Capote had a nervous breakdown, collapsing under a ton of drugs and drink. Later on he tended to downplay and reattribute his distress. He never liked the Very Rich anyway. Those published sections were no more than warning shots; the novel was burgeoning away in its hothouse. He wasn't scared. 'Just wait', he said, 'till they see the rest of it.'

Gore Vidal, for one, never believed that there *was* any 'rest of it'. From an interview in 1979:

As this is America, if you publicise a nonexistent work enough, it becomes positively palpable. It would be nice if he were to get the Nobel on the strength of *Answered Prayers*, which he, indeed, never wrote. There were a few jagged pieces of what might have been a gossip-novel published in *Esquire*. The rest is silence; and litigation and . . . noise on TV.

And unfortunately Vidal was right. This posthumous novel consists of only three sections, 'Unspoiled Monsters', 'Kate McCloud' and 'La Côte Basque'. The putative fourth, 'Mojave', was roped into the stopgap collection *Music for Chameleons* (1980), and left there. A fifth and sixth, 'Yachts and Things' and 'A Severe Insult to the Brain', though often and fondly discussed by Capote, have failed to surface. Even with running heads, broad margins and fancifully aerated line-spacing, *Answered Prayers* is nothing more than a frazzled novella. Far from nursing the book through the years to tender fruition, Capote, I suspect, barely looked at it. This seems clear from internal evidence alone, for in every sense *Answered Prayers* is quite without finish. In the preface to *Music for Chameleons* Capote noted with satisfaction how his prose was crystallizing into an untrammelled purity. 'Most writers, even the best, overwrite. I prefer to underwrite. Simple, clear as a country creek.' But *Answered Prayers* is slangy, coarse, unbuttoned – regressive. And while the scandalous snippets might have done for *Esquire*, it is hard to imagine a fully operative Capote passing them for hard covers. Capote was a craftsman, and *Answered Prayers* feels ragged.

'A rollicking soldier-sailor-marine-marijuana-saturated Denny-Jean cross-country high-jinks', for instance, 'or a pasta-bellied whale-whanged wop picked up in Palermo and hog-fucked a hot Sicilian infinity ago'. This is Venice: 'Sea mist drifts through the piazzas and the silvery rustle of gondola bells shivers the veiled canals.' This is rural Pennsylvania: 'A rolling farm filled with fruit trees and roaming cows and narrow tumbling creeks.' Rolling and roaming? The style is as promiscuous as the narrator. 'Her pubic hair and her shoulder-length honey-red hair were an exact colour match; she was an authentic redhead, all right.' (Who is this? Chandler? Spillane?) 'I massaged the nape of her neck, rippled my fingers along her spine, and her torso vibrated, like a purring cat.' And who is *that*? Velma? Zelda?

This is a novel about the Very Rich, so the imagery tends towards the exotic – or at any rate the expensive. Colette's friend Miss Barney speaks 'in tones chilled as Alpine slopes'. On the facing page, Colette herself has 'slanted eyes, lucent as the eyes of a Weimaraner dog, rimmed with kohl'. Whatever that might look like. A corgi wearing a pair of cheap sunglasses would be equally evocative, though a lot less opulent. Similarly, an ordinary anecdote about drunken speechlessness is still an ordinary anecdote, even when the speechless drunk is Montgomery Clift.

It isn't that the beau monde was too big for Capote's talents. The beau monde was too small for Capote's talents. Here, at least, in human terms the Very Rich are very poor. Interestingly, they are not interesting; incredibly, they are not even *credible*. They are certainly not the 'unspoiled monsters' of Capote's chapter title: they are spoiled mediocrities, they are boring freaks. The backgammon bums, the sweating champagne buckets, 'the Racquet Club, Le Jockey, the Links, White's', 'Lafayette, The Colony, La Grenouille, La Caravelle', 'Vuitton cases, Battistoni shirts, Lanvin suits, Peal shoes': how keen can a writer afford to be on all this?

Truman Capote spent the last ten years of his life pretending to write a book that was never there. Why? He was far too tough, I think, to fear further reprisals or ostracism from high society. He didn't write the book because the book was never there – artistically. Capote must have been mortified by a sense of creeping fraudulence. And such feeling as survives in *Answered Prayers* has to do with anticipated rejection, with finding out that your friends are strangers, and always were. An assignation with a ruined playwright:

> What I thought was: here's a dumpy little guy with a dramatic mind who, like one of his own adrift heroines, seeks attention and sympathy by serving up half-believed lies to total strangers. Strangers because he has no friends, and he has no friends because the only people he pities are his own characters and himself – everyone else is an audience.

Observer November 1986

Don DeLillo's Powers

Mao II by Don DeLillo

Post-modernism in fiction was never a school or a movement, like symbolism or surrealism, and had none of the revolutionary trappings – executive committees, special handshakes, manifestos cobbled together in cafés by ambitious young drunks. It was, instead, evolutionary: something that a lot of writers everywhere began finding themselves doing at roughly the same time. Even its exponents could see, in post-modernism, the potential for huge boredom. Why all the tricksiness and self-reflection? Why did writers stop telling stories and start going on about *how* they were telling them? Well, nowadays the world looks pretty post-modern in many of its aspects. It is equally fantastical and wised-up, and image-management vies for pride of place with an uninnocent reality. Post-modernism may not have led anywhere much; but it was no false trail. It had tremendous predictive power.

Don DeLillo is an exemplary post-modernist. And perhaps he is also pointing somewhere beyond. Whereas his contemporaries have been drawn to the internal, the ludic and the enclosed, DeLillo goes at things the other way. He writes about the new reality – realistically. His fiction is public. His dramatis personae are icons and headliners: politicians, assassins, conspirators, cultists. His society has two classes: those who shape the modern mind, and those whose minds are duly shaped. It is entirely fitting that the hero of DeLillo's longest, best and most recent novel, *Libra*, should be Lee Harvey Oswald: a sleepwalking ideologue who, in a single act, achieved iconic immortality, becoming a kind of flux-tube of national paranoia.

As a package, *Mao II* could hardly look more sprucely post-modern and transmedial. The title, which sounds like its own sequel, refers not to the Mao silkscreen on the cover but to the 1973 line drawing – by Warhol, naturally, the great displacer or degrader of images and icons. Each section of the book is preceded by a beautifully hazed photograph: a rally in Peking, a mass Moonie wedding, the tortured crowd on the terraces at Hillsborough, Khomeini's funeral, the cracked streets of Beirut. The documentary feel is appropriate. DeLillo is giving it to us straight: there's never the slightest doubt about what's going on. We move freely, in brightest light. It is the protagonists who grope and stumble. A blurbist might call the cast of characters 'unlikely', but they are more or less familiar players in the DeLillo game: a terrorist, a hostage, a terrorist broker or PR man, a reclusive (indeed wraithlike) American novelist, his obsessive fan and archivist, a monomaniac photographer, and an only partly deprogrammed disciple of Master Moon.

We are in an intensified millennial present, the Last Days – what the Moonies call 'hurry-up time'. 'When the Old God leaves the world,' DeLillo writes, 'what happens to all the unexpended faith?' It's not that people will start believing in anything: they will start believing in everything. 'When the Old God goes, they pray to flies and bottletops.' Karen, who first appears as one of the brides in the Mexican-wave, blind-date Moonie wedding at Yankee Stadium, is only the most extreme symptom of an (apparently) general condition. The post-modern world magnifies the self to the point of insupportability; those who can't take it will need to surrender to an idea or – easier still – a personality. The icon of this overlordship is of course the inscrutable Chairman, who tried to replace the thoughts of a billion people with the thoughts of Mao. At the same time Mao heroized the masses, the dark crowds to whom, DeLillo hints, the future 'belongs'.

Brita is the driven photographer. She used to photograph derelicts, but now she's switched to writers (any writers, all writers). Her lifework is a kind of 'species count', a pictorial census of the breed. 'I'm not interested in photography,' she tells Karen: 'I'm interested in writers.' And Karen very sensibly asks: 'Then why don't you stay home and read?' But we all know that second-hand isn't close enough any more. Or better say third-hand. The event or the person is first-hand. TV is second-hand. Print is third-hand.

A break comes Brita's way when she is asked to photograph the world-famously reclusive writer Bill Gray. Bill is also world-famously blocked, or burnt-out. His two 'lean novels' are agreed to be classics, but he has spent more than twenty years on number three – and it's a dud. Bill lives in elaborate obscurity with the devoted Scott, a personable heterosexual 'in his absurdly early thirties', who is almost the kind of fan American celebrities need least: the kind that shows up with the gun and 'the roguish smile he's been preparing for weeks'.

Practically blindfolded, Brita is brought to Bill's house. She takes her photographs, and talks and listens, and spends the night, as planned. And yet somehow her visit turns out to be pivotal, entraining Bill's dramatic re-emergence, and his eventual death. It is, one gathers, the simple theft and dissemination of his likeness ('the image world is corrupt') that releases Bill from his mythic solitude. Release him, in fact, into the heart of the contemporary action, into the 'event glamour', to use Saul Bellow's phrase, which leads Bill to New York, to London, to Athens, to Nicosia, to Beirut.

The main difficulty with *Mao II* is knowing how seriously, or respectfully, we are meant to take Bill and Bill's ideas, many of which struck this reader as neither true nor interesting. DeLillo is wonderfully good with his 'ordinary' crackpots: Scott and Karen are done with unimprovable inwardness; and the glazed pages about the Beirut hostage, although they at first seem dutifully virtuoso, are frequently exquisite. But Bill is lopsided. As a novelist inside a novel, he has an automatic post-modern authority, and he gradually becomes the book's spokesman or compère. Soon, everyone starts talking like the hero (a common tendency in the novel of ideas). And everyone keeps agreeing with him: 'I like your anger.' 'Interesting.' 'Very nice indeed.' At one point Karen says, 'I never think about the future.' Then we get: '"You come from the future," Bill said quietly.' When main characters say things 'quietly', you know it's meant to be good stuff.

Bill thinks that there's 'a curious knot that binds novelists and terrorists' and that 'terror is the only meaningful act' and that 'what terrorists gain, novelists lose . . . The danger they represent equals our own failure to be dangerous.' Too often the novel seems to bear Bill out – to weave a circle round him thrice. Brita compares his study to 'a bunker'; on her way to Bill's place, she feels she is 'being taken to see some terrorist chief at his secret retreat'. 'Some' terrorist chief? Which terrorist chief lives in Westchester or wherever it is, writing fiction and shunning publicity?

DeLillo does better – does wonderfully – when he interprets rather than propounds. His topography is unique: hard-edged, metallic, riveted into place, like Moonie Karen's brainstorms, which come 'with a shining, an electrochemical sheen, light from out of nowhere, brain-made, the eerie gleam of who you are'. He writes about the city ('the deep stream of reflections, heads floating in windows, towers liquefied on taxi doors, bodies shivery and elongate'), and then says: 'Nothing tells you what you're supposed to think of this.' But DeLillo is telling you, all the time. This is Bill, talking to an answering machine:

> The machine makes everything a message, which . . . destroys the poetry of nobody home. Home is a failed idea. People are no longer home or not home. They're either picking up or not picking up.

Independent on Sunday September 1991

Underworld by Don DeLillo

Expect a lot from the next sentence. Among its other virtues, the title of Don DeLillo's heavily brilliant new book gives a convenient answer to the Big Question about the American novel: where has the mainstream been hiding? The grand old men, the universal voices of the late-middle century (predominantly the great Jews, and John Updike), are getting older and grander, but the land they preside over looked to be shrinking. Furthermore, it seemed that their numbers were not being replenished by writers of comparable centrality. Was this an epochal change, a major extinction? No. It was a strategic lull.

Something atomized the mainstream. The next wave of genius was there, but not visibly, not publicly. Inasmuch as the mainstream was an institution, these writers could not work within it. They went underground, they sought an underworld of codes and shadows: incognito, incommunicado, and quietly dissident, their literary reputations largely cult-borne. But now the condition that caused the great discontinuity in American letters has come to an end. The novelists are climbing out of the bunker. Don DeLillo's exact contemporaries, Robert Stone and Thomas Pynchon, seem poised for a fuller expansion. DeLillo himself, however, suddenly fills the sky. *Underworld* may or may not be a great novel, but there is no doubt that it renders DeLillo a great novelist.

Needless to say, his was already a redoubtable body of work. Here is a writer of high intellect and harsh originality, equipped with extraordinary gifts of eye and ear – and of nose, palate and fingertip. Right from the start – *Americana* (1971) – DeLillo appeared tricked out and tooled up, his prose hard-edged, pre-stressed, sheet-metalled. As a young writer, naturally, he was only intermittently in full control of his energies. The next four novels, which include the little diamond of comic invention, *End Zone*, and the big, bountiful and necessary failure, *Ratner's Star*, showed a similar erratic intensity; as narratives, they felt defiantly shapeless and almost humorously static. They didn't head towards a destination; they went down culs-de-sac, performing frequent U-turns and handbrake skids; and they waited in jams. In particular, they didn't 'end'. They just stopped. DeLillo's alienation was never facile or reflexive; it was rich, dark and dangerous. But he was still a turbulent tributary searching for a river.

Running Dog (1978) signalled the fresh surge. This lean, mean, inch-perfect political thriller was followed by a long and improbably mellifluous departure, *The Names*, DeLillo's European – or Mediterranean – novel. Of course, DeLillo has always been a literary writer: deeply literary, and also covertly literary. In *The Names* the high style often feels stiff and inelastic; he can do it, but he looks musclebound. The experiment, in any event, was clearly salutary, because hereafter we hit the mother lode. First, that beautifully tender anxiety-dream, *White Noise*. And then *Libra*, the through-the-roof masterpiece. And then the cool formal artistry of *Mao II*. And then this.

The new novel is Don DeLillo's wake for the cold war. According to its argument, the discontinuity in American cultural life had a primary cause: nuclear weapons. The hiatus was inaugurated on the day that Truman loosed the force from which the sun draws its powers against those who brought war to the Far East; and it was institutionalized four years later when the Soviet Union started to attain rough parity. Cosmic might was now being wielded by mortal hands, and by the State, which made the appropriate adjustments. The State was your enemy's enemy; but nuclear logic decreed that the State was no longer your friend. In one of the novel's childhood scenes, the schoolteacher (a nun) equips her class with *dog-tags*:

> The tags were designed to help rescue workers identify children who were lost, missing, injured, maimed, mutilated, unconscious or dead in the hours following the onset of atomic war . . . Now that they had the tags, their names inscribed on wispy tin, the drill was not a remote exercise but was all about them, and so was atomic war.

Nuclear war never happened, but this was the nuclear experience, unknowable to anyone born too soon or too late. In order to know what it was, you have to have been a schoolchild, crouched under your desk, hoping it would protect you from the end of the world. How people arranged their lives around this moral void, with its exorbitant terror and absurdity, is DeLillo's subject. Perhaps it always has been. The new novel, at any rate, is an 827-page damage-check.

Underworld surges with magisterial confidence through time (the last half-century) and through space (Harlem, Phoenix, Vietnam, Kazakhstan, Texas, the Bronx), mingling fictional characters with various heroes of cultural history (Sinatra, Hoover, Lenny Bruce). But its true loci are 'the white spaces on the map', the test sites, and its main actors are psychological 'downwinders', victims of the fallout from the blasts – blasts actual and imagined. DeLillo, the poet of paranoia and the 'world hum', pursues his theme unstridently; he is tenacious without being tendentious. Yet even his portraits of bland, hopeful, pre-post-modern American life – his Americana – glow with the sick light of betrayal, of innocence traduced or abused. The 'great thrown shadow' has now receded and terror has returned to the merely local. MAD (Mutual Assured Destruction) was exploded; and the bombs did not detonate. Still, the press-ganged children who wore the dog-tags must live with a discontinuity in their minds and hearts. DeLillo's prologue is called 'The Triumph of Death', after the Breughel painting. In the end, death didn't triumph. It just ruled, for fifty years. I understand DeLillo to be saying that all our better feelings took a beating during those decades. An ambient mortal fear constrained us. Love, even parental love, got harder to do.

The protagonist, Nick Shay, works for a company called Waste Containment. And *Underworld* is among other things a witty and dramatic meditation on excreta, voidance, leavings, garbage, junk, slag, dreck. A drunken spectator at the 1951 Dodgers–Giants playoff leans forward and disgorges a length of 'flannel matter. He seems to be vomiting someone's taupe pajamas.' A newlywed on his honeymoon finds that 'his BMs' (daily 'hygiene' is another euphemism) 'are turning against him': 'that night Marvin had to make an emergency visit to the hotel toilet, where he unleashed a fire wall of chemical waste'. This is human waste, forgivable waste. But then there is nuclear waste: the stuff that never goes away and makes heaven stop its nose. In the exceptionally inspired epilogue, entitled 'Das Kapital', Shay visits the Museum of Misshapens in Semipalatinsk and confronts foetuses preserved in Heinz pickle-jars. Then he visits the radiation clinic and sees, among others, a 'woman with features intact but only half a face somehow, everything fitted into a tilted arc that floats above her shoulders like the crescent moon'.

In *White Noise* the famous 'airborne toxic event' was the result of a military-industrial accident. But it was also DeLillo's metaphor for television – for the virulent ubiquity of the media spore. Explaining a recent inanity committed by his daughter, Shay's co-worker 'made a TV screen with his hands, thumbs horizontal, index fingers upright, and he looked out at me from inside the frame, eyes crossed, tongue lolling in his head'. DeLillo's way with dialogue is not only inimitably comic; it also mounts an attack on the distortions, the jumbled sound bites, of our square-eyed age. 'I'll quote you that you said that.' 'She's got a great body for how many kids?' 'They put son of a bitches like you behind bars is where you belong.' 'I'm a person if you ask me questions. You want to know who I am? I'm a person if you're too inquisitive I tune you out completely.' 'Which is the whole juxt of my argument.'

It should be said in conclusion that those who stay with this book will experience an entirely unexpected reward. *Underworld* is sprawling rather than monumental, and it is diffuse in a way that a long novel needn't necessarily be. There is an interval, approaching halfway, when the performance goes awful quiet. But then it rebuilds, regathering all its mass. As I noticed the surprising number of approximations DeLillo settles for ('a kind of sadness', 'sort of semidebonaire', 'a certain funky something'), my feelings about the author began to change. Reading his corpus, sensing the rigour of his language, the near-inhuman discipline of his perceptions and the severity of his gaze, you often feared for the man's equilibrium. Yet who was the man? DeLillo is normally quite absent from his fiction – a spectral intelligence. *Underworld* is his most demanding novel but it is also his most transparent. It has an undertow of personal pain, having to do with fateful irreversibilities in a young life – a register that DeLillo has never touched before. This isn't Meet the Author. It is the earned but privileged intimacy that comes when you see a writer whole – what Leavis called the 'sense of pregnant arrest'.

'But the bombs were not released . . . The missiles remained in the rotary launchers. The men came back and the cities were not destroyed.' Just so. Now that the cold war is gone, the planet becomes less 'interesting' in the Chinese sense (ancient animadversion: May you live in interesting times). But it isn't every day, or even every decade, that one sees the ascension of a great writer. This means that from now on we will *all* be living in more interesting times. Which is my whole juxt.

New York Times Book Review October 1997

Even Later

The Actual by Saul Bellow*

Novelists don't age as quickly as philosophers, who often face professional senility in their late twenties. And novelists don't age as slowly as poets, some of whom (Yeats for instance) just keep on singing, and louder sing for every tatter in their mortal dress. Novelists are stamina-merchants, grinders, nine-to-fivers, and their career curves follow the usual arc of human endeavour. They come good at thirty, they peak at fifty (the 'canon' is very predominantly the work of men and women in early middle age); at seventy, novelists are ready to be kicked upstairs. How many have managed to pace themselves through and beyond an eighth decade? Saul Bellow's *The Actual* has a phrase for this kind of speculation: 'cemetery arithmetic'. The new book also confirms the fact that Bellow, at eighty-two, has bucked temporal law.

And bucked it twice over, it may be. Fifteen years ago, I believed that Late Bellow, as a phase, had begun with *The Dean's December*. The visionary explosiveness of Bellow's manly noon (*Augie March*, *Herzog*, *Humboldt's Gift*) seemed to have hunkered down into a more pinched and wintry artistry; the air was thinner but also clearer, colder, sharper. Then came the unfailingly mordant and accurate *Him with His Foot in His Mouth and Other Stories*. And then came *More Die of Heartbreak*, which now looks like yet another transitional work: a final visitation from the epic volubility of the past. The author had turned seventy. But this wasn't Late Bellow. Late Bellow, or Even Later Bellow, was just about to crystallize.

In an essay of 1991 Bellow quoted Chekhov: 'Odd, I have now

* See also pp. 447–69.

a mania for shortness. Whenever I read my own or other people's works it all seems to me not short enough.' And he added: 'I find myself emphatically agreeing with this.' Later Bellow consists of three novellas (*A Theft*, *The Bellarosa Connection*, *The Actual*) and two short stories ('Something to Remember Me By' and 'By the St Lawrence'), the whole running to about 300 pages. Shortness, certainly, is to some extent enforced. And when one casts about for comparable examples of literary longevity (Singer? Welty? Pritchett?), one seems to be moving naturally and inevitably towards a realm of sparer utterance.

Of course, the picture may change all over again (see below). Pretty well the only useful sentence in the thoroughly superfluous memoir by Harriet Wasserman (*Handsome Is: Adventures with Saul Bellow*), the author's former agent, reports the existence of two uncompleted novels, which may still emerge. And even that disclosure feels impertinent. When I reflect that the Wasserman volume (my proof copy has had the final section physically sheared out of it, doing little for its general deportment) is a mere look-see compared to James Atlas's massive anatomy, the *Life*, due in 2000, I find that my protective instincts are strongly stirred. Among many other things, *The Actual* reminds us that the fiction is the actual, the truthful record. As its narrator, Harry Trellman, observes:

> Your inwardness should be, deserves to be a secret about which nobody needs to get excited. Like the old gag. Q: 'What's the difference between ignorance and indifference?' A: 'I don't know and I don't care.'

Although Bellow has spoken of 'the more or less pleasant lucidity' attainable 'at this end of the line', it is not the kind of lucidity that deals in apothegms, admonitions, 'answers' ('nobody expects to complete their feelings any more. They have to give up on closure. It's just not available'). *It All Adds Up* was Bellow's cheerful title for his collection of discursive prose, but the imaginative life allows for no confident aggregations. The author of *Dangling Man* (1944) was far more inclined to assert and propound than the author of *The Actual*. And whereas, for example, *Mr Sammler's Planet* presented the Holocaust as a graspable historical event, *The Bellarosa Connection* refuses it all understanding. The story 'By the St Lawrence' contains a deeply apposite figure: 'Intensive-care nurses had told him that the electronic screens monitoring his heart had run out of graphs, squiggles and symbols at last and, foundering, flashed out nothing but question marks.' Later Bellow is a distillation, but not a distillation of wisdom. Capability has gone negative, confining itself to what can decently be said. These meditations are concerned with human attachments, most obviously or publicly the consanguinity peculiar to the Jews.

Confronted by the obsessive torments of a middle-European refugee, the narrator of *Bellarosa* silently advises: 'Forget it. Go American.' The advice is of course frivolous, a symptom of the 'American puerility' he detects in himself; but it's a popular option. Ravaged and haunted, the surviving elders look on helplessly as their children submit to American lunkification, homogenized by a carnal culture. The Jews have a special centrality, reconferred on them by the twentieth century; but now they are shedding their peculiarity, their ties of remembrance, and their talent for the transcendental. Towards the end of *Bellarosa* the narrator encounters just such a Jew-gone-native, who mocks him for his old-style sentiments. The last page beautifully registers the weight of what is being lost:

> Suppose I were to talk to him about the roots of memory in feeling – about the themes that collect and hold the memory; if I were to tell him what retention of the past really means. Things like: 'If sleep is forgetting, forgetting is also sleep, and sleep is to consciousness what death is to life. So that the Jews ask even God to remember, "*Yiskor Elohim.*"'
>
> God doesn't forget, but your prayer requests him particularly to remember your dead.

Loved ones can absent themselves without dying, and Later Bellow is adorned with many variations of amorous regret, grief, nostalgia, and thought-experiment. Seen from both points of view, by the way: let me drown out certain fashionable murmurs by trumpeting the assurance that no one writes more inwardly about women than

Saul Bellow. Look at Sorella, look at Mrs Adletsky; look at Clara Velde, from *A Theft*, fully incarnated in a single sentence (students of literary economy should examine its comma): 'The mouth was very good but stretched extremely wide when she grinned, when she wept.' While you love, that which is innate in you becomes malleable; so love shapes you. In 'Something to Remember Me By' and 'By the St Lawrence' this shaping goes all the way back to moments of youthful awakening, qualified by a complementary accession to death. The con-girl seductress, the child in the coffin, the wait outside the bordello, the body on the railtrack: Bellow makes us feel the mortal hold of these raw configurations.

The Actual is even more scrupulously written than its immediate predecessors. We notice the 'dried urban gumbo of dark Lake Street', we glimpse a silhouette 'in the gray bosom of the limo TV'; an ancient billionairess is 'like a satin-wrapped pupa'. But after eighty years of passionate cohabitation, the author's relationship with language has evolved into something like sibling harmony. The desire for vatic speech is undimmed, yet no riffs, no party pieces, accompany it. Bellow's prose remains a source of constant pleasure because of its manifest immunity to all false consciousness. It plays very straight. 'There is great variety in my dreams,' one Bellow hero confides. 'I have anxious dreams, amusing dreams, desire dreams, symbolic dreams. There are, however, dreams that are all business and go straight to the point.' Later Bellow is something like that: all business.

As I was putting this piece to bed, the launch issue of a literary magazine arrived on my desk: *The Republic of Letters*, edited by Saul Bellow and Keith Botsford. Its lead piece is a new Bellow story, entitled 'View from Intensive Care' and tagged 'from a work in progress'.* Picking up on certain details in 'By the St Lawrence', it

---

* 'View from Intensive Care' became part of *Ravelstein* (2000). *Ravelstein* is a full-length novel. It is also, in my view, a masterpiece with no analogues. The world has never heard this prose before: prose of such tremulous and crystallized beauty. (Incidentally, the James Atlas biography, mentioned earlier, turned out to be a moral disaster; hostile, inaccurate and ill-written, it is a dramatized inferiority complex lasting 600 pages.)

describes a medical close call with heroic, terrifying, and near-comical detachment: 'Taking note is part of my job-description. Existence is – or was – the job.'

Well, existence still is the job. And while the new story increases the scope of Later Bellow, nothing qualitative has changed. There is a great deal going on in these short fictions, tangled plots (for tangled lives) and intense formal artistry. But what accounts for their extraordinary affective power? When we read, we are doing more than delectating words on a page – stories, characters, images, notions. We are communing with the mind of the author. Or, in this case, with something even more fundamentally his. Bellow's first name is a typo: that 'a' should be an 'o'.

Observer August 1997

Obsessions
and Curiosities

Chess Is Their Life

Searching for Bobby Fischer: The Adventures of a Father and his
Brilliantly Gifted Son in the Obsessional World of International Chess
by Fred Waitzkin

Earlier this summer I played Nigel Short, the world number three,
at what chessers call a charity 'simul', or simultaneous display. And I
lost. The game was one-sided, and the defeat severe; but I suppose my
humiliation was quieter than it might have been against other world
number threes — quieter than if, say, I had dared Boris Becker to
present himself at Paddington Sports Club, on Castellain Road, there
to face the fury of my rising backhand slice. Two other grandmasters
were in the hall that day and I appealed to them for advice, which
they gave freely, and at high speed. This was no help. It was like
listening to the road directions of some hypermanic yokel: by the
end of the third paragraph you just want to ask whether it's right or
left at the end of the street. Young Nigel (he was born in 1965) had
about thirty other games to attend to, and at first his visits to my board
were relaxingly infrequent; later on, though, as positions simplified,
and opponents resigned, he seemed to be constantly presenting me
with his round, bespectacled, full-lipped face. This face was not so
much ageless as entirely unformed: you felt that it would still light up
at the sight of a new chemistry set, or a choc-ice. But somehow his
hands bestowed terrible powers on the white pieces. Those linked
central pawns of his — oh, what they could *do* to me. They weren't
pawns in the normal sense; they had grown, fattened; they were more
like bishops, or rooks. No, they were like queens, I thought, as they
worked their way into the very crux of my defence.

Searching for Bobby Fischer is a vivid, passionate and disquieting
book. Throughout, it runs a light fever of anxious pride and anxious

love. As a 'chess parent', a journalist, and a sane man, Fred Waitzkin is articulately aware of what he is doing. And what he is doing isn't always pretty. Full of bafflement, doubt, persistent self-reproach and comically vulgar ambition, he continues to preside over his son's distorted boyhood. His wife Bonnie, a moderating influence, 'frequently reminded us that there is life after chess'; but Fred Waitzkin never quite admits that, so far as little Josh Waitzkin is concerned, there has been no life before it. In every sport, in every exceptional endeavour, the coaching, caddying parent must gamble a compromised present against an uncertain future. But in no other activity is the gamble so discrepant and extreme. Every player in America is 'searching for Bobby Fischer' or his reincarnation, in a millennial quest for a Messiah, a deliverer, another world champ. But where is the old redeemer now, and what is he up to? He is, as Waitzkin will eventually reveal, a corny megalomaniac and flophouse miser, curled up on a bed somewhere in Los Angeles with *The Myth of Six Million Dead* and *The Protocols of the Elders of Zion*.

The book hinges on this kind of contrast: the purity and other-worldliness of the game, and the human mess and wreckage that almost always surround it. The contrast happens to be at its wildest in the Waitzkins' home town: 'With its dense architecture and crafty manipulations, its subtle attacks, intensity and unexpected explosiveness, chess is like the city' – and that city is New York. Little Josh discovered chess in Washington Square Park when he was six years old; he pestered his mother to take him there; 'he said he liked the way the chess pieces looked'. But did he like the players, and the way *they* looked? Israel Zilber, an International Master 'who reeked of urine and raged at the voices in his head'; Jerry, 'a strong A player', also an alcoholic who has gunfights with his wife; or the more typical Vinnie, a master-level player who is 'often short of change for a subway token'? They are addicts, hustlers, inveterates, recidivists – geniuses, idiots. This is Hoffmann, who dropped out of Columbia twenty years ago:

The chess-hustling business is bad. It's down with the economy, and O.T.B. [off-track betting] and Lotto have hurt. It's not a good

game for a gambler, because chess players are too rational and
conservative. You have to find a true compulsive who happens
to play chess – someone who's essentially masochistic and enjoys
being humiliated. One of my best customers was a rabbi . . .
While I beat him, he cursed and screamed, begging me to have
mercy on him. I'd tell him, 'What a fish you are. I'm gonna
crush you.' I took a lot of money from him. Unfortunately, he's
dead now.

Even when you begin to move up the professional scale, the
contrast remains sharp. Josh's chess tutor, Bruce Pandolfini, is
Manager of the Manhattan Chess Club, which sounds quite grand
until you glimpse him scrubbing its toilet. Major congregations of
chess talent take place in sorrowful front rooms over pizza parlours,
with stained walls, torn rugs and 'electrical wires dangling from
holes in the ceiling'. Even at the best tournaments 'the players
are a ragtag group, sweaty, gloomy, badly dressed, gulping down
fast food, defeated in some fundamental way'. And there is no
companionship; there is no human curiosity. The chess freaks
will occasionally mutter a few words about giving up the game
and doing something different with their lives, 'which is reasonable, considering that even the most brilliant are impoverished'.
Apart from that, it's just the wooden pieces, and the sixty-four
squares.

This is the American way: chess on the free market, with the
genius as bum. Early on in the book Fred takes Josh to Moscow for the
Karpov/Kasparov World Championship. Before they go, Waitzkin
talks to a Soviet defector who is keen to locate the dissident chess
champion Boris Gulko:

You'll need to contact a man I know who is a well-known
grandmaster, an expert in the endgame. He is also a KGB
agent, but don't worry, he is totally corrupt. The first day
you meet him, give him a present worth fifteen or twenty
dollars – a digital watch, maybe . . . He will suggest dinner.
During this meal present him with pornographic books and

magazines; then the chances are he will arrange for you to meet Gulko.

And we duly experience the Soviet version: politicking, match-fixing, drug-taking and institutionalized anti-Semitism – chess on steroids, with a gun at the player's temple. In the United States, a former national champion may be jobless and sleeping rough; in the Soviet Union you can watch him being singled out in the street and beaten up by the police. Normally one's instinct would be to blame the society for these characteristic injustices. After *Searching for Bobby Fischer*, though, one is more inclined to blame the game. Why is it that nearly every major chess event is a havoc of scandal, venality and hysteria? As David Spanier pointed out in *Total Chess*, only outsiders are surprised by such tawdriness. Real players know that this is the way chess is.

Dutifully, without the least hope of success, Waitzkin finally undertakes a literal search for Bobby Fischer, the man who brought chess to America and then, it seemed, 'took it away'. He doesn't find him but he brings back a haunting silhouette of the 'strongest' player who ever lived. For a while Fischer looks like the classic *idiot savant*. This is from Brad Darrach's biography:

When he loses interest in a line of thought, his legs may simply give out, and he will shuffle off to bed like an old man. Once, when I asked him a question while he was eating, his circuits got so befuddled that he jabbed his fork into his cheek.

In a variety of disguises Fischer moves through LA's Skid Row, 'from one grungy hotel to the next', usually registering as 'Mr James'. He gets a discount at the local anti-Semitic bookstore, so valued is his custom there. Not long ago he had all his fillings removed; he didn't want anything artificial in his head, in case he picked up radio transmissions. We only need a figure like Mick Jagger in here to complete the miserable pentagram of modern schizophrenia, with its fantasy electronics, media flotsam and sniggering blood libels.

It is quite a road that young Josh is walking; and Josh is the book's hero, a humorous, endearing and honourable little boy. When he plays, his face 'becomes serene' and 'he doesn't look like a seven-year-old'. He calls out chess moves in his sleep, and plucks at his hair, developing a small bald patch. But he conducts himself with certainty among the ragged putzes and patzers, the blitzers and kibitzers. When Josh loses, Fred confesses that he finds it difficult to embrace his son, and notices an extra distance between them as they walk down the street. And yet their shared intensity is in some way enviable. You feel the poeticism is earned when Waitzkin recalls his fishing trips with his brother and father:

> While we pulled in our fish, he stood behind us and rooted like any Little League father, as if we were accomplishing life's great deeds. Sometimes I felt as if I were reeling in his love.

The matter of anti-Semitism runs through the book like a recurrent illness. As I read *Searching for Bobby Fischer* my own little boys were, as usual, marching or creeping round the house, both armed to the teeth. It has often occurred to me that I could very easily turn them into anti-Semites, into stout little Nazis. Of course, I have little heart for the project. Certainly it would be far more time-consuming to turn them into chess prodigies. One's reluctance, in the latter case, is not equivalent but it is comparable. Chess genius lives, or windmills its arms, on the outer rim of sanity, as Nabokov knew; but Luzhin's confusions in *The Defence* (1929) already seem romantically antique. In *More Die of Heartbreak*, another book about a 'pure' scientist, Saul Bellow writes: 'Crazies are always contemporary, as sandpipers always run ahead of the foam line on beaches.' This is one chess combination – mental imbalance, in the contemporary setting – that can only become more and more unlovely. It has taken an exceptionally candid book to remind us that chess is beautiful, and to confirm the hidden or buried suspicion that it is also, somehow, unclean.

The Times Literary Supplement July 1989

Mortal Games by Fred Waitzkin;
Chess Is My Life by Viktor Korchnoi;
Kasparov–Short: 1993 by Raymond Keene

The face of chess is changing. For one thing, it is getting handsomer. Gone, it seems, are the bespectacled eccentrics, the mumbling autists and reeking regressives of yesteryear. The Grand Master Analysis Room no longer resembles the soundstage of *Revenge of the Nerds*. And look at the TV team: Daniel King could be a stand-in for Daniel Day-Lewis; John Speelman is the romantic image of the struggling artist, hard-up but head-in-air – the young Courbet, perhaps; once a GM and now a busy chess middleman, Raymond Keene has evolved from cautious pedagogue to broad-handed entrepreneur, to white-suited impresario. Until very recently chess players tended to look like Nigel Short, i.e., like child prodigies catapulted into adulthood. Now they tend to look like Garry Kasparov. Short, with his ripe and inconvenienced stare, is still fascinating to watch, perhaps because he more faithfully conforms to the outsider's ideas about the game. He expresses its ponderous anguish: the low blink-rate, the dreamlike retardation of gesture and reaction time. Whereas Kasparov, for all his famous intensity, now looks thoroughly secular. He looks as though he is at another kind of board meeting – at the IMF, say, okaying that fifty billion for the Brazilians.

Himself a considerable chess problemist, Vladimir Nabokov wrote two novels about chess, or around chess. In *The Real Life of Sebastian Knight* (1941) the interest is structural and metaphorical: the elusive Sebastian moves like a chessman, the knight, the only piece (other than the rook as it castles) capable of leaving the board and then returning to it. He is a figure for the ethereality of the game. The earlier novel, *The Defence*, is much more solidly, even grossly naturalistic. Here we encounter the slow-moving body and racing mind of a chess master, Luzhin, whose obsessive and tragic quest is for the impregnable 'defence' – against the white pieces, and against life. Luzhin will do as the archetypal GM of the pre-modern era. Pure scientist, crazy professor, arrested adolescent. The moment she sets eyes on him, his shadowy sweetheart knows that here is a man who will have to be inspected on his way out of the door every morning: odd socks, unbuttoned fly, a gout of shaving-cream in either ear. Such erotic feelings as he awakens in her are almost exclusively maternal. His besetting vulnerability will lead to breakdown, and then to suicide. Seedy, solipsistic, gullible, pitiable, abstracted, tormented and doomed: this, surely, is our platonic ideal of the chess genius.

No longer. The days of slobs and inverts, of fag ash and crumbs-in-the-beard, are all behind us. Modern chess has become professionalized, technicized – and glamorized. With its ranks of VDUs, its laptops, its display screens and mimic boards, the press room has submitted to the TV burnish: the burnish of the modern. All is fingertip and button-punch. The GMs are practically in lab coats. Information flashes and whirrs like the figures on the computer database. 'We're out of the book!' shouts one analyst to another, around move twelve, when one player unveils (as chess machismo dictates) his latest 'novelty': that novelty, he hopes, is on its way to becoming an innovation. Attacks and defences, we notice, are no longer called 'openings': they are now called *systems*. The backstage scene feels like a dramatization of the switch from the old notation to the new. '1 . . . P-QB4', for instance, has become the brisk, the ruthless, the digitalized '1 . . . c5'.

Garry Kasparov became world champion in 1985. Unquestionably, his has been a style-setting administration, like that of a two-term President. You see the role-model trickledown everywhere, from the Analysis Room to the chess pub or coffee house; maybe even to Washington Square Park, the world of hustlers and misfits (where every bum and babbler is a jinxed GM), so beautifully caught by Fred Waitzkin in *Searching for Bobby Fischer*. During these years Kasparov has refused to be straitened and caricatured by his own eminence. His self-esteem is still wonderfully sincere (it is without blindspots); he still twists and bounces around while he talks; his laughter is till dismayingly anarchical. Yet he has found amplitude; chess is his energy, but not his trap.

'I lost my childhood. I never really had it,' he tells Fred Waitzkin in *Mortal Games*. 'For some, chess is stronger than the sense of childhood.' Viktor Korchnoi gave his autobiography the generically blinkered title, *Chess Is My Life*. What kind of statement is this? A boast, a confession, a helpless confirmation of the obvious? Like most fields of contemporary endeavour, chess obeys the law of ever-increasing specialization. In 1985, aged twenty-two, Kasparov already looked specialized to the point of inanity. And then something happened. Chess might have taken his childhood; but he seems to be hanging on to his maturity.

Clearly the expansion has been partly political. I do not refer here to the bold clash of interests and personalities which saw Kasparov and Short break away from Fide to form their alternative body (the wobbly PCA). Nor yet to the largely symbolic opposition between Kasparov and Karpov, in which Karpov played White, or White-Russian (standing for the apparat and the empire), and Kasparov played Black (standing for ethnicity, decentralization and democracy). In the winter of 1989–90, Kasparov's home city of Baku in Azerbaijan became a kind of control experiment – conducted by Gorbachev, Kasparov believes – in hardline federal policing, or in brutalist race-management. As in Bosnia, a successful multicultural society was forcibly reinfected with racial atavisms. The bloodbath that followed was Gorbachev's signal to his restless republics. Kasparov was there; he was involved, he was endangered, he helped the people he could help. And he was never the same. These events not only destroyed his past – they contaminated it. He really had no choice but to reinvent himself.

All Russian chessplayers are prominent political beings, whether they like it or not. Korchnoi and Karpov seemed to form the two ends of the visible spectrum: Korchnoi was conscientiously persecuted before and after his defection, whereas Karpov (to say the least of it) became a consummate placeman, an air-sniffer, a seat-warmer. Such were the traditional options of the intellectual, and the artist, and the sportsman. It was Solzhenitsyn who, in far harder times and for far higher stakes, showed that there was a third way: he showed how you could leap right off the board. If you were a figure of sufficient size, you could confront the state directly, and as an equal, because world opinion was ready and waiting to redress the disparity.

Kasparov has shown that the chess player can also be a political player. He isn't just a pawn; and he isn't just a database either, an inflated cerebellum, a throbbing maniac in the closed system of the sixty-four squares. The effect has been roundly liberating. It has brought air to the cave of chess, and given colour to the etiolated faces of the players. You could warily argue that the chess genius, whose thoughts are about nothing else but the disposition of power, is in crucial need of the other dimension, to stay steady. Fischer was not coerced into a political life, so his paranoia invented one; and it was a mess. So here's the simple message that Kasparov sends: diversify if you dare. Play sublime chess while staying active in the world we know. Many of his rivals hate him for this – for his betrayal of the collegiate monomania. Many others see the force of Kasparov's move, and will emulate him.

Handsomely figureheaded, freshly configured, and at least partly humanized, chess waits in the wings, taking deep breaths, ready to burst on to the stage as a planetary spectator sport. This is the idea. This is certainly Kasparov's idea. Chess offers its audience the soap opera of opposed personalities in genuinely bitter combat, deploying an unbounded repertoire of feint, bluff, trap, poeticism, profundity, brilliancy, together with a complementary array of blunders, howlers, squanderings, bottlings, clawbacks, pratfalls, chokejobs . . . What stands in its way? Not the epic slowness of the game, nor its frieze-like immobility. What stands in its way is the gap, the chasm, the abyss that lies between the watcher and the watched. The difficulty is the thing separating the ordinary player from Garry Kasparov. The difficulty is the difficulty.

Here is an average chat in the Analysis Room, with the personable purists lounging over the chess boards, the chess computers, the chess mags and chess printouts, following the game on the closed-circuit TV. 'Then you hang me on e7.' 'We're trying to get Nd1.' 'You were going Bf4, e5, Be3, then d5.' 'Nf2!' 'Are we winning the piece? Qd7?' 'I always think with f3 it's nothing.' 'This is all right. No. It looks horrible.' 'Give me that line again? Quickly?' 'Kh8.' 'Kh8?' 'Kh8.' 'E3.' 'Not f4.' (Loud sneering.) 'Bg5.' 'Aren't we meant to have a swinging rook?' 'Nigel's taken it.' 'What about Nc7?' 'No way was he going e7.' 'Nd4, Qc4, Qd2, E5?' 'D5?' 'I'd consider going a5.' 'What about Nd7 again?' 'F4!' (Loud laughter.)

Now we move to the Savoy Theatre, where the combatants sit centre-stage. In the background the two arbiters lurk like resentful porters in a gentlemen's club, occasionally brandishing a sign marked 'Silence'. The audience follows the game on the giant screens, coached over their headphones by the invisible commentary team. In their perch the rotating GMs are rather more disciplined than in the Analysis Room, but just as unstoppably jokey, catty, sarky and cliquey. What you get here is the same blizzard of notation plus much empathetic squirming as the positions solidify and sharpen. During the speed games, the previous week, the GMs gave up all pretence at mediation and simply jabbered and gloated and cheered among themselves. They are very excited, and excitement is pretty well all they can communicate. The analysis is conducted at a speed and with a second-nature familiarity that put it well beyond the civilian's grasp. Still, as one sits there not understanding the GMs, it's at least nice to think that the GMs are understanding Short and Kasparov. But they aren't.

Take Game 19. Kasparov opened with the Ruy Lopez and Short defended with the Deferred Steinitz (4 . . . d6). By move twelve, Short, typically, had wrecked his own pawn structure in the daring hope of greater activity for his bishops and open files for his rooks. At move twenty the Savoy GMs were all in agreement that the game was level. After White's twenty-second move they were all in agreement that Black was losing. After Black's twenty-second move they were all in agreement that Black had lost.

'What's Nigel got that we haven't seen?' 'Nothing!' 'It's over.' 'Finished.' 'Goodnight, Charlie!' The game ended after White's twenty-sixth move, at which point the GMs all assumed that Short had resigned. Not so: down on stage the players were coolly shrugging and leering over the pieces, having settled on a draw. Subsequent analysis seemed to confirm that the position was unwinnable. But who knew? 'Let's face it,' said Short (according to Raymond Keene's quickie, *Kasparov–Short: 1993*), 'we don't have a clue what's happening.' 'The final position is a mess,' said Kasparov. 'It's extremely complicated.'

The ladder of incomprehension, at any rate, is clear enough. I don't understand the arcana of the GMs; the GMs don't understand the arcana of Short and Kasparov; and Short and Kasparov don't understand the arcana of their own positions. None of us understands. How cheering. Chess-promoters shouldn't try to meddle with or minimize the near-infinite difficulty of the game: they are absolutely stuck with it. It is what surrounds the board with holy dread – the exponential, the astronomical. So what are they up to out there, approximately? Because no one really knows. It would seem that comparatively little time is spent doing what you and I do at the chess board: hectically responding to local and immediate emergencies (all these bolts out of the blue). We are tactical, at best; they are deeply strategic. They are trying to hold on to, to brighten and to bring to blossom, a coherent vision which the arrangement of the pieces may or may not contain. And of course they are never left alone to pursue this search. Chess is savagely and remorselessly interactive: it is both mental game and contact sport. What's it like? All-in wrestling between octopuses? Centipedal kickboxing? In its apparent languor, its stealthy equipoise, as each player wallows in horrified fascination, waiting to see what his opponent has seen, or has not seen, one may call to mind a certain punitive ritual of the Yanomani. Only one blow at a time is delivered by the long stave. The deliverer of the blow spends many minutes aiming; the receiver of the blow spends many minutes waiting. Garry Kasparov is the best there's ever been at it, and he knows what chess is. 'The public must come to see that chess is a violent sport,' he says. 'Chess is mental torture.'

Independent on Sunday November 1993

The Sporting Scene: White Knights of Reykjavik by George Steiner

Chess, with its combination of the profound and the banal, the cerebral and the spurious, its autodynamic symmetries and nebulous structures, has obvious affinities with George Steiner's criticism and thought. It has obvious attractions for him too: in common with music and mathematics, chess produces prodigies, many of them Jewish; although the game is clearly 'finite', computers, flatteringly, are less good at it than we are (our fastest calculator would need many thousand times the age of the earth to compute the opening twenty-five moves); it concentrates the nervous system with such an intensity that the board's sixty-four squares become subject (in Steiner's phrase) to 'the unbounded exactitudes of art'. What's more, the resonances of the 1972 Fischer–Spassky world championship – political tension, unprecedented publicity, the clash of old and new chess values – must have further flared the nostrils of the panoptic, polymathic, polysyllabic Doctor as he stepped out on to the Reykjavik tarmac.

Yet one of the most attractive things about Steiner's new book is how refreshingly unSteineresque it is. There's not one detailed comparison between a middle game and Bach's *Die Kunst der Fuge*. Page after page goes by without any reference to Auschwitz. Nor, with a couple of exceptions, is he reduced to slinky *aperçus* on, say, the entropic tendencies of chess praxis. Originally a series of articles for the *New Yorker*, the book is literary reportage rather than a specialist monograph. It is the human drama and intellectual excitement that catch Steiner's imagination – and no one who enjoys either can afford to miss *The Sporting Scene*.

Although the subtitle refers to the contestants as the 'White' knights of Reykjavik, Fischer, in Steiner's eyes, is morally always playing Black. True, Spassky was under pressure from Moscow, was repeatedly humiliated by Fischer's antics, behaved throughout with a courtly pathos and dignity, and had everything to lose; Fischer, on the other hand, with everything to gain, seemed an ignorant, avaricious, *Playboy*-reading, commie-bashing exhibitionist. Steiner accordingly gives a touching portrait of Spassky, but sympathy is often absent from his treatment of Fischer. For instance, we are nagged about Fischer's 'infantile greed' – an obvious simplification, since Fischer's cavortings and bust-ups regularly ran counter to his material interests. Similarly, 'when matters were not going well', clucks Steiner, 'Fischer would instantly revert to irascible histrionics'. Not so: Fischer reverted to these as late as the eighteenth game, threatening to 'terminate summarily' a match he was by then in no danger of losing. Svetozar Gligoric points out that Fischer had little real sense of what was at stake, in terms either of money or self-aggrandizement; just as Fischer is rumoured to sit in hotel rooms shrieking 'Zap!', 'Chop!' and 'Crunch!' when playing chess with *himself*, his demands and tantrums are expressions purely of surplus combative will – a quality Spassky was eventually shown to lack, perhaps to his credit. It may seem inadequate to observe that Fischer, like many other grandmasters, is merely insane, but it needs to be said that for all his predatory genius he remains something of an innocent.

As Steiner moves from psychological to philosophical conjectures the fit reader begins to regard the book askance. Some grand-sounding, though plausible, links are forged between chess and the other autonomous non-verbal constructs of music and maths before Steiner (riskily) attempts to evoke what Nabokov calls 'the full horror of the abysmal depths of chess'. In several respects these are thrilling pages; but when unleashed on the abstract Steiner is never very far from the old apocalyptic beefcake:

Even before the start of play, the pieces, with their subtle insin-uation of near-human malevolence, confront each other across an electric silence. At the first move, that silence seems to shred like stretched silk [on 1 N-QR3, maybe, as your opponent splits his sides, but hardly on 1 P-K4] . . . all mass and energy interact in a lattice so finespun, so multidimensional that we cannot even conceive of a model. The dynamic dovetailing of the whole game, the unfolding ramifications of its crystalline armature are implosive in the very first move . . . As one breathes the first scent of victory – a musky, heady, faintly metallic aura, totally indescribable to a non-player – the skin tautens at one's temples, and one's fingers throb. The poets lie about orgasm.

Now wait: if it *is* indescribable, don't describe it. Characteristically, there is a spark of meaning somewhere in this gaudy bonfire – but such apprehensions must be evoked with hesitance, irony, self-effacement, everything, in short, that Steiner lacks, here as elsewhere. It may be invidious to quote so many bad sentences from a book containing so many good ones; however, it is time Steiner ceased to be blinded by his own immense gifts, and time he noticed the important distinctions between brilliance and dazzle.

New Statesman April 1973

Football Mad

The Soccer Tribe by Desmond Morris

Readers of the *London Review of Books* who like football probably like football so much that, having begun the present article, they will be obliged to finish it. This suits me down to the ground. Pointy-headed football-lovers are a beleaguered crew, despised by pointy-heads and football-lovers alike, who regard our addiction as affected, pseudo-proletarian, even faintly homosexual. We have adapted to this; we keep ourselves to ourselves – oh, how we have to cringe and hide! If I still have your attention, then I assume you must be one of us, pining for social acceptance and for enlightened discussion of the noble game. This puts me in the happy position of not really caring what I write. You will read me anyway. Ho-hum. If I could render a whistle on the page (a strolling, nonchalant whistle, hands in pockets, head held high), then that is what I would render . . . But let's talk football for a while.

I am writing this piece, by the way, several days before the England v. Hungary encounter on 18 November 1981. By the time you read me, anything might be happening. Brian Clough or Bob Stokoe or Elton John could be the new England manager, nursing bruised dreams for the World Cup in 1986. On the other hand, Sir Ron Greenwood might even now be contentedly inspecting the hotels in Bilbao, hoping to find a likely venue for the lads next summer. Thanks to a series of hilarious flukes, England need only a draw against Hungary to qualify, and so it's a fair bet that the team will be gouged through into the Finals. However, this would be no vindication of anything or anybody. English honour has already been lost, on the playing fields of Norway and Switzerland. The predicament is unaltered. What are our realistic prospects? Where can we look for solace, for succour, in Spain?

Did you notice, during the Norway game, how the *faces* of our stars degenerated as the match went on? Kevin Keegan, a cross between Marc Bolan and Donny Osmond when he spun the coin in the centre circle, resembled a grimacing Magwitch by half-time. Paul Mariner, a picture of pampered, hammy self-love at club level, reminded me, as he trudged from the park, of the standard, traumatically chinless mod who puts in depressingly regular appearances at south-coast magistrates' courts after Bank Holiday weekends. Trevor Francis, usually the identikit poet, dreamer and heart-throb of the lower sixth, looked like a mean and frazzled brawler when he missed that easy header in the second half. As for Terry McDermott, who cuts a pretty unreliable figure at the best of times . . . By the final whistle, England looked like a scratch team from a remedial borstal, whereas the Norwegians, their blond locks bouncing in the air, were romping about like cosseted college boys.

It is curious that many of the automatic metaphors of football commentary, written and spoken, are connected with the idea of education. A thoughtful pass, a cultured back-heel. A football brain. Indeed, an educated right foot. You didn't need to watch, as I did, all the episodes of the recent inside-football series on BBC2 to satisfy yourself that these concepts aren't much in use on the training field. 'Magic', 'class', 'great', 'nice', 'terrific' and 'unlucky' seem to be the main epithets on offer there. In the post-goal frenzy, when the players roll and cuddle and leap in that delightful way, what are they saying to each other? 'Sapient!'? 'Profound!'? 'Erudite!'? 'Perspicacious!'? Unlikely, on the whole. I am trying to suggest that, conceivably, our football suffers from the dominance of its working-class ethos. They don't seem to have this trouble in the rest of Northern Europe – where, in fact, they appear to have dispensed with the working classes altogether. It has been said that our footballers are paid too much money. Perhaps they should be paid in something else: book-tokens, lecture coupons, night-class dockets, culture vouchers.

A slight digression. One Sunday lunchtime, some years ago, I found myself in a high-priced restaurant on the Embankment – an

expense-account, no-account gin palace, with tuxed pianist, brawny
escort girls and many a spendthrift loudmouth yelling in the padded
gloom. Who should be at the bar but Malcolm Allison (then manager
of Crystal Palace) and Martin Chivers (then centre-forward for Spurs
and England). Perched on stools, these big modern princes were
talking intimately and earnestly, their heavy shoulders tensed over
their drinks. Naturally I edged up close to Chiv and Big Mal, hoping
to hear – what? Fluent, allusive talk of set-pieces, short corners,
long throw-ins, one-against-one situations, professional fouls, banana
kicks. What I heard went something like this.

'The more you learn, the more you know.'
'This is it.'
'This is it.'
'The more you know, the more you learn.'
'This is it.'
'In this life, if you learn something, you –'
'You don't forget it.'
'This is it.'
'So that –'
'As you go on –'
'In this life –'
'You're always –'
'Learning things.'
'This is it.'

But Mal and Big Chiv weren't talking football. They were talking
philosophy.

What went wrong for England, on the night, on the park, during
those two vital qualifiers in Norway and Switzerland? 'Five minutes of
madness' was how Ron Greenwood explained the Norway debacle,
whereas it had previously taken only 'two minutes of madness' to cost us
the game in Switzerland. In these seven mad minutes, England conceded
four goals to teams made up partly of amateurs – teams, we were sternly
reminded by the press, that would 'struggle in our Second Division'. In
both cases, the hysteria produced in the England team by conceding one

goal led instantly to the concession of a second. 'And it's gone in! It's a goal!' said commentator Brian Moore, in a tender, incredulous moan; and before the great man could even clear his throat he was required to add: 'And . . . another goal! Disaster for England.' God, what a croak it was. Any team might have let this happen once (and the Swiss goals, at least, were beautifully set up). But twice?

Of course, it is all too easy to blame Ron Greenwood. Yet I think we should blame Ron Greenwood, whether it is all too easy or not. The selection of Ray Clemence in Norway cost us the first goal, and the first goal cost us the second (thanks also to a skilful 'tap-on' from Terry McDermott to the lone Norwegian in the England penalty area). Big Ray was plainly in a terrible state after his nightmare inauguration at Tottenham. He came cartwheeling off his line to flail at innocuous crosses; all night he looked capable of being nutmegged by a beachball. It was very typical of Greenwood to fly in the face of popular counsel and 'show faith' in his man. But this display of purposeful calm clearly spooked the rest of the team. Much has been written to the effect that our players lack skills. Perhaps they do. The other thing they lack is the confidence to show the talents they do have. At the moment the team is quite without psychological cohesion. Greenwood doesn't give players confidence: he gives them the horrors.

It is convenient, for the purposes of analysis, to look at the history of England managership since 1970 as a drama, or tragedy, in three parts or phases. Part One could be entitled *The Nervous Breakdown of Alf Ramsey*, Part Two *The Nervous Breakdown of Don Revie* and Part Three, which is still running, *The Nervous Breakdown of Ron Greenwood*. Each part culminates in or leads towards the same crisis or 'recognition': failure to qualify for the World Cup.

All three tragic heroes played their parts in a distinct style. Alf Ramsey was mild, defensive, strenuously elocuted, buoyed up by past glories and a secure knighthood. The visage of Don Revie, after his first few matches, became a disturbingly familiar sight: a mask of tanned and glittering desperation. Revie,* of course, resigned halfway through the fifth act, having leaked the news to his pal Jeff Powell

* 'Revie', in my typescript, was here misprinted as 'Review'.

on the *Mail*, and split for Dubai, thereby embracing a wonderful opportunity to safeguard the financial security of his family.

Greenwood's style is something else again. *The Nervous Breakdown of Ron Greenwood* might even now develop an epilogue or sequel, one very tentatively entitled *The Remarkable Recovery of Ron Greenwood*; but the lineaments of Ron's tragedy are already clear. In this case, the grim psychodrama is bodied forth in terms of unpierceable *serenity*. The serenity is cultivated, precarious and, in fact, non-existent; yet serenity is the keynote of the performance. Do you remember the smile of beatific repose that Greenwood found himself sporting throughout the defeat by Scotland at Wembley in the Home Internationals this year? A ghastly spectacle, much lingered on by the television cameras. The smile suggested that this defeat, like all the others, was yet another feint or shimmy in a vast and inscrutable battle-plan which only Ron knew about. I need hardly add that the whole veneer has subsequently deteriorated and is barely visible behind the hot mists of paranoia which Greenwood now candidly exudes. Poor guy! But he has done nothing in the England job, except to distance the memory of Don Revie.

Where, then, do we look for our next Motivator, the next candidate for the prime time and the valium? According to the Voice of Sport – I mean, *The Sun*'s Frank Clough – the 'people's choice' is Brian Clough, who is no relation. According to Brian Glanville on the *Sunday Times*, it is Jack Charlton – an extraordinary finding. Charlton, I suppose, has a head start on his rivals, in that he already suffers from onomastic aphasia, and keeps getting all the players' names wrong. But what else has Jack got going for himself? The main thing about Charlton, as a figure, as a force, is his reputation for being one of the most 'physical' players ever to pull on an England jersey. This is what the people who make the people's choice must be yearning for: a return to the 'traditional strengths' of the English game.

Brian Clough, of course, is mad already, but he isn't anything like as mad as he used to be and would perhaps enjoy a certain amount of immunity in the England job. Malcolm Allison, too, went mad some time ago now, when Crystal Palace were relegated twice in successive seasons. The most common reservation about the amiable Bobby

Robson concerns one central fear: we hear talk of his 'excitability'. And as for Mad John Bond of Norwich and Manchester City . . . It is tempting to conclude that being a football manager drives a man insane. But I still think that this diagnosis is too simple. It's not being a football manager that drives them mad. It's going on television that really does it.

Perhaps, then, we may modestly envision a quieter role for the England manager of the future: more cloistered, more thoughtful, more bookish. Under no circumstances, however, should the Gaffer be left alone with Desmond Morris's new work: he would almost certainly go mad, or else simply die of inanition. In *The Soccer Tribe* Morris maps out the connection between 'ancient blood sports' and 'the modern ball game'. Nowadays, the goalmouth is 'the prey', the ball 'the weapon', and the attempt to score 'a ritual aim at a pseudo-prey'. Is this true? Or, more important, is this interesting? Morris goes on to say that 'in England, there are four "divisions", presenting a parody of the social class system'. He then traces the analogies between football and religion: 'Star players are "worshipped" by their adoring fans and looked upon as "young gods".' Later on, he develops a far more compelling thesis, arguing that . . .

Ah, but the sands of space are running out. That's enough football for today. I only have time to add that Morris's book is handsomely packaged, that the pictures are great, magic, brill, etc., and that the text is an austere, an unfaltering distillation of the obvious and the obviously false.

London Review of Books December 1981

Among the Thugs by Bill Buford

Early on in *The Silence of the Lambs*, when the first victim has been hauled out of the river – a small-town teenage girl, naked, flayed, bloated – and is lying on the coroner's deck, the author writes: 'Sometimes the family of man produces, behind a human face, a mind whose pleasure is what lay on the porcelain table.' Thomas Harris opened up that hidden mind, and made it cohere. In *Among the Thugs* Bill Buford realizes a similarly alien world. One transgressor acts in a crowd, the other is irreducibly alone, but the thug and the serial murderer have plenty in common: sociopathy, delirium, motivelessness, and an utter dedication to the ugly.

Every British male, at some time or another, goes to his last football match. It may very well be his first football match. You stay home, thereafter, and watch it on TV. At my last football match, I noticed that the fans all had the complexion and body-scent of a cheese-and-onion crisp, and the eyes of pitbulls. But what I felt most conclusively, above and below and on every side, was ugliness – and a love of ugliness. One day in 1983, Buford found himself in the Shed, at Chelsea, wedged into the solid mass of swearing, sweating, retching, belching humanity. For most of us, this situation would represent a personal catastrophe, to be escaped and recovered from and never repeated. Instead of wanting less, however, Buford wanted more.

Buford is an American; and, as the creator of *Granta*, he is, to put it no higher, one of the eminent literary middlemen of his time. I expected *Among the Thugs* to follow a formula: respectable figure pursues horrible subject in search of the bad time that will make a good book. But such an approach, honourable enough in its way, wouldn't have worked for the thugs. A natural aversion, not to mention a natural terror, would have set in far too early. Buford was possessed by a genuine fascination, necessarily perverse, and bound up with his own susceptibilities. He began the book because he 'wanted to know why young males in England were rioting every Saturday'. Answer: because they like it. Buford wrote the book because he liked it, too. He liked the crowd, and the power, and the loss of self.

Being American helped, as Buford hoped it would. *Among the Thugs* is full of minor solecisms. (Listen, mate: the top bit's the *bar* not the post, and it's two *legs* not two games, and you don't *tie* the score, and you might say *the* Fulham Road but you never say *the*

Fulham Broadway. OK?) But as Buford starts sampling the London grounds, we start re-experiencing their squalid exoticism. 'The Den on Cold Blow Lane opposite the Isle of Dogs.' Now that's really *good*. At first it seems that Buford is taking us nowhere we haven't already been. But when were we last there? Aren't we insulated by irony, weariness and disgust? Haven't we all spent years looking the other way?

Before you know it, Buford is flying to Turin with the lads of Man U. Abroad, of course, is the place where the football fan sheds his diffidence and starts to come alive. There he stands, in a Renaissance setting, with Union Jack underpants on his head, with the words BRYAN ROBSON tattooed across his brow, stripped to the waist, fat, pale, ankle-deep in sick, menacing the local women and children, peeing into a fountain, singing 'Fuck the Pope' and 'God Save the Queen', and blind drunk. This is before the match. This is nine o'clock in the morning.

After the match, the whisper starts making the rounds. 'It's going to go off . . . it's going to go off.' Then the chant: United. United. United. United. Buford is in the middle of a tight mob of 200, walking fast but not running, hands on the shoulders of the man in front, moving in on the city. Sammy, the leader, with his personal pack of juvenile sheepdogs, runs backwards down the line intoning: 'The energy . . . the energy is very high. Feel the energy.' Then it goes off: violence, breakage, ecstatic transgression, naturally escalating with every fresh jolt of shattered glass and sickening impact, until Sammy is saying: 'The city is ours . . . ours, ours, ours.' Buford also recalls the words of another lad, as it starts to go off. He said 'that he was very, very happy, that he could not remember ever being so happy . . .'

There is, as they say, a question-mark over Buford's fitness – his fitness to participate, and then to describe. He cops a full beer-can and a nightstick in Turin, has his head banged against a lamp-post by a National Fronter in Bury St Edmunds, and gets a thorough spanking from the riot police in Sardinia. 'I will not describe the violence,' he says, more than once. How much violence did Buford commit, and at whose expense? True, he isn't in top nick for much of the action: on page 71, for instance, he is 'very, very drunk', whereas on page 144 he is merely resolving to *get* 'very, very drunk'. And as the book wears on, and the obsession wears out, he is increasingly and understandably 'bored', 'indifferent', 'exhausted'. We are allowed only one glimpse of his largely unexplored brutalization, when, on his return from Turin, an elderly couple impede his progress on a staircase in the Underground. He shoves them 'forcefully' aside, moves past, turns, and says: 'Fuck off. Fuck off, you old cunts.'

At the outset Buford believed that football violence had a cause, or at least an explanation. Protest/rebellion/alienation/class/unemployment/football itself. 'It's a religion.' 'We do it for England.' 'It's like war.' Buford turns to Elias Canetti (*Crowds and Power*) and stylistically to Hemingway, and even, one suspects, to Marlon Brando in *Apocalypse Now*: 'Nothingness is what you find there in a crowd. Nothingness in its beauty, its simplicity, its nihilistic purity.' One by one, though, all the 'reasons' fall away. 'I couldn't believe', writes Buford, 'that what I saw was all there was.' But he does come to believe it: what he sees is all there is.

At one point in the late Alan Clarke's remorseless and masterly TV movie, *The Firm*, our central football hooligans are lounging around watching a documentary about football hooligans. Why do football hooligans do what they do? 'It's a search for *meaning*,' says the on-screen sociologist. And one of the lads – Nunky – pitches in: 'Why don't he just say we like ittin people?' Then, to the tune of 'Here We Go', the lads start singing: 'Wank-wank-wank, wank-wank-wank, wank-wank-wank. Wank-wank-wank, wank-wank-wank, wank-wank-wank . . .' Why people like hitting people is of course an eternal mystery. Becksie, the top thug in *The Firm*, is asked this question by his wife: why? 'I need the buzz,' he whispers, almost in apology. She replies: 'Well buy a bloody bee-yive!' No, a beehive definitely wouldn't do it – not for Becksie. A beehive wouldn't help him in his violent struggle with impotence and (above all) with boredom.

Independent on Sunday October 1991

The School of Doyle

The Biggest Game in Town by A. Alvarez

Anyone who started *sitting down* early in life will always be susceptible to the cool ostentation of poker. *Stud, check, burn, raise, kick a buck, deuce, lady, freeze out, call, fold, flop*: you never get a chance to sound so boastful and cinematic when playing cribbage or canasta. Money, they say, is 'the language of poker', but poker-talk has its own fascination too. Like drug-talk or crime-talk, poker-talk is clandestine, male-supremacist and incurably Yankophone, tending towards self-dramatization and heroic monologue. My big poker period was in my teens. Ever tell you about the time I lost my busfare at lowball?

'Ungar broke Bill Smith when he flopped a flush against Smith's pair of sixes and straight draw . . .' A. Alvarez is a lifelong poker addict and a feared member of various schools in London and New York. For the purposes of this vivid little book, however, he doesn't mess about with his own vicissitudes at the table. He goes straight to the top: to the World Series No Limit Hold 'Em Championship in Las Vegas.

We would all be so much better at poker – or at chess, snooker or shove-ha'penny – if we did nothing else the whole time. In Las Vegas, they do nothing else the whole time: twelve hours a day, seven days a week. 'I feel I'm anteing myself to death,' says one glazed dude. 'I've already been playing professional for twenty years. In the same game, really. I mean, how long is a poker game?' The spooks of the Glitter Gulch poker parlours simply play, eat, sleep and occasionally 'grab a broad'. There are veterans of Binion's Horseshoe who have never heard of the Vietnam War.

Such suspension and torpor, as Alvarez explains, are built into the

Las Vegas ecology. By 10 a.m., it is too hot for golf or tennis, or even for swimming. Apart from quick marriages, quick food, pornography, prostitutes and pawnshops, the sand-locked town has nothing to offer but hazardry. There are no clocks, no windows; there is no outer reality. On a certain morning in 1976, the banner headline of the Las Vegas *Review Journal* read 'DEALERS LOSE TO IRS!' In the bottom corner was a taciturn paragraph headed 'Jimmy Carter New Pres.'

'The guy who invented gambling was bright,' the New York dicer Big Julie once observed, 'but the guy who invented the chip was a genius.' Chips are legal tender in Las Vegas, toy money that buys food, drink, sex and goods. By the same self-hypnotic process, bets of a 'nickel', a 'dime' and a 'big dime' translate as bets of $500, $1,000 and $10,000 respectively. Thus, five big-dime bets – five slivers of innocuous plastic – and you've lost your house.

Of course, this conspiracy of cool is a definite plus when it comes to gulling the suckers, the losers, the 'dogs' – the troupes of spangled, mink-Stetsoned, blue-rinsed, Big Mac-ravaged punters who hit town every year to surrender their savings, pensions, social-security cheques and disability allowances. Yet the survivors, the million-a-year pirates of the system, are precisely those who connive most thoroughly with the prevailing unreality. As Alvarez makes clear, the true highroller has no concern for money whatever.

Money is the language of poker, but for the pro that language has no further currency. 'It is just an instrument, and the only time you notice it is when you run out.' Similarly, when the highroller makes a killing he quickly blows his winnings on random and ignorant wagers. The 1981 poker champ, Stu Ungar, was asked what he would do with his purse of $375,000. 'Lose it,' he yawned. The highrollers exult in their freedom as outsiders, subversives, buckers of the work-and-earn establishment. But they are paralysed in their turn by the psychotic lineaments of their strange talent.

Las Vegas is an island on the travelogue archipelago, trampled flat by pundits. Alvarez doesn't always triumph over cliché ('at those dizzy altitudes', 'a stable point in a notoriously shifting world', 'glanced furtively', 'winked meaningfully'). But *The Biggest Game in Town* will be scooped up by all poker-players, gamblers, gamesmen, addicts – by all observers of extremes. A man of wide interests, a poet, a scholar, Alvarez is true to his vulgar and vainglorious passion, and so remains undemeaned by it. His book has the heated quirkiness one might expect when the author of *The School of Donne* turns his attention to the school of Doyle Brunson, Crandall Addington, Puggy Pearson, Byron Cowboy Wolford and Crazy Mike Caro.

Observer September 1983

Believe It or Else

The Guinness Book of Records

The review notes to this, the eighteenth edition, give a preview of 'a few items which illustrate the pace at which records seem to get broken'. These items tell us that, among other things, the pickled-onion-consumption record has been smashed, a nonagenarian golfer has holed in one, and that a celebrated Copenhagen toad probably *isn't* fifty-four years old after all. Also, a world's-fattest-goalkeeper record was set as long ago as *c.* 1900 and has, presumably, just come to light. I see here the beginnings of a stimulating cross-fertilizing process between the existing categories. I look forward next year to hearing about America's tallest bungalow, London's least-patronized restaurant, the world's most fertile librarian, and so on.

The *GBOR* is a revamped yearbook, and obviously Guinness Superlatives Ltd have urgent reasons for trying to give the impression that it's all their staff can do to keep up. But if new records are thin on the ground there are always new fields in which fresh records can get established. The respective worlds of competitive omelette-cooking, pram-pushing, smoke-ring-blowing, pub-crawling, and face-slapping have been pretty well revolutionized since last October, and you can now get the definitive word on the biggest totem-pole, the earliest-recorded slipped disc, and the world's most well-travelled typewriter. And this edition is much bigger than the last one. Its 320 pages are bulked out by an expanded Sports chapter (complete with the long-awaited Beagling and Gaelic Football sections), and all the facts in the book are much more conscientiously documented. There is, actually, a certain scholarly prolixity which fills out the paragraphs very nicely: a 200 IQ rating 'has been attributed to Johann Wolfgang von Goethe

(1749–1832) of Frankfurt-am-Main, West Germany'. They mean Goethe.

Nevertheless, the book is nicely put together and handsomely illustrated, and it is probably worth replacing any earlier edition you might already possess, especially if it has Chester Dufort, or whoever, clocking 95 mph as the new land-speed record. Also, much of the attraction of this book consists of quite incidental information, put in irresistibly mysterious form:

> If the age of the Earth is likened to a single year, Handy Man arrived at about 8.35 p.m. on 31 December, Britain's earliest inhabitants arrived at 11.32, the Christian era began 13 seconds before midnight.

> In Chinese, the fourth tone of 'I' has 84 meanings, varying as widely as 'dress', 'hiccough', and 'licentious'.

Furthermore, it would be dishonest to deny the remarkable believe-it-or-else compulsion of this durable series. Every superlative in the book does something towards increasing one's conception (there is – unfortunately – no other way of putting it) of what being *Homo sapiens* entails. This applies most directly to 'The Human Being', the first section, which I always read with annually renewed horror and fascination. Here there are few breakthroughs, except for the recent discovery of a new world-class giantess. I see that Hopkin Hopkins (31 in.) is still the smallest UK man, and that Bob Hughes is still the world's fattest, and his coffin, a converted piano-case, still had to be lowered by crane. I see also that the longevity record has come *down* two years (the compilers complain bitterly about inveterate deceit, dotard vanity, etc.) and is now a disappointing 113.

Another virtue of this section is that it makes you feel very lithe and well-made. The grotesque regularly stops being funny and starts being sad. Consider these two cases. Max Taborsky, at the age of twenty-one, was 3 ft 10 in.; ten years later he was over seven feet; he was severely weakened and died at the age of fifty-one, having beguiled the intervening years confined to his bed. Nineteen-year-old

Calvin Phillips measured twenty-six inches and weighed less than a stone with all his clothes on; he died two years later of progeria, a rare affliction, characterized by 'dwarfism' and teenage senility.

Spectator December 1971

No Laughing Matter

The Best of Modern Humour edited by Mordecai Richler

A sense of humour is a serious business; and it isn't funny, not having one. Watch the humourless closely: the cocked and furtive way they monitor all conversation, their flashes of panic as irony or exaggeration eludes them, the relief with which they submit to the meaningless babble of unanimous laughter. The humourless can programme themselves to relish situations of human farce or slapstick – and that's about it. They are handicapped in the head, or mentally 'challenged', as Americans say (euphemism itself being a denial of humour). The trouble is that the challenge wins, every time, hands down. The humourless have no idea what is going on and can't make sense of anything at all.

For instance, is it funny that a Canadian should be asked to compile an anthology of funny prose? 'The Cream of Canadian Humour', after all, is a regular contender in those jocose short-book competitions – along with 'Australian Etiquette', 'Italian War Heroes' and so on. Mordecai Richler is an accomplished comic novelist, though of the manic, buttonholing, spray-fire variety: a glance back through his stuff confirms that he is funniest when being least 'humorous'. And *humour* itself is a bad word, isn't it, in such 'best-of' contexts? The humourless will buy this book in hope that it will wonderfully improve their laughter quotas and joke-recognition profiles. But it will only multiply their confusions.

Like Richler's fiction, the anthology divides fairly equally into two unrelated categories: first, prose that is incontestably, fanatically, apoplectically funny and is (therefore) not funny at all; and, second, prose that is going about its business as prose should and is only incidentally or secondarily funny, or quite funny, or (in many cases) not funny at all. Mr Richler clearly likes a good laugh. It would be idle to accuse him of humourlessness. I would say with some confidence that, on the whole, Mr Richler boasts a sense of humour. But we all have our blind-spots, and humour is a funny thing.

Of obvious appeal to the humourless is the writer who comes on stage in a clown outfit or King Kong suit, with party hat and harem slippers, with banana skins and custard pies. Now here's a humorist. Such writing takes six main forms:

1. *The whimsical travesty.* 'Gertrude raised her head and directed towards the young nobleman two eyes so eyelike in their expression as to be absolutely circular, while Lord Ronald directed towards the occupant of the dogcart a gaze so gazelike that nothing but a gazelle, or a gas-pipe, could have emulated its intensity.' No one laughs at this kind of facetiousness except the author himself (Stephen Leacock), whose chortlings are audible, and ruinous. I'm afraid J.B. Morton comes under this grouping too. People I think are funny think 'Beachcomber' is funny. But he isn't funny. He might once have cheered you up in a surgery waiting room. A few years on, though, and between hard covers? Lady Nausea ('Babs') Bottleown? Celery Vowpe? Lord Lochstock and Barrel?

2. *The prose parody* (which must always announce itself as such, just in case). The appropriate form for parody is the short poem. Perelman's Chandler is fun, and so is E.B. White's Hemingway, and so is Wolcott Gibbs's mimicking exposé of *Time* magazine; but they exhaust you with their surplus brilliance after less than half a page. As for cases like Jean Kerr on Françoise Sagan: why compound the tedium when the original author has done so much of the work?

3. *The autobiographical anecdote.* This genre is another clunker, though inoffensively represented here by Nora Ephron, John Mortimer and Jessica Mitford. The tone is cosy and collusive. The narrator tends to be in a bit of a scrape but comes through okay in the end. 'We peered cautiously out of the window', 'we quickly dashed round a corner', and so on.

4. *The comic column.* It remains a sound rule that funny journalism can only flourish as the offshoot or sideline of something larger. No funny journalist who is that and nothing more will ever write anything

lastingly funny. Thus the more recent stuff (by Alan Coren, Garrison Keillor, Ian Frazier) looks good, because the contemporary *frissons* it deals in are still current. The less recent stuff looks bad. And the more recent stuff will soon look like the less recent stuff.

5. *The mock-heroic, in whatever guise.* One example, from Alexander Theroux: 'It was high tea: the perfervid ritual in England which daily sweetens the ambiance of the discriminately invited and that nothing short of barratry, a provoked shaft of lightning, the King's enemies, or an act of God could ever hope to bring to an end.' This elaborate banality might serve as a lesson to all fifth-formers. The sentence is a wreck: ugly, untrue and illiterate; even in the interests of pseudo-elegant variation, you cannot start a clause with a *which* and then switch to a *that*.

6. *The party turn.* Extended charades or word games, diverting enough in the workaday hands of Thomas Meehan, Dan Greenburg and George S. Kaufman. It is bathetic, however, to see Flann O'Brien, a writer of comic genius, represented only by his lugubrious 'Keats and Chapman' concoctions. '"There's a nip in the heir," said Keats.' '"His B. Arch is worse than his bight," said Keats.' Puns are cues or triggers to the humourless, and double puns are obviously twice as funny as single ones. Poor Flann! He must have cranked out these duds after lunch, in drunken scorn or cynical despair.

Mr Richler does lesser but considerable disservice to many of his writers by catching them left-handed or wrong-footed. Such capable middleweights as Truman Capote, Terry Southern, Bruce Jay Friedman and Wilfrid Sheed are included merely as jocular journalists; the exuberant Saul Bellow is thrown away with a travel piece; the great innovator Peter de Vries is shamed by a dull parody of Faulkner. Showing remarkable assiduity, the editor has also managed to track down and rootle out a wholly ill-judged critique by Kenneth Tynan and a completely unfunny article by H.L. Mencken.

Otherwise, Mr Richler includes decent-sized extracts from the mainstream fiction of Eudora Welty, Thomas Berger, Stanley Elkin, Beryl Bainbridge, John Cheever, V.S. Naipaul, Kurt Vonnegut, Joseph Heller and – the most successful piece in the book – Philip Roth. Some of these offerings are no more than mildly funny, and were never meant to be. They are loosely comic as opposed to humorous, comedy being definable as a world where the greatest sins are folly and pretension, and where the ultimate deliverance is merely one of laughter. Your response to these writers at their best, is a persistent smile of admiration – a response that Mr Richler should perhaps have aimed for all along.

There is something whorish about looking for laughs, or laughs only, and there is certainly a good deal of excruciation in following such a quest. Seldom have I eyed a half-finished book with more vivid dread. Give me an 800-page extravaganza by a Guatemalan magical realist; give me a book on German accountancy. Well, only the meek and put-upon reviewer has to trudge through the whole thing. It *can* be done. As in all life's crises and trials, you just have to keep your sense of humour.

Observer July 1984

John Updike

Life Class

Picked-Up Pieces by John Updike

The adversaries of good book-reviewing are many and various, but the chief one is seldom mentioned – perhaps because of its ubiquity. We hear a lot, especially from academics, about reviews not being academic enough; and it is true that 'name' reviewing of the Evel-Knievel-on-Kierkegaard variety often shows the reviewer hideously stretched. We hear a lot, especially from publishers, about reviewers using books as springboards for tangential musings; and it is true that the book trade might well improve if the blurb-transcribing sots of yesteryear were reinstated. And we hear a lot, especially from authors, about 'showing off', about metropolitan spite, and about the unearned asperity of the menial scribbler – 'i.e., cheek', as F.W. Bateson once labelled the tendency. These vices exist, perhaps, but they don't seriously diminish that corner of intellectual life which literary journalism inhabits. The crucial defect is really no different from that of any other kind of writing: it is dullness. The literary pages throng with people about whom one has no real feelings either way – except that one can't be bothered to read them.

As a literary journalist, John Updike has that single inestimable virtue: having read him once, you admit to yourself, almost with a sigh, that you will have to read everything he writes. At a time when the reviewer's role has devolved to that of a canary in a pre-war coalmine, Updike reminds you that the review can, in its junior way, be something of a work of art, or at least a worthy vehicle for the play of ideas, feeling and wit. His stance is one of ultimate serviceability: the alert and ironic layman unanxiously detached from the world of literary commerce (indeed, 'I must be one of the few Americans with a bachelor-of-arts degree who has never met either Robert Lowell or

Norman Mailer'). And the fizzy pungency of his prose is answered by
the intense, if erratic, strength of his responses. Updike's reviewing is
high-powered enough to win the name of literary criticism – which
is to say, it constantly raises the question (a question more interesting
than it at first sounds), 'What is literature?'

A rather workaday grumble to be made about *Picked-Up Pieces* is
that many of its pieces ought never to have been picked up – at least
not without emendation. Complaints about the price of particular
novels or a book's margin-sizes may look well enough in the columns
of the *New Yorker* but appear footling between hard covers. Several
books-received notices on humdrum theologians should have been
exorcized, and it is hard not to be startled by a sixty-word citation to
Thornton Wilder (which carries a fifty-word footnote humourlessly
defending its inclusion). Include away: here, plainly, Updike is
more interested in his personal filing-system than in his normal
courteousness towards the reader. And then, too, the hot snort of
the hobby-horse can be felt on and off throughout books of this kind.
Updike is mad about golf, for instance, and three excitable articles on
this pastime are duly reprinted. Part of the trouble, no doubt, is that a
regular reviewer will often have to gouge standard-length pieces out
of sub-standard books. And, inevitably, Updike will sometimes look
like an Olympic swimmer in a bathtub.

The heart of *Picked-Up Pieces*, however, is its fiction reviews,
where Updike can always revert to first principles and so remain
unimplicated by the frequent banality of his material. Updike goes
at fiction with a firm idea of what he takes a novel to be, but he is
incomparably good at conveying the *weight* of an author's prose, the
lineaments of the talent behind it. Even when he is scorning what
seems admirable or praising what seems mischievous, there is never
any clouding of the issues involved. Yet the readings are intractably
didactic, even polemical; and although Updike's methods are close
to irreproachable, one can only react polemically to his findings.

For some reason, most of the novels Updike has chosen to
review are translations. I thought at first that Updike must have some
gluttonous craving for local colour, judging by his preparedness to
read the likes of Simone Schwarz-Bart, Yambo Ouologuen, Ezekiel

Mphahele, Paul van Ostaijen, etc. Surely, one reads even the foreign classics in translation as a guilty duty, to get some blotched silhouette, as one might look at snapshots of inaccessible paintings. But Updike regards the language barrier as a rut which any frog could straddle:

> Distinctly unmusical, at least in translation . . . at least for a reader deprived of the original Polish . . . [the translator], who for all I know has done the best of all possible jobs . . . also excellent, at a guess, is the translation from the Dutch . . .

Updike can keep a straight face while noting the linguistic tang of translated 'Arab and Bantu exclamations'; and he is perfectly capable of talking about the *style* of a novel translated from the French translation of the Polish – which is like analysing the brushstrokes in a Brownie. It is an insensitivity that points to an imbalance in Updike's view of how novels work, and it loiters in everything he says about fiction.

Even Nabokov's fiction – and the seven essays on Nabokov are perhaps the most valuable thing in the book. The swagger of Updike's prose provides the ideal window for the teeming haughtiness of Nabokov's, from his excesses ('his prose has never menaced a cowering reader with more bristling erudition'), to, very nearly, his essence: 'Nabokov's is really an amorous style . . . it yearns to clasp diaphanous exactitude into its hairy arms.' Here, you feel sure, is a critic unimprovably equipped for and attuned to his author. But here too, suddenly, Updike's linguistic blindfold (e.g., Dmitri Nabokov's adjectives in his translation of *Glory* are caressingly praised, as if for all the world they were Vladimir's) is whipped off to reveal tightly closed eyes. 'Is art a game? Nabokov stakes his career on it'; he makes 'airtight boxes . . . detached from even the language of their composition'. If you substituted 'embodied in' for 'detached from even' you might get within hailing distance of Nabokov's art, but by now Updike is in full retreat. Nabokov, *horribile scriptu*, spurns 'psychology and sociology', confronting us 'with a fiction that purposely undervalues its own humanistic content'.

Uh-oh, one thinks. Updike is a Protestant of the small-town Dionysian sort, and that does his writing no harm; yet he is also a

Humanist, of the numinous Apollonian sort, and this does seem to account for that vein of folksy uplift which underlies his novels as well as his criticism. Thus, Auden's 'technical displays cast doubt upon the urgency of his inspiration' (presumably, then, Updike's ignorance of the form of the haiku, revealed in the previous paragraph, is an oblique tribute to Updike's urgency). Thus, Erica Jong's appallingly written and irreducibly autobiographical *Fear of Flying* is a 'lovable, delicious novel', because, well, in Updike's view Erica Jong has a lovable and delicious lifestyle. Would Updike defend this on the grounds that a writer's life can 'matter more than his works'? Or because, as Updike says five pages later, books can 'exist less as literature than as life'?

Life. 'Life.' Some people seem very keen on stressing their approval of this commodity, almost as if the rest of us had no time for the stuff. Updike, who likes fiction to believe in 'improvement' and 'a better world', crucially asserts that 'by a novel we understand an imitation of reality rather than a spurning of it', and grades them accordingly. But what's the difficulty? Life goes on regardless, and reality won't mind if a novel spurns it. The confusion is age-old, answering as it does to an authentic pang. If Updike granted art the same reverent autonomy he grants life, some 'improvement' would indeed take place: he would become a better critic. Meanwhile, get to grips with this Christian gentleman. His gallantry reliably extends to whatever is disadvantaged, homely, long-suffering, foreign or feminine. Kind to stragglers and also-rans, to well-meaning duds and worthies, and correspondingly cautious in his praise of acknowledged stars and masters, Updike's view of twentieth-century literature is a levelling one. Talent, like life, should be available to all.

New Statesman March 1976

Roger's Version by John Updike

If the strong nuclear force were 2 per cent stronger than it is, the universe would consist entirely of helium; if it were 5 per cent weaker, the sun wouldn't burn. If the *weak* nuclear force were any weaker than it is, there would be no heavy elements, no structures, in space. And if the mass of the neutron were only .998 of its actual value, there would be no atoms at all. In short, the universe – the world, human life – is a preposterous fluke. You could fill the rest of this page with zeros and have little notion of the odds against:

> 'Everywhere you look,' he instructed me, 'there are these ter-rifically finely adjusted constants that have to be just what they are . . . and there's no intrinsic reason for those constants to be what they are except to say God made them that way. God made Heaven and Earth. It's what science has come to. Believe me.'

The speaker is Dale Kohler, a spotty, pallid, wised-up eternal student, who wants a grant that will enable him to prove the existence of God – on his computer. The listener, appropriately, is an expert on heresy: Roger Lambert, our narrator, one-time Methodist minister, now a divinity-school professor in New England. (As he puts it, he used to be in the 'distribution' end of the religion business, but these days he's in 'quality control'.) Roger is repelled and intrigued by Dale – and by almost everyone and everything else (this is a novel of weighty dualities). In Dale, perhaps, he sees a version of his younger self, though one hopelessly degraded by modern 'head-culture', by the era of big brains and microscopic sensibilities.

At any rate Roger adopts Dale and helps him get the grant for his doomed and blasphemous project. In return Dale reacquaints Roger with a lost relative, sassy and foul-mouthed young Verna. A single parent in a housing project, Verna is Roger's runaway niece, the daughter of his half-sister: there is just enough consanguinity to lend an incestuous flavour to their entanglement. Meanwhile, via feats of empathy which teeter on psychosis or fictional innovation (what one might call the Wandering or the Floating Narrator), Roger starts to 'live through' Dale, to see through his eyes, to yearn through his loins. This is a particularly absorbing hobby for Roger, because Dale is now dividing his time between his quest for the evident God and a rather more successful quest for Esther, Roger's neglected little wife.

All according to Roger, of course. This is merely Roger's version, the gospel according to Roger. It is never quite clear, for instance, whether Dale is really having an affair with Esther, or whether Roger is indulging in extended erotic fantasy as he pictures their couplings and ungluings, their squattings and squirtings. Here too we encounter one of Updike's few faults or excesses, his undifferentiated love of detail. Faced with a character's genitals, we don't get the phrase or sentence we think we could make do with: we get a paragraph of close-up. On the other hand, maybe the obsessiveness can be granted structural status here: it is Roger's obsession, and provides an overlong but necessary glimpse of his duplicitous, sublimating, sleepwalking soul.

Even by the standards of late-middle Updike, Roger is a grossly paradoxical figure, exalted and demonic, heartless and sentimental, magnanimous and mean: a 'dour, tweedy villain', 'with every pinch that lust and spite had delivered in a half-century of egoism some- where remembered in the slack and creviced texture of [his] cunning, cautious face'. He is caught between heaven and hell – or between heaven and earth, which will do these days. Equally keen on pornography and theology, he is alike addicted to the 'rat scrabble' of Dale's God-seeking computer and to the helpless *nostalgie* that leads him back to the smells and secretions of Verna's two-room walk-up. She calls him 'evil' – and he is flattered. He revels in his own heresy: 'that of committing deliberate abominations so as to widen and deepen the field in which God's forgiveness can magnificently play'.

This is a tremendously expert novel. Updike, by now, is the 'complete' player, an all-court wrong-footing wizard who has lost none of his speed. As with Roger, the book's cargo of disgust (disgust

for the corporeal, disgust for the contemporary) is perfectly offset by
the radiance of the humour, the perceptions, the epiphanies. Dale
Kohler seeks the designer universe. I direct him to the fiction of
John Updike. It is a very dinky place – too dinky, perhaps. I sense
genius, but not the heavy impact of greatness, not yet. I feel like
Roger, tiptoeing through the projects (and this is a typically nifty
strophe):

> Two limber black youths were mounting the steel stairs three at
> a time, in utterly silent bounds. They rose towards me at great
> speed, in their worn stovepipe jeans, their shiny basketball jackets
> and huge silent jogging shoes, and passed on either side of me like
> headlights that turn out to be motorcycles.

Observer October 1986

Self-Consciousness: Memoirs by John Updike

'These memoirs', John Updike writes, 'feel shabby . . . forced . . .
[they] struggle to expose what should be – in decency, to conserve
potency – *behind.*' *Self-Consciousness* is Updike's cobbled-together
autobiography, written, or cobbled together, in response to the news
that someone *else* was about to write the Life. It has huge faults, and
huger (unrelated) virtues. But the 'shabbiness' that haunts Updike is
generic – it comes with the territory; and funnily enough it is the
shabbiness of imposture. The novelist cowers in the boiler-room of
the self, where he works in his stinking singlet, his coccyx-baring
jeans. In the autobiography he takes you back down there on an
official tour or PR walkabout, dressed in a foreman's crisp rompers.

The autobiographer has all these *duties* to discharge. Of course,
one is prepared for a certain amount of personal history, of deep
background; and sure enough the screens and porches, the back
streets and back yards, that toy, that field, that texture – the real
estates of childhood – are exhaustively evoked. Updike was an
obedient child 'oversold' on school ('the faithful little *habitué* of
the Shillington playground'), and he remains a methodical adult.
We therefore get personal *pre*-history, too – and a sudden collapse,
on Updike's part, into near-sadistic garrulity. These forty pages are
by many magnitudes the worst he has ever written.

Updike may lack the pedigree of an Anthony Powell, who, in
his memoirs, I seem to remember, traced himself back to someone
like Beowulf, via Glendower and Robin of Loxley. But he apprises
us all the same of Cousin George and Aunt Bessie and Uncle Arch.
Then we read this:

A cheerful slant on the New Jersey Updikes is offered by *The Op
Dyck Genealogy*, written by Charles Wilson Opdyke and privately
printed in Albany, New York, in 1889. Hartley's grandfather, Peter,
appears on page 333 . . .

Page 333? And now it's George Opdyke and Gysbert op den Dyck
and Louris Janesen op Dyck who begot Johannes Opdyck who begot
Lawrence Updick. 'Robust stock', 'a big bumptious race' – oh, that
hardy breed! When you learn that 'Gysbert himself owned all of
Coney Island', you have to remind yourself that you're not reading
something very funny by John Cheever. But you're not: you're
reading something very unfunny – something very po-faced and
glazed-over – by John Updike. After an hour of this, I was reduced
to recalling my own interest in personal lineage, which ended when
I was sixteen, suspiciously soon after I looked up *Amis* in a dictionary
of surnames and saw something like: 'assoc. with the lower classes,
esp. slaves'. It probably isn't vainglory that animates Updike's pages;
it feels more like hobbyism or authorial thrift. Anyway, here we see
Updike nude, without a stitch of irony or art.

All fiction reveals the self, but it is the best – or the most interesting

– self available, heated and purged into something a bit more rarefied. There is no reason, for instance, why a novelist's opinions or 'positions' should be of special value, let alone special authority. And so it proves with Updike, who here frames his socio-political beliefs in an essay in cautious support of the Vietnam War. With his genius for place goes a genius for time, and 'On Not Being a Dove' is an expert recreation of the American Sixties, with its shamelessness and hysteria, its youth-worship, its intellectual stampedes. Updike wore 'dashikis and love beads', and 'frugged' to Janis Joplin, and he liked the promiscuity; but he didn't like the radicalism – he didn't like the promiscuity of the mind. Thus he seems to have supported the war largely out of a dislike for its opponents.

The peace movement becomes, for him, an inexplicable excrescence ('now along came this movement') rather than a direct symptom of what the war was actually doing to *America*. Updike's prose writhes in jargon, sentence-length cliché, and prissy sarcasm:

> It was all very well for civilised little countries like Sweden and Canada to tut-tut in the shade of our nuclear umbrella and welcome our deserters and draft evaders, but the US had nobody to hide behind. Credibility must be maintained. Power is a dirty business . . .

Updike wisely confesses to something primitive in his response. But no atavism should lead him into such calibrated falsehood: 'Under the banner of a peace movement . . . war was being waged by a privileged few upon the administration and the American majority that had elected it.' In *Rabbit Redux* (1971) these sentiments almost got Harry Angstrom laughed out of town – and *that* town was Brewer, Pennsylvania. Even Harry, moreover, confronts a question that Updike avoids. There's only one thing you need ask yourself about prosecuting a war you're too old for: how would your stomach feel, in the provincial airport, as you waved your sons off to fight it?

What's the matter with him? Brooding in his tent, does he thirst for action? Here's yet another hitch with the literary autobiography, though it is one that Updike eventually profits from: writers never go out. Whereas the memoirs of, say, Genghis Khan would have a guaranteed appeal, the novelist is nothing – is no novelist – without his aeons of repetitively anxious solitude. This makes for a curious self: static, self-tasting, most alive when alone. The book's unchallengeable success is its exploration of this cloistered quiddity. As usual, Updike has much to say about the human soul; but what distinguishes his book is its commentary on the human body.

Updike's body, a strange and endearing instrument, tricked out with all that wonky genes and a nervous disposition can viciously devise: psoriasis, asthma, claustrophobia, hydrophobia, arachnophobia, insomnia, poor teeth, a tendency to choke and a spectacular stammer. He writes of this, not with shame, but with ardour, like an articulate animal. Updike is above all an *embarrassing* writer: it is his recurrent weakness, and his unifying strength. He is always successfully taking you to where you don't quite care to follow.

The last section of the book, 'On Being a Self Forever', is to my knowledge the best thing yet written on what it is like to get older: age, and the only end of age.

> Insomnia offers a paradigm: the mind cannot fall asleep as long as it watches itself. At the first observed lurch into nonsensical thought we snap awake in eager anticipation, greedy to be asleep.

Writing like this wins one's deepest assent; it seems to enlarge the human community. But by now I find myself thinking that such sentences are too good, too universal, for a work of discourse and belong in a work of art (where, I hope and trust, they will shortly reappear). *Self-Consciousness* emerges as a crankily original way of showing how the photograph on the front of the book (Johnny at five: stubborn, querying, amused) became the photograph on the back. It has many brilliant pages. But the best page is unnumbered and comes near the beginning. It is the one that says he wrote *Bech: A Book* and *Rabbit is Rich*.

Observer May 1989

Rabbit at Rest by John Updike

About halfway through *Rabbit at Rest*, the reader will start to hear a
hoarse whisper in the background. You may feel it is your own heart
that is doing the murmuring (for the book is all about ageing, about
seizure and closure: it is itself an ending). Later on, though, the noise
becomes more raucous and more generalized: perhaps it belongs to
the sports arena or the auditorium; there is something of the herd
instinct in it, involving you in a pleasant loss of individuality. At last
you acknowledge that this is nothing other than the sound of applause,
American applause: the ows and yays, the stomp of feet, the vociferous
whistling. With *Rabbit, Run* (1960), *Rabbit Redux* (1971) and *Rabbit is
Rich* (1981), John Updike loaded the bases. *Rabbit at Rest* is the home
run. We can see him again now, in slow motion, the old batter
jogging round the diamond, his pumped arm, his solemn high-fives
with officials and trainers. With his head shyly inclined, he returns to
the plate – to the bench-clearing welcome, and the big burbly roar
of the crowd.

Updike calls them 'the Angstrom novels', but we know them
more familiarly as the Rabbit books. They span thirty years and
1,500 pages. And they tell the story, from youth to death, of
a Pennsylvanian car salesman: averagely bigoted and chauvinistic,
perhaps exceptionally gluttonous and lewd, but otherwise brutally
undistinguished. It is as if a double-sized *Ulysses* had been narrated,
not by Stephen, Bloom and Molly, but by one of the surlier
underbouncers at Kiernan's bar.

What Updike is saying – or conclusively demonstrating – is
something very simple: that the unexamined life is worth examining,
that indeed it swarms with instruction and delight. Among prose
works which address the American century, Rabbit has few obvious
betters. *The Adventures of Augie March*. Probably *Lolita*. Possibly Joseph
Heller's *Something Happened*. Then what? If Updike lacks something
in the way of vision and attack, he makes up for it in tirelessness

and will. Like Anthony Burgess, he is a man of nineteenth-century amplitude. He'll write his twenty letters and thirty pages in the morning, run for high office in the afternoon, go hunting at teatime, then look up from his pre-prandial epopee and say to his wife, 'Fie upon this quiet life: I want work.'

Rabbit at Rest opens and shuts in Florida, at the end of the Reagan era, in the fading glow of America's elaborately doctored well-being. Harry Angstrom is retired now, and he is going to die pretty soon, so where else should he hang out but in the Sunset State, more specifically in a condo-complex called Valhalla (*COD*: 'palace in which souls of slain heroes feasted')? The malls are full of 'sunstruck clinics – dental, chiropractic, cardiac, legal, legal-medical' and prosthesis parlours; the corridors smell 'of air freshener, to mask the mildew that creeps into every closed space'. 'In Florida everybody is so cautious, as if on two beers they might fall down and break a hip. The whole state feels brittle.'

> The highways are full of big white soft-shocked power-steered American cars being driven by old people so shrunken they can barely see over the hood. Any time you get somewhere without a head-on collision is a tribute to the geriatric medicine in this part of the world, the pep pills and vitamin injections and blood thinners.

Tall, sedentary Harry has just turned fifty-five. Rabbit is rich, but he's fat now too, 'a float of a man' who sleeps curled up, giving 'his belly room to slop into'; 'shaving each morning, he seems to have acres of lather to remove.' On the beach he stares at his feet: 'so white and papery! As if he is standing up to his knees in old age.' The 'inner dwindling' of *Rich* has become, in *Rest*, a sense of sclerotic and solitary doom. Soon, the doctors are telling Harry that he has 'a typical American heart'. But this we already knew. The wife-and-children business quickly 'palled for him'; and 'other people, even so-called loved ones', are just a strain on his routine. The reason he can't leave his wife, Janice, Rabbit tearfully confesses to an ex-mistress, 'is, without her, I'm shit'. His heart, then, is typical: 'It's tired and stiff and full of crud.'

Another and more surprising kind of expansion has happened to
Harry: intellectual growth. He is still a brute and a rube, still hemmed
in by jargon and junk; and Updike doesn't deny us the expected
comedy. On the wall in the car showroom there hangs 'a *Playboy*
calendar, the girl for this month dressed up as a bare-assed Easter
bunny, which Harry isn't so sure strikes quite the right note'; later,
receiving a Toyota executive, Harry babbles: '"Miss Oshima, I mean
Mr Shimada"' – Harry had been practising the name, telling himself
it was 'like Ramada with shit at the beginning'. Yet the indulgent
distance between author and hero has been partly closed. One of
the biggest laughs in *Rabbit is Rich* comes when Harry, in proud
contemplation of his 'den', wonders if 'in this room he might begin
to read books, instead of just magazines and newspapers, and begin
to learn about history, say'. Well, it has come to pass. He may not
know much about geography (in a discussion about Portugal: 'The
only country over there I've ever wanted to go to is Tibet'), but he
has taken up history, in his final death-driven surge towards 'the big
picture'.

Harry, after all, will soon be history himself. The big picture
is what Updike is going for, too. Rabbit tarries in Florida for
only half the year. The rest of the time he is back in Brewer, in
rustbelt Pennsylvania. Florida has history, glimpsed early on in a
couple of guided tours of the local arcana. But history has called
it a day down there; it is static, necrotic. Brewer is the scene of
the continuing American experience. Here, in several passages of
lordly brilliance, Updike gives a sense of the abject demographics of
the city: upheaval and reinvention, the churnings and devourings of
'development', the human and material detritus of decay. Harry has
been there, with his typical American heart. And by the time you
start wondering whether he has what it takes to become a national
metaphor, Rabbit is duly asked to lead a Fourth of July parade,
as Uncle Sam. The set-piece that follows is a quietly frightening
apotheosis.

Flanked by a great press of young humanity and all its troubled
dynamism, Rabbit marches, weeping with emotion ('from the oceans,

white with foam'), his heart thumping 'worse and worse', sick and giddy, 'as if he has been lifted up to survey all human history'. Harry Angstrom, 'as a loyal American', isn't going to attempt any radical critique of his homeland. But certain tormented gropings are allowed him. At one point (his hugely charmless son Nelson has just returned from a rehab clinic), Harry feels stifled by 'induced calm and steadiness'. He turns to his granddaughter, 'looking for an opening, a crack, a ray of undoctored light'. And doesn't get it. 'Undoctored': Harry is surrounded by doctoring (he watches his own angioplasty on a monitor, as if it were just something else on TV); and he is surrounded by doctored thought, doctored language, doctored feeling. 'I need to process', 'you should reinforce him', 'I was getting reacclimated.' The professionalization of ordinary existence: this is the enemy within.

In *Rabbit at Rest* the most candid prognosis on America is given by the Toyota executive, the one whose name is like Ramada with shit at the beginning. He says that America must change her ways. But Rabbit won't change his. 'They should just let people die,' he says. 'It's modern science, you should be grateful,' says his wife, utilitarian Janice, with her 'blunt little knob of a nose, a nose with no more character than a drawer pull'. And the nature of Harry's death, beautifully arrived at, suggests the countervailing forces of illusion and nostalgia. Uncle Sam, elderly now, dancing in worship of his vanished vigour.

American superabundance is everywhere saluted and memorialized in Updike's pages. Indeed, the rhythm of the Rabbit books always tends towards the enumerative, the encyclopaedic. This is a side-effect of Updike's boyish braininess and easy mastery; like the author of *Cursor Mundi*, he puts down everything he knows, as a kind of analogy of divine knowledge. In two recent novels, *The Witches of Eastwick* and *Roger's Version*, Updike crammed himself to PhD level in such areas as cosmology, computers, theology, Darwinism, necromancy, pottery and the cello. *Rabbit at Rest* throws in nutrition, addiction, heart surgery and real estate. The big picture is made up of lots of little pictures. Similarly in the external world, promiscuously absorbed, with hand following eye at great speed of scrutiny and encapsulation, Updike's ravenousness makes you frown and shake your head in appalled admiration.

An unfettered style is the central gamble of the tetralogy. It is a style that sees the big picture – time and space – in every passing snapshot and billboard. Updike is sometimes accused of overburdening Harry's huddled mind; but the Rabbit books would be paltry things if they were exercises in mere mimesis. He lets the ordinary man sing and soar. For the ordinary man sings and soars in any case, but silently, until the novelist intercedes. Not for Updike the kind of prose that takes a vow of poverty. Such vows, besides, are more easily taken by the pauper than by the prince. And Updike is happy in his counting house. This novel is enduringly eloquent about weariness, age and disgust, in a prose that is always fresh, nubile and unwitherable. Here, on a small-hours drive across lowly Brewer, Updike's prose takes Rabbit 'over there', to Portugal, to Tibet:

> The cars parked along the curbs display a range of unearthly colours, no longer red and blue and cream but cindery lunar shades, like nothing you can see or even imagine by daylight . . . The trimmed large bushes of the groomed yards, the yews and arborvitae and rhododendrons, look alert by night, like jungle creatures come to the waterhole to drink and caught in a camera's flash.

Independent on Sunday October 1990

Odd Jobs: Essays and Criticism by John Updike

We often think in terms of literary pairs: Hemingway and Fitzgerald, and so on. But what about literary opposites? Jorge Luis Borges versus Joyce Carol Oates, Nicholson Baker versus Leon Uris, Thomas Pynchon versus C.P. Snow, Norman Mailer versus Anita Brookner. John Updike has no obvious soulmate or near equivalent (though Anthony Burgess harbours a similarly hyperactive cortex). But he does have an opposite, and a diametrical one: Samuel Beckett.

Beckett was the headmaster of the Writing as Agony school. On a good day, he would stare at the wall for eighteen hours or so, feeling entirely terrible; and, if he was lucky, a few words like NEVER or END or NOTHING or NO WAY might brand themselves on his bleeding eyes. Whereas Updike, of course, is a psychotic Santa of volubility, emerging from one or another of his studies (he is said to have four of them) with his morning sackful of reviews, speeches, reminiscences, think-pieces, forewords, prefaces, introductions, stories, playlets and poems. Preparing his cup of Sanka over the singing kettle, he wears his usual expression: that of a man beset by an embarrassment of delicious drolleries. The telephone starts ringing. A science magazine wants something pithy on the philosophy of subatomic thermodynamics; a fashion magazine wants 10,000 words on his favourite colour. No problem – but can they hang on? Updike has to go upstairs again and blurt out a novel.

Odd Jobs is his fourth cuboid volume of higher journalism, following *Assorted Prose* (1965), *Picked-Up Pieces* (1975) and *Hugging the Shore* (1983). It shows us a huge mind at once crammed and uncluttered. If writers – if people – are either clean-desk or messy-desk (and I write these words from under the familiar haystack), then Updike is a spotless work-surface above tightly packed drawers: he is organized. He is also, apparently, omniscient, as *au fait* with evolution, for example ('asteroidal or cometary causation' set against 'punctuated equilibrium'), as with scriptural scholarship ('it is roughly true that

Matthew = Mark + Q and that Luke = Mark + Q + the considerable
body of narrative and preachment present only in Luke'). Or how
about this:

> Edward is the son of the famous painter Jesse Baltram and his
> mistress, Chloe Warriston, and Stuart of the famous writer Casimir
> Cuno's son Harry, who married Chloe when she was pregnant with
> Edward, and Harry's first wife, Teresa, née O'Neill, a Catholic
> from New Zealand who, like Chloe, died young, having produced
> one male child.

John Updike even knows what's going on in a novel by Iris
Murdoch.

On the whole, he is modest about his formal education. 'I peaked,
as a scholar, in my junior year,' he writes, 'and capped my academic
career with a dull thesis and a babbling display of ignorance at my oral
examination.' Since then, in a trance of evergreen precocity, he has
been educating himself: doing his homework and writing his essays.
It is a commonplace that autodidacts are trying to impress somebody
– mother, father, a sainted schoolteacher, their own platonic selves.
But there's no need to ask whose approval Updike is after. He aspires,
in his own way, to something seraphic while heeding various New
Testament recommendations about kindness, self-abnegation, and the
value of suffering.

It isn't the first or indeed the second thing that strikes you, but
Odd Jobs is a record of near-biblical torment. (Maybe the second half
of the title should be pronounced with a long *o*.) 'The prose', Updike
stoically notes at one point, reviewing *Children of the Arbat* by Anatoly
Rybakov, 'comes across as colorless and rarely gets off the ground':
the book is 685 pages long. And still the supposed masterworks are
heaping up on the mat, from Chile, from Paraguay, from Austria,
from Albania. You have only to look at the bibliographical lead-ins
to feel your lower lip tremble: '*Cities of Salt*, by Abdelrahman Munif,
translated from the Arabic by Peter Theroux. 627 pp.' 627 pages
from the Arabic . . . Yet Iron John dispatches that one, and is
ready for more. Often he is to be found chirpily welcoming a

'sprightly first novel' or the latest from a 'brave little publishing house'. Although many writers leave Updike unstirred (deficient in juice, in warmth, in life), only a handful succeed in disheartening him: Yevgeny Yevtushenko, Thomas Bernhard, Jacques Derrida.

In one of the four admiring essays on John Cheever, Updike fondly recalls a trip they made together in 1964 to Russia, where Cheever's 'lively fancy and brave ebullience' made the grim tour 'as gay as an April in Paris'. We therefore share Updike's consternation ('It was with some surprise that I read . . .') a few pages later, when he comes across the following from *The Letters of John Cheever*:

> Updike, whom I know to be a brilliant man, traveled with me in
> Russia last autumn and I would go to considerable expense and
> inconvenience to avoid his company. I think his magnaminity
> [*sic*] specious and his work seems motivated by covetousness,
> exhibitionism and a stony heart.

Still reeling from that, we then get S.J. Perelman writing to Ogden Nash about 'the characteristic nausea that attacks me when this youth performs on the printed page'. Updike takes this hard, but he takes it; and his admiration doesn't falter. On the way up, the aspirant sees literary eminence as an ocean liner, with a champagne reception awaiting him in first class. Once there, he encounters 'a kind of Medusa's raft', littered with snarling skeletons.

Actually, the density of *Odd Jobs* is not just an indication but a proof of Updike's magnanimity. As Karl Barth says of Mozart, 'Joy overtakes sorrow without extinguishing it . . . The Yea rings louder than the ever-present Nay'; and Updike has always been spiritually committed to the Yea. Oddly, it is his generosity that causes the only kind of trouble he ever gets into – trouble with the bien-pensant left. His recent, quirky autobiography, *Self-Consciousness*, contained a contorted essay on Vietnam. Here, Updike's selective blindness, his reluctance to think ill, led him to reject the radical package of malaise, conspiracy and paranoia – and thus to support the war. Included in *Odd Jobs* is a speech entitled 'How Does the State Imagine?', given in 1986 as part of the forty-eighth International PEN Congress, in which Updike sings a sunny little hymn to the US Postal Service. A postscript tells us how very badly the speech went down, in the 'goblin air of fevered indignation and reflexive anti-Americanism'. Updike sometimes seems a lonely and anachronistic figure in this age of irony and dread. But only a cynic would accuse him of cynicism, for cynics are condemned to see cynicism everywhere.

In *Self-Consciousness* Updike revealed that his father, in later years, took to wearing a wool Navy watch cap: 'It kept his head warm, yet also made him look like a cretin.' This is one of the perverse consolations of ageing, Updike argued: pleasure in looking foolish, whimsicality, *un*selfconsciousness. One can see a similar strain, perhaps, in Updike Jr (who now wears a watch cap himself, all winter, inside and out). There is a trundling quality, increasingly indulged: too much trolley-car nostalgia and baseball-mitt Americana, too much ancestor worship, too much piety. In his collected art criticism, *Just Looking*, Updike often seemed happier with the hack than with the genius. Here, too, you feel he is more relaxed with the likes of Sherwood Anderson and William Dean Howells than with, say, Saul Bellow and Vladimir Nabokov – his only obvious superiors in the second half of the American century.

But let's be clear. This book is a torrent of finely phrased justice: the 'rather blithely morbid sensibility' of Graham Greene; 'the ailment of excessive clear-sightedness' suffered by Tolstoy; Umberto Eco's permanent 'orgy of citation and paraphrase'; John O'Hara, in whose work 'all sorts of irrelevancies stick up, almost like bookmarks'; the 'slightly unctuous stiffness of tone' in a biography of T.S. Eliot, as if '[Peter] Ackroyd were trying to make adequately stuffy conversation with an odd old type with whom he has been condemned to spend a fiendishly prolonged sherry hour'; or the sensation, in Kafka,

of anxiety and shame whose center cannot be located and therefore cannot be placated; a sense of an infinite difficulty within things, impeding every step; a sensitivity acute beyond usefulness, as if the nervous system, flayed of its old hide of social usage and religious belief, must record every touch as pain.

New York Times Book Review November 1991

Ultramundane

Here Comes Everybody

Who's Who in Twentieth Century Literature
by Martin Seymour-Smith

It is said that Coleridge was the last man to have read everything. He isn't any longer. Mr Martin Seymour-Smith is. The author of the four-volume *Guide to Modern World Literature* (a work so panoptic that hardly anybody dared review it) now brings us the equally far-flung *Who's Who in Twentieth Century Literature*. And here, again, Seymour-Smith not only gives the impression that he has read everything ever written by and about everyone in every language: he also gives the impression that he has read everything ever written by and about everyone in every language *twice*.

Genuinely humbling though much of Seymour-Smith's erudition is, the constant parade of omniscience is not, to put it mildly, without its funny side. He makes no apologies for knowing everything, and indeed it is his tundra-like humourlessness on the point that makes the book so diverting. Having read, in the 'A' section, successive essays on a Romanian poet, an Argentinian novelist, an Alsatian sculptor, a French playwright and a Guatemalan 'fiction writer', I went back to a remark I had noticed in the introduction. There it was: 'The resultant selection is therefore necessarily biased towards British and American authors.' Muttering not just 'who's who?' but occasionally 'who dat?' I stumbled on through the gobbets about Danish polemicists, Senegalese poets, Italian memoirists, Afrikaans poetesses, Nigerian playwrights, Basque philosophers, German essayists, Russian syncretists . . .

A bemusing habit of Seymour-Smith's is to make a remark of truly galactic learning – and then dwarf it by revealing a whole new universe of bibliomania in the background. Daniel Fagunwa is the first important writer in Yoruba and *Ogboju ode ninu igbo irunmale* is assuredly his best book. Ah, but he did not build up an account of Yoruba cosmogony as poetically as did 'Tutuola (q.v.)'. The Icelander Halldór Laxness's fiction, we're all agreed, is 'not wholly integrated'. Were you aware, however, that he owed much to the 'untranslated' Thórbergur Thórdarson 'who is perhaps the superior writer'?

Similarly, opinions so exotic that you can't imagine anyone human holding them are frequently made to sound banal and secondhand by the World-weary Seymour-Smith. 'It is now fashionable', for instance, 'to dismiss his poetry while acknowledging his enormous influence.' Who might this be? Rubén Dario, the Nicaraguan poet who died in 1916. Well, if it *is* fashionable, I shall start dismissing Dario's poetry at once, while naturally acknowledging his enormous influence. How, you wonder, can Seymour-Smith keep in touch with so many cultures? Do people ring him up from time to time and say, 'Someone else has learnt to read and write down here'? I went through the book half-expecting the 'X' section to be the longest: there, surely all the *really* unknown writers would find a home.

Unfair, of course. Despite the fact that Seymour-Smith's oeuvre includes *The Bluffer's Guide to Literature*, I am inclined to credit at least half of the scholarship exhibited here – in itself a colossal accolade. How much use this book will be to anyone but George Steiner, though, remains debatable. On those writers who do ring a bell with me, Seymour-Smith is by turns impartial, biased, mean, forgiving, prurient, sympathetic, hamfisted, delicate, trivial and profound. Is Willa Cather 'one of the more important American writers of this century', Pirandello 'the greatest short-story writer of the century', Kenneth Burke 'the most rewarding English-language critic of this century'? Was Graves 'ultimately rejected' by Laura Riding? Was Kipling '(unconsciously) in love' with his second wife's brother? God knows, and so does Mr Seymour-Smith, but what is a beginner to do with such questions?

Digests of this sort should be the work either of committees or of humdrum minds. Seymour-Smith is not a committee and his mind is not humdrum. On the contrary, his response to literature is at once busy and deep. The main question posed by the book, which is a plea for internationalism rather than a directory, is whether it will make readers less parochial or more so. Having been drawn into Seymour-Smith's surreal world of – what next? – Kampuchean controversialists, Chelyabinskian concretists, Maharashtrian manifestoists, Kalmykovoan typewriter-repairers, Liaoningian paperclip-dealers, I have decided to get round to reading *The Merry Wives of Windsor* first. Then we'll see.

Observer June 1976

Russian Ghost

Islanders and *The Fisher of Men* by Yevgeny Zamyatin.
Translated by Sophie Fuller and Julian Sacchi

Along with Bely, Bunin and Bulgakov, Yevgeny Zamyatin rode
the last wave of Russian fiction. 'Having become the most fantastic country in all present-day Europe,' he wrote, in an essay on
Wells published in the early Twenties, 'post-revolutionary Russia
will undoubtedly reflect this . . . in a literature of fantasy.' But of
course the literature never happened; it was collectivized, immured,
eliminated, and now persists only in scattered and contorted forms.
Its ghost is visible in the Nabokov of *Bend Sinister* and *Invitation to
a Beheading*, in the skittish mysticism of 'unborn' Russian writers
like Saul Bellow, and in the satirical epics of such banished survivors
as Alexander Zinoviev; and of course there is Solzhenitsyn.★ Bely's
Petersburg, Bulgakov's *The Master and Margarita* and Zamyatin's *We* –
exalted, ecstatic, fizzing with humour and licence – are the flagships
of a vanished literature.

The present volume contains the previously untranslated novella
Islanders and the companion story 'The Fisher of Men'. And the
book is remarkable in every way, not least in its provenance and
implications. A naval architect, Zamyatin spent most of 1916 and
1917 in Newcastle, overseeing the construction of ten ice-breakers
for the Tsar: an appealingly eerie happenstance, as if D.H. Lawrence,
say, had designed aeroplanes in Vladivostok. Both stories are set in
England – *Islanders* was written there – and they reveal Zamyatin's
complicated attachment to our national ethos. (Among the Russian

★ There is also, unquestionably, Vasily Grossman. His monumental *Life and
Fate* was published, posthumously, in 1985.

bohemians of his day the tweed-suited Yevgeny was known as 'The Englishman'; he translated Sheridan and Wells, and wrote on Bacon and Shaw, among others.) In Zamyatin's quirky diagnosis, the natives emerge as fastidious and fantastical, dogged and capricious, busy rationalizers of their abiding repressions. *Islanders* predates *We* by three years and anticipates it in detail, despite the radical switch in setting and timescale. For a while, one entertains the extraordinary thought that *We* is not a futuristic satire on mature Soviet tyranny so much as a gentle lampoon of British utilitarianism. The Benefactor, the Big Brother in *We*, is Lenin all right; but he is also Dickens's Gradgrind, hideously magnified.

Just as the One State in *We* is ruled by Hourly Commandments, so the Reverend Dewley in *Islanders* is smugly in thrall to a life of self-imposed timetables. On one timetable, 'which particularly concerned Mrs Dewley ... every third Saturday was marked' – for amorous play, again prefiguring *We*, with its Sexual Days and copulation coupons ('She held out to me her tiny pink mouth – and her small pink ticket. I tore off the stub'). The English bourgeoisie secretly yearns for the Great Machine of State, which will eradicate human volatility and variance. Even the effusiveness of nature is repellent to the well-regulated citizen: the 'ill-bred' sun shines 'scandalously bright', the birds sing 'inexcusably', and the flowers ruin the 'respectable, well-clipped' trees. As in *We*, mendacity is saluted as an evolutionary accomplishment (lying alters messy reality; besides, animals can't do it, so it must be good); and the nightlife of dreams is feared and hated, because it represents chaos, creativity and desire, the three things that the good citizen is most anxious to suppress.

The point is, of course, that Zamyatin was himself imaginatively drawn towards the tendencies he vilified and satirized. Artist and engineer, he responded to an impossible vision of human order and mechanical harmony. The comic masterstroke of *We* (the title is marvellously triumphal, with its proud denial of all singularity) was to make the narrator, D-503, a passionate *fan* of the One State, pompously exulting in the horrors that surround him. Zamyatin had the imagination of a Futurist and the heart of a Luddite; and in that rift his genius lived. Like Bernard Guerney's *We*, the translation is wonderfully supple and elegant – perhaps because Zamyatin's 'Englishness' eases the passage of his prose. We now await the resurrection of the essays and the plays.

Observer November 1984

Nothing is Deserved and Everything is Accepted

The Complete Short Stories of Franz Kafka; The Complete Novels of Franz Kafka. Principal translators: Edwin and Willa Muir

Much has been said and written about Kafka's guilts and alienations, his obsessive love for his father and for Milena Jesenská, his sickness of body and distemper of mind, the prescient universality of the Kafka 'predicament'. These handsome volumes, published halfway through the centenary year of his birth, provide a chance to re-glimpse an aspect of Kafka often lost among the punditry and scholarly gossip, and among the half-impressions subsumed by that woolly watchword 'Kafkaesque' (used, nowadays, to describe a train delay or a queue in the post office). Namely, the stuff itself – the work, the art.

The Penguin *Complete Short Stories* cunningly opens with 'Two Introductory Parables' – 'Before the Law' and 'An Imperial Message' – neither of them much more than a page in length. In the first story, a man from the country approaches the gate to the Law and begs its formidable doorkeeper for admittance. 'Not at the moment' is the repeated reply. Should the man venture through the gate, there will be other door-keepers, each more formidable than the last. 'The third doorkeeper', says the first doorkeeper, 'is already so terrible that even I cannot bear to look at him.' The man sits and waits, for months, for years. Now withered by age, the man asks with his last breath why no one else has ever come to seek admittance to the gate of the Law. The doorkeeper shouts into the ear of the dying man: 'No one else could ever be admitted here, since this gate was made only for you. I am now going to shut it.'

In the second piece, 'An Imperial Message', a dying Emperor has dispatched a message to you – 'to you, the humble subject, the insignificant shadow cowering in the remotest distance before the imperial sun'. The message is so important that the Emperor has it whispered back to him as he sprawls on his deathbed. 'A powerful, an indefatigable man', the messenger immediately sets out on his journey through the thronged anterooms. But the multitudes are illimitable, the chambers endless, and a lifetime will pass before he can escape even the innermost halls of the palace. 'And if at last he should burst through the outermost gate – but never, never can that happen – the imperial capital would lie before him, the centre of the world, crammed to bursting . . .' So the message will never reach you. 'But you sit at your window when evening falls and dream it to yourself.'

'Before the Law' points fairly obviously to *The Trial*, 'An Imperial Message' to *The Castle*. But the two parables point further than that, and can be seen as forming the twin poles of Kafka's world – or the double-sided coin of its currency. On the one hand, there is the sense of constriction, pointless vigil, invidious exclusion ('The Metamorphosis', 'In the Penal Colony', 'A Report to an Academy'); on the other (in 'The Refusal', 'A Little Woman', 'The Great Wall of China'), there is the sense of painful boundlessness, of repetition and duplication, of human worthlessness in the face of an indifferent infinity. It has been said, for instance, that *The Trial* is 'about' divine justice, that *The Castle* is 'about' divine grace. Yet every reader knows that Kafka's art lies much closer to home.

In Kafka, the two nightmares – one claustrophobic, one agoraphobic – are really the same nightmare; and it doesn't end when morning comes. It has always been tempting to negotiate Kafka as an interpreter of the hidden world of dreams. Certainly no one can read him without feeling that they have already dreamed him: the freefalls and turn-arounds, the abolition of cause and effect, the excruciations of proximity and remoteness, the evanescent temptresses, the pains proliferated, the pleasures deferred. In a sense, though, we distance ourselves from Kafka if we demote him to the outback of the unconscious. The jokes and jumps of his prose have as much to tell us about the futilities of the waking consciousness, which is never more than a neurotic babble, occasionally and briefly forced into some expedient order.

Kafka is the antic poet of everyday fear, shame and stoical yearning. The art is subversive, even playful. He deals in savage inequities that are never resented, pitiful recompenses that are tearfully cherished. Nothing is deserved and everything is accepted, with hilarious, inhuman pedantry. We tend to keep a straight face for writers who daunt us with their modernity. After the due process of assimilation, however, we can see that only the art is innovatory and that the concerns belong to the mainstream of life, to its humour and its pathos.

Jorge Luis Borges – whose debt to the master, while often acknowledged, is increasingly manifest – recently claimed that the primacy of 'atmosphere' in Kafka renders the stories superior to the novels. This feels accurate. As a work of art, the short story 'The Stoker' is more fully evolved than the novel *America*, of which it forms the opening chapter. The novels are attritional – deliberately so. 'They are epics of suspension and postponement, and could never be finished into art.' It is in the stories that Kafka's genius shines most unmistakably: in modulation, pacing, indirection, in the exquisite pregnancy of his endings. Take the closing lines of 'A Hunger Artist', the story of a circus performer whose 'act' consists of forty-day fasts completed alone behind the bars of a cage. Slowly the art of fasting falls out of fashion; forgotten, the hunger-artist dies unnoticed behind his bars:

> 'All right, deal with this mess!' the foreman said, and they buried the fasting-artist together with the straw. Into the cage they now put a young panther. It was a palpable relief even to the most stolid to see this savage animal thrashing about in the cage that had been bleakly lifeless for so long. He lacked nothing . . . even freedom he did not appear to miss; that noble body, endowed almost to bursting-point with all it required, seemed to carry its very freedom around with it – somewhere in the teeth, apparently; and sheer delight at being alive made such a torch of the beast's breath that the spectators had difficulty in holding their ground against it. With a conscious

effort, however, they crowded round the cage and, once there, would not budge.*

The coda has the same violent, distorted poignancy as that of 'The Metamorphosis': the starved and festering beetle dies alone in his room, and the family travel to the countryside, where the parents note with pleasure that their daughter is the first to stand up, 'stretching her young body'. Despite or because of the Jewish lineaments of his consciousness, Kafka saw the artist's isolation as Christlike – an infinitely gentle, infinitely suffering thing, yet capable of wincing laughter. Grateful as we are for the reissues of the *Diaries* and the *Letters*, intrigued as we will doubtless be by the forthcoming picture books and pop-up albums, we need no further testimony to Kafka's pain and how he bore it.

Observer July 1983

---

* Translated by J.A. Underwood, whose *Stories 1904–1924* is often superior to the Muirs' *Complete Short Stories*.

Educated Monsters

The Chip-Chip Gatherers by Shiva Naipaul

In *The Pleasures of Exile* George Lamming scolded V.S. Naipaul, as he no doubt would his younger brother Shiva, for taking too soft a line on Trinidadian social conditions, for being smug when he ought to be angry, for writing 'castrated satire'. This, of course, is like calling 'The Windhover' a castrated epic. What the Naipauls write is irony, not satire, and irony is by definition non-militant. Should they decide to give up creative prose in favour of pamphleteering, then Mr Lamming's remarks would carry weight; as it is, Caribbean social conditions have for them, *qua* novelists, an imaginative significance only.

It is true that a primitive society offers a Hobson's choice of styles to its authors: tantrumese, noble-savagery, or a combination of irony and pathos. But like all limitations this brings special liberties. Irony and pathos are essentially downward-looking viewpoints, so a society of grotesques, fools, snobs, show-offs, martinets and ingénues who think and talk in illiterate clichés has obvious perks for a writer with as delicate a touch as Shiva Naipaul. One sentence from his first novel, *Fireflies*, the story of Baby Lutchman's struggle to be free of her family and make a life of her own with her husband, illustrates the comic discrepancy between the author's sophistication and that of his characters: 'It was generally agreed that Mrs Lutchman was being deliberately awkward [in wanting some independence], "too big," as Urmila had put it, "for she boots."' Although Mr Naipaul must, so to speak, keep his distance, this doesn't cut off sympathy but creates an undertow of restrained emotion (as in the almost definitive poignancy of the Lutchman marriage). The compassion is there in the sheer quality of the writing and never has to become explicit.

Naipaul's second novel, like his first, is predominantly concerned with one question about Trinidadian life: what happens when a backward people starts to educate itself? The most imaginatively appealing answer is that the old atavistic instincts are not transcended, merely adulterated: what used to express itself in abuse and beatings turns into inarticulate malice; worry becomes anxiety, nostalgia becomes regret, apathy becomes morbidity, vague aspiration becomes obsessive ambition. This, like so much else, can best be observed through child–parent relationships, and Naipaul again requires a broad canvas and a forty-year period in which to encompass it.

The Chip-Chip Gatherers opens in 'the Settlement', a Gypsy-like community in the Trinidad sticks. Here, aggressive, Quilp-like Ramsaran and the weedier, more malleable Bholai are planning (like everyone else there) to get out of the Settlement and (like every Trinidadian) to get into the professional classes. Ramsaran goes, Bholai stays; gradually, the broader ironies develop. Ramsaran, having married ostentatiously beneath himself, produces a son whom he sets about traumatizing with his own repressions. Back at the Settlement, Bholai, having married obsequiously above himself, produces a son to whose emancipation he dedicates his own wasted life. The predatory Ramsaran rears the morose Wilbert; the morose Bholai rears the predatory Julian. Ramsaran does 'his best to see that Wilbert received . . . a distorted life's experience', while Bholai, faced with the open scorn of his comparatively cultivated children, can only shrug that 'it have nothing surprising in the way they turn out. Is how we wanted them to be after all – to be different from us. To be better.' Wilbert duly wanders into a pleasureless marriage with the nastiest Bholai girl. Julian duly jilts his Ramsaran-ménage sweetheart to take up a scholarship abroad. The last thing we hear Bholai tell his children, finally goaded into a kind of befuddled eloquence, might serve as the book's sententia:

> You have education – or say you have. What you do with it?
> Where you hiding it? Monsters. That is the only name for all-you.
> Educated monsters, which is the worst kind of monster it have.

On the novel's last page we leave the rich, doomed, loveless Wilbert watching Trinidad's poor, the chip-chip gatherers, scavenging in the sea-beds for morsels of food, undeterred 'by the disproportion between their labours and their gains', 'on this wind-swept, shimmering beach of starving dogs, chip-chip gatherers and himself'.

If the book isn't quite as successful as the shockingly mature *Fireflies*, it is because Naipaul has started to deal with the problem of focus. He is concentrating on nuance rather than ambience, shaving down his sentences, and holding his vast – perhaps Dickensian – comic talents carefully in check. But for a writer in his twenties these are further precocities, not constraints, and there can be little doubt that his next novels will establish him as one of the most accomplished, and most accessible, writers of his generation.

New Statesman April 1973

Black and White by Shiva Naipaul

What was going on in Jonestown, Guyana – before that day in November 1978, when Pastor Jim Jones came on the tannoy and summoned his flock to the waiting vats of Kool-Aid and cyanide?

While running his San Francisco ministry, Jones had been a pillar of Californian society. He won the praise not only of proven gulls like Jane Fonda and Tom Hayden but also of hard politicians like Jerry Brown and Walter Mondale (who considered Jones 'an inspiration'). Jones cared for people whom no one cared for – the Moorlocks, the underground proletariat, the junked: exploded hippies, dropouts, addicts, sociopaths, whores, the old, the crippled, the unemployable. In 1976 the *Los Angeles Herald* named Jones as their Humanitarian of the Year. Fostering his (mostly black) community, Jones entertained paranoid fears of fascist-racist reprisal. But his subsequent move to Guyana was an act of hope and liberation, a move towards conscious utopianism.

According to many reports, that utopia was brilliantly realized. In the remote jungle of South America the Jonestowners led a life of lyrical freedom and productivity. They gorged themselves on protein-rich food and sang in the fields. This was communism, and it worked. They lived in hygienic 'cabins'; education and medical care were first-rate, and Jim was always on hand to exhort and, sometimes, to heal; the elderly smiled all day and danced all night. Visitors from all over the world continued to be 'impressed' by the noble experiment.

According to other reports, the horror of Jonestown was, from the start, unrelieved. By February 1978, half of the 1,000 congregants were suffering from diarrhoea and malnutrition. The town was putrefying. 'Dark circles under one's eyes or extreme loss of weight were considered signs of loyalty.' Children were regularly tortured. The lowlier blacks were treated like slaves. Worst of all, perhaps, the ailing, drug-racked Jones never tired of airing his megalomania over the public-address system – often for six hours a day, sometimes much longer. When the end came, most of the Jonestowners must have been ready to go.

Shiva Naipaul is fascinated by the contradictory nature of these reports – black and white with nothing in between. They are testimony to the hysteria that was inseparable from Jim Jones, and possessed his followers as well as his enemies. 'Their hysteria goaded Jonestown towards extinction.' Reciprocally, Jones did not protect and solace his marooned parishioners; he traumatized them with his own fears. In a sense the Jonestown Thousand were saying to the world what all suicides say: look what you have made me do.

It has been argued that the People's Temple was a tragic instance of idealism gone wrong. For Naipaul, it had never gone right, and was the efflorescence of a larger vacuity. 'Jim Jones was a beachcomber,' Naipaul writes, 'picking up the flotsam and jetsam washed ashore from the Sixties shipwrecks.' His championship of the black cause was no more than opportunism: 'Church was nothing, a handful of old bigots, till I brought in some blacks,' Jones privately boasted. 'And that is how the goddamned religious career got rolling.' In one of his most jolting paragraphs, Naipaul argues that Jones felt nothing but hatred

for the blacks he had salvaged – 'a hatred so deep-seated, so tormenting, that, in its fury, it turned itself inside out and called itself Love'.

Black and White (and note the absence of any subtitle) is no highbrow quickie on the Jonestown disaster. It is a serious, possibly over-ambitious book about racial distortion and perversity. At the same time Naipaul is always engaging and acute. As in *North of South*, his travel book about Central Africa, he places himself and his neuroses at the hub of the narrative. He has the Naipaulian confidence that what he finds interesting will interest us. It is not high-energy reporting; Naipaul doesn't probe and scurry about for information – he just hangs around with his whole sensibility on hire. The result is haphazard, all the same. Naipaul's pacing and priorities often seem suspect. There are over-generous digressions on the South American political background and the Californian cults; and Naipaul is rather too happy to sit back with an illiterate Guyanese pamphlet, a Jonestown brochure, a hippie manifesto, and jeer his way through it.

It is intriguing, meanwhile, to speculate on the course of Shiva Naipaul's career. His two early novels, *Fireflies* (1971) and *The Chip-Chip Gatherers* (1973), were precocious masterpieces, and they shine disturbingly in the memory. I'm sure Naipaul doesn't need reminding that he has published no work of fiction for nearly a decade. Many writers could have tackled Jonestown, though perhaps not as ably. But only one writer can tackle the fiction of Shiva Naipaul.*

Observer November 1980

★ I append the following:

Anyone who knew – or read – Shiva Naipaul will feel horribly robbed and violated by his death, last week, at the age of forty.

The moment I finished his first novel, *Fireflies*, I felt delight in being alive at the same time as such a writer. I passed the book round to friends (I must have bought half-a-dozen of those Penguins), and there are many people with whom I can initiate a long train of quotation – and laughter – from that book alone: Ram Lutchman's torments at the hands of his hobby, photography (he takes to developing his own film, under the bed: 'There go another sonofabitch. Is

MARTIN AMIS

---

like a goddamn lake in here'); his subsequent refrain, at any humbling reverse
in his troubled and frustrating life: 'Is just like that sonofabitch camera'); and
the ostracism his wife Baby must endure from her family, having settled on the
lowly Ram: 'It was generally agreed that Baby was being deliberately awkward,
"too big," as Urmila had put it, "for she boots."'

I quote from memory. Perhaps this is what one is always obliged to
do with the dead — quote from memory. The second novel, *The Chip-Chip
Gatherers*, fully maintained the great promise, and the great achievement.
I got to know him about that time (the early Seventies), a humorous,
recalcitrant and denunciatory figure. He was still not yet thirty. Many people
felt impatience at the tum his career then took. His travel books, *North of
South* and *Black and White*, were brilliant, and characteristically brilliant; but
where were the novels?

The novels were simmering away. Shiva's third, *A Hot Country*, signalled a change
of direction and a toughening-up, a wheeling round of the guns. In losing him, we have
lost thirty years of untranscribed, of vanished genius: the hard political intelligence,
and the beautiful comedy, which dealt in the most forgiving pathos and irony, as
bearish and affectionate as the man.

With Shiva, you usually found yourself having five-hour sessions in exasperated but
needy Greek restaurants. I once asked him what he thought of an editor we both
knew, an editor I liked. 'To kill such a man', smiled Shiva, 'could not be accounted
murder.' It turned out that this editor had once cut three lines of Shiva's copy, or
had been a day late with payment. Such vehemence was partly play, for he was a
gentle presence. The other day I parped my horn as I drove past him in the street,
and saw him wave and smile and level his accusing eyes. I felt more warmth for him
than for people I know far better. He had a talent for warmth, as for much else. He
was one of those people who caused your heart to lift when he entered the room.

No Way

A Journey in Ladakh by Andrew Harvey

Reviewing Joan Didion in the *Sunday Times*, Paul Theroux remarked that *Salvador* was a good book about 'being nervous' but not much of an account of Salvador. Travel writing remains a predominantly European genre – a genre that the New World has yet to get around to. Explanations and exceptions immediately present themselves. In *To Jerusalem and Back*, Saul Bellow pointed out that America is more like a world than a country; and perhaps this is why the best American travel writing is almost invariably domestic. In England, a new generation of talented tourists has recently emerged: we have Bruce Chatwin and Jonathan Raban; and V.S. and Shiva Naipaul by adoption. In America, there is no such tradition to be maintained. (You have Theroux, true, but he lives with us in London now.) The embarrassing answer may be that the England-based traveller is emboldened by the vestiges of an imperial unreflectiveness. *We* aren't nervous: we've done all this before. Combining intrepidity with lack of imagination, the Brit strides out into the world and brings back the story, dead or alive.

There is one road, however, that even the cultural colonist treads warily. This is the Way, or the Path – the 'hippie trail' to the Enlightenment centres and Revelation strongholds of the East. The literature of these journeys has dwindled in modern times: the travellers fall prey to dysentery or dope, or forget how to write, or never come back, or return with an understanding too ineffable for syntax. The Eastern road is a humbling one; the trekker treks on tiptoe, or on all fours, cruelly burdened by his knapsack of Western guilt and self-loathing; he longs to prostrate himself before the first smiling guru who will redeem and legitimize him, and kiss away his confusion and his cares. You begin Andrew Harvey's book feeling like an averagely soiled and venal Westerner. You finish it in far worse shape. I don't know whether the reader will want to retrace the steps of Harvey's quest, but he will certainly contemplate a brief visit to a health farm. At the very least, the book reminds all of us here in the West, as we sweat it out in our mangled cityscapes, that it might be time to cut down on the smoking and the drinking, the adult videos and the Big Macs.

As the preposition in its title half-suggests, *A Journey in Ladakh* describes a spiritual odyssey. Yet the journey begins conventionally enough, in all respects. Enervated by the 'bitterness and solitude' of his twenties, harassed by 'the complex civilised ironies and melancholies of Europe', Harvey, a talented and tempestuous Oxford academic, makes his long-anticipated pilgrimage to Ladakh, in northern India, 'one of the last places on earth . . . where a Tibetan Buddhist society can be experienced'. He sets off from Delhi, pondering a saying from the Dhammapada: 'By oneself the evil is done, by oneself the evil is undone, no one can purify another.' An experienced traveller, Harvey is none the less struck by the 'splendour and majesty' of the mountains and the 'age and uncomfortableness' of the buses. In Leh, he acquires the usual gushing guide, the usual Ahmed. 'You name it, I am knowing it very fully. This is truth, sir.'

Not yet searching for Truth, Harvey is free to write rapturously and hungrily about the crispness of the Ladakhi landscapes, the gentleness and simplicity of the people. Ladakh, it transpires, is a land that time forgot – or a land that time is just beginning to recall. It is an endangered culture, threatened by the twentieth century and by its own prelapsarian innocence. But then, Harvey sounds innocent too, in his yearning generosity, and the reader isn't sure what goes unobserved while the 'silent splendour' proceeds to 'rinse' the author's mind 'of everything but calm'. 'I have seen very little cruelty,' Harvey is assured by an American psychologist. 'Once I saw a child tormenting a dog. That's about all – in three years.' Ladakhis are taught that every living thing has been their mother in a previous incarnation. There are no unhappy lovesongs in Ladakhi folk culture, and there is no concept of tragedy in Ladakhi literature.

Harvey meets with much kindness, hospitality, and good humour – a teasing gaiety. Right up to the highest levels of Enlightenment, he finds that the (Tibetan) Buddhist emphasis is on pleasure rather than asceticism. 'Don't worry,' a monk tells him, as they share a flask of chang. 'Padma-sambhava himself drank. A great deal.'

Meanwhile, as Harvey encounters the familiar crew of Western searchers and finders, seekers and seers, he eventually notes with regret that there is also 'ugliness' in Ladakh, to which he devotes a brief paragraph. This is the first suggestion that Harvey is visiting a deprived area in one of the poorest countries on earth. There are, for example, 'mangy flearidden dogs nosing for food in the gutters'. My first thought, on reading this, was that Harvey hadn't really looked at the dogs – 'mangy' and 'flearidden' are received, automatic adjectives; and what else do pariah dogs do but nose for food in gutters? (Indian dogs are in fact highly distinctive creatures: they look like abruptly promoted rats, bemused by their sudden elevation, and pining for a quiet return to the rodent kingdom.) Harvey reminds us a dozen pages later that he spent much of his childhood in India; and we must again acknowledge how this fact, so little emphasized in the text, crucially slants *A Journey in Ladakh*.

Harvey's Indian childhood provides him with all kinds of vaccinations and culture-shock-absorbers denied to that mental traveller, the reader. In *An Area of Darkness* V.S. Naipaul speaks of the Indian facility for 'ignoring the obvious' – for ignoring the suffering, the excrement, and the stench that initially stupefy the Westerner. Indians do not see what we see. Nor does Harvey. Eclectic myopia is the necessary mysticism of India; it is what Kipling is referring to when he talks of the 'ecstatic' quality of the ordinary, the urban, the unknown Indian, whose life is variegated and sustained by a fabric of religious consolations. Harvey has something of this otherworldliness. To an extent that he doesn't sufficiently discuss or allow for, he is not the pilgrim so much as the prodigal son.

Halfway through the book, however, Harvey has yet to set off down the Path. He has had many rambles, on foot and in conversation. He tells of his troubling dreams and his husky crying-jags up in the mountains. But his moments of uplift are not readily distinguishable from mere pantheistic euphoria. The extreme, cleansing beauty of Ladakh is summoned in these pages not by description but by Harvey's detailed reports on the joy these landscapes give him. Even the most blemished readers will feel that they could improve their spirituality without really trying if they spent more time in Ladakh and less time in, say, Piccadilly Circus. At this point, though, and quite inadvertently, Harvey stumbles across his guru, his Rinpoche (pronounced Rinpochay), and from here on *A Journey in Ladakh* follows Harvey's tutorials at the feet of the great man.

The book gets less enjoyable around now but much more original, as Harvey's own temperament becomes its dramatic core. Throughout, Harvey presents himself openly, unpointedly, as if the book were simply a diary that had somehow fallen into the hands of a publisher. He comes across as eager, un-self-sparing, perhaps rather helpless in his pain and narrow in his humour, charged with tearing desire; and the reader feels protective of his fragile excitability.

Thuksey Rinpoche has none of the lisping hucksterism of the Bhagwan Rajneesh or the Maharishi. He emerges as endearing and likeable, and convincingly holy and wise. He got that way by the following means: abstinence, prayer, study, meditation, and spending ten years alone in a cave. Spending ten years alone in a cave is obviously the hard bit. Your only chance of skipping this stage is by being an Incarnation right from the start, like Drukchen Rinpoche, another voluble genius – a spiritual princeling at twenty, happy in his 'simple monk's robe' and his 'small bare room'. Harvey's induction begins. Time is short, but he manages to make the big breakthrough on his very last night, up there with the old Rinpoche: having experienced Emptiness, his first glimpse of the Void, Harvey is finally led into the Way of Compassion.

Here the reader is in the position of anyone buttonholed by a convert's account of revelation. You are obliged to ask yourself, however reluctantly, Why is he telling me this? Harvey certainly fails to commemorate or enshrine the moment with any new intensity in his writing. There isn't much difference in energy, or indeed in content, between Harvey's exaltation when he alights from the bus –

... each winding dark stream, each small shrub clawing the sides of the road, each bird, seemed to be so full of its own essence that it hovered on the brink of dissolution, so brimming with energy that I feared often it could not survive itself ...

– on page 15, and his climactic trance of 'Sunyata', thirty pages from the end:

Each object looked at once startlingly, intensely real – and completely fabricated ... Even the Rinpoche looked at once imposing and a doll ... The fruit in front of him seemed at once solid and so fragile that a breath could blow it away or break it.

There are other things that trouble the reader, the Westerner marooned in his own inner city. Approximately half the book is in the form of dialogue, or distributed monologue, with Harvey allowing the munshis and mystics their full say. Now, it is hard to imagine Harvey asking the Rinpoche, 'Will you teach me the meditation on Avalokiteshvara?' with one finger tensed on the REC button of a Sony. Jam Yang, a Ladakhi acquaintance, mentions Harvey's 'big black notebooks, full of illegible writing'. But when did all the transcription take place? Is Harvey also granted Perfect Recall? The questions become more pressing towards the end, by which point Harvey is too blissed out to do much more than bask in the Rinpoche's gaze. And yet the jotting got done somehow, pages of complicated and technical instruction, all in immaculate English.

One has always understood, furthermore, that an initiation such as Harvey underwent is as non-transferable as a mantra. Yet Harvey holds nothing back. Indeed, he would seem to have written a book about it all. Isn't it 'materialist', or at any rate paradoxical, to popularize and profit from an experience in which the author triumphantly turns his back on worldly preferment? Even if it should transpire that the royalties are going straight to a Ladakhi children's home, certain anxieties would still hold, and Harvey ought to have helped purge them.

In his Western incarnation, Harvey is a poet and a teacher. His poetry has always erred on the side of precocity and dazzle, but *A Journey in Ladakh*, as an act of writing, is a subdued performance. This is deliberate: early on, Harvey abjures the temptation 'to fling names at things' and learns to treasure 'the gift of silence'. One of his key questions to the Rinpoche involves the conflict between spirituality and art. If spirituality grows, doesn't art begin to end? The Rinpoche's riposte is a good one. He concludes:

> With time and sincerity you will discover a way to work and write that does not harm you spiritually, that does not tempt you to vanity, that is the deepest expression of your spirituality. You will find a voice that is not your voice only, but the voice of Reality itself, and free from all delusion and stain of personality.

Harvey made his journey in 1981. He doesn't tell us whether his illuminations survived re-entry. He doesn't tell us – he probably doesn't yet know – whether his art can now prosper in the weak and wanton West, where the gods are Talent and Hard Work and Immersion in the Consensus Reality. Religion used to be a part of that consensus. It isn't any longer, and Harvey will have to choose which gods to honour. *A Journey in Ladakh* is not the kind of book in which the reader follows the free play of perception and inquiry; it doesn't seek inclusion in the corner of art that travel writing inhabits. It is bleached by exposure to a higher light.

Atlantic Monthly July 1983

More Bones

Finding the Centre by V.S. Naipaul

'You are a damn good writer, boy,' an elderly voyager tells V.S. Naipaul early on in *The Middle Passage* (1962). 'Yes, man, I watch you at the post office in the Azores. Writing off those cards so damn fast I couldn't even read what you was writing.'

One often speculates about the content of Naipaul's postcards. 'Not having nice time'? Or to an enemy. 'Wish you were here'? James Fenton said recently in *Granta* magazine that travel writing is always 'hedonistic' in tendency. But the form has its stoical, even its self-punitive practitioners. Disquiet, futility, corruption, half-made societies, areas of darkness: these are the things that excite Naipaul, and inspire his best work.

At first, *Finding the Centre* looks like an opportunist or desk-tidying volume. It consists of two unrelated 'narratives' written one after the other and 'offered as a book principally for that reason'. And, at first, both pieces seem surprisingly low on energy and impact, the pacing hesitant, the prose listless, unmodulated, under-rehearsed. Wavering readers, however, are urged to put the book aside for a while and fortify themselves with the scandalous brilliance of *Among the Believers*, say, or *The Overcrowded Barracoon*. On their return they will discover that *Finding the Centre* is, in its quiet way, an original and highly artistic piece of work. The two narratives form a subtle and satisfying whole, and Naipaul's instinct was sound when he chose to publish them in tandem.

The opening section, 'Prologue to an Autobiography', begins with an endearing glimpse of the young Vidya, just down from Oxford, working in Langham House as a freelance for the BBC Caribbean Service. He sits at the typewriter with his knees drawn up, his shoes resting on the top rung of the chair 'in something like a monkey crouch' – the characteristic posture of Indian vigil. With superstitious self-effacement he writes his first sketches of Trinidadian life; he writes *Miguel Street*. Unable to face a return to his benighted island (even on the death of his father), Naipaul finds that fiction offers a form of mental repatriation, of homecoming. 'Without having become a writer, I couldn't go back . . . I wrote my book; I wrote another. I began to go back.'

The journey was hard then, and it is hard now. One sees, in the diffidence and difficulty of this essay, how little of the self is present in Naipaul's work. In the novels, a past is used, but a self is not used. In the travel writing, a controlling intelligence is present, but the self remains inscrutable and undisclosed (even during his frequent losses of self-command). There is a natural fastidiousness in him, a brahmin distance, which has to be mollified or appeased; and there are strange origins to be assimilated.

In his mental travel at Langham House, Naipaul practised 'magic' – and not only the conjurations of literary talent. Naipaul's magic was superstitious, propitiatory. He always used stolen 'non-rustle' BBC paper ('it seemed less likely to attract failure'). He never numbered his pages, 'for fear of not getting to the end'. And on the typescripts of his first four books, he never wrote his own name. 'Such anxiety; such ambition.' Such modest voodoo. But this too was a necessary re-enactment of the hidden past.

Naipaul's father, Seepersad Naipaul, 'had made himself into a journalist' on the *Trinidad Guardian*: a tremendous achievement for this morose autodidact, himself the son of an immigrant farmer. He wrote local – i.e., rural, Indian, Hindu – news stories, bylined 'The Pundit' (in the loose sense of 'guru'). Young Vidya took enough interest in Seepersad's work to share his distress when it ceased. But it wasn't until 1970 that he discovered the startling reasons for his father's professional humiliation and personal decline.

Investigating one of many Hindu feuds, a horrified Seepersad reported a blood sacrifice in rural Chaguanas. He then received a death threat: he would die within a week unless he performed 'the very ceremony he had criticised'. And he submitted: 'the goat anointed and garlanded with hibiscus . . . the cutlass on the tree stump'. The quarrel becomes public, and Naipaul Sr has no choice but to bluff his way through an account of his own supplication to Kali:

He will never sacrifice again, he says; he knows his faith now. And he records it as a little triumph that he didn't wear a loincloth . . . The odd, illogical bluster continues the next day, on the front page of the Sunday paper. *Mr Naipaul Greets you! – No poison Last Night.* 'Good morning, everybody! As you behold, Kali has not got me yet . . .'

Soon afterwards he is demoted. He becomes mentally ill; he starts to die. In 1972 V.S. Naipaul asked his mother what form her husband's madness had taken. 'He looked in the mirror one day,' she replied, 'and couldn't see himself. And he began to scream.'

Less need be said about the second narrative, 'The Crocodiles of Yamoussoukro', a more conventional exercise in Naipaulian travel. It is a familiar self-exposure of nerves and senses, forming a psychiatric report on the condition of an emergent nation. In this instance the Ivory Coast is on the couch; and here, for the first time, Naipaul glimpses 'light at both ends of the African tunnel', the possibility of African 'completeness'. On the one hand there is prosperity, spread wealth; on the other, there is an undiminished (if illusory and often repellent) sense of cultural integrity, the African night-world of fantasy and totemic power coexisting with the sober routines of day. In a delightfully insidious way, the second narrative enacts the themes that the first narrative only states. As its beautiful title suggests, it is about magic and order; it is about naming and identifying; it is about writing.

Finding the Centre is not, perhaps, one of Naipaul's most important books, though it may turn out to be of great transitional significance. Both narratives are, in effect, success stories: the Ivory Coast towers over its neighbours ('Liberia, illiterate, impoverished', 'Guinea, a murderous tyranny' – this is the more recognizable voice); and while Seepersad Naipaul suffered the nullity of the writer *manqué*, his son has resplendently fulfilled that lost ambition. Paradoxically, though,

Naipaul is happiest with misery, and most deeply stirred by failure. After all, the postcard that tells of fine weather and good food is less fun to write – and to read – than the postcard that tells of missed connections, belly trouble, snatched passports and collapsing hotels.

One could go a little further. In all his work Naipaul writes about civilization by writing about its absence. His great theme is that of the exile, the emigrant, the man without a society. We accept this as a central twentieth-century experience but we probably underestimate its harshness. It is not a Nabokovian experience of elegy and playful alienation. It is an experience of despair, fear and above all hatred – the journey of the silent travellers in *In a Free State*, who will never know

> what bus we will take when we get to the station, or what other train, what street we will walk down, what gate we will go through, and what door we will open into what room.

('Tell Me Who to Kill')

Observer May 1984

The Return of Eva Peron, with *The Killings in Trinidad*
by V.S. Naipaul

While planning the murder of Gale Ann Benson, Michael X also found time to start work on a novel. The narrator is a thirty-year-old Englishwoman called Lena Boyd-Richardson, but the hero, or the star, is Michael X himself. At the outset, Lena is of the opinion that 'these natives are all shiftless good for Nothings'. Then she encounters the enigmatic Michael. She becomes strangely drawn to this strange man ('something about him drawing you to him'); she sees him 'leaning against the Coconut tree like some statue on a Pedestal, some god'; there is talk of 'the fantastic following he had in the country'; she hears shouts in the street – 'We go crown him king.' One day Lena visits the strange man at his imposing house. He plays her 'the Thihikosky 1812' and she admires his 'gigantic bookshelf': 'I discover that he not only have the books but actually reads and understands them I was absolutly bowld, litteraly. I took a seat, and gazed upon this marvel, Mike.'

Michael X's illiterate fragment was clearly a gift for V.S. Naipaul – and not just for his journalism. 'The Killings in Trinidad' was written in 1973. Naipaul then came home and reworked the whole story, as fiction. In *Guerrillas* (1975), Jimmy Ahmed, the black-power hustler, is writing a novel, or a fantasy; he is the hero, but it is the spellbound white girl, Clarissa, who narrates: 'This man fills my whole mind to the exclusion of all other trivial concerns . . . a woman of my class can see what he really is . . .' In the novel, Naipaul's novel, Jimmy murders his 'Clarissa', just as in Michael's novel Mike would no doubt have been obliged to murder Lena Boyd-Richardson. And in the real world, glimpsed through these phantom projections, Michael X really did murder Gale Benson.

The story is brilliantly told by Naipaul. After his period of celebrity in England, Michael X formed a commune in Trinidad. An ex-pimp and hoodlum, flattered by British journalists, rock-stars and rich kids, Michael X was waiting to lead a revolution that would never come. His head was full of dangerous trash – jargon and self-love. Gale Benson just happened to be in the wrong place at the wrong time. She was a middle-class dropout, a guerrilla groupie, the adoring mistress of one of Michael's lieutenants. The murder was motiveless but not meaningless. Michael's 'novel', with its flopped aspirations, its shamed yearning for inclusion in the white world, tells us all we need to know – certainly far more than Michael X could ever have consciously articulated. The novel is the key to the girl's death, as Naipaul quickly sensed: 'This was a literary murder, if ever there was one.'

Michael X had something like an anti-talent for fiction: coarse, self-serving and, above all, pitiably transparent. 'But when he transferred his fantasy to real life,' as Naipaul says, 'he went to work like the kind of novelist he would have liked to be. Such plotting, such symbolism!' Michael and his men loosened up for the deed by killing a calf and drinking its blood. They spoke of the necessity of spilling the girl's heartblood; Michael 'wanted the heart'. The girl struggled in the ditch as Michael's men clumsily hacked at her; then the death-blow was administered, in the throat, by Steve Yeats, Supreme Captain of the Fruit of Islam, Lieutenant Colonel of Michael X's Black Liberation Army. The girl's body was buried in manure. The men cleansed themselves in the river, lighting a pyre on the bank . . . Within a few weeks, Michael's commune had fallen apart. There was another pointless murder, a drowning, a fire – then Michael cut out for Guyana, on the run. He was hanged at the Royal Jail in Port of Spain, in May 1975.

Trinidad looms over the story of Michael X. It is as if his dissolution is no more than a theatrical reply to the nullity and abandoned squalor in which Naipaul locates him. In the fiction of Shiva Naipaul, Trinidad is reimagined as a Dickensian hinterland of comedy, pathos and ebullient caricature; but Vidya, the elder brother, sees only the pervasive terrors of political breakdown and economic rot. 'Black carrion corbeaux guard the entrance to Port of Spain . . .' In his peripatetic journalism, V.S. Naipaul is turning into the prose-poet of the earth's destitute; he is also becoming world-weary – or Third World-weary, anyway. Perhaps this is the condition of the exile: compelled to travel, condemned to find nothing new.

> It was a good place for getting lost in . . . after years, it defined itself
> into a jumble of clearings separated by stretches of the unknown,
> through which the narrowest of paths had been cut.

Where is this? Trinidad? Uganda? Borneo? No. It is Naipaul's description, written in 1964, of his first visit to London.

'The Return of Eva Peron' – the other major piece in the present book – takes Naipaul to Argentina and Uruguay. His method of assimilating a place is by now familiar. He begins with a passionately tendentious run-through of the country's recent history, in a style that could be regarded as the demonic opposite of a *Look at Life* documentary (in which, for example, a clotted refugee camp might be described as a hardy work-force crying out to be tapped). A century ago the Argentines, marooned Spaniards and Italians, sought out and annihilated the native Indians. They built 'vast *estancias* on the stolen, bloody land'. Within a few pages Naipaul has casually referred to 'the desolate land', 'the alien land', 'the blighted land'. The scene is set, and so is the mood. With Naipaul, they are more or less the same thing.

Naipaul then goes on to produce a gloomy cacophony of local voices: 'the film-maker says', 'the publisher-bookseller says', 'the ambassador's wife says', 'the provincial businessman says'. What they say is always elegiac, paranoid, discordant. Next, Naipaul settles the hash of whatever indigenous culture happens to be on offer. This being Argentina, he has a bigger fish to fry than usual, in the person of Jorge Luis Borges; but he settles down to the task, allotting Borges a chapter of his own, 'Borges and the Bogus Past'. 'For the contemplation of his country's history Borges substitutes ancestor worship', and so on. Naipaul's own fiction has been denounced for its socio-political shortcomings, and it is puzzling to watch him haul Borges through the same old hoops. I have never valued Borges as a pundit on Argentina's problems, nor seen him as much of a contemplator of its history. But of course he does do these things, inevitably, as all artists do. Stories like 'The Lottery in Babylon' and 'The Library of Babel' could be read as intensely vivid reflections of Argentine inertia, sterile frenzy and wasted *espiritismo*. Naipaul's sympathy and responsiveness, however, are held in check, and Borges is duly pressed into his vision of degeneracy and decline. 'And Borges is Argentina's greatest man.' In other words – is that the best they can do?

Finally, and most memorably, Naipaul prowls out to mingle with the people: a peeled sensorium. We see him sighing and suffering in airports, walking among ruins, disaffectedly lending his presence at strained dinner-parties, sparring with bureaucrats, inspecting street scenes, monuments, hotel rooms – always on the lookout for mimicry, falsity, any pretence at civilization. He is isolated, alone with his preoccupations, which tend to be sexual, scatological and demonic. Naipaul mingles with the braying *machos* who parade the streets of Buenos Aires: 'Money makes the macho. Machismo requires, and imposes, a widespread amateur prostitution; it is a society spewing on itself.' In the short piece on Zaire which follows, Naipaul watches two old men in Kinshasa strolling out with their teenage whores: 'Old men: their last chance to feed on such young blood.' By this stage Naipaul is ready to label the country, or the continent, with the kind of sonorous abstraction (preferably alliterative) that his readers have come to expect: 'the Indian emptiness', 'the Argentine sterility and waste', 'the South American nightmare', 'the nihilism of Africa', 'the abjectness of Africa'.

Naipaul's best book about the Third World is *An Area of Darkness*. It is likely to remain his best book about the Third World. Written in the early Sixties, it has a dimension of human richness absent from his later travel writing. That dimension has to do with Naipaul's historical ties with India, naturally, but it is more a question of the untempered traveller confronting his own neuroses. 'I was longing for greater and greater decay, more rags and filth, more bones.' By the time he returned in 1975/6 to write *India: A Wounded Civilisation* his style had hardened, had become public and 'responsible'. Such a narrowing of focus was perhaps a necessary form of self-protection. Naipaul has seen enough bones by now.

The new book ends with a short piece on Conrad – 'Conrad's Darkness', as opposed to Naipaul's. It records a personal journey and a personal debt:

> But in the new world I felt that ground move below me. The new politics, the curious reliance of men on institutions they were yet working to undermine, the simplicity of beliefs and the hideous simplicity of actions, the corruption of causes, half-made societies that seemed doomed to remain half-made: these were the things that began to preoccupy me.

The 'political panic' which possessed the young Naipaul has not gone away. It has been assimilated into a stance, a rhetorical attitude. He writes about peoples as if they were people – patients on the psychiatrist wing, with their 'hysteria', 'frenzy', 'withdrawal symptoms' and 'spiritual distress'. But the stance is punitively moral – and, of course, intensely literary. There is a fashionable temptation to see history as a process of helplessness, of blind movement. Naipaul does not submit to this. He thinks that everyone has choices to make, even if they haven't made them yet, and probably never will.

New Statesman July 1980

Great Books

Broken Lance

The Adventures of Don Quixote de la Mancha by Miguel de
Cervantes. Translated by Tobias Smollett

While clearly an impregnable masterpiece, *Don Quixote* suffers from
one fairly serious flaw – that of outright unreadability. This reviewer
should know, because he has just read it. The book bristles with beauties, charm, sublime comedy; it is also, for long stretches (approaching
about 75 per cent of the whole), inhumanly dull. Looming like one
of the Don's chimerical adversaries, it is a giant 'with legs like lofty
steeples, and arms resembling the masts of vast and warlike ships;
while each eye, as large as a millwheel, beams and burns like a
glass furnace'. But the giant has a giant weight problem, and is
elderly, and soft-brained. Reading *Don Quixote* can be compared
to an indefinite visit from your most impossible senior relative, with
all his pranks, dirty habits, unstoppable reminiscences, and terrible
cronies. When the experience is over, and the old boy checks out
at last (on page 846 – the prose wedged tight, with no breaks
for dialogue), you will shed tears all right: not tears of relf or
regret but tears of pride. You made it, despite all that *Don Quixote*
could do.

Written in the days before novel-reviewing – indeed, in the days
before novels – *Don Quixote* was probably never intended to be read
in the modern manner: that is, straight through. Group or family
recitations of a chapter a night were, in all likelihood, the most that
Cervantes expected anyone to manage. His epic is epic in length
only; it has no pace, no drive. An anthology, an agglomeration, it
simply accrues. The question 'What happens next?' has no meaning,
because there is no next in *Don Quixote*'s world: there is only more.
Through *Don Quixote* we stare into the primal soup of fiction,

steaming, burping, fizzing with potential life, thick with crude and pungent prototypes.

In his introduction Carlos Fuentes (whose surname, by a pleasant coincidence, is glossed in the text: 'Fuentes signifies . . . fountains') salutes *Don Quixote* as the central, all-encompassing supernovel. With its antic bookishness and its rival realities, Quixote plainly sets off deep stirrings in the blood of Fuentes's own work. But his tradition is not our tradition. The Latin-American novel has always been Quixotic – playful, self-conscious, magical-realist. In the fiction of the North Atlantic mainstream, however, realism provides a heavier undertow, modified not by magic but by irony. Furthermore, while we are obliged to adapt to the great strange books of the past, they are obliged to adapt to us, changing through time (in the way that Jane Austen was 'modernized' by Lionel Trilling and others) to greet each rising generation. How does 'the Quixote', in Borges's glamorous phrase, shape up to the twentieth century and its wizened reality? How does it cope?

The following will give some idea of what the book is like to read. Its first twenty chapters are squalid, savage, and attritional – rather well suited, in fact, to modern tastes. In his copious free time, 'which engrossed the greatest part of the year', a humble gentleman called Alonzo Quixano grows addicted to books of chivalry, and, like all addicts, soon pauperizes and deracinates himself in lone gratification. Now the newly styled Don Quixote de la Mancha – 'so long, so lank, so lean', or, as Cervantes later describes him, 'so long, so lank, so lean, so yellow' – sallies forth in quest of adventure on his horse Rosinante, 'so long and raw-boned, so lank and meagre'. With him, after a while, rides Sancho Panza, who with Hispanic panache has 'deserted his wife and children', without a farewell, the better to serve his master. That golden age of chivalry was always a fiction; now, in 1605, it isn't even a memory. But off they go. The knight impelled by madness and high ambition, the squire by stupidity and greed, they burst out into the unchivalrous reality ('this detestable age', 'these iron times', 'these degenerate times') of rural Spain.

Here are their achievements. Unprovoked except by chivalric paranoia, Don Quixote beats up a carrier ('with such good will', 'so effectually mauled') and shatters the skull of his innocent companion. Interfering in a squabble, he then causes a blameless young rustic to be flogged 'so severely, that he had like to have died on the spot'. Next, attempting to beat up a merchant, the Don crashes from his horse and is flogged himself ('so severely'). Now comes the business with the windmills, in which 'knight and steed are whirled aloft ['with so much fury'] and overthrown in very bad plight upon the plain'. During an altercation in which it is Sancho's turn to be beaten 'so unmercifully', Quixote tries to murder a Biscayan traveller, who strikes back 'with such force and fury' that he slices off half the Don's ear.

'Ragged and lousy' from all his encounters with these 'rascally scum', Don Quixote attacks some more carriers (giving one 'such a hearty stroke, as laid open . . . a large portion of his shoulder'), who in return stave him 'with infinite eagerness and dexterity', leaving him senseless at Rosinante's feet. Brawling at an inn, Quixote receives 'such a terrible blow . . . as bathed his whole countenance in blood', and is moreover drenched in boiling oil. The next day, imagining a flock of sheep to be an advancing army, the Don wades in, chopping up 'about seven' little lambs before the shepherds send over a hail of stones ('the least of which was as large as an ordinary fist') that break two of his ribs and smack out half his teeth. As Sancho inspects the damage, his 'stomach turned, and he emptied his bowels upon his master . . . a handsome pickle'. Continuing on his sociopathic way, Quixote assails some defenceless mourners, robs a barber, and pummels an itinerant prison guard ('such wonderful dispatch', 'dangerously wounded'), thus freeing a band of convicts, who then turn on their liberator ('with such force', 'a most furious application'), leaving him robbed, stripped, and soundly trounced.

At this point it dawns on the reader that there are still 700 pages to go. Cervantes, you feel, will have to change tack pretty soon – while his principals remain in one piece. And so it proves. Although my notes continue to be dotted with havoc ('most miserably mauled', 'most handsomely drubbed', 'sufficiently pummeled', 'such a thwack'), and although there is many a clubbing and drubbing and sousing and scalding along the way, Cervantes does begin to diversify. He begins to pad.

And goes on padding. Sancho and the Don are reduced to helpless onlookers as Cervantes just goes on padding, using all the trash, all the hay and straw, of popular contemporary literature. It is a bizarrely shameless spectacle, as if Señor Fuentes, say, had bulked out *The Death of Artemio Cruz* with half a dozen supermarket romances. Here is the goatherd's tale, the muleteer's tale, the captive's tale; here is a thirty-page digression of labyrinthine intrigue (which even the Penguin translator implores you to skip); here are ditties, serenades, the swoonings and weepings of thwarted love; here are gross coincidences, surprise reunions, instant rehabilitations. Piling error upon inconsistency, excrescence upon excrescence, Cervantes maintains the cheerful havoc as Volume I enters its final tailspin and eventually wafts and flutters to a close.

The author took a decade to recover from the first part of *Don Quixote* before completing and publishing the second. The modern reader, of course, enjoys no such holiday, and soon finds himself eyeing the fortress of Volume II. Luckily, and for various conflicting reasons, it is immeasurably more accomplished than its predecessor. It seems that the comedy of humours (where the Hispanic tradition does cross paths with our own) works by a dual process of attrition and sedation: to win your somnolent and exhausted assent, the characters need do no more than what they have always done. And by this stage, also, the intransigent greatness of the book has begun to press in on you. Crossing and uncrossing your legs, and always wondering what else you could be doing, you follow the poor enchanted knight and the swag-bellied lurcher towards their remote epiphany.

Since the technique of *Don Quixote* is that of periphrasis, of lapidary duplication, of saying everything (at least) twice, it is appropriate that the second half should be a mirror image of the first – with one important reversal. Both in the actual world of Cervantes and in the fictional world of the novel, Volume I has been published, to vast international acclaim. Don Quixote has not read *Don Quixote* and awaits news of its reception with suitable diffidence. His 'Adventures', he learns, have been criticized on predictable grounds – the digressions, the 'inadvertencies' (whereby, for instance, Señora Panza is given three different Christian names), the remorselessness of 'those infinite drubbings' – but the Don is now as famous as he could ever have wished, if for all the wrong reasons. Sallying out once again with his squire, he is universally humoured and hoaxed by a colluding reality. His baseless imaginings of Volume I are, through a series of elaborate deceptions (often as cruel and gratuitous as the beatings the Don earlier dispensed), given sham life in the observable world. Don Quixote was driven mad by books; now he enters a reality driven mad by *Don Quixote*.

The subversion or pre-emption of his dream-life is a kind of moral tragedy for Don Quixote. It is a hideously protracted humiliation, as cynical reality steadily usurps and degrades the knight, divesting him of his once rampant creativity. Encountering many a symbolic hell and dungeon, Quixote is jeered and hounded back to his village, savaged by cats, pinched by governesses, teased by maidens, unhorsed by guttersnipes, vanquished in arms, trampled first by bulls, then by swine. We leave him 'pensive, melancholy, mauled, and meagre', crushed by actuality, as the Manchean music fades.

Had he lived, Quixote would have repaired to a pastoral setting, to give 'full scope to his amorous sentiments'. These have been directed throughout the novel at a woman he hardly knows. She is just a country wench, but Quixote has adorned her with the name Dulcinea del Toboso and also with a beauty she has never possessed. 'I am enamoured', he tells Sancho, 'for no other reason but because it is necessary that knights-errant should be in love.' On one level he knows her to be what she is, and yet 'I paint her in my fancy, according to my wish'. All his exploits were committed in her name, though she neither knew nor cared. It is the saddest story. Don Quixote de la Mancha, the great artist *manqué*: he attempted to live what he could not write.

Incarcerated in convention and garrulity, *Don Quixote* remains a beautiful idea. And it should be stressed that when a great book enters a period of dormancy in any particular age, then the age is the loser: the age is judged, as well as the book. Tobias Smollett's neglected translation is astonishingly vigorous, a work of genuine symbiosis, though perhaps erring on the side of Anglo-Saxon joviality. He gives us a Quixote for the eighteenth century; what he cannot do is give us a darker, more Hispanic Quixote for the twentieth. I suggest with respect, and some spite, that Carlos Fuentes or one of his peers should now face such an enterprise. It will require much cutting and mauling and chopping and slicing. It will require infinite drubbings.

Atlantic Monthly March 1986

Force of Love

Pride and Prejudice by Jane Austen

The first challenge you face when writing about *Pride and Prejudice* is to get through your first sentence without saying, 'It is a truth universally acknowledged . . .' With that accomplished (with *that* out of the way), you can move on to more testing questions. For example: why does the reader yearn with such helpless fervour for the marriage of Elizabeth Bennet and Mr Darcy? Why does the reader crow and flinch with almost equal concern over the ups and downs of Jane Bennet and Mr Bingley? Jane and Elizabeth's mother, Mrs Bennet (stupid, prattling, coarse, greedy), is one of the greatest comic nightmares in all literature, yet we are scarcely less restrained than she in our fretful ambition for her daughters. Jane Austen makes Mrs Bennets of us all. How?

And, even more mysteriously, this tizzy of zealous suspense actually survives repeated readings. Finishing the book for perhaps the fifth or sixth time, the present writer felt all the old gratitude and relief: an undiminished catharsis. These days, true, I wouldn't have minded a rather more detailed conclusion – say, a twenty-page sex scene featuring the two principals, with Mr Darcy, furthermore, acquitting himself uncommonly well. (Such a scene would take place, of course, not in a country inn or a louche lodging house in town but amid all the comfort and elegance of Pemberley, with its parklands and its vistas and its ten thousand a year.) Jane Austen, with her divine comedies of love, has always effortlessly renewed herself for each generation of readers (and critics, too: moralists, Marxists, myth-panners, deconstructors – all are kept happy). One may wonder what she has to say to the current crop of twenty-year-olds, for whom 'love' is not quite what it was. Today love faces new struggles:

against literalism, futurelessness, practicality, and nationwide condom campaigns. But maybe the old opposition, of passion and prudence, never really changes; it just sways on its axis.

Let us begin by pinpointing the moment at which love blooms – for Mr Darcy, and for every male reader on earth. It blooms on page 33 of my edition (the *Oxford Illustrated Jane Austen*, 1923). We have had the Meryton assembly, the straitlaced *thé dansant*, at which the local community thrills to the entrance of the eligible gents and their entourage; and we have protectively endured Mr Darcy's audible humiliation of our heroine: 'She is tolerable; but not handsome enough to tempt *me* . . .' Soon afterwards Jane Bennet – meek, sweet, uncomplicated – is invited to dine with the fashionable newcomers. 'Can I have the carriage?' she asks her mother. 'No, my dear, you had better go on horseback, because it seems likely to rain; and then you must stay all night.' Jane rides, it rains, she falls ill – and cannot be moved. Elizabeth's anxiety is one we can easily share: experienced in the ways of nineteenth-century fiction, we know that these frail beauties can fall apart more or less overnight. So, the next morning, impelled by sibling love, Elizabeth strides off through the November mud to Netherfield, that fortress of privilege and disdain. She arrives unannounced, and scandalously unaccompanied, 'with weary ancles, dirty stockings, and a face glowing with the warmth of exercise'. By now the male reader's heart is secure (indeed, he is down on one knee). But Darcy's palpitations are just beginning.

As for female susceptibilities – as for falling in love with *him* – Mr Darcy, I think, ravishes the entire gender on his very first appearance:

Mr Darcy soon drew the attention of the room by his fine, tall person, handsome features, noble mien; and the report which was in general circulation within five minutes after his entrance, of his having ten thousand a year.

That, plus this –

'You have a house in town, I conclude?'
Mr Darcy bowed.

– will about do it. Auden, among many others, was shocked by Jane Austen's celebration of 'the amorous effects of brass': that is, of money, and *old* money, too. Money is a vital substance in her world; the moment you enter it you feel the frank horror of moneylessness, as intense as the tacit horror of spinsterhood. Funnily enough, our hopes for Elizabeth and Darcy are egalitarian, and not avaricious, in tendency. We want love to bring about the redistribution of wealth. To inspire such a man to *disinterested* desire, non-profit-making desire: this is the romantic hinge.

Elizabeth Bennet is Jane Austen with added spirit, with subversive passion, and, above all, with looks. Although writers' lives are no more than optional extras in the consideration of their work, the dull fact of Jane Austen's spinsterhood – her plainness, her childlessness, her virgin death – invests her comedies with disappointment, and with a sense of thwarted homing. It also confirms one's sense of the diminishing physicality of her later heroines: inconspicuous, undetectable Fanny Price; the regal Emma (with her avuncular Mr Knightley); the poignant staidness of Anne Elliot. Incredibly, Jane Austen was about the same age as Elizabeth when she began *Pride and Prejudice* ('I am not one and twenty'), and Elizabeth remains her only convincingly sexual heroine. Even her father, indolent Mr Bennet, is sufficiently aware of her passionate nature to deliver an exceptional warning: 'discredit and misery' would await her, she 'could be neither happy nor respectable', in a loveless marriage. *His* marriage is loveless, and so is everybody else's; and they have all settled for it. But he knows that Elizabeth would never settle for anything less than love.

How do we get a sense of this society, this universe, with its inhibition, its formality, its echelonized emotions? It comes to us most clearly, perhaps, in its language. Mr Darcy's first name is Fitzwilliam, which is a nice name – but Elizabeth will never use it. She will call him 'Mr Darcy' or, occasionally, 'My dear Mr Darcy'. You call your mother 'Madam' and your dad 'Sir'. When the dance floor is 'crouded', young ladies may get a 'headach'. You may 'teaze' a gentleman, should you 'chuse', and should he consent to be 'laught' at. If it be the sixth of October, then 'Michaelmas' will have been celebrated 'yesterday se'nnight.' 'La', what 'extacies' we were in! Everyone is much 'incumbered' by 'secresy' and the need to watch their 'expences'. A rich man must marry a rich girl, to avoid 'degradation' or even 'pollution'. But a poor man must marry a rich girl too, in order to achieve a 'tolerable independence'. So who is to marry all the *poor* girls – the poor girls, how will they find 'an husband'? How will they swerve between passion and prudence, between sensibility and sense, between love and money?

Two extreme cases are explored in *Pride and Prejudice*. Or, rather, they are unexplored, unexamined; they define the limitations of Jane Austen's candour and, perhaps, the limitations of her art. First is the marriage that is all sense, all money (and not very much money either): the marriage of Mr Collins and Charlotte Lucas. Charlotte is Elizabeth's neighbour and her closest friend. Mr Collins is, of course, a world-class grotesque; he has a slimy vigilance that Mr Podsnap might have envied. 'Can he be a sensible man, sir?' Elizabeth asks her father, having acquainted herself with Mr Collins's introductory letter. Mr Bennet responds with typically droll and fateful laxity:

No, my dear: I think not. I have great hopes of finding him quite the reverse. There is a mixture of servility and self-importance in his letter, which promises well. I am impatient to see him.

Mr Collins comes to stay. Because of the famous 'entail' in Mr Bennet's estate, the girls will be bypassed, and cousin Collins is next in line to inherit. He therefore feels obliged to marry one of the many Bennet daughters. His gaze first alights on Jane, then (one day later) on Elizabeth, to whom (eight days later) he unsuccessfully proposes before fixing on Charlotte Lucas (one day later). He proposes to *her* one day later. And she accepts him.

Jane Austen expends little energy on physical description. Her characters are 'handsome' or 'pleasing' or 'not at all handsome'. The feature-by-feature inventory she leaves to the hags and harpies (this is Miss Bingley on Elizabeth: 'Her face is too thin . . . Her nose wants character . . . Her teeth are tolerable, but not out of the common way'). She deals in auras, in presences; her creations fill a certain space with a certain personal style, and they are shaped by their idiolects. Of the Reverend William Collins we are told only this: 'He was a tall, heavy looking young man of five and twenty.' But his immense physical dreariness is none the less fully summoned. (The twenty-page sex scene is in this case not sorely missed. 'I crave your indulgence, my dear Mrs Collins, if, at this early juncture . . .')

Anyway, Charlotte repairs to what Collins calls his humble abode. And that's her life gone. Jane Austen interprets the matter with a kind of worldly savagery: Charlotte accepts Collins 'from the pure and disinterested desire of an establishment'; marriage is 'the only honourable provision' for women so placed, and 'must be their pleasantest preservative from want'. Elizabeth is not so hard-barked about it, but her 'astonishment' at her closest friend's expediency soon modulates into the quiet conviction 'that no real confidence could ever subsist between them again'. And by the time she pays a visit to the newlyweds, she has decided that 'all the comfort of intimacy was over'. Isolation, then, is part of the price Charlotte pays, and expects to pay. Elizabeth feels she can discuss her best friend's situation with Mr Darcy, whom at this stage she thoroughly dislikes ('[Mr Collins's] friends may well rejoice in his having met with one of the very few sensible women who would have accepted him'); but she doesn't feel she can discuss her best friend's situation with her best friend. Why not? Well, people didn't, then. There is no reason why it should occur to Elizabeth to question this miserable silence. But perhaps it ought to have occurred to Jane Austen. Elizabeth is quick to find rueful humour in the business, and Jane Austen is even quicker to find non-rueful humour in it (we hear Charlotte's mother enquiring 'after the welfare and poultry of her eldest daughter'). The marriage is pitiful and creepy; but it is routinely pitiful and creepy. It is everyday.

The other escape from the love–money, passion–prudence axis is the escape undertaken by Elizabeth's youngest sister, Lydia: all love, or at least all passion, or at any rate no prudence (and certainly no money). Little Lydia elopes with the feckless Lieutenant Wickham.

Now, in Jane Austen's universe, elopement is a tractable delin-quency, provided the absconders marry very soon, preferably before nightfall. Should she neglect the wedlock end of it, however, the woman will face an isolation far more thoroughgoing than Charlotte Lucas's: 'irremediable infamy', ostracism, demi-mondainedom. Lydia languishes for two whole weeks with Wickham before the affair is patched and pelfed together (largely by Mr Darcy, it transpires); thus Lydia's virtue is precariously and, as it were, retroactively preserved. Wickham consents to make an honest woman of her, after heavy bribes.

So what are we meant to feel about Lydia? Slimeball Mr Collins writes to Mr Bennet, at an early stage in the scandal, 'The death of your daughter would have been a blessing in comparison of this.' In a later letter, having 'rejoiced' that the 'sad business has been so well hushed up', Collins adds,

> I must not . . . refrain from declaring my amazement, at hearing that you received the young couple into your house as soon as they were married. It was an encouragement of vice . . . You ought certainly to forgive them as a christian, but never to admit them in your sight or allow their names to be mentioned in your hearing.

'*That*', says Mr Bennet, 'is his notion of christian forgiveness!' But what is Jane Austen's notion of it? We may well believe that as a Christian she forgives Lydia. But we will want to know whether as an *artist* she forgives her.

Installed in 'all the comfort and elegance' of Pemberley, Elizabeth sends the Wickhams odd bits of spare cash, and 'occasionally' receives her sister there. Lydia, so to speak, is wheeled off on to a siding, lost to serious consideration, and lost to her sister. And this despite the following mitigations (which gallantry, as well as conscience, obliges one to list): that Lydia's fall was precisely and vividly foretold by Elizabeth; that its likelihood was blamed on parental and familial laxity; that Elizabeth was at one point entirely gulled by Wickham's charms and lies; and that Lydia, during the course of the novel, only just turns sixteen. Calling on her privilege as the local omniscient,

Jane Austen consigns Lydia's marriage to the communal grave ('His affection for her soon sunk into indifference; hers lasted a little longer'), underlining her exclusion from the circumambient happy ending. Lydia, so beautifully evoked (brawny, selfish, clumsy, wholly transparent: after the ball at Netherfield 'even Lydia was too much fatigued to utter more than the occasional exclamation of "Lord, how tired I am!" accompanied by a violent yawn'), is now summarily written out. And here, I think, the reader begins to feel that artists should know better than that; we expect them to know better than that. We expect artists to stand as critics not just of their particular milieu but of their society, and of their age. They shouldn't lose sight of their creations at exactly the same point that 'respectability' – or stock response – loses sight of them.

For all its little smugnesses and blindspots, despite something airless and narrow, *Pride and Prejudice* is Jane Austen's most sociable book – and, strangely, her most socially idealistic. The impulse is in fact strongly present. And because this is a romantic comedy, the impulse expresses itself through the unlikely personage of Fitzwilliam Darcy. Darcy doesn't account for the novel's eternal humour and élan, but he does account for its recurrent and remorseless power to move. Elizabeth's prejudice is easily dealt with: all she needs is the facts before her. Yet the melting of Darcy's pride demands radical change, the difference between his first declaration ('In vain have I struggled') and his second ('You are too generous to trifle with me'). The patching-up of the Lydia business involves Darcy in some expense, but it also forces him to descend into the chaos of unrestrained dreads and desires – an area where Jane Austen fears to linger, even in her imagination. The final paragraph gives us the extraordinary spectacle of Darcy opening his house, and his arms, to Elizabeth's aunt and uncle, who make what money they have through *trade*. Darcy, Jane Austen writes, 'really loved them'. This is the wildest romantic extravagance in the entire corpus: a man like Mr Darcy, chastened, deepened, and finally democratized by the force of love.

Atlantic Monthly February 1990

The War Against Cliché

Ulysses by James Joyce

This year's new edition of *Ulysses* incorporates about 5,000 emendations, most of them 'accidentals': slips and skips, previously unretrieved corrections, errors caused by the incredulity of earlier typesetters or by the author's failing eyesight or faulty memory – gremlins, of one kind or another. True, some corrections are quite substantial: the summoning telegram that Stephen received in Paris, 'Mother dying come home father', now reads 'Nother dying come home father', 'heave under embon *senorita* young eyes Mulvey plump bubs me breadvan Winkle red slippers she rusty sleep wander years of dreams return' is, I suppose, a clear gain on 'heave under embon *senorita* young eyes Mulvey plump years dreams return', and 'Nes. Yo' certainly makes a change from 'Yes. No'. But the new edition will not reverberate far. It will scupper the odd doctorate, embarrass a few commentary footnotes, upend one or two learned articles, and that's about all. If, like me, you have tried *Ulysses* before, and got about halfway through (its common fate with the common reader), then the refurbished text simply provides another excuse to try again. Take my word for it: you won't notice the difference.

What, nowadays, is the constituency of *Ulysses*? Who reads it? Who *curls up* with *Ulysses*? It is thoroughly studied, it is exhaustively unzipped and unseamed, it is much deconstructed. But who reads *Ulysses* for the hell of it? I know a poet who carries *Ulysses* around with him in his satchel. I know a novelist who briefly consults *Ulysses* each night upon retiring. I know an essayist who wittily features *Ulysses* on his toilet bookshelf. They read it – but have they read it, in the readerly fashion, from beginning to end? For the truth is that *Ulysses* is not reader-friendly. Famously James Joyce is a writers' writer. Perhaps one could go further and say that James Joyce is a writer's writer. He is auto-friendly; he is James Joyce-friendly.

He is also a genius. One says this with some confidence: he makes Beckett look pedestrian, Lawrence look laconic, Nabokov look guileless. Throughout the course of his oeuvre one watches Joyce steadily washing his hands of mere talent: the entirely approachable stories of *Dubliners*, the more or less comprehensible *Portrait*, then *Ulysses*, before Joyce girds himself for the ultimately reader-hostile, reader-nuking immolation of *Finnegans Wake*, where every word is a multilingual pun. The exemplary genius, he is also the exemplary Modern, fanatically prolix, innovative and recondite, and free of any obligation to please a reading public (in place of government grants or protective universities, Joyce had patronage). Unreined, unbound, he soared off to fulfil the destiny of his genius; or, if you prefer, he wrote to please himself. All writers do this, or want to do this, or would do this if they dared. Only Joyce did it with such crazed superbity.

It is both comic and appropriate that *Ulysses* started out as a short story, to be added to *Dubliners*. In a way, that is how *Ulysses* ended up: a short story of a third of a million words, a short story into which Joyce put everything he knew. The mad inclusiveness of the novel is offered as an ironic sacrament, a human version of divine knowledge: Joyce really is the Omniscient Narrator. Still, one can imagine how the original tale might have gone, recounted with the decorous obliquity of the early work. Gentle, fortyish Jew strolls the streets of Dublin, tormented by prospective sexual jealousy as his wife prepares for a fresh infidelity; reckless, twentyish Catholic takes a parallel route, tormented by retrospective guilt about his dead mother; they meet; they talk; they part. End of story. In the quietness and austerity of the tale, in its constrictions of time and place, Joyce saw – or willed into being – the frame of epic: degraded epic, modern epic.

There is only one event in *Ulysses*: the meeting between Bloom and Stephen. (It is a hundred-page anticlimax; but then this is an anti-novel.) All the rest is 'Life, life', in Bloom's phrase. 'Every life is many days, day after day,' as Stephen puts it: 'We walk through ourselves, meeting robbers, ghosts, giants, old men, young men, wives, widows, brothers-in-love, but always meeting ourselves.' The presiding life-force of the book is traditionally thought to be Molly – crooning, yearning, bleeding, squirming, two-timing Molly Bloom. Yet the real superanimator is Joyce's prose, this incredible instrument, half wand, half weapon. In fact the prose and the heroine have a good deal in common, equally fickle, headstrong and vain. One moment she is readied for the tryst, primped and prinked, all lilt and tease, bristling with bedroom know-how and can-do; the next she is immersed in a sour and impenetrable sulk. We know only this: she will have her way.

Let us look at this prose and its scales of intensity. First, the yellow pages. The gardener: 'aproned, masked with Matthew Arnold's face, he pushes his mower on the sombre lawn watching narrowly the dancing motes of grasshalms'. The barmaid: 'She set free sudden in rebound her nipped elastic garter smackwarm against her smackable a woman's warmhosed thigh.' The dairywoman: 'Crouching by a patient cow at daybreak in the lush field, a witch on her toadstool, her wrinkled fingers quick at the squirting dugs. They lowed about her whom they knew, dewsilky cattle.'

On into the animal world. A bat: 'Like a little man in a cloak he is with tiny hands. Weeny bones. Almost see them shimmering, kind of a bluey white.' A rat: 'An obese grey rat toddled along the side of the crypt, moving the pebbles. An old stager: greatgrandfather: he knows the ropes. The grey alive crushed itself in under the plinth, wiggled itself in under it.' A cat: '– Mrkrgnao! the cat said loudly. She blinked up out of her avid shameclosing eyes, showing him her milkwhite teeth. He watched the dark eyeslits narrowing with greed till her eyes were green stones.'

Until we reach the inanimate, the lifeless. Smoke: 'Frail from the housetops two plumes of smoke ascended, pluming, and in a flaw of softness softly were blown.' Dust: 'Dust slept on dull coils of bronze and silver, lozenges of cinnabar, on rubies, leprous and winedark stones.' Water: 'White breast of the sea. The twining stresses, two by two. A hand plucking the harpstrings, merging their twining chords.' Space – and the book's most ravishing sentence: 'The heaventree of stars hung with humid nightblue fruit.'

The Joyce corpus maps a journey into language and away from life – life, which never stays put or holds still for quite long enough. *Ulysses* was his consummation of the human world, a loving and languid farewell; no one has written more entrancingly about the rhythms and the furniture of daily life. But Joyce wanted more: he wanted the dream world, the word world of *Finnegans Wake*, his own Book of the Dead. We watch him crystallizing.

Beautiful prose came so naturally to Joyce that he often indulged a perverse attraction to its opposite: to hideous prose, to mirror-cracking, clock-stopping prose. *Ulysses* parodies everything from the *Cursor Mundi* to the tabloid headline. There are jewels: '*All the dollarbills her husband gave her were spent in the stores on wondrous gowns and costliest frillies. For him! For Raoul!*' But most of the parodies feel like a deliberate strain on the reader's patience. What fun – at least in theory – when the exquisite stylist starts sounding like a bailiff or a telephone directory or a drunk or a scripture. The scene in the cabman's shelter is said to be a parody of dud journalism; but it is more like a parody of *writing*, a nightmare of repetitions, tautologies, double negatives, elegant variations, howlers, danglers: 'Mozart's *Twelfth Mass* he simply revelled in, the *Gloria* in that being, to his mind, the acme of first class music as such, literally knocking everything else into a cocked hat.' And so on: the *tour de force* of lugubrious cliché is ten times longer than this review. It is as if Joyce used dead prose and swingeing tedium – epic boredom, biblical boredom – as a counterweight to all that is fresh and vital elsewhere. Structural cliché, structural boredom: Joyce is a stern master.

It occurs to you that *Ulysses* is *about* cliché. It is about inherited, ready-made formulations, fossilized metaphors – most notably those of Irish Catholicism and anti-Semitism. After all, prejudices are clichés: they are secondhand hatreds. How devastatingly Joyce combines his themes when, in the citizen's chapter, the debt-collector staggers out of the bar to the latrine, convinced that Bloom has secretively made a killing on the day's big horse race. It is a mark of Joyce's modernity that he follows his creations not only into the bedroom but into the bathroom:

... gob says I to myself I knew he was uneasy ... in his mind
to get off the mark to (hundred shillings is five quid) and when
they were in the (dark horse) pisser Burke was telling me card
party and letting on the child was sick ... all a plan so he could
vamoose with the pool if he won or (Jesus, full up I was) trading
without a licence (ow!) Ireland my nation says he (hoik! phthook!)
never be up to those bloody (there's the last of it) Jerusalem (ah!)
cuckoos.

'There's a jew for you!' he later reflects. 'All for number one. Cute
as a shithouse rat.' But we have already seen the shithouse rat, hoiking
and phthooking his bitterness and mediocrity into the drowned urinal.
In the next chapter (one of the greatest passages in all literature) we see
the citizen's granddaughter, Gerty MacDowell, disintegrating beneath
her legacy of stock-response: she is herself a beautiful slum of clichés.
Joyce never uses a cliché in innocence. When he says, of a gloomy
building, 'Whole place gone to hell', we remind ourselves that it
once housed a murderer.

Ulysses takes about a week to read, if you do nothing else. There is
much laughter; there is, for many a stretch, the steady smile of envious
admiration; there is the authentic shiver, the sense of pregnant arrest,
at the close. There is also much swearing and shouting and shuddering.
The book has two main presences, Stephen and Bloom. Like his
creator, Stephen is a virtuoso earbender, a coruscating pedant:

It is susceptible of nodes or modes as far apart as hyperphrygian and
mixolydian and of texts so divergent as priests heihooping round
David's that is Circe's or what am I saying Ceres' altar and David's
tip from the stable to his chief bassoonist about the alrightness of
his almightiness.

Enough! Even if he knew when to stop, Stephen would keep going;
Stephen would hang in there. Throughout you long for Bloom, for
the logical and lyrical Joycean music. This writer has the power to
take you anywhere (nothing is beyond him); but he keeps taking you
where you don't want to go.

The scholars have assured us that *Ulysses*, like *Finnegans Wake*, 'works out'. Which is good to know. We like difficult books, said Lionel Trilling, and the remark became one of the slogans of modernism. Yet who are *we*, exactly? Academics and explicators like difficult books, and Joyce helped create the industry they serve; with modern geniuses, you must have the middlemen. The reader, I submit, remains unconsulted on the matter. Tell a dream, lose a reader, said Henry James. Joyce told a dream, *Finnegans Wake*, and he told it in *puns* – cornily but rightly regarded as the lowest form of wit. This showed fantastic courage, and fantastic introversion. The truth is Joyce didn't love the reader, as you need to do. Well, he gave us *Ulysses*, incontestably the central modernist masterpiece; it is impossible to conceive of any future novel that might give the form such a violent evolutionary lurch. You can't help wondering, though. Joyce could have been the most popular boy in the school, the funniest, the cleverest, the kindest. He ended up with a more ambiguous distinction: he became the teacher's pet.

Atlantic Monthly September 1986

The American Eagle

The Adventures of Augie March by Saul Bellow

The Adventures of Augie March is the Great American Novel. Search no further. All the trails went cold forty-two years ago. The quest did what quests very rarely do: it ended.

But what was that quest, anyway – itself so essentially American? No literary masterpiece or federal epic is mentioned in the Constitution, as one of the privileges and treats actually guaranteed to the populace, along with things like liberty and life and the right to bear computerized machine-guns. Still, it is easy enough to imagine how such an aspiration might have developed. As its culture was evolving, and as cultural self-consciousness dawned, America found itself to be a youthful, vast and various land, peopled by non-Americans. So how about this place? Was it a continental holding-camp of Greeks, Jews, Brits, Italians, Scandinavians and Lithuanians, together with the remaining Amerindians from ice-age Mongolia? Or was it a nation, with an identity – with a soul? Who could begin to give the answers? Among such diversity, who could crystallize the American experience?

Like most quests, the quest for the Great American Novel seemed destined to be endless. You won't find that mythical beast, that holy grail, that earthly Eden – though you have to keep looking. As with the pursuit of happiness, the pursuit was the thing; you were never going to catch up. It was very American to *insist* on having a Great American Novel, thus rounding out all the other benefits Americans enjoy. Nobody has ever worried about the Great French Novel or the Great Russian Novel (though it is entirely intelligible that there should be some cautious talk about the Great Australian Novel). Trying to find the Great American Novel, rolling up your sleeves

447

and trying to *write* it: this was *American*. And so it would go on, for ever, just as literature never progresses or improves but simply evolves and provides the model. The Great American Novel was a chimera; this mythical beast was a pig with wings. Miraculously, however, and uncovenantedly, Saul Bellow brought the animal home. He dedicated the book to his father and published it in 1953 and then settled down to write *Seize the Day*.

Literary criticism, as normally practised, will tend to get in the way of a novel like *Augie March*. Shaped (loosely) as an odyssey, and well stocked with (unsystematic) erudition – with invocations and incantations – the book is very vulnerable to the kind of glossarial jigsaw-solver who must find *form*: pattern, decor, lamination, colour-scheme. But that isn't how the novel works on you. Books are partly about life, and partly about other books. Some books are largely about other books, and spawn yet other books. *Augie March* is all about life: it brings you up against the dead-end of life. Bellow's third novel, following the somewhat straitened performances of *Dangling Man* and *The Victim*, is above all *free* – without inhibition. An epic about the so-called ordinary, it is a marvel of remorseless spontaneity. As a critic, therefore, you feel no urge to interpose yourself. Your job is to work your way round to the bits you want to quote. You are a guide in a gallery where the signs say Silence Please; you are shepherding your group from spectacle to spectacle – awed, humbled, and trying, so far as possible, to keep your mouth shut.

A brief outline. *The Adventures of Augie March* is about the formation of an identity, of a soul – that of a parentless and penniless boy growing up in pre- and post-Depression Chicago. Augie's mother is 'simple-minded' and so is his younger brother Georgie, who 'was born an idiot'. Simon, his older brother, is hard-headed; and Simon is all he's got. The domestic configuration is established early on, with typical pathos and truthfulness:

Never but at such times, by necessity, was my father mentioned.

I claimed to remember him; Simon denied that I did, and Simon was right. I liked to imagine it.

'He wore a uniform,' I said. 'Sure I remember. He was a soldier.'

'Like hell he was. You don't know anything about it.'

'Maybe a sailor.'

'Like hell. He drove a truck for Hall Brothers laundry on Marshfield, that's what he did. *I* said he used to wear a uniform. Monkey sees, monkey does; monkey hears, monkey says.'

His mother sewed buttonholes at a coat factory in a Wells Street loft and his father was a laundry driver; and Augie is simply 'the byblow of a travelling man'.

What comes across in these early pages – the novel's first act – is the depth of the human divide between the hard and the soft. The home, with its closed circle, tries to be soft. The outside world is all hard – isn't it? (It certainly *looks* hard.) Georgie is soft. He puts 'his underlip forward' in search of a kiss, 'chaste, lummoxy, caressing, gentle and diligent'. Given his chicken gizzard at noon, he 'blew at the ridgy thing more to cherish than to cool it'. Later, Georgie sits at the kitchen table 'with one foot stepping on the other' while his grim future is grimly discussed. This leads to the famously unbearable scene where Augie accompanies his brother to the institution:

We were about an hour getting to the Home – wired windows, dog-proof cyclone fence, asphalt yard, great gloom . . . We were allowed to go up to the dormitory with him, where other kids stood around under the radiator high on the wall and watched us. Mama took off Georgie's coat and the manly hat, and in his shirt of large buttons, with whitish head and big white, chill fingers – it was troubling they were so man-sized – he kept by me beside the bed while I again showed him the simple little stunt of the satchel lock. But I failed to distract him from the terror of the place and of boys like himself around – he had never met such before. And now he realized that we would leave him and he began to do with his soul, that is, to let out his moan, worse for us than tears, though many grades below the pitch of weeping. Then Mama slumped down and gave in utterly. It was when she had the bristles of his special head between her hands and was kissing him that she began to cry. When I started after a while to draw her away he tried to follow. I cried also. I took him back to the bed and said, 'Sit here.' So he sat and moaned. We went down to the car stop and stood waiting by the black, humming pole for the trolley to come back from city limits.

Mama, too, simple, abandoned, a fool for love, is soft. As with Georgie, when Augie evokes his mother he accords her the beauty and mystery of a child. Family disruptions (of which there are many) frighten her: 'she was upright in her posture and like waiting for the grief to come to a stop; as if this stop would be called by a conductor'. But her distress is also adult, intimidating, unreachable. After the decision is made to commit Georgie, Mama

made no fuss or noise nor was seen weeping, but in an extreme and terrible way seemed to be watching out the kitchen window, until you came close and saw the tear-strengthened color of her green eyes and of her pink face, her gap-toothed mouth . . . she lay herself dumbly on the outcome of forces, without any work of mind . . .

In Augie's childhood world, with its hesitancy and its raw senses, it is as if everybody is too delicate to be touched. Too soft, or too hard – like Simon. Simon is Augie's parallel self: the road not travelled. All Simon ever does is set himself the task of becoming a high-grade American barbarian; but on the page he becomes a figure of Shakespearean solidity, rendered with Dickensian force. And there is a kind of super-charged logic here. To the younger brother, the older brother fills the sky, and will assume these unholy dimensions. Simon sweats and fumes over the novel. Even when he is absent he is always there.

Parentless and penniless: the basic human material. Penniless, Augie needs employment. If the novels of another great Chicagoan,

Theodore Dreiser, sometimes feel like a long succession of job interviews, then *Augie March* often resembles a surrealist catalogue of apprenticeships. During the course of the novel Augie becomes (in order) a handbill-distributor, a paperboy, a dimestore packer, a news-vendor, a Christmas extra in a toy department, a flower-deliverer, a butler, a shoe-salesman, a saddle-shop floorwalker, a hawker of rubberized paint, a dog-washer, a book-swiper, a coal-yard helper, a housing surveyor, a union organizer, an animal-trainer, a gambler, a literary researcher, a salesman of business machines, a sailor, and a middleman of a war profiteer. As late as page 218 Augie is still poring over magazines in search of 'vocational hints'.

'All the influences were waiting for me. I was born, and there they were to form me . . .' Malleable and protean, 'easily appealed to', busy 'trying things on', Augie is a natural protégé, willing prey for the nearest 'reality instructor': would-be 'big personalities, destiny molders, and heavy-water brains, Machiavellis and wizard evildoers, big-wheels and imposers-upon, absolutists'. First there is Grandma Lausch (no relation), the old widow who directs and manipulates the March family with the power-crazed detachment of a eugenicist. 'Her eyes whitely contemptuous, with a terrible little naked yawn of her gums, suck-cheeked with unspoken comment', Grandma Lausch is definitely of the *hardness* party. But she is old-world, Odessan, '*Eastern*'; and Augie's subsequent mentors are embodiments of spe-cifically American strategies and visions, as their names suggest: Mr Einhorn, Dingbat, Mrs Renling, Joe Gorman, Manny Padilla, Clem Tambow, Kayo Obermark, Robey, Mintouchian, Basteshaw (and Simon. Always Simon). With each of these small-cap 'universalists' – who believe that wherever they happen to be standing 'the principal laws [are] underfoot' – Augie goes a certain distance until he finds himself 'in the end zone' of his adaptability. Then he breaks free.

So what are all these roles and models, these outfits and uni-forms, these performances? Augie is on a journey but he isn't going anywhere. If he has a destination, it is simply a stop called Full Consciousness. In a sense, Augie is heading to the point where he will become the author of his own story. He will not necessarily be capable of writing it. He will be capable of thinking it. This is what the convention of the first person amounts to. The narrator expresses his thoughts, and the novelist gives them written shape. Like all narrators, Augie is a performing artist (as a young man). And it is Bellow who provides his Portrait.

The artist, perhaps uniquely and definingly, gets through life without belonging to anything: no organization, no human conglomerate. Everybody in Augie's familial orbit is eventually confined to an institution – even Simon, who commits himself to the association of American money. A leaf in the wind of random influences, Augie wafts through various establishments and big concerns, leagues, cliques and syndicates. As he does so it becomes increasingly clear that whatever identity is, whatever the soul is, the institution is its opposite and its enemy. This commonplace does not remain a commonplace, under Augie's gaze. Human amalgamation attacks his very sensorium, inspiring animal bafflement, and visionary rage. Dickens's institutions are eccentric; Bellow's are psychopathic. Small isn't always beautiful, but big vibrates with *meshuggah* power.

This is the dispensary:

> like the dream of a multitude of dentists' chairs, hundreds of them in a space as enormous as an armory, and green bowls with designs of glass grapes, drills lifted zigzag as insects' legs, and gas flames on the porcelain swivel trays – a thundery gloom in Harrison Street of limestone county buildings and cumbersome red streetcars with metal grillwork on their windows and monarchical iron whiskers of cowcatchers front and rear. They lumbered and clanged, and their brake tanks panted in the slushy brown of a winter afternoon or the bare stone brown of a summer's, salted with ash, smoke, and prairie dust, with long stops at the clinics to let off clumpers, cripples, hunchbacks, brace-legs, crutch-wielders, tooth and eye sufferers, and all the rest.

This is the dimestore:

that tin-tough, creaking, jazzy bazaar of hardware, glassware, chocolate, chickenfeed, jewelry, drygoods, oilcloth . . . and even being the Atlases of it, under the floor, hearing how the floor bore up under the ambling weight of hundreds, with the fanning, breathing movie organ next door and the rumble descending from the trolleys on Chicago Avenue — the bloody-rinded Saturday gloom of wind-borne ash, and blackened forms of five-story buildings rising up to a blind Northern dimness from the Christmas blaze of shops.

And this is the old folks' home, where Grandma goes:

We came up the walk, between the slow, thought-brewing, beat-up old heads, liver-spotted, of choked old blood salts and wastes, hard and bone-bare domes, or swollen, the elevens of sinews up on collarless necks crazy with the assaults of Kansas heats and Wyoming freezes . . . white hair and rashy, vessel-busted hands holding canes, fans, newspapers in all languages and alphabets, faces gone in the under-surface flues and in the eyes, of these people sitting in the sunshine and leaf-burning outside or in the mealy moldiness and gravy acids of the house.

Such writing is of course animated by love as well as pity and protest. And there are certain institutions and establishments to which Augie is insidiously drawn. The poolhall, for instance, and the anti-institution of crime. Here is Augie, in a new kind of uniform:

Grandma Lausch would have thought that the very worst she had ever said about me let me off too light, seeing me in the shoeshine seat above the green tables, in a hat with diamond airholes cut in it and decorated with brass kiss-me pins and Al Smith buttons, in sneakers and Mohawk sweatshirt, there in the frying jazz and the buzz of baseball broadcasts, the click of markers, butt-thumping of cues, spat-out pollyseed shells and blue chalk crushed underfoot and dust of hand-slickening talcum hanging in the air. Along with the blood-smelling swaggeroos, recruits for mobs, automobile thieves,

stick-up men, sluggers and bouncers . . . neighborhood cowboys
with Jack Holt sideburns down to the jawbone, collegiates, tinhorns
and small-time racketeers and pugs . . .

That *frying* jazz! Criminals are attractive because their sharply indi-
vidualized energies seem to operate outside the established social
arrangement. Augie is deeply candid, but he is not especially *honest*.
Invited along on a housebreaking job, Augie doesn't give any reason
for saying yes; he simply announces that he didn't say no.

'Are you a real crook?' asks Mr Einhorn. 'Have you got the
calling?' At this point Mr Einhorn, the crippled property-broker
('he had a brain and many enterprises, real directing power'), is still
Augie's primary mentor. Mr Einhorn knows how the world works; he
knows about criminals and institutions. And here, in one of the book's
most memorable speeches, he lets Augie have it. One hardly needs
to say that Bellow has an exquisite ear, precise and delighted in its
registers: Guillaume, for example, the dog-handler who has become
over-reliant on his hypodermic ('Thees jag-off is going to get it!'); or
Happy Kellerman, Simon's much-abused coalyard manager ('I never
took no shit in bigger concerns'); or Anna Coblin, Mama's cousin
('Owgie, the telephone ringt. Hear!'). Naturally, Bellow can do all
this. But from time to time he will also commandeer a character's
speech for his own ends, keeping to the broad modulation of the
voice while giving them a shove upwards, hierarchically, towards the
grand style. Seasoned Bellovians have learnt to accept this as a matter
of convention. We still hear Einhorn, but it is an Einhorn pervaded
by his creator:

'Don't be a sap, Augie, and fall into the first trap life digs for you.
Young fellows brought up in bad luck, like you, are naturals to
keep the jails filled – the reformatories, all the institutions. What
the state orders bread and beans long in advance for. It knows
there's an element that can be depended on to come behind bars
to eat it. Or it knows how much broken rock for macadam it can
expect, and whom it can count on to break it . . . It's practically
determined. And if you're going to let it be determined for you

too, you're a sucker. Just what's predicted. Those sad and tragic things are waiting to take you in – the clinks and clinics and soup lines know who's the natural to be beat up and squashed, made old, pooped, farted away, no-purposed away. If it should happen to you, who'd be surprised? You're a setup for it.'

Nevertheless, as the novel nears the end of its second act, Augie continues to feel the urge to bottom out. At least the bottom is solid, when there's no further to fall – and nothing else in his life seems solid. Soon after Einhorn's speech Augie goes on another incautious jaunt (in a hot car) with the *same* hustler (Joe Gorman, the housebreaker), up north, Toledo way. Augie escapes the state troopers but gets incarcerated on another charge, in Detroit:

> 'Lock 'em all up.'
>
> We had to empty our pockets; they were after knives and matches and such objects of harm. But for me that wasn't what it was for, but to have the bigger existence taking charge of your small things, and making you learn forfeits as a sign that you aren't any more your own man, in the street, with the contents of your pockets your own business: *that* was the purpose of it. So we gave over our stuff and were taken down, past cells and zoo-rustling straw . . . An enormous light was on at all hours. There was some-thing heavy about it, like the stone rolled in front of the tomb.

Augie's durance, though, on his detour in the Midwest, unmoored from Chicago, is internal and spiritual. Here for the first time he sees human misery stretched across a natural landscape: war veterans, the unemployed, 'factor-shoved' bums, haunting the railtracks (they 'made a ragged line, like a section gang that draws aside at night back of the flares as a train comes through, only much more numerous') and sleeping in heaps on the floors of disused boxcars:

> It was no time to be awake, or half awake, with the groaning and sick coughing, the grumbles and gases of bad food, the rustling in paper and straw like sighs or the breath of dissatisfaction . . . A

bad night – the rain rattling hard first on one side and then on the other like someone nailing down a case, or a coop of birds, and my feelings were big, sad, comfortless, of a thinking animal, my heart acting like an orb filled too big for my chest

– 'not from revulsion,' Augie adds, 'which I have to say I didn't feel.' And we believe him. Passively, directionlessly, Augie is visiting the dark and bestial regions occupied by his mother and younger brother – alike incapable of 'work of mind'. Some pages earlier, after an extreme humiliation, Augie has said,

I felt I had got trampled all over my body by a thing some way connected by weight with my mother and my brother George, who perhaps this very minute was working on a broom, or putting it down to shamble in to supper; or with Grandma Lausch in the Nelson Home – somehow as though run over by the beast that kept them steady company and that I thought I was safely away from.

And by the time Augie limps back to Chicago his family is gone. Simon has taken off, in obscure disgrace; Mama has been farmed out; and Grandma Lausch ('My grates couldn't hold it. I shed tears with my sleeve over my eyes') is dead. Childhood – act one – ended with the house getting 'darker, smaller; once shiny and venerated things losing their attraction and richness and importance. Tin showed, cracks, black spots where enamel was hit off, threadbarer, design scuffed out of the center of the rug, all the glamor, lacquer, massiveness, florescence, wiped out'. The second act – youth – ends when there is nothing to go back to, because the home is no longer a place.

Georgie Mahchy, Augie, Simey
Winnie Mahchy, evwy, evwy love Mama.

So Georgie used to sing, on the novel's opening page. And it wasn't quite true. Winnie, Grandma Lausch's poodle ('a pursy old overfed dog', 'a dozy, long-sighing crank'), didn't love Mama; and it remains painfully questionable whether Simon ever loved anybody. Georgie might have amended his song, so that it concluded: evwy evwy Augie love. Simon tells Augie, with full Chicagoan contempt, 'You can't hold your load of love, can you?' And it's true. Tallish, dark, flushed, 'rosy', with 'high hair', always 'vague' but always 'stubborn', Augie is unembarrassably amorous. When it comes to love, Augie just refuses to get real.

This marks him out, locally, as an effeminate anachronism – as does his goodness. 'You don't keep up with the times. You're going against history,' says Manny Padilla. 'The big investigation today is into how *bad* a guy can be, not how good he can be.' Generally, in literature, goodness has always been bad news. As Montherlant said, happiness – the positive value – 'writes white'. Only Tolstoy, perhaps, has made happiness swing on the page. And goodness writes purple. We'll never know how Russian novelists would have done modern goodness. In his Russian novels, as opposed to his American novels, Nabokov's goodies exude an aristocratic triumphalism (it's his one dud note), striding, blaring, munching, guffawing. But Bellow is a Russian, too, as well as an American; and he makes goodness swing. Of course, Augie *is* an anachronism. Empathetic on a broad scale, he remains unalienated. His sufferings are reactive rather than existential. He is not a discontent: civilization, if he could get any, would suit him fine. He believes in the soul, and in human perfectibility. For the hero of a mid-twentieth-century novel, Augie is anomalously allegro; he is daringly, scandalously spry.

With women, Augie displays an almost satirical susceptibility. First love, or first yearning, smites him as a high-school sophomore:

I took sick with love, with classic symptoms of choked appetite and utter absorption, hankering, great refinements of respect in looks . . . with a miserable counterfeit of merely passing, secretly pumped with raptures and streaming painfully, I clumped by . . . I didn't stop this sadhearted, worshipful blundering around or standing like painted wood across the street from the tailor shop in the bluey afternoon. Her scraggy father labored with his needle, bent over, and presumably thinking nothing of his appearance to the street in the lighted glass; her chicken-thin little sister in black gym bloomers cut paper with the big shears.

Augie never addresses a word to Hilda Novinson, the tailor's daughter. But he gets a little bit further with his next love-object, Esther Fenchel. At this point Augie is under the tutelage of wealthy Mrs Renling, togged up in 'dude-ranch' style and holidaying in a fancy hotel on Lake Michigan. In the meantime he has become acquainted with 'the sexual sting' (and will soon be noticing, for instance, that Guillaume's girlfriend is 'a great work of ripple-assed luxury with an immense mozzarella bust'). Nevertheless, Augie continues to love Esther from afar, and in the high style: 'the world had never had better color, to say it exactly as it strikes me, or finer and more reasonable articulation. Nor ever gave me better trouble. I felt I was in the real and the true . . .' One night Augie glimpses Esther alone in the music room; 'troubled and rocky', he approaches her, saying,

> 'Miss Fenchel, I wonder if you would like to go with me some evening to the House of David.' Astonished, she looked up from the music. 'They have dancing every night.'
>
> I saw nothing but failure, from the first word out, and felt smitten, pounded from all sides.
>
> 'With you? I should say not. I certainly won't.'
>
> The blood came down out of my head, neck, shoulders, and I fainted dead away.

As always, Augie is surrounded by exemplars and counter-exemplars, showing him what to do about love and what not to do about it, in pre-war Chicago. First there is the conventional road, brutally described by Mrs Renling and duly followed by Augie's old friend Jimmy Klein – and by tens of millions of others. This is the arrangement where loss of virginity coincides with unwanted pregnancy and unwanted marriage: marriage as an institution, and nothing more. Alternatively there is the bohemian path (in outline: illegal abortion, puerperal fever, septicaemia) followed by Augie's fellow boarder, Mimi Villars. 'Women are no good, Augie,' she warns him. 'They're no f—— good.' (These Bowdler dashes date the book far more noticeably than, say, the references to Sandino's activities in Nicaragua or the unpadded picador horses in the Spanish bullring. *Augie March* is not otherwise dated, incidentally, and feels as immediate as the end of the millennium.) 'They want a man in the house,' says Mimi. 'Just there, in the house. Sitting in his chair.' Augie demurs, and then beautifully reflects:

> I wasn't enough of an enemy of such things but smiled at such ruining wives too for their female softnesses. I was too indulgent about them, about the beds that would be first stale and then poisonous because their manageresses' thoughts were on the conquering power of chenille and dimity and the suffocation of light by curtains, and the bourgeois ambering of adventuring man in parlor upholstery. These things not appearing so threatening to me as they ought to appear, I was . . . a fool to [Mimi], one who also could be stuck, leg-bent, in that white spiders' secretion and paralyzed inside women's edifices of safety.

There is another way: Simon's way. 'I am an American,' says Augie, at the very outset. But he is not as American as Simon: 'I want money, and I mean *want*; and I can handle it. Those are my assets.' Later, when Mr Einhorn is giving Augie the lowdown on labour unions, he pronounces, with superb cynicism, 'One more big organization. A big organization makes dough or it doesn't last. If it makes dough it's *for* dough.' Meaning on dough's side: pro-dough. Simon, quintessentially, is pro-dough. And this enables him to free his head of all distractions.

He enters an arranged marriage with a girl he has never seen, Charlotte Magnus, the scion of a big-boned kindred of Chicago merchants and burghers, themselves an institution, close-knit Netherlandish folk – Simon's patrons or backers. Their world is summoned in terms of furniture and textures, the 'carpeted peace and gravy velour' of the vast apartments, the 'mobile heraldry' of their cars rushing on soft tyres 'toward the floating balls and moons' of the great hotels and their

'Jupiter's heaviness and restless marble detail, seeking to be more and more, introducing another pot too huge for flowers, another carved figure, another white work of iron'. At the Magnuses', at night, the 'riches-cluttered hall' is 'partly inventoried' by the moonlight. Watching Charlotte preparing for her nuptials, Augie observes:

> Neither her ladies' trimming and gewgawing, the detail of her tailored person, nor the decorating of the flat when they furnished one . . . was of real consequence. But in what related to the bank, the stock, the taxes, head approached to head discussing these, the great clear and critical calculations and confidences made in the key to which real dominion was set, that was what wedlock really rested on.

The deal here – and it *is* a deal – turns out to be unambiguously Faustian. Although the Magnuses are prepared to stake him, Simon has to deliver on his promised ability to make a rich man of himself, worthy to join the community of American money.

> In spring he leased a yard, at the end of the coal season. It had no overhead track, only a long spur of siding, and the first rains made a marsh of the whole place . . . I was spending a good amount of time at the office; for when [Simon] grabbed my wrist and told me, almost drunkenly, with the grime and chapping of the mouth that comes of long nervous talking, saying low, huskily, viciously, 'There's got to be somebody here I can trust. *Got* to be!' I couldn't refuse.

In the brilliant – and crucial – pages that follow, the coalyard becomes a figure for Simon's marriage and Simon's life:

> Over the way was a stockyards siding, dusty animals bawling in the waiting cars, putting red muzzles to the slats; truck wheels sucked through the melting tar, the coal split and tarnished on the piles, the burdocks died on the stalk. There were rats in a corner of the yard who did not stir or go away for anyone, whole families, nursing, creeping, feeding there.

a lushed-up dealer called Guzynski tore onto the scale out of the slushy yard with white steam gushing from his busted radiator . . . I told a hiker to clear the scale, but Guzynski was standing over his coal with a shovel and swung on him when he came near. Happy Kellerman was phoning for a squad car when Simon arrived . . . in the narrow space between the truck and the office wall, Simon caught him, had him by the throat, and hit him in the face with the side of the gun. This happened right below Happy and me; we were standing at the scale window, and we saw Guzynski, trapped, square teeth and hideous eyes, foul blue, and his hands hooked, not daring to snatch the gun with which Simon hit him again. He laid open Guzynski's cheek. My heart went back on me when the cuts were torn, and I thought, Does it make him think he knows what he's doing if the guy bleeds?

The misery of his look at this black Sargasso of a yard in its summer stagnation and stifling would sometimes make my blood crawl in me with horror . . . Simon's patience and swallowing were worse to me than his wrath or flamboyance – that shabby compulsory physical patience. Another such hard thing was his speaking low and with an air of difficult endurance to Charlotte on the telephone and answering her questions with subdued repetitiousness, near the surrender point.

It is as if all the institutional weights and fetters, the gravity of the large agencies and big concerns, are pressing in on Simon; and Augie, who has swung his life on to his brother's parallel track (he even has a stern Magnus daughter to court), must suffer this pressure vicariously, fraternally, but with utterly unwelcome clarity. The novel's opening page bears a famous line about suppression: 'Everybody knows there is no fineness or accuracy of suppression, if you hold down one thing you hold down the adjoining.' And we have now reached the place where that sentence was pointing. Much later, after Augie has broken clear from Chicago, he returns to the city with a disinfected eye, and he can see this suppression daubed all over the landscape like paint:

461

Well, here it was again, westward from this window, the gray snarled city with the hard black straps of rails, enormous industry cooking and its vapor shuddering to the air, the climb and fall of its stages in construction or demolition like mesas, and on these the different powers and sub-powers crouched and watched like sphinxes. Terrible dumbness covered it, like a judgment that would never find its word.

But now the third-act climax is approaching. From this deep entanglement, from this junction of bad roads (Simon; engagement to the Magnus girl and the Magnus money; love and what to do about it), Augie must absent himself. And he escapes the only way he ever escapes anything: through inadvertency. New Year's Eve is approaching. Neglecting his festive duties as a squire to the Magnuses, Augie accompanies Mimi Villars to a backstreet abortionist. This loyal and innocent deed is discovered and misinterpreted, spelling the end of his apprenticeship at the feet of American money. The moment is signalled by another prose epiphany, in a hospital (the penultimate institution), where Augie has taken the ailing Mimi. Here we come to understand all that Augie is not ready for:

I passed through to another division where the labor rooms were, separate cubicles, and in them saw women struggling, outlandish pain and huge-bellied distortion, one powerful face that bore down into its creases and issued a voice great and songlike in which she cursed her husband obscenely . . . And just then, in the elevator shaft nearby, there were screams. I stopped and waited for the rising light I saw coming steadily through the glass panels. The door opened; a woman sat before me in a wheel chair, and in her lap, just born in a cab or paddy wagon or in the lobby of the hospital, covered with blood and screaming so you could see sinews, square of chest and shoulders from the strain, this bald kid, red and covering her with the red. She too, with lost nerve, was sobbing, each hand squeezing up on itself, eyes wildly frightened; and she and the baby appeared like enemies forced to have each other . . .

'What are you doing here?' said the nurse with angry looks. I
had no right to be there.

A sonnet can be perfect, a short story pretty well unimprovable,
a novella near-flawless, a novel just a few blemishes away from its
platonic ideal. But the art of the long novel is an inexact art. A long
novel, at its conception, bids farewell to exactitude, and to other
constraints. Now, something strange, something passing strange,
happens to *The Adventures of Augie March* as it enters its fourth act.
On page 358, Augie is very much where we expect him to be: hiding
out in a cinema on Madison Street, Chicago, after a union bust-up in
the linen room of the Northumberland Hotel. On page 388 he is in
another cinema, in Nuevo Laredo, Mexico, with a fully-grown *eagle*
on his arm. What has happened in the interim? The answer is Thea
Fenchel (the older sister of Esther, back at the Lake Michigan resort).
Augie March, and *Augie March*, have been swept off their feet.

Thea is both lover and mentor, perhaps an untenable combination. Augie has grown used to eccentrics by now, as has the reader;
but Thea, a wealthy and resolute young woman, is eccentric simply
because she *wants* to be – not forced into a weird shape by heredity
or personal history or blind circumstance. In any event, tricked out
in a new uniform, Augie escorts Thea south. Their plan is to buy an
eagle which they will then train to hunt giant iguanas, 'these huge
furious lizards, mesozoic holdouts in the mountains south of Mexico
City'. And we follow them, eagerly but dazedly, over the Rio Grande,
through the smells and shapes and the aromatic heat, and through the
fluctuations of their anxious, lopsided, intensely realized passion. And
the eagle?

Before setting out from Chicago, Augie pays a visit to the zoo –
to get the general idea:

[The eagle] perched on a trunk inside a cage forty feet high and
conical like the cage of a parlor parrot, in its smoke and sun colors
dipped somewhat with green, and its biped stance and Turkish or

Janissary pants of feathers – the pressed-down head, the killing eye, the deep life of its feathers. *Oy!*

Up close, with their own eagle ('Caligula'), Augie finds that 'this open shadow would shut out your heart with its smell and power – the Etna feathers and clasped beak opening', the 'almost inaudible whiff of his spread wings' and 'the fan of the pinions with hidden rust and angel-of-death armpit':

> He was, however, powerfully handsome, with his onward-turned head and buff and white feathers among the darker, his eyes that were gruesome jewels and meant nothing in their little lines but cruelty, and that he was here for his own need; he was entirely a manifesto of that . . . trees, bushes, stones, as explicit as glare and the spice of that heat could make them. The giant bird, when Thea brought him out, seemed to shoulder it with a kind of rise of sensuality. I felt dizzy from long sleep and the wires of radiant heat curling up from road to rock.

Caligula is one of the most lavishly vivid animals in all literature (more lavish, even, than the lion in *Henderson the Rain King*). But for all this you have to share Augie's bafflement, and feel partly second-guessed, when he asks himself: 'what did there have to be an eagle for?' You know the novel is in trouble here because you keep seeking refuge in – of all things – literary criticism. Is the eagle (*aguila*) Augie, or what remains of his beast nature? Is the eagle *money*, as the twenty-five-cent coin still declares it is? Is the (American) eagle simply America? But *Augie March* isn't a *meaning* novel: it is a *gut* novel. It depends not on equivalences but on the free flow of voice and feeling.

Caligula carries you, magically; it is only when he is gone (and Thea is gone, and love has failed) that you see the violence he has done to the novel's unities. After all, it wouldn't be right if the Great American Novel didn't have something wrong with it. 'You're not special,' Thea tells Augie, in parting. 'You're like everybody else.' And what the novel now charts is Augie's drift into the ordinary. After the fever and voodoo of Mexico, he is re-embraced by sombre

Chicago, failed in love, his youth evaporating, his youthful illusions absenting themselves from his thoughts. Poor Augie babbles about his dreams (sad dreams, of disappointment and deformity), and nurses hopeless visions of reunion with idiot Georgie and blind Mama, in a little house in the country, with children and animals all around. These ordinary sadnesses are perhaps his birthright and inheritance. It may be that Augie was on to something inescapable, when he stared at the sky on his way south to Mexico:

> For should I look into any air, I could recall the bees and gnats of dust in the heavily divided heat of a street of El pillars – such as Lake Street, where the junk and old bottleyards are – like a terribly conceived church of madmen, and its stations, endless, where worshipers crawl their carts of rags and bones. And sometimes misery came over me to feel that I myself was the creation of such places. How is it that human beings will submit to the gyps of previous history while mere creatures look with their original eyes?

The novel regathers itself very powerfully towards its close. When we last see him, Augie is established in the exhausted, yawning, pinch-yourself unreality of post-war Europe. He is an illicit trader ('there was this Florentine uncle of a Rome bigshot I had to pay off, and he was one of those civilized personalities with about five motives to my one'), and he has an unreliable wife, Stella (perhaps 'a Cressida type', 'a double lifer'). He can declare himself free of all influences, all Machiavellis ('I took an oath of unsusceptibility'), before adding, with comic prescience, 'Brother! You never are through, you just think you are!' Sure enough, Simon – tormentor, anti-mentor, hugely loved, hugely pitied – lends his shattered presence to the gradual and reluctant conclusion. We are left, finally, with images of toil and isolation. But creative labour, and creative loneliness. Augie has fallen into the habit of going to a café every afternoon, 'where I sat at a table and declared that I was an American, Chicago born, and all these other events and notions'. So he is preparing himself to write – or just to imagine – his story:

all the time you thought you were going around idle terribly hard work was taking place. Hard, hard work, excavation and digging, mining, moling through tunnels, heaving, pushing, moving rock, working, working, working, working, working, panting, hauling, hoisting. And none of this work is seen from the outside. It's internally done. It happens because you are powerless and unable to get anywhere, to obtain justice or have requital, and therefore in yourself you labor, you wage and combat, settle scores, remember insults, fight, reply, deny, blab, denounce, triumph, outwit, overcome, vindicate, cry, persist, absolve, die and rise again. All by yourself! Where is everybody? Inside your breast and skin, the entire cast.

Attentive readers will, I hope, have noticed that this is an extraordinarily *written* novel. There are mannerisms or tics in the way the words squirm up against each other. The compounds – 'worry-wounded', 'lair-hidden', 'bloody-rinded', 'pimple-insolence', 'gum-chew innocence' – which, in Bellow's heavily sprung rhythms, sometimes career into train-wreck compression: Trafton's gym, with its 'liniment-groggy, flickety-rope-time, tin-locker-clashing, Loop-darkened rooms'. There are the verb-couplings: trams 'lumbered and clanged', billiard balls 'kissing and bounding', traffic 'dived and quivered', cars 'snoring and trembling' or 'fluddering and shimmering'. It is a style that loves and embraces awkwardness, spurning elegance as a false lead, words tumbling and rattling together in the order *they* choose: 'glittering his teeth and hungry', 'try out what of human you can live with', 'the long impulse from well out in ocean bobs the rotten oranges', 'a flatfooted, in gym shoes, pug-nosed old woman', '[he] sobbed in the brakes of, he thought, most solitude', 'I hoped there'd something show on the horizon', 'I could not find myself in love without it should have some peculiarity', 'hypocritic', 'honestest', 'ancientest', 'his brittle neck would be broke', 'waked-up despair', 'loud-played music'. Why is 'loud-played music', in a dimestore, so much better than 'loud'? Because it suggests wilfulness, vulgarity and youth, whereas 'loud' is just *loud*. *Augie March* isn't written in English; its job is to make you feel how beautiful *American* is, with its jazzy verbs: 'it sent my blood happy', 'to close a deal', 'to run [a nickel] into a fortune', 'we were making twelve knots', 'cover the house' (get around it), 'beat a check' (leave without paying it), 'to make time with Mimi' (seduce), 'This is where I shake you, Augie' (reject). Never mind the p's and q's of fine prose. Whatever works . . .

Style, of course, is not something grappled on to regular prose; it is intrinsic to perception. We are fond of separating style and content (for the purposes of analysis, and so on), but they aren't separable: they come from the same place. And style is morality. Style judges. No other writer and no other novel makes you feel surer about this. It is as if Bellow is turning himself inside out and letting the observable world poke and prod at him nerve by nerve. Things are not merely described but registered, measured and assessed for the weight with which they bear on your soul.

The river:

At last [Simon] answered me coldly, with a cold lick of fire in his eyes, on the stationary wintriness of the cold black steel harness of the bridge over the dragging unnamable mixture of the river flowing backward with its waste.

The street guy:

He was never anything but through and through earnest when the subject was loyalty or honor; his bony dukes were ready and his Cuban heels dug down sharply; his furrowed chin was already feeling toward its fighting position on the shoulder of his starched shirt, prepared to go into his stamping dance and start slugging.

Mimi Villars, on the telephone:

'You'll never live to hear me beg for anything,' were Mimi's last words to Frazer, and when she slammed phone and hook together with cruelty it was as a musician might shut the piano after he had finished storming chords of mightiest difficulty without a single flinch or error.

The recovery ward:

Shruggers, hobblers, truss and harness wearers, crutch dancers, wall inspectors, wheelchair people in bandage helmets, wound smells and drug flowers blossoming from gauze, from colorful horrors and out of the deep sinks.

The copshop:

And as the mis-minted and wrong-struck figures and faces stooped, shambled, strode, gazed, dreaded, surrendered, didn't care . . . you wondered that all was stuff that was born human and shaped human . . . And don't forget the dirt-hardness, the dough fats and raw meats, of those on the official side.

The Chicago roofscape:

In its repetition it exhausted your imagination of details and units, more units than the cells of the brain and the bricks of Babel. The Ezekiel caldron of wrath, stoked with bones. A mysterious tremor, dust, vapor, emanation of stupendous effort traveled with the air, over me on top of the great establishment, so full as it was, and over the clinics, clinks, factories, flophouses, morgue, skid row.

The sea:

In beauty or doom colors, according to what was in your heart, the sea and skies made their cycles of day and night, the jeweled water gadding universally, the night-glittering fury setting in . . . Meanwhile the boat sauntered through glassy stabs of light and wheewhocked on the steep drink.

Augie March, finally, is the Great American Novel because of its fantastic inclusiveness, its pluralism, its qualmless promiscuity. In these pages the highest and the lowest mingle and hobnob in the vast democracy of Bellow's prose. Everything is in here, the crushed and the exalted and all the notches in between, from the kitchen stiff –

> The angry skin of his dish-plunging arms and his twist horse-gauntness, long teeth and spread liquidness of eyes in the starry alley evening . . . Under the fragile shell of his skull he leakily was reasoning

– to the American eagle. When an eagle flies, it isn't a matter of 'the simple mechanics of any little bird that went and landed as impulse tickled him, but a task of massive administration'. This is Caligula, taking to 'the high vibrations of blue'. And this is Saul Bellow, at thirty-eight, over and above the eagle – not an individual but a messenger:

> Anyway, it was glorious how he would mount away high and sit up there, really as if over fires of atmosphere, as if he was governing from up there. If his motive was rapaciousness and everything based on the act of murder, he also had a nature that felt the triumph of beating his way up to the highest air to which flesh and blood could rise. And doing it by will, not as other forms of life were at that altitude, the spores and parachute seeds who weren't there as individuals but messengers of species.

Atlantic Monthly October 1995

Nabokov's Grand Slam

Lolita by Vladimir Nabokov

Like the sweat of lust and guilt, the sweat of death trickles through *Lolita*. I wonder how many readers survive the novel without realizing that its heroine is, so to speak, dead on arrival, like her child. Their brief obituaries are tucked away in the 'editor's' Foreword, in nonchalant, school-newsletter form:

> 'Mona Dahl' is a student in Paris. 'Rita' has recently married the proprietor of a hotel in Florida. Mrs 'Richard F. Schiller' died in childbed, giving birth to a stillborn girl, on Christmas Day 1952, in Gray Star, a settlement in the remotest Northwest. 'Vivian Darkbloom' has written a biography . . .

Then, once the book begins, Humbert's childhood love Annabel dies, at thirteen (typhus), and his first wife Valeria dies (also in childbirth), and his second wife Charlotte dies ('a bad accident' – though of course this death is structural), and Charlotte's friend Jean Farlow dies at thirty-three (cancer), and Lolita's young seducer Charlie Holmes dies (Korea), and her old seducer Quilty dies (murder: another structural exit). And then Humbert dies (coronary thrombosis). And then Lolita dies. And her daughter dies. In a sense *Lolita* is too great for its own good. It rushes up on the reader like a recreational drug more powerful than any yet discovered or devised. In common with its narrator, it is both irresistible and unforgivable. And yet it all works out. I shall point the way to what I take to be its livid and juddering heart – which is itself in prethrombotic turmoil, all heaves and lifts and thrills.

Without apeing the explicatory style of Nabokov's famous Lectures (without producing height-charts, road maps, motel bookmatches, and so on), it might still be as well to establish what actually happens in *Lolita*: morally. How bad is all this – on paper, anyway? Although he distances himself with customary hauteur from the world of 'coal sheds and alleyways', of panting maniacs and howling policemen, Humbert Humbert is without question an honest-to-God, open-and-shut sexual deviant, displaying classic ruthlessness, guile and (above all) attention to detail. He parks the car at the gates of schoolyards, for instance, and obliges Lo to fondle him as the children emerge. Sixty-five cents secures a similar caress in her classroom, while Humbert admires a platinum classmate. Fellatio prices peak at four dollars a session before Humbert brings rates down 'drastically by having her earn the hard and nauseous way permission to participate in the school's theatrical programme'. On the other hand he performs complimentary cunnilingus when his step-daughter is laid low by fever: 'I could not resist the exquisite caloricity of unexpected delights – Venus febriculosa – though it was a very languid Lolita that moaned and coughed and shivered in my embrace.'

Humbert was evidently something of a bourgeois sadist with his first wife, Valeria. He fantasized about 'slapping her breasts out of alignment' or 'putting on [his] mountain boots and taking a running kick at her rump' but in reality confined himself to 'twisting fat Valechka's brittle wrist (the one she had fallen upon from a bicycle)' and saying, 'Look here, you fat fool, *c'est moi qui décide.*' The weakened wrist is good: sadists know all about weakspots. Humbert strikes Lolita only once ('a tremendous backhand cut'), during a jealous rage, otherwise making do with bribes, bullying, and three main threats – the rural fastness, the orphanage, the reformatory:

> In plainer words, if we two are found out, you will be analysed and
> institutionalized, my pet, *c'est tout*. You will dwell, my Lolita will
> dwell (come here, my brown flower) with thirty-nine other dopes
> in a dirty dormitory (no, allow me, please) under the supervision
> of hideous matrons. This is the situation, this is the choice. Don't

you think that under the circumstances Dolores Haze had better stick to her old man?

It is true that Humbert goes on to commit murder: he kills his rival, Clare Quilty. And despite its awful comedy, and despite Quilty's worthlessness both as playwright and citizen, the deed is not denied its primal colorations. Quilty is Humbert's 'brother', after all, his secret sharer. Don't they have the same taste in wordplay and women? Don't they have the same voice? 'Drop that pistol,' he tells Humbert: '*Soyons raisonnables*. You will only wound me hideously and then rot in jail while I recuperate in a tropical setting.' Quilty is a heartless japer and voyeur, one of the pornographers of real life. Most readers, I think, would assent to the justice of Humbert's last-page verdict: 'For reasons that may appear more obvious than they really are, I am opposed to capital punishment . . . Had I come before myself, I would have given Humbert at least thirty-five years for rape, and dismissed the rest of the charges.' Quilty's death is not tragic. Nor is Humbert's fate. Nor is *Lolita*. But Lolita is tragic, in her compacted span. If tragedy explores thwarted energy and possibility, then Lolita is tragic – is flatly tragic. And the mystery remains. How did Nabokov accommodate her story to this three-hundred-page blue streak – to something so embarrassingly funny, so unstoppably inspired, so impossibly racy?

Literature, as has been pointed out, is not life; it is certainly not public life; there is no 'character issue'. It may be a nice bonus to know that Nabokov was a kind man. The biographical paraphernalia tells us as much. Actually, everything he wrote tells us as much. *Lolita* tells us as much. But this is not a straightforward matter. *Lolita* is a cruel book about cruelty. It is kind in the sense that your enemy's enemy is your friend, no matter how daunting his aspect. As a critic, Nabokov was more than averagely sensitive to literary cruelty. Those of us who toil through Cervantes, I suspect, after an initial jolt, chortlingly habituate ourselves to the 'infinite drubbings' meted out and sustained by the gaunt hidalgo. In his *Lectures on Don Quixote*, however, Nabokov can barely bring himself to contemplate the automatic 'thumbscrew' enormities of this 'cruel and crude old book':

The author seems to plan it thus: Come with me, ungentle reader, who enjoys seeing a live dog inflated and kicked around like a soccer football; reader, who likes, of a Sunday morning, on his way to or from church, to poke his stick or direct his spittle at a poor rogue in the stocks; come . . . I hope you will be amused at what I have to offer.

Nevertheless, Nabokov is the laureate of cruelty. Cruelty hardly exists elsewhere; all the Lovelaces and Osmonds turn out, on not very much closer inspection, to be mere hooligans and tyrants when compared to Humbert Humbert, to Hermann Hermann (his significant precursor) in *Despair*, to Rex and Margot in *Laughter in the Dark*, to Martha in *King, Queen, Knave*. Nabokov understood cruelty; he was wise to it; he knew its special intonations – as in this expert cadence from *Laughter in the Dark*, where, after the nicely poised 'skilfully', the rest of the sentence collapses into the cruel everyday:

> 'You may kiss me,' she sobbed, 'but not that way, please.' The youth shrugged his shoulders . . . She returned home on foot. Otto [her older brother], who had seen her go off, thumped his fist down on her neck and then kicked her skilfully, so that she fell and bruised herself against the sewing-machine.

Now Humbert is of course very cruel to Lolita, not just in the ruthless *sine qua non* of her subjugation, nor yet in his sighing intention of 'somehow' getting rid of her when her brief optimum has elapsed, nor yet in his fastidious observation of signs of wear in his 'frigid' and 'ageing mistress'. Humbert is surpassingly cruel in using Lolita for the play of his wit and the play of his prose – his prose, which sometimes resembles the 'sweat-drenched finery' that 'a brute of forty' may casually and legally shed (in both hemispheres, as a scandalized Humbert notes) before thrusting 'himself up to the hilt into his youthful bride'. Morally the novel is all ricochet or rebound. However cruel Humbert is to Lolita, Nabokov is crueller to Humbert – finessingly cruel. We all share the narrator's smirk when he begins the sexual-bribes chapter with the following sentence: 'I am now faced with the distasteful task of recording a definite drop in Lolita's morals.' But when the smirk congeals we are left staring at the moral heap that Humbert has become, underneath his arched eyebrow. Irresistible and unforgivable. It is complicated, and unreassuring. Even so, this is how it works.

Lolita herself is such an anthology piece by now that even non-readers of the novel can close their eyes and see her on the tennis court or in the swimming pool or curled up in the car seat or the motel twin bed with her 'ridiculous' comics. We tend to forget that this blinding creation remains just that: a creation, and a creation of Humbert Humbert's. We have only Humbert's word for her. And whatever it is that is wrong with Humbert, not even his short-lived mother – '(picnic, lightning)' – would claim that her son was playing with a full deck. (Actually his personal pack may comprise the full fifty-two, but it is crammed with jokers and wild cards, pipless deuces, three-eyed queens.) A reliable narrator in the strict sense, Humbert is not otherwise reliable; and let us remember that Nabokov was capable of writing entire fictions – *Despair*, *The Eye*, *Pale Fire* – in which the narrators have no idea what is going on *at all*. *Lolita*, I believe, has been partly isolated and distorted by its celebrity. 'The greatest novel of rapture in modern fiction,' states the cover of the first Penguin, which also informs us, on the back, that Humbert is English.

Haven't we been conditioned to feel that *Lolita* is *sui generis*, a black sheep, a bit of tasteful, indeed 'beautiful' erotica, and that Nabokov himself, with this particular novel, somehow got 'carried away'? Great writers, however, never get carried away. Even pretty average writers never get carried away. People who write one novel and then go back to journalism or accountancy ('Louder, bitch!') – *they* get carried away. *Lolita* is more austere than rapturous, as all writing is; and I have come to see it, with increasing awe, as exactly the kind of novel that its predecessors are pointing towards. It constructs a mind in the way that a prose Browning might have gone about it, through rigorous dramatic monologue. Perhaps Lolita herself, at least to begin with, is a sadder, triter and more ordinary being than Humbert Humbert is willing or able to fix (resembling the 'decidedly homely kid' that her mocked mother sees). It may be that Lolita, so identified with 'the geography of the United States' which her story puts 'into motion', is to some degree an exile's delirious invention. She is more than a figment (she is more than Don Quixote's Dulcinea), but she is also an externalization of Humbert's glittering quiddity.

Humbert is a narcissist. One hesitates to explore the psychological connexions, if any, between narcissism and classical paedophilia (and Freud must have been *some* good, one suspects, to have bedevilled the great Nabokov so), yet both conditions are clearly regressive or anorexic, showing a reluctance to abandon the sentimentally scaled-down perfection of youth. 'Rope-skipping, hopscotch . . . Ah, leave me alone,' moans Humbert, 'in my pubescent park, in my mossy garden. Let them play around me for ever. Never grow up.' Even earlier in the novel, when recalling his child love Annabel, Humbert describes a lost snapshot of their group: Annabel 'did not come out well' (she was bending over her *chocolat glacé*); 'but I,' enthuses Humbert,

> sitting somewhat apart from the rest, came out with a kind of
> dramatic conspicuousness: a moody, beetle-browed boy in a dark
> sport shirt and well-tailored white shorts, his legs crossed, sitting
> in profile, looking away.

Dramatic, moody, well-tailored, looking away: now that is the grist of romance. The path of self-love is always a rocky one. But the love shared by Humbert and Humbert, for all its rough and smooth, is unquestionably the real thing.

No narrator in literature, I think, goes on about his physical splendour as passionately and comically as the narrator of *Lolita*. With his 'striking if somewhat brutal good looks', the younger, Paris-based Humbert knows all too well that he could obtain, at the snap of his fingers, his choice of 'the many crazed beauties' who lash his 'grim rock':

Let me repeat with quiet force: I was, and still am, despite *mes malheurs*, an exceptionally handsome male; slow-moving, tall, with soft dark hair and a gloomy but all the more seductive cast of demeanour. Exceptional virility often . . . [etc., etc.]

When he first encounters Lolita, Humbert cruises past her in what he feels to be his 'adult disguise (a great big handsome hunk of movieland manhood)'. 'I have all the characteristics', he goes on to expound,

> which, according to writers on the sex interests of children, start the responses stirring in a little girl: clean-cut jaw, muscular hand, deep sonorous voice, broad shoulder. Moreover, I am said to resemble some crooner or actor chap on whom Lo has a crush.

A few pages on he wonders if he might quickly avail himself of a movieland clinch: 'A modern child, an avid reader of movie magazines, an expert in dream-slow close-ups, might not think it too strange, I guessed, if a handsome, intensely virile grown-up friend – too late.' Very soon Humbert is trying on a new pair of bathing trunks before the mirror, and duly becomes (he has married the mother by now) 'a bronzed glamour boy' at Hourglass Lake.

About a third of the way through the novel, with Humbert's corny gorgeousness now massively established, Nabokov has Humbert say, with inimitable tentativeness:

> I do not know if in these tragic notes I have sufficiently stressed the peculiar 'sending' effect that the writer's good looks – pseudo-Celtic, attractively simian, boyishly manly – had on women of every age and environment. Of course, such announcements made in the first person may sound ridiculous. But every once in a while I have to remind the reader of my appearance much as a professional novelist, who has given a character of his some mannerism or a dog, has to go on producing that dog or that mannerism every time the character crops up . . . There may be more to it in the present case. My gloomy good looks should be kept in the mind's eye if my story is to be properly understood. Pubescent Lo swooned to Humbert's charm as she did to hiccuppy music . . .

'Hiccuppy' more than adequately summons the tonsil-swallowing vocalists of the period, those 'throb-and-sob' idols of a teen's 'dream male' pantheon, where, as Humbert later reminds Lolita, he was once privileged to stroll. In his Afterword, when Nabokov speaks of the exhilarations of 'philistine vulgarity', he doesn't just mean Lolita, or motels, or America. 'There is no intrinsic difference between Palearctic and Nearctic manners [i.e., between Old and New worlds]. Any proletarian from Chicago can be as bourgeois (in the Flaubertian sense) as a duke.' Humbert, with his 'pleasantly arched thick black ad-eyebrows', has picked his prey well, for Lo 'it was to whom ads were dedicated: the ideal consumer, the subject and object of every foul poster'. Like the poster gummed to the wall above Lo's bed: 'A full-page ad . . . It represented a dark-haired young husband . . . Lo had drawn a jocose arrow to the haggard lover's face and had put, in block letters: H. H.' The resemblance, Humbert allows, was 'striking'. 'First time I've seen a man wearing a smoking jacket, sir,' says a 'queerly observant' schoolmate of Lo's, '– except in movies, of course.' No doubt the Lo–Hum story would have worked out wonderfully, in Hollywood, in dreamworld or ad-land. But this is only America, car-tool and lawn-sprinkler America, and Hum is Lo's stepfather, and three times her age, and for two years he rapes her at least twice a day.

Indeed Humbert's situation is fantastically contorted and extreme. It is the central miracle of the novel that the tiny madman in his tiny cell becomes, artistically, by a series of radical shifts in context, a lord of infinite space. In bald structure, *Lolita* is a tale of chronic molestation – not the most liberating of narrative schemes. One can see why certain publishers wanted Nabokov to refit the novel to a setting of appropriate grimness and deracination. From the author's Afterword:

> . . . one reader suggested that his firm might consider publication if I turned my Lolita into a twelve-year-old lad and had him seduced by Humbert, a farmer, in a barn, amidst gaunt and arid surroundings, all this set forth in short, strong 'realistic' sentences ('He acts crazy. We all act crazy, I guess. I guess God acts crazy', etc.).

As it happens, Nabokov finds an uncovenanted freedom in Humbert's dark confinement, and writes with the freshness of discovery about parenthood, marriage, jealousy, America, art and love. The angle is a tortured squint but the vistas are boundless.

Parents and guardians of twelve-year-old girls will have noticed that their wards have a tendency to be difficult. They may take Humbert's word for it that things are much more difficult – are in fact entirely impossible – when your twelve-year-old girl is also your twelve-year-old girlfriend. The next time you go out with your daughter, imagine you are *going out* with your daughter. We know that 'limits and rules' apply in the matter of parental caresses, that 'girlish games are fluid, or at least too childishly fluid for the senior partner to grasp'; but the ambitious molester had better learn the ropes, and quick, if his charge is not 'to start back in revulsion and terror'. All but the childless will nod in quiet sympathy when Humbert talks of Lo's 'fits of disorganized boredom, intense and vehement griping, her sprawling, droopy, dopey-eyed style, and what is called goofing off – a kind of diffused clowning . . .' Or how about this (aren't they awful?):

There was the day when having withdrawn the functional promise I had made her on the eve (whatever she had set her funny little heart on – a roller rink with some special plastic floor or a movie matinee to which she wanted to go alone) I happened to glimpse from the bathroom, through a chance combination of mirror aslant and door ajar, a look on her face . . . that look I cannot exactly describe . . . an expression of helplessness so perfect that it seemed to grade into one of rather comfortable inanity just because this was the very limit of injustice and frustration – and every limit presupposes something beyond it . . .

And, because of Nabokov's nerve and truthfulness (and because the artistic opposite of cruelty is not kindness but vulnerability), Lolita's innocence is never more piercingly evoked than during the fateful night at The Enchanted Hunters: when the (lightly drugged) Lo sits up in bed 'staring at me, and thickly calling me "Barbara"'; when she 'frees herself from the shadow of my embrace – doing this not consciously, not violently, not with any personal distaste, but with the neutral plaintive murmur of a child demanding its natural rest'; or when, having been given water, 'with an infantile gesture that carried more charm than any carnal caress, little Lolita wiped her lips against my shoulder'.

Similarly, every father feels a pang when his daughter begins to take a healthy interest in the opposite sex. But how much more incandescent the pain (this is Freud made real) when the daughter's suitors are the father's rivals. Again there is great comic veracity in the horror and fastidiousness with which Humbert views the repulsive *galère* of Lolita's admirers: 'goons in luxurious cars, maroon morons near blued pools', 'golden-haired high school uglies, all muscles and gonorrhoea', 'odious visions of stinking high school boys in sweat-shirts and an ember-red cheek pressing against hers' – indeed every variety of gangling, reeking adolescent, 'from the perspiring nincompoop whom "holding hands" thrills, to the self-sufficient rapist with pustules and a souped-up car'. (Acne is everywhere: even a truck sports its 'backside carbuncles'.) And when the rival is Quilty, an adult, a 'brother' (who physically resembles a cousin of Humbert's), and when the admiration is requited by the 'vile and beloved slut', then the prose congests with a lyrical disgust; the disgust is authentic, because it is ultimately self-directed. At the swimming pool:

> There he stood, in the camouflage of sun and shade, disfigured by them and masked by his own nakedness, his damp black hair or what was left of it, glued to his round head, his little moustache a humid smear, the wool on his chest spread like a symmetrical trophy, his navel pulsating, his hirsute thighs dripping with bright droplets, his tight wet black bathing trunks bloated and bursting with vigour where his great fat bullybag was pulled up and back like a padded shield over his reversed beasthood.

A husband, too, can on occasion find his wife a little wearing, particularly if she is a self-constructed simulacrum of the perfect

American homemaker (all poise and how-to), and even more particularly if he is planning to drug and rape her twelve-year-old child.
Humbert married his first wife, Valeria (the 'animated merkin', the
'brainless *baba*'), as 'a piteous compromise': what attracted him was
'the imitation she gave of a little girl'. He marries Charlotte out of
the coldest expediency; and what follows, in these implacably talented
early pages, is a vicious parody of marital cheer: Charlotte beautifies
the lovenest and pores over *Your Home Is You*, while Humbert
handsomely glowers and gloats, with 'a cesspoolful of rotting monsters
behind his slow boyish smile'. With his feelings quite unengaged ('My
solemn exasperation was to her the silence of love'), Humbert is free
to celebrate 'the coarse pink skin of her neck', or the way the wings of
her nose shine 'having shed or burned up their ration of powder', or
the 'tasteless reveries' in which she predicts that the soul of the child
she lost (another dead child) would return 'in the form of the child she
would bear in her present wedlock'. With Valeria, Humbert managed
to perform sexually by having her dress up in a girl's plain nightshirt
('I derived some fun from that nuptial night and had the idiot in
hysterics by sunrise'). With Charlotte he relies on good liquor, 'two
or three kinds of vitamins' and 'the richest foods available', and also
contrives to engage her in Lolita's bedroom, where he experiences
'some initial trouble, for which, however, he amply compensate[s]
her by a fantastic display of old-world endearments'. Thereafter, in
the fifty days of their cohabitation, it is genetic consonance that alone
sustains him:

> So I tom-peeped across the hedges of years, into wan little win-
> dows. And when, by means of pitifully ardent, naively lascivious
> caresses, she of the noble nipple and massive thigh prepared me
> for the performance of my nightly duty, it was still a nymphet's
> scent that in despair I tried to pick up, as I bayed through the
> undergrowth of dark decaying forests.

Even by locally prevailing standards Charlotte is egregiously
traduced in *Lolita*. Poor Charlotte: rigid, religious, snobbish and
formidable, an exponent of the fake candour that eternally precludes

the real thing (not that Humbert has much use for candour). The novel kills her off, of course, yet she survives as a character; and her resilience is the resilience of young America. Nabokov has scoffed at the notion, but the descent of Humbert Humbert, a boho among bohunks, with his intricate ironies and lusts, on the *fruit vert* of America is in some sense a paedophiliac visitation. Like Lolita, America is above all *young*, 'with a quality of wide-eyed, unsung, innocent surrender that my lacquered toy-bright Swiss villages and exhaustively lauded Alps no longer possess'. With unsurpassed sharpness of eye and ear Nabokov captures the rhythms of the American road. But for Humbert the circumambient 'wilds' represent a humiliation and, again, a travesty; their openness and freedom are a continual reproach to his own furtiveness and ignoble constraint. Admire this supreme modulation, in which the swiftness of disdain gradually slows in the heavier water of anxiety:

> *Nous connûmes* the various types of motor court operators, the reformed criminal, the retired teacher and the business flop, among the males; and the motherly, pseudo-ladylike and madamic variants among the females. And sometimes trains would cry in the monstrously hot and humid night with heartrending and ominous plangency, mingling power and hysteria in one desperate scream.

Or here, where Humbert allows himself the dejected clarity of hindsight:

> And so we rolled East . . . We had been everywhere. We had really seen nothing. And I catch myself thinking today that our long journey had only defiled with a sinuous trail of slime the lovely, trustful, dreamy, enormous country that by then, in retrospect, was no more to us than a collection of dog-eared maps, ruined tour books, old tyres, and her sobs in the night – every night, every night – the moment I feigned sleep.

It has often been suggested that the 'morality' of *Lolita* is not inherent but something tacked on at the end, like the last scene of Hitchcock's *Psycho*, in which a swarthy psychiatrist is produced to explain in neat jargon the very different depravities in a very different motel. As if, after a 260-page debauch (Nabokov having been 'carried away'), the author sobered up, gave his phallus a brisk downward chop with the side of his hand, and started tricking out his denouement with a few face-saving spiritual mottoes. Humbert on the hillside begging forgiveness of Lolita and the American landscape, Humbert paying his last call on the plain and pregnant Mrs Richard F. Schiller (where, we should note, his cruelty is indiluted: 'leave your incidental Dick, and this awful hole . . .'), Humbert's last memories of Lolita as the entirely ordinary little girl she kept on being, throughout everything: these scenes are justly famous (they can still make the present reader shed tears as hot as Humbert's), and even the dissenting critic will allow them a certain emotional power. But we are not moved by artful editorials. We are moved by the ending of *Lolita*, by its finality and justice, because – perhaps only subliminally – we have seen it all coming. Even today, after two of Lolita's lifespans, people are still wandering up to Dmitri Nabokov and asking him what it was like, having a dirty old man for a father. Even sophisticated readers still think that Nabokov had something to feel guilty about. Great novels are shocking; and then, after the shock dies down, you get aftershocks.

The presiding image of *Lolita*, so often missed by the first-time reader (I know I missed it, years ago), is adumbrated in its Foreword: Lolita in childbed, dead, with her dead daughter. Let us see what forms and colorations Nabokov gives to this stark silhouette. In Paris, when Humbert is confining himself to visiting prostitutes 'whose mere youth warranted [his] catching some appalling disease', he contacts a specialist *qui pourrait arranger la chose*, and, the next day,

> an asthmatic woman, coarsely painted, garrulous, garlicky, with an almost farcical Provençal accent and a black moustache above a purple lip, took me to what was apparently her own domicile, and there, after explosively kissing the bunched tips of her fat fingers to signify the delectable rosebud quality of her merchandise, she

theatrically drew aside a curtain to reveal what I judged was that part of the room where a large and unfastidious family usually slept. It was now empty save for a monstrously plump, sallow, repulsively plain girl of at least fifteen with red-ribboned thick black braids who sat on a chair perfunctorily nursing a bald doll.

Those last five words may be swamped by the bounty of their predecessors; but they exactly answer to 'the dreadful grimace of clenched teeth tenderness' which, on the previous page, Humbert sees in an accusing mirror while dallying with another small whore in another 'small Eden'. Such are the travesties of familial feeling ('almost farcical', 'theatrically'), among 'very young harlots disguised as children'. Images of deformity, of half-aliveness, of cruel displacements in mortal time, give *Lolita* a glow no less numb and waxy than its heroine's corpse.

For the novel is shot through with these bald dolls and wizened mannequins – with the old made young and the young made old. On the eve of the seduction, the 'lethal' delectation, Humbert writes: 'I should have known (by the signs made to me by something in Lolita – the real child Lolita or some haggard angel behind her back) that nothing but pain and horror would result from the expected rapture.' The next morning, as he prepares to leave the hotel:

> I was forced to devote a dangerous amount of time . . . to arranging the bed in such a way as to suggest the abandoned nest of a restless father and his tomboy daughter, instead of an ex-convict's saturnalia with a couple of fat old whores. Then I finished dressing and had the hoary bellboy come up for the bags.

On the next page Lolita is both an 'immortal daemon disguised as a female child' and 'the small ghost of somebody I had just killed'. In death Charlotte is a doll, a 'doll-like wee career girl', diagrammatized (this *is* very American) by the man who ran her over. Shopping for Lo, on his way to camp to claim her, Humbert is surrounded by 'lifesize plastic figures of snubbed-nose children with dun-coloured, greenish, brown-dotted, faunish faces'. These figures reappear, mutilated, in a later storefront, just before Lolita finally takes off: 'wigless and armless ... On the floor ... there lay a cluster of three slender arms, and a blonde wig. Two of the arms happened to be twisted and seemed to suggest a clasping gesture of horror and supplication.' All these pathetic fragments and progeriac transpositions will be hideously jumbled, under an Alp-weight of pain, in the dreams Humbert has when Lo is gone:

> she did haunt my sleep but she appeared there in strange and ludicrous disguises as Valeria or Charlotte, or a cross between them. That complex ghost would come to me, shedding shift after shift, in an atmosphere of great melancholy and disgust, and would recline in dull invitation on some narrow board or hard settee, with flesh ajar like the rubber valve of a soccer ball's bladder. I would find myself, dentures fractured or hopelessly mislaid, in horrible *chambres garnies* where I would be entertained at tedious vivisecting parties that generally ended with Charlotte or Valeria weeping in my bleeding arms and being tenderly kissed by my brotherly lips in a dream disorder of auctioneered Viennese bric-à-brac, pity, impotence and the brown wigs of tragic old women who had just been gassed.

In his Afterword Nabokov explains that the first 'shiver' of *Lolita* was inspired by a newspaper story about an ape, 'who, after months of coaxing by a scientist, produced the first drawing ever charcoaled by an animal: this sketch showed the bars of the poor creature's cage'. Inspiration needn't be very apposite; but the appositeness of this 'first little throb' has perhaps been misemphasized. It's not so much that Lolita has been encaged and enslaved, though she has been. Humbert's crime is to force her out of nature – to force a child through the hoops of womanhood, insulting and degrading her childish essence. Nabokov says that the initial impulse had 'no textual connection' with the fiction that followed, but in fact there are at least a couple of backward glances. Valeria, soon to die in childbirth, spends some of her last days imitating an animal, on a diet of bananas and dates, as part of a paid ethnological experiment. And on his travels Humbert visits a zoo 'where a large troop of monkeys lived on [a?] concrete replica of Christopher Columbus' flagship', and thus spend their lives mutely symbolizing America. Lolita is 'trained' (i.e., pampered and terrorized); she subsists on apples and sugarlumps given in exchange for her animal repertoire. Only once is she specifically imagined in this way; it is one of those moments of extraordinary expansion, where Nabokov's prose streaks off like a tracer bullet in a dark sky. The sexual act has taken place on a hilltop:

> I remember that the operation was over, all over, and she was weeping in my arms – a salutary storm of sobs after one of the fits of moodiness that had become so frequent with her in the course of that otherwise admirable year! . . . and so we lay, when with one of those jolts that have ended by knocking my poor heart out of its groove, I met the unblinking dark eyes of two strange and beautiful children . . . [followed by] a stout lady with a raven-black bob, who automatically added a wild lily to her bouquet, while staring over her shoulder at us from behind her lovely carved bluestone children . . . With the quiet murmured order one gives a sweat-stained distracted cringing trained animal even in the worst of plights (what mad hope or hate makes the young beast's flanks pulsate, what black stars pierce the heart of the trainer!), I made Lo get up, and we decorously walked, and then indecorously scuttled down to the car . . . and with a scrunch and a skid we drove off, Lo still struggling with her clothes and swearing at me in a language that I never dreamed little girls could know, let alone use.

Shockable Humbert, who finds bad language so 'disgusting'. I shudder to think how his ghost, attired in its ghostly smoking-jacket, would round on me for calling him a vulgarian and a philistine. Actually he is of a more dangerous and rarer breed (though one very fully represented in Nabokov's corpus): such people, because they cannot make art out of life, make their lives into art. Humbert is the artist *manqué*. To see the magic of nymphets 'you have to be an artist and a madman', claims Humbert early on ('oh, how you have to cringe and hide!'). Wangling yet more powerful sleeping pills from the family doctor (on which to gorge the limp nymphet), he comes away with violet-blue capsules 'intended not for neurotics whom a glass of water would calm . . . but only for great sleepless artists who had to die for a few hours in order to live for centuries'. The weeping Humbert sheds above-average teardrops, 'hot, opalescent, thick tears that poets and lovers shed'. He is 'her Catullus', he is 'poor Catullus': 'The gentle and dreamy regions through which I crept were the patrimonies of poets – not crime's stamping ground.' This is all blasphemous flannel, naturally. Who but Hum could refer to the gauged postponement of his orgasm (on the sofa, with a still innocent Lo) as 'a nicety of physiological equipoise comparable to certain techniques in the arts'? 'Emphatically, no killers are we,' Humbert pleads: 'Poets never kill.' But this one does. Before he pulls the trigger he recites a poem: a parody – under the circumstances, a travesty – of 'Ash-Wednesday'. And Nabokov never had much time for Eliot.

Necessarily uncensorious himself (a neighbour is a 'retired executioner or writer of religious tracts – who cared?'), Humbert Humbert, all his life, has longed for great disasters, explosions, earthquakes, situations where 'nothing really mattered', where 'nothing mattered any more, and everything was allowed' ('A shipwreck. An atoll. Alone with a drowned passenger's shivering child. Darling, this is only a game!'). In art, in a sense, nothing really matters; no one gets hurt; it *is* only a game. But an artistic reckoning must be completed, and, in Nabokov, art itself provides the reproach and the punishment. His *manqué* figures pay a steep price for their presumption, for their monkeying around with the order of things: Albinus in *Laughter in the Dark*, with his plan to cartoonify the Old Masters; Kinbote in *Pale Fire*, with his epic and vandalously solipsist misreading of John Shade's poem; Hermann Hermann, another autist, in *Despair*, with his doomed crime and his doomed novel. Inasmuch as *Lolita* is Humbert's creation, then he is partly redeemed, leaving us this book which has 'bits of marrow sticking to it, and blood, and beautiful bright-green flies'. Those flies: we think, rather, of their 'horribly experienced' brethren, 'zigzagging over the sticky sugar-pour' in some foul diner, in some dismal ex-prairie state. Not all the book comes from Humbert's pen. He isn't responsible for the Foreword, where we learn of Lolita's death, in childbed. Humbert's sin is biological, a sin against the ordinary. He has made ordinary biology impossible: marriage, childbirth, a daughter, ordinary happiness, ordinary health, in 'Gray Star, a settlement in the remotest Northwest' and 'the capital town of the book', as Nabokov notes. It may or may not surprise Humbert to learn that the book he has written is not a love story but a travesty.

What makes human beings laugh? Not just gaiety or irony. That laughter banishes seriousness is a misconception often made by the humourless – and by that far greater multitude, the hard of laughing, the humorously impaired or under-gifted. Human beings laugh, if you notice, to express relief, exasperation, stoicism, hysteria, embarrassment, disgust and cruelty. *Lolita* is perhaps the funniest novel in the language because it allows laughter its full complexity and range. We hear its characteristic edge when Humbert uses his 'pet' for the play of his wit and his prose: this is the laughter we hear (not too often, I hope) when we recognize the outright *perfection* of our moral sordor. 'Sordid' is a word largely conspicuous by its absence in Humbert's tale. Its one self-directed appearance, I think, comes (in brackets) at The Enchanted Hunters, when he concedes that the sleeping-pill business is 'a rather sordid affair, *entre nous soit dit*'. The mock-genteel French tag is an important constituent of Humbert's corrosive mask. And there is a feeling of all laughter spent when, reluctantly admiring the shapely hands of Richard F. Schiller (Mr Lo), Humbert writes:

> I have hurt too much too many bodies with my twisted poor hands
> to be proud of them. French epithets, a Dorset yokel's knuckles,
> an Austrian tailor's flat fingertips – that's Humbert Humbert.

At one point, comparing himself to Joyce, Nabokov said: 'my English is patball to [his] champion game'. At another, he tabulated the rambling rumbles of *Don Quixote* as a tennis match (the Don taking it in four hard sets). And we all remember Lolita on the court, her form 'excellent to superb', according to her schoolmistress, but her grace 'so sterile', according to Humbert, 'that she could not even win from panting me and my old fashioned lifting drive'. Now, although of course Joyce and Nabokov never met in competition, it seems to me that Nabokov was the more 'complete' player. Joyce appeared to be cruising about on all surfaces at once, and maddeningly indulged his trick shots on high-pressure points – his drop smash, his sidespun half-volley lob. Nabokov just went out there and did the business, all litheness, power and touch. Losing early in the French (say), Joyce would be off playing exhibitions in Casablanca with various arthritic legends, and working on his inside-out between-the-legs forehand dink; whereas Nabokov and his entourage would quit the rusty dust of Roland Garros for somewhere like Hull or Nailsea, to prepare for Wimbledon on our spurned and sodden grass. We still talk about Joyce in the pavilion, constantly: the footwork, the flow, the dream backhand, the maybes, the might-have-beens, the time he won the Italian with his left hand shackled to his right leg. Then we move on to the great Russian, and the eye strays to the honours board – and Nabokov's fat wedge of Grand Slams.

When they come across something wise or witty, or fond, or funny, or something obviously necessary to the whole, warmed readers make a little vertical mark on the page with their bookside pencils. Accordingly, then, the perfect novel would have perfect verticals running down the length of every margin. It never works out quite like that, because the novel is a tangled thing, and shifts its shape over the years. I have read *Lolita* eight or nine times and not always in the same edition; but the margins of my staple hardback bear a Pompeiian litter of ticks, queries, exclamation marks, and lines straight and squiggly and doubled and tripled. My pencilled comments, I realize, form a kind of surrealistic summary of the whole:

but you can't . . . steady insult . . . ear . . . disguise . . . playing with Dostoevsky . . . love proceeds . . . v. v. good . . . travelling eye . . . one pup and at least three important dogs . . . vampire again . . . oh, oh . . . Flaub. . . . co-ed . . . the bike . . . poor, poor Dolly . . . brimming . . . quite mad . . . now alone . . . sobbing over sneaker . . . all along! . . . all dead . . . horribly experienced . . .

Clearly, these are not a scholar's notes, and they move towards no edifice of understanding or completion. They are gasps of continually renewed surprise. I expect to read the novel many more times. And I am running out of clean white space.

Atlantic Monthly September 1992

Index